PHILOSOPHICAL FOUNDATIONS OF TAX LAW

Philosophical Foundations of Tax Law

Edited by

MONICA BHANDARI

OXFORD
UNIVERSITY PRESS

OXFORD
UNIVERSITY PRESS

Great Clarendon Street, Oxford, OX2 6DP,
United Kingdom

Oxford University Press is a department of the University of Oxford.
It furthers the University's objective of excellence in research, scholarship, and education by publishing worldwide. Oxford is a registered trade mark of Oxford University Press in the UK and in certain other countries

First Edition published in 2017

Impression: 1

Published in the United States of America by Oxford University Press
198 Madison Avenue, New York, NY 10016, United States of America

British Library Cataloguing in Publication Data
Data available

Library of Congress Control Number: 2017930568

ISBN 978–0–19–879843–9

Printed and bound by
CPI Group (UK) Ltd, Croydon, CR0 4YY

Acknowledgements

Most of the chapters here first appeared as papers at the Bentham House Symposium held at UCL in May 2015. This was an exciting and stimulating conference, bringing together academics from different disciplines and practitioners, for challenging and thought-provoking debate. The papers benefited greatly from the discussion and I would like to thank the CIOT for its funding of the conference and also the law faculty at UCL for hosting the conference and the support through the Bentham House Conference funding (particularly Charles Mitchell and James Penner for their support of this project and Lisa Penfold for helping the symposium to run so smoothly). Thanks also to my research assistant James Webb for his assistance with the conference and in the editing of this book, as well as Maxwell Myers for his help with ensuring the chapters met with house style. Of course thanks also to the contributors for bearing with us and our demands, and for being patient with the publication of this collection, as well as OUP for their help and support in bringing this collection to life.

Contents

List of Contributors

Monica Bhandari is a Senior Lecturer in Taxation Law at University College London.

Jennifer Bird-Pollan is the James and Mary Lassiter Associate Professor of Law at the University of Kentucky College of Law.

Dominic de Cogan is a University Lecturer and Fellow of Christ's College, Cambridge.

Charles Delmotte is a PhD Candidate and teaching assistant at Ghent University, Law Faculty and Adam Smith Fellow at George Mason University.

David G. Duff is Professor of Law and Associate Dean at the University of British Colombia.

Patrick Emerton is an Associate Professor at the Faculty of Law, Monash University.

Stuart P. Green is Distinguished Professor of Law and Nathan L. Jacobs Scholar at Rutgers School of Law.

Kathryn James is a Senior Lecturer in Law at the Faculty of Law, Monash University.

Miranda Perry Fleischer is Professor of Law at the University of San Diego.

John Prebble QC is a Professor of Law at the Victoria University of Wellington, a Gastprofessor at the Institut für Österreichisches und Internationales Steuerrecht, Wirtschaftsuniversität Wien, and an Adjunct Professor of Law, Sydney School of Law, The University of Notre Dame Australia.

Theodore P. Seto holds the Frederick J. Lower, Jr. Chair at Loyola Law School.

John Snape is an Associate Professor at Warwick University.

John Stanton-Ife is a Senior Lecturer at the Dickson Poon School of Law, King's College London.

Henk Vording is Professor of General Tax Law at the University of Leiden.

Introduction to Philosophical Foundations of Tax Law

Monica Bhandari

The idea for this collection came about many years ago, when John Stanton-Ife (contributor of Chapter 2) and I taught a small mini-option on the LLB creatively named Tax and Jurisprudence. We wanted to show the students different aspects of our core subjects—that tax was better understood when adding a philosophical dimension to its study and that jurisprudence, contrary to their perceptions, has a real place in the practical world. It is this coming together of two areas which are considered so very different, that the authors of this edited collection wanted to explore further.

Tax law changes at a startling rate—most academics in this area will some days wish they had chosen a more 'stable' subject when rewriting their lecture notes for the umpteenth time in a year. Not only does society change and demand change in the tax system, but changes in the political climate will force change, as well as many other competing pressures. At the time of writing this introduction the global political scene is in a state of flux, with much uncertainty ahead. This in turn causes change and uncertainty in the tax system and its direction. By the time of publication these issues will be closer to a resolution, but a new set of issues will surface. Hence the constant state of flux in the system. With this pace of change, it is easy to focus on the practical and forget the core underpinnings of the system, to drive the system in a direction with fits with its philosophical justifications. Thus, taking a pause to remind ourselves of those principles and how they can operate in the modern tax system is crucial to ensure that the tax system does not diverge too far from what it should be or could be. Given the controversy that surrounds tax, particularly in a turbulent economic environment, it is an excellent time to explore tax from a philosophical perspective. It is essential that we have a complete understanding of the answers to some of the seemingly basic questions which surround tax, before we can begin to think about what a tax system should look like. Questions such as what in fact is a tax? Why should we tax? How much should we tax and on whom should tax be levied? What should taxes be used for? How do ideas of fairness and justice tie in with the tax system? The consideration of all these questions is crucial to a complete understanding of the tax system and the future of the tax system.

The starting point for many, as it was for us many years ago when teaching the undergraduates, has been Murphy and Nagel's *The Myth of Ownership*.[1] It is this work that starts to bring the strands of the philosophical foundations of tax law together in

[1] Liam Murphy and Thomas Nagel, *The Myth of Ownership* (Oxford: Oxford University Press, 2002).

Philosophical Foundations of Tax Law. First Edition. Edited by Monica Bhandari.

modern times.[2] The authors consider ideas of justice within the conception of property rights and how taxes fit in with those ideas. It is essential reading for anyone exploring this area and readers will see many references to the work in this collection, some using it as a springboard for their ideas. The idea of justice in the tax system and notions of property and wealth are key in this collection and the foundations of considering tax from a philosophical perspective. The aim of this collection was to bring together legal philosophers and tax lawyers to bring a cohesive approach to the area and give a broad understanding on the questions we face when considering the tax system in this way.

The collection is structured in three parts. The first part focuses on the justification for tax and enforcement. This forms the backdrop to what follows. It is by understanding that we should have a tax system, that we need to tax and that it is right to demand that taxpayers contribute to the system, that we can begin to consider how the system should function.

It was important for this collection to challenge the notion that a philosophical perspective on tax law is of abstract and academic interest only. Thus we move to practical issues for the remaining chapters. The second and third parts consider the design and mechanics of the tax system. The second part focuses on general principles regarding the design and mechanics of a tax system, including the notion of an income tax and how it should operate. Income tax is one of the core elements of any tax system, and the one which usually raises the most revenue.[3] The third part focuses on the specific area of wealth and property. Wealth and the related concept of property are fundamental concepts in considering the philosophical foundations of tax law—property was the starting point for Murphy and Nagel and many of the authors of the chapters in this part look to challenge and develop their ideas.

Turning to the chapters themselves, we start in the first part on the justification for tax, ethics, and morality with John Snape's chapter 'The "Sinews of the State": Historical Justifications for Taxes and Tax Law'. Snape considers historical levies of tax and their purposes, as public purpose is a core element of identifying a charge as a tax in modern taxation. In considering purpose, he discusses the purpose of levies in the context of differing social and political orders, to argue for the constitutive importance of tax and the importance of historical ideals in the shaping of purpose, and further that it is essential to consider political justification to classify a charge as tax. We must thus understand tax law as a fundamental part of the law, but also as a part of public law.

We then move to John Stanton-Ife's chapter 'Must We Pay for the British Museum? Taxation and the Harm Principle'. Stanton-Ife explores and challenges James Fitzjames

[2] This is not to say that there have been no other notable writings in this area. Many of the contributors to this collection, and other academics, have written articles in the arena of tax philosophy before now.

[3] In the UK in the 2015–16 tax year, total revenue raised was £533.7 billion in tax receipts, of which income tax was by far the greatest revenue generator. Income Tax and National Insurance Contributions together raised £282.152 billion—over half the revenue for the year. The rest of the receipts were made up of other taxes such as VAT (£115.4 billion), Corporation Tax (£44.4 billion), Capital Gains Tax (£7.1 billion), Inheritance Tax (£4.7 billion), and other duties. See *HM Revenue and Customs*, HMRC Tax & NIC Receipts for more detail, https://www.gov.uk/government/uploads/system/uploads/attachment_data/file/539194/Jun16_Receipts_NS_Bulletin_Final.pdf.

Stephen's argument that compulsory taxation to support artistic, cultural, or esoteric purposes is a violation of Mill's harm principle. He argues that whilst the harm principle has not historically been widely explored in the context of tax law by liberals, certain aspects of it can form a philosophical foundation of tax law, and uses Feinberg's work as a point of departure for his discussion.

In considering the justification for tax, we must also consider that if it is right to impose tax, how can we ensure that it is paid? Thus the final two chapters of this part consider enforcement, by looking at conceptions of tax evasion and tax avoidance.

In 'Tax Evasion as Crime', Stuart P. Green explores the offence of tax evasion in the context of criminal law theory. He considers how tax is different from other financial penalties in order to understand why the evasion of tax is considered morally wrong, and explores the factors which play a part in defining its moral content. Concluding that tax evasion is wrong principally on the basis that it constitutes cheating, Green goes on to consider whether the same analysis can determine tax avoidance as morally wrong.

This leads us to John Prebble's chapter on a tool against tax avoidance. In 'Kelsen, the Principle of Exclusion of Contradictions, and General Anti-Avoidance Rules in Tax Law' Prebble considers general anti-avoidance rules (GAARs) which are present now in many tax systems. He analyses them using Kelsen's principle that two norms that contradict one another within the same legal system breach the philosophical principle of exclusion of contradictions and therefore cannot both be valid at the same time. Prebble argues that GAARs can be viewed as a contradiction of norms and thus a breach of the principle of exclusion of contradictions, but that tax law nonetheless justifies and requires the existence of GAARs.

The second part of the collection on the design and mechanics of the tax system commences with Dominic de Cogan's chapter. This chapter begins the focus on design and mechanics as it considers the design of a tax system in its entirety. In 'Michael Oakeshott and the Conservative Disposition in Tax Law' de Cogan considers how change can be implemented in the tax system. He argues that the system is both complex and resistant to legal change, but that by exploring the work of Oakeshott, it is apparent that the resistance has a basis. He considers the rationale for the resistance; discusses rationalism, tradition, and conservatism; and considers methods of driving change in the tax system.

Moving on to the specifics of income tax, Patrick Emerton and Kathryn James' chapter considers the notion of justice in a tax system and its requirement of income tax. In 'The Justice of the Tax Base and the Case for Income Tax' Emerton and James argue that the choice of a tax base is a fundamental and foundational aspect of tax. They argue that there are principles which are prior to the tax structure, that these must be taken into account by the tax system, and that these mean that income taxation is the most favourable tax base. They also highlight threats to the income tax at a global level, arguing that the need for income tax from the perspective of justice demands that these be threats be eliminated.

In 'Tax Policy and the Virtuous Sovereign: Dworkinian Equality and Redistributive Taxation' David G. Duff considers, in part, how an income tax should be designed. He demonstrates that a just tax system requires an income tax which is progressive in nature. He also argues for wealth transfer taxes. He analyses aspects of redistributive justice, using Dworkin's theory of equality of resources. Furthermore, he argues that Dworkin's approach is favourable to welfare-based theories, Rawlsian theory, and classical libertarianism. He highlights the deficiencies of each of these approaches, and comes to the conclusion that whilst Dworkin's theory cannot necessarily be taken on in its entirety, equality of resources gives us the best guidance to the structure of the tax system.

The final part of this collection focuses on wealth and property as a basis for taxation, in its different forms. It is no surprise that this part has the most chapters, as it is here that we find the most debate on the issue of the basis and underpinnings of tax. The extent to which citizens own pre-tax property was a fundamental part of Murphy and Nagel's work. Therefore, notions of property and wealth see much debate stem from this concept, as we see in this part.

The first chapter here, Theodore P. Seto's 'A Forced Labour Theory of Property and Taxation', gives us a historical perspective on property and tax law. Seto seeks to challenge two oppositions to taxation: first Nozick's idea, as extrapolated by later theorists, that taxation amounts to theft, and second that without taxation citizens would work and save, and thus taxation distorts these choices. He considers theories of property law to support his claims and concludes that property law and taxation work together and are foundational in civilized society.

Jennifer Bird-Pollan's 'The Philosophical Foundations of Wealth Transfer Taxation' considers the desirability of taxing wealth transfers. Bird-Pollan argues that this type of taxation is underutilized, particularly when compared to income tax, yet it is taxation of wealth and wealth transfers that more effectively achieve the redistributive aims of taxation. Whilst this form of taxation may be unpopular, it more closely aligns with philosophical ideals.

Henk Vording in 'Talents, Types, and Tags: What Is the Relevance of the Endowment Tax Debate?' considers wealth from the perspective of whether an endowment tax is morally preferable to an income tax. Given that two people might earn the same income but have very different financial positions when considering wider factors, can an income tax actually achieve a just outcome or should we focus on wealth? He argues against the prominence of the concept of 'slavery of the talented' as put forward by Rawls and Dworkin and rather focuses on the difference between endowment and personal choice.

This takes us to Miranda Perry-Fleischer's chapter 'How Is the Opera Like a Soup Kitchen?' which explores relative wealth from the perspective of taxation and tax exemptions in the arena of charities. Given the redistributive outcomes of these exemptions, she analyses the system using the concept of distributive justice, focusing on the fact that there is a plethora of charities which serve very different segments of society, from the wealthy to the needy. Thus can the aims of distributive justice be met by having the same rules for these different types of charities? Perry-Fleischer considers that account must be taken of expensive tastes versus ordinary tastes and thus it is in fact possible to meet distributive aims in this way.

The final chapter focuses on as aspect of the mechanics of taxing wealth. In 'The Right to Autonomy as a Moral Foundation for the Realization Principle in Income

Taxation' Charles Delmotte uses the work of Thomas Piketty as a starting point and explores the need for capital and wealth taxes in order to reduce the wealth gap. Delmotte looks at how we can begin to find a suitable technique to assess wealth and capital. Taking a normative approach, he compares the mark-to-market and realization methods, arguing that the latter is favourable on the basis of efficiency and redistribution.

The chapters in this collection tie together some of the major themes in unpicking the philosophical foundations of tax law and tackle the difficult questions that surround this area. They provide a coherent and fulsome analysis of the basis for tax law, which allows us to consider how tax systems should move forward in the modern world, with a sound philosophical basis, to provide the practical tax system that the state requires and the citizens deserve.

PART I

JUSTIFICATION FOR TAX AND ENFORCEMENT

1

The 'Sinews of the State'

Historical Justifications for Taxes and Tax Law

John Snape

I. Introduction

Twentieth-century jurisprudence defined the concept of a tax as having four constituent elements. Besides being payable under legal compulsion, to be a tax a levy must be: exacted under legislative authority; assessed and collected either by government itself or by an institution carrying out functions of a public nature;[1] and 'intended for a public purpose'.[2]

This chapter concentrates on the last of these four: the intended purpose. The chapter adduces three interrelated arguments about the purposes of taxes and about the nature of tax law. First, it is maintained that historically specific ideals go a long way to shaping the purposes of levies imposed under different social and political orders. Secondly, that the nature and scope of viable purposes is a function of the social and political relations created by those orders. Thirdly, that it is the presence or absence of a political justification for the chosen purposes that affirms or denies both the status of a levy as a tax and the categorization of tax law as public law. All three arguments draw attention to the range of levies imposed at various times and under different historical social and political conditions. The titular and ancient image of taxes or, more specifically, the revenues raised by them as 'the sinews of the state'[3] underlines taxation's constitutive importance. The title therefore explicitly excludes from the scope of the chapter ecclesiastical levies, while acknowledging their historical importance.

To illustrate each of the arguments, four different societal orders are predicated: 'the feudal realm'; 'the absolutist state'; 'the parliamentary state'; and 'the administrative state'. The latter two expressions have been used by the public lawyer Martin Loughlin, and others, to illustrate a crucial shift in the nature of the state over the eighteenth to the twentieth centuries.[4] The former two are in wide use by medieval and early modern scholars. They are all used here as 'ideal types'. They each serve a function similar to Joseph Alois Schumpeter's concept of 'the tax state',[5] which encompasses all but the

[1] *Australian Tape v Commonwealth* (1993) 176 CLR 480.

[2] *Re Eurig* (1998) 165 DLR (4th) 1, 10; M. Barassi, 'The Notion of Tax and the Different Types of Taxes,' in B. Peeters et al. (eds), *The Concept of Tax* (Amsterdam: IBFD, 2005), 59–73, 61; M. Bowler Smith and H. Ostik, 'Towards a Classification of the Central London Congestion Charge as a Tax', [2011] *British Tax Review* 487–508.

[3] Marcus Tullius Cicero, quoted in S. Smith, *Taxation: A Very Short Introduction* (Oxford: Oxford University Press, 2015), 3.

[4] M. Loughlin, *Foundations of Public Law* (Oxford: Oxford University Press, 2010), 259, 435.

[5] J.A. Schumpeter, 'The Crisis of the Tax State', in R. Swedberg (ed.), *J.A. Schumpeter: The Economics and Sociology of Capitalism* (Princeton: Princeton University Press, [1918] 1991), 99–140.

Philosophical Foundations of Tax Law. First Edition. Edited by Monica Bhandari.

feudal realm. It is not suggested that each of the four orders fosters a unique and distinct purpose, or purposes, for a levy. Nor is it argued that history either discloses clear demarcations between each one or that any follow(s) sequentially upon the other(s). Rather the argument is that, in each societal order, one purpose or other seems to predominate. Within all but one are concealed other social orders of world-changing significance. In all times, antecedent purposes persist, purposes that are more or less occluded by later ones. The bloody struggles of England's history yield every possible example, every conceivable unsettling idea.

Discussion turns first to the feudal, since this awakens a consciousness of often-unremarked features of the other orders. Most importantly, although various levies form part of the feudal order, they should not be thought of as taxes in the sense described above. Recognizing this is essential here, because it illuminates later justifications for taxes properly so called. The term 'levies' is used neutrally to comprise impositions that do not satisfy the definition of a tax as well as ones that do. The intention is thereby to illuminate the philosophical issues in this particular chapter by avoiding anachronistic categorization. Such fastidiousness is not always necessary when writing of the history of taxation ideas but it is important for present purposes.

The writer has analysed at length elsewhere the implications of a public law characterization of tax law. This chapter will seek to demonstrate the historical and philosophical significance of purposes and justifications in that characterization. In the process, it will show how tax law became a particular type of public law.

II. The Feudal Realm

The purposes of levies within a feudal realm were shaped by the need to observe God's will and to perform deeds conducive to personal salvation. The feudal realm can usefully be understood as a web of personal allegiances, rather than as a political society, with pre-political law and adjudication, rather than politics, as its main constitutive elements. Ideas of the state relate to types of social ordering rather different from the feudal and law has not always had a political complexion. Feudal justifications recognized the natural law significance of levies but, given these premises, there could be no public law of taxation.

A. Feudal Ideals and Feudal Levies

The ordering of feudal society by a hierarchy of intermediate lords, with the 'pyramidal' structure culminating in the king as lord paramount,[6] implied that levies were either incidents of feudal landholding or well-established types of levy imposed generally.

A strong feudalism lasted in England from the eleventh century and the Norman conquest[7] into the reigns of John (1199–1216) and of his son, Henry III (1216–72). By contrast,

[6] *Mabo v Queensland (No 2)* (1992) 175 CLR 1, 48 (Brennan J); K. Gray and S.F. Gray, *Elements of Land Law*, 5th edn (Oxford: Oxford University Press, 2009), 64.

[7] Gray and Gray, n. 6, 8.

on the European continent and in Asia, in Romanov Russia and Tokugawa Japan,[8] feudalism endured until the latter part of the nineteenth century. The order conferred jurisdictional and coercive powers on lords over 'aristocratic vassals', legally enforceable powers 'which enabled them to extract rents, services and other dues'.[9] It relied 'on the granting of land (fiefs) in exchange for military and administrative services'.[10] Feudalism was about *persons*, rather than purposes. It antedated any public–private distinction, and at its core were ideas of reciprocal rights and obligations, first as between lord and vassal,[11] and then in relation to things ('proprietary rights').[12] The feudal law, in combination with German customary law, came to be what the English referred to as 'the common law'.[13] Besides being strongly coercive, Anglo-Norman feudalism conferred on the judges of the common law an authority superior even to that of the barons. When, around the 1190s, Richard I instituted the Court of Exchequer ('with judges called barons'), this authority was extended to stewardship of the revenue.[14]

The feudal order generated two categories of levy: dues annexed to fiefs and levies imposed as general tribute. Feudal dues constituted much of the royal 'pension', which was generated both by the crown's retained land (the royal demesnes) and land granted away to barons in 'knight-service'.[15] Such dues had always been payable in pennies rather than in kind.[16] A king could unilaterally augment his pension by increasing these dues.[17] Henry II did so in 1159, to move against the Count of Toulouse, adding two marks to a knight's fee worth £20 per year, where the knight did not accompany the king to France.[18] The cash substitute for knight-service was known as 'scutage' and the assessment was based on the number of knights with which a tenant-in-chief was required to furnish the king.[19]

General tribute was well-known.[20] The king could levy 'tallages' in his own demesnes.[21] He could also impose general levies on his tenants-in-chief, ideally with conciliar—that is, curial—advice from the barons.[22] These general levies took the form of 'carucages' (assessed on land),[23] and 'thirteenths' (assessed on movables).[24]

[8] P. Gatrell, 'The Russian Fiscal State, 1600–1914', in B. Yun-Casalilla et al. (eds), *The Rise of Fiscal States: A Global History 1500–1914* (Cambridge, UK: Cambridge University Press, 2012), 191–212, 192, 206; M. Nakabayashi, 'The Rise of a Japanese Fiscal State', in Casalilla, n. 8, 378–409, 380–8.

[9] C. Dyer, *Making a Living in the Middle Ages* (New Haven: Yale University Press, 2009), 71.

[10] Ibid., 8; R. Allen Brown, *Origins of English Feudalism* (London: Allen & Unwin, 1973), 23. Thanks to Peter Cook for referring me to this work.

[11] Schumpeter, n. 5, 103–4; R. Tombs, *The English and Their History* (London: Allen Lane, 2014), 49. Schumpeter was discussing feudalism in the continent but the point holds good for England.

[12] A.W.B. Simpson, *A History of the Land Law*, 2nd edn (Oxford: Clarendon, 1986), 36–7.

[13] Tombs, n. 11, 65–6; R.C. van Caenegem, *An Historical Introduction to Private Law* (Cambridge, UK: Cambridge University Press, 1992), 2–3.

[14] J.H. Baker, *An Introduction to English Legal History*, 4th edn (London: Butterworths, 2002), 17–18, 47–8; Tombs, n. 11, 50 See, further, Baker, ch. 2, esp. 14–22.

[15] Simpson, n. 12, 3–4.

[16] Tombs, n. 11, 49.

[17] S.A. Morgan, *The History of Parliamentary Taxation in England* (New York: Moffat Yard, 1911), 30.

[18] Ibid., 32–3.

[19] D. Carpenter (ed.), *Magna Carta* (London: Penguin, 2015), 126, 468.

[20] R. Bonney, 'Revenues', in R. Bonney (ed.), *Economic Systems and State Finance* (Oxford: Clarendon, 1995), 423–505, 447.

[21] G.L. Harriss, *King, Parliament, and Public Finance in Medieval England to 1369* (Oxford: Clarendon, 1975), 12.

[22] Morgan, n. 17, 41.

[23] Harriss, n. 21, 9–10, 14–16.

[24] Morgan, n. 17, 69 (35, 43–4).

B. Feudal Relationships

If the feudal realm is understood not as a political society—or 'state'—but rather as a web of personal allegiances, the effect is suggestive. For example, a feudal realm did not even need to have geographical borders.[25] It is true that Anglo-Norman England was anomalous because it was mapped onto the Anglo-Saxon kingdom that the Normans had conquered. However, not even that kingdom could be described as an entity that, besides requiring its subjects' allegiance, had 'the monopoly of the legitimate use of physical force within a given territory', not least since the precise extent of that territory was for long far from clear.[26]

With personal allegiance at the centre of the feudal order, tallages and other levies were governed by law rather than politics. It was not until the 1240s that the barons took some control over the king's expenditure.[27] Moreover, even after *Magna Carta* in 1215, the societal order was not a representative one.[28] Barons who promised to make payments to the king, promises binding on their own vassals, made personal commitments as lesser despots, rather than as representatives of those vassals.[29]

The law of God, as expressed in part in judicial decisions, regulated the conduct of a king. The sanctions for wrongdoing were real. Though there was no way of saying whether, or how, sanctions would be visited in this world, they would certainly be enacted in the next. Bracton (d.1268) affirmed that the feudal realm was dependent upon the duties that the king and subject owe both to each other and to God. Obedience to the law was due both to God and to man. Whilst '[t]he king has no equal within his realm', said Bracton, he has to respect the laws, as did Christ Himself:

> The king must not be under man but under God and under the law, because law makes the king, /Let him therefore bestow upon the law what the law bestows upon him, namely rule and power./ for there is no *rex* where will rules rather than *lex*.[30]

The king was thus 'the vicegerent on earth' of Christ, whose obedience to the laws was an example to earthly kings because He himself used 'not the power of force but the reason of justice'.[31]

If kings were governed by the divine law and the divine was ascertained through the natural law, positive law was largely about adjudication in individual cases. Chapter 12 of *Magna Carta*, traditionally portrayed as the beginning of the public law of taxation in England, was—on the view advocated here—not that exactly. It read:

> No scutage or aid is to be levied in our kingdom, save by the common counsel of our kingdom, save for the ransoming of our body, and the making of our first-born son

[25] M. Oakeshott, 'On the Character of a Modern European State', in *On Human Conduct* (Oxford: Clarendon, 1975), 185–326, 207.

[26] M Weber, 'Politics as a Vocation', in H.H. Gerth and C. Wright Mills (eds), *From Max Weber* (London: Routledge and Kegan Paul, [1919] 1948), 77–128, 78, quoted in M. Loughlin, *The Idea of Public Law* (Oxford: Oxford University Press, 2003), 6. See also R.R. Davies, *The First English Empire: Power and Identities in the British Isles 1093–1343* (Oxford: Oxford University Press, 2000), ch. 3, esp. 67.

[27] Morgan, n. 17, 89. [28] Ibid., 91–2. [29] Ibid., 91.

[30] S.E. Thorne (ed. and trans.), *Bracton on the Laws and Customs of England*, vol. 2 (Cambridge, MA: Belknap, 1968), 33.

[31] Ibid.

> a knight, and for the marrying a single time of our first-born daughter; and for these things there is only to be a reasonable aid.[32]

An aid was either '[a] payment demanded by a lord (including the king) from his tenants by knight-service' or a general levy, while 'the common counsel' of the kingdom referred to the king's council of tenants-in-chief, namely barons.[33] This wording, with its generous exclusions, did not therefore refer to taxes in the modern sense, nor did it protect vassals against extraordinary impositions.[34] Shepard Morgan points out that Chapter 12 made no specific mention of carucages, nor of thirteenths. Later versions of the charter emasculated even the limited assurance offered by the original Chapter 12.

C. Feudal Justifications

Feudal levies were justified, not by public purposes, but by personal rights and obligations having a theological origin and expressed in the common law.

Philosophers who wrote during the flourishing of this order alluded to features of feudalism while yearning for the lost *states* of the ancients and to the possibilities of taxes in such states. John of Salisbury (*c.*1115–80), sometime Bishop of Chartres, in his 'Mirror for Princes' work, *Policraticus* (1159), envisaged the societal order as a human body, with the 'Treasurers and record keepers … [resembling] the shape of the stomach and intestines'.[35] But 'there is surprisingly little [in *Policraticus*] that depends consciously on the feudal organization of society which actually … prevailed when John wrote'.[36] John nonetheless accepted that a levy may not be imposed merely to satisfy an avaricious motive of a king.[37]

The justice or otherwise of levies was addressed a century later by the Dominican friar, Thomas Aquinas (*c.*1224–74), who argued that that nonexcessive contributions could be raised by a ruler 'without sin' from citizens in general, it being 'just that the citizens should contribute what is necessary to promote the common interest'.[38] 'The rulers of countries [Aquinas wrote] are appointed a pension which should suffice for their needs, and which removes any excuse for the spoliation of their subjects.'[39] Only a common emergency could justify a general levy.[40] Aquinas assumed features of the

[32] Carpenter, n. 19, 43. For a significantly different assessment, see J. Frecknall-Hughes, 'King John, Magna Carta and Taxation', in R.J. Holland (ed.), *Magna Carta: Muse & Mentor* (Thomson Reuters and Library of Congress, 2014), 191–225.

[33] Carpenter, n. 19, 170, 461.

[34] Morgan, n. 17, 30.

[35] C.J. Nederman (ed.), *John of Salisbury: Policraticus* (Cambridge, UK: Cambridge University Press, 1990), 67. A 'Mirror for Princes' work contained 'instructions to rulers on how to govern correctly' (see J. Fried, *The Middle Ages*, P. Lewis (trans.) (Cambridge, MA: Harvard University Press, 2015), 290.

[36] G.H. Sabine, *A History of Political Theory*, 3rd edn (London: Harrap, 1963), 246. It is important to note that *Policraticus* pre-dates the appearance of William of Moerbecke's translation of Aristotle's *Politics* in 1264 (see Fried, n. 35, 290).

[37] Nederman (ed.), n. 35, 38.

[38] Aquinas, 'On the Government of Jews', in AP d'Entrèves (ed.), *Aquinas: Selected Political Writings* (Oxford: Blackwell, 1959), 93. 'Common good' might be a more apposite translation than 'common interest' (see J. Snape, *The Political Economy of Corporation Tax: Theory, Values and Law Reform* (Oxford: Hart, 2011), 119–22).

[39] AP d'Entrèves (ed.), n. 38, 85–95, 91.

[40] Ibid., 93.

feudal order while seeking to fashion from Aristotle an idea of the state as the perfect community, intrinsically unique, creating laws that were authoritative because they were deliberated over and containing everything necessary for life.[41] Aquinas's natural law system relied on the argument that 'there is an eternal law, implicit in the fact that God constructed the universe on rationally intelligible principles and for rationally endorsable ends'.[42]

The compilation of Domesday Book (1086) had, much earlier on, illustrated the fact that revenue-raising was what the 'gradual and often interrupted extension of royal justice' was all about.[43] Indeed, impelled by the fact that the monarch had to 'increase the income of the crown',[44] revenue-raising was the justification for 'a king's first adventures in "legislation"'.[45] Danegeld, for which there had been a motive, if not a justification, took the form of a carucage when it was reimposed in 1194 during the reign of Richard I (1189–99).[46] It had been abolished *c.*1051 by Edward the Confessor (1042–66) when the king, entering his treasury, saw 'the devil seated upon the money'.[47] John levied the thirteenth of 1207 on the grounds of an anticipated general emergency.[48] A general levy of 1232, imposed on a similar basis, brought down Henry III's Treasurer of the Exchequer, Peter des Rivaux (d.1262). The king, like Christ himself, had to be obedient to natural and positive laws alike. John's failures in this respect were important reasons why he was considered a bad man; it was the appropriate feudal order that the barons sought to reinstate in *Magna Carta*. Indeed, Bracton seemingly authorized them to do so: 'The king has a superior, namely, God. Also the law by which he is made king. Also his *curia*, namely, the earls and barons, because if he is without bridle, that is without law, they ought to put the bridle on him.'[49] A feudal order thus denies the possibility of political justifications but facilitates justifications of a nonpolitical kind. Strategic behaviour, of which William the Conqueror (1066–87) had been the exemplar, and which the thirteenth-century barons had mastered, was nonetheless not political behaviour because there was no state and no intelligible concept of politics. There was a natural law, as well as a divine law, but no conception of taxation as public law.

Thus we have two important components of the analysis. Though the feudal realm knows no public law of taxation, because it is not a state, it creates a common law of property in land. Since it is therefore a pre-political order, it provides a pre-political justification for property—or proprietary—rights, whether in royal grant or as a result of legal adjudication.

[41] Ibid., xxv. Although *Policraticus* (n. 35) 'explicitly labels itself as 'political [*politica*]', this medieval sense does not correspond to Aristotle nor (see below) to Machiavelli (see S. Elden, *The Birth of Territory* (Chicago: Chicago University Press, 2013), 158) and does not therefore predicate a state.

[42] A. Ryan, *On Politics* (London: Allen Lane, 2012), 240.

[43] Oakeshott, n. 25, 208; M. Morris, *The Norman Conquest* (London: Windmill, 2013), 308ff.

[44] Oakeshott, n. 25, 209. [45] Ibid. [46] Harriss, n. 21, 9–10.

[47] H.T. Riley (trans.), *The Annals of Roger de Hoveden*, vol. 1 (London: Bohn, 1853), 132, recounted in Morgan, n. 17, 7; also B.A. Abraham, '"Danegeld"—From Danish Tribute to English Land Tax: The Evolution of Danegeld from 991 to 1086', in J Tiley (ed.), *Studies in the History of Tax Law*, vol. 6 (Oxford: Hart, 2013), 261–82, 272.

[48] Harriss, n. 21, 3, 9, 18–20. [49] Thorne (ed.), n. 30, 110.

III. The Absolutist State

The absolutist state defined the purposes of levies by reference to the prince's judgment and to the intrinsic virtue of obedience. Absolutism reduced the web of feudal allegiances to the nexus of sovereign and subject within precise geographical borders. The prerogatival nature of absolutist levies meant that they were not constituted by law and, not being taxes, were not the subject matter of a public law of taxation. The characteristics of levies under absolutism were refracted by those of *taxes* under its nemeses: the short-lived republic in Britain (1649–60)[50] and the enduring Dutch republic (1581–1795).[51]

A. Absolutist Ideals and Absolutist Levies

Absolutist levies were justified by public purposes with a quasi-theological source upon which the king and his principal advisers[52] had deliberated and the king himself had adjudicated.

In England, effective absolutism tended to be associated with 'the personal rule' of Charles I (1629–40), as well as with certain elements of that of his father James I (1603–25). Charles's sons, Charles II (1660–85) and James II (1685–8), grasped at it somewhat ineffectually.[53] Much earlier, Edward I (1272–1307) stood on his prerogative as, later, did all of the Tudor monarchs, notably Henry VII (1485–1509), his son Henry VIII (1509–47), and Henry VIII's younger daughter Elizabeth I (1558–1603). In France, absolutism's archetype was the long reign of Louis XIV (1643–1715). More recent exemplars of absolutist monarchies have been Saudi Arabia, Jordan, and pre-1979 Iran.[54]

Absolutism, as Alan Ryan explains, had both a theological and a political significance.[55] In theological terms, it signified an order in which a divinely anointed prince governed willing subjects in furtherance of a public interest as to which he adjudicated.[56] In legal terms, absolutists agreed that 'the king was bound by his own laws *until* he chose to suspend them; but they insisted that he had the power to suspend them and was not bound once he had exercised that power'.[57] If feudalism was about *persons*, then absolutism was about *purposes*, and the highest of those purposes was the safety of the people: *salus populi suprema lex esto*.[58]

The contrast between feudal and absolutist orders was thus dramatic and comprehensive. What was at stake was a move from a pre-political order, based on gradations of status and feudal property law, to a political one based on prerogative alone. Such

[50] T.C. Barnard, *The English Republic 1649–1660* (Harlow: Longman, 1982).

[51] J. Israel, *The Dutch Republic* (Oxford: Clarendon, 1995), 285–91.

[52] Notably, William Laud (1573–1645) and the Earl of Strafford (1593–1641) (see J.P. Kenyon, *The Stuart Constitution, 1603–1688* (Cambridge, UK: Cambridge University Press, 1966)).

[53] S. Pincus, *1688: The First Modern Revolution* (New Haven: Yale University Press, 2009), 256–7.

[54] M. Herb, *All in the Family* (Albany: State University of New York Press, 1999), 168, 217–18 (264–6).

[55] Ryan, n. 42, 303, 514.

[56] Ibid., 302–3.

[57] Ibid., 514–15.

[58] M. Oakeshott, *The Politics of Faith and the Politics of Scepticism* (New Haven: Yale University Press, 1996), 39–42.

purposes were the essence of levies in the absolutist state. This is not to characterize absolutism as a monolithic conception. There were wide variations, even in seventeenth-century Europe.[59] But it nonetheless embodies a serviceable interpretation.

Prerogatival levies tended to manifest themselves in terms of customs duties because of an ancient ambiguity as to their control by Parliament. It was this ambiguity that the Exchequer Barons sought to clarify in *Bate's Case*[60] in 1606. A London merchant, John Bate, refused to pay a duty of customs (an 'imposition') on the importation of currants at five-shillings-and-sixpence a hundredweight because the amount of tax was assessed and charged under the prerogative alone.[61] The justification for imposing the duty was the king's right to open and close 'the king's ports' as he saw fit, ports being 'the gates of the king'.[62] In confirming the propriety of the duty, Sir Thomas Fleming CB famously distinguished between the 'ordinary' prerogative and the 'absolute' prerogative[63] of the king,[64] the power of imposing customs duties falling within a range of acts constituting the latter category. The king's ordinary prerogative, not at issue, was exercised by his judges in the formation of the common law ('*jus privatum*'), which 'cannot be changed, without parliament'.[65] The king's absolute prerogative, however, under which customs duties were imposed, was exercised by the king in person for 'the general benefit of the people' and was not contained in legislation.[66] Such a power of imposition was one of the 'great prerogatives of the crown',[67] said Clark B, its revenues constitutive of kingship and inseparable from the crown itself.[68] When, in 1372, statute had banned Edward III (1327–77) from levying customs duties under the prerogative, that ban bound only Edward himself, since the right to customs 'is a principal part of the crown of England, which the king cannot diminish'.[69] Ironically, perhaps, Bate's counsel unsuccessfully urged on the court the passage from Bracton quoted above.[70] This was nothing to the point, though; Michael Oakeshott draws attention to the fact that, in speaking of 'the general benefit of the people', Fleming CB subtly widened the scope of *salus populi* beyond 'public safety'.[71] In response, James I issued, under the Great Seal, his prerogatival book of customs duties.[72] James wrote:

> princes ... may according to their several occasions raise to themselves such fit and competent means by levying of customs and impositions upon merchandise transported out of their kingdom or brought into their dominions ... as to their wisdoms and discretions may seem convenient.[73]

[59] Pincus, n. 53, 480 (England), 360 (Denmark), 360–1 (France).

[60] (1606) 2 St Tr col 371.

[61] J.S. Hart, Jr., *The Rule of Law, 1603–1660* (Harlow: Pearson, 2003), 91–8.

[62] (1606) 2 St Tr col 371, cols 386, 389 (see G.D.G. Hall, 'Impositions and the Courts 1554–1606', 69 *Law Quarterly Review* (1953), 200–18).

[63] Hart, n. 61, 96; L.A. Knafla, *Law and Politics in Jacobean England* (Cambridge, UK: Cambridge University Press, 1977), 66.

[64] (1606) 2 St Tr col 371, col 389.

[65] Ibid.

[66] Ibid.; T. Poole, 'Hobbes on Law and Prerogative', in D. Dyzenhaus and T. Poole (eds), *Hobbes and the Law* (Cambridge, UK: Cambridge University Press, 2012), 85.

[67] (1606) 2 St Tr col 371, col 383.

[68] Ibid.; also R. Barber, *Edward III and the Triumph of England* (London: Allen Lane, 2013), 129, 580.

[69] (1606) 2 St Tr col 371, col 385; 45 Edw III (1370–1371) c 4 (customs) (see Morgan, n. 17, 242n).

[70] Hart, n. 61, 96.

[71] Oakeshott, n. 58, 40.

[72] Morgan, n. 17, 244–5; Poole, n. 66, 84.

[73] G.W. Prothero (ed.), *Select Statutes and Other Constitutional Documents*, 4th edn (London: Oxford University Press, 1913), 354, quoted in Morgan, n. 17, 245.

Reasoning similar to that of the Exchequer Barons in *Bate's Case* was used two decades later in the *Case of Ship-Money* (*R v Hampden*),[74] to justify the prerogatival imposition, on noncoastal counties, of the obligation either to provide royal ships or contribute to their maintenance.[75] There were, however, extra dimensions to the later decision. The judicial approach in *Bate* was quite legalistic (to which prerogative do customs belong?), while in *R v Hampden* it was more wide-ranging, even theologico-political. Like *Bate's Case, R v Hampden* prioritized historical precedent ahead of the claims of old ideas of natural law. Before the issuing of the earliest ship-money writs in 1634, there had been an appeal to history to justify the running of writs to inland counties. Morgan depicts Sir William Noy A-G locking himself in the Tower of London 'for some days' so 'that he might better consult the ancient authorities'.[76] Never mind the justice: for Charles the expedience of precedent was the thing.

B. Absolutist Relationships

Effective absolutism was extremely short-lived in England but, as eventually theorized, it did come to rely on a new conception of natural law based upon a science of mankind.

The proprietary nature of the absolutist tie between king and subject was expressed in Louis XIV's aphorism: '*l'état c'est à moi*'.[77] Edward I's 1303 prerogatival imposition of 'tunnage and poundage' explicitly recognized both the distinction between subject and alien[78] and the geographical parameters of the English state. Absolutist levies were not tributary: rather they were the appropriation by the king of resources the property in which was in a sense *already his*.

Within the absolutist state, feudal ties had gradually been dissolved, although there was no single point of national manumission of unfree subjects.[79] The Tenures Abolition Act of 1660[80] affirmed that the realm was not dependent on reciprocal obligations of king and subject nor of each to God. The Act, which compensated the crown for the loss of its dues and abolished knight-service, made the tenure of all nonecclesiastical land, except copyhold, freehold tenure. The 1660 Act confirmed a Commonwealth measure of 1656. From now on, freeholders owed nothing to the crown merely by virtue of holding an estate in land, while copyholders paid rent to the lord of the manor and all subjects paid amounts on account of indirect levies (e.g. excise duties) to the sellers of commodities. Still, the king was God's vicegerent,

[74] (1637) 3 St Tr 825.

[75] D.L. Keir, 'The Case of Ship-Money', 52 *Law Quarterly Review* (1936) 546–74; Hart, n. 61, 148–57; C. Cooper et al., 'The Stuarts, the Civil War and After,' in J. Banbury et al. (eds), *Woodstock and the Royal Park* (Oxford: Andrews, 2010), 45–6.

[76] Morgan, n. 17, 281.

[77] H.H. Rowen, '"L'État c'est à moi": Louis XIV and the State', 2 *French Historical Studies* (1961) 83–98; Schumpeter, n. 5, 108.

[78] Morgan, n. 17, 158.

[79] I.S. Leadam, 'The Last Days of Bondage in England', 9 *Law Quarterly Review* (1893) 348.

[80] 12 Charles II c 24 (1597–1672) 7 *Statutes at Large*, 472.

with the important difference from feudalism that this vicegerent was guided by expedient judgment only.[81]

It was in the work of Thomas Hobbes (1588–1679) that the role of natural law in absolute monarchy was rethought. Hobbes's was a new kind of natural law, conceived as 'a science of virtue and vice and of good and evil'.[82] He was a theorist of absolutism but his work was ambiguous, as would be demonstrated much later by its importance to the administrative state. Hobbes, tutor to an aristocratic Derbyshire family, was a legal and political philosopher of incomparable breadth and depth. Appalled by the losses of the two Civil Wars, Hobbes concluded that Charles I's ideas had been right but his methods too soft.[83] The ties of feudal society needed to be reimagined in terms of a single political body, a 'mortal god' stronger than anyone or anything else, to which all individual wills were surrendered and which was endowed with the supreme purpose of saving the people:[84]

> [T]he multitude so united in one person, is called a COMMONWEALTH, in Latin CIVITAS. This is … that great LEVIATHAN, or rather, to speak more reverently … that *mortal god*, to which we owe under the *immortal God*, our peace and defence.[85]

Salus populi was 'the end, for which … [the sovereign representative was] trusted with the sovereign power'.[86] It followed that all relationships had to be reconfigured in political terms on the basis both of 'expedience' and a 'law of nature' understood in terms of 'the known natural inclinations of mankind'.[87] There was no scope for a curial bridle to be put on the sovereign. The account that the sovereign had eventually to give of the people's safety would have to be made 'to God, the author of that law [of nature] and to none but him'.[88] Promoting the people's safety meant revisiting Aquinas' ideas on taxation, as read by Hugo Grotius.[89] '[B]y safety here [said Hobbes], is not meant a bare preservation, but also all other contentments of life, which every man by lawful industry, without danger, or hurt to the commonwealth, shall acquire to himself'.[90] It was therefore necessary and, by definition, just, for what Hobbes significantly referred to as 'Taxes' to be 'equal', not according to ability to pay, but according to the benefit gained: 'To equal justice, appertaineth also the equal imposition of taxes; the equality whereof dependeth not on the equality of riches, but on the equality of the debt that every man oweth to the commonwealth for his defence.'[91] The consequence, if this and other axioms were not followed, would be the death of the mortal god. Hobbes gives

[81] King James VI and I, 'The Trew Law of Free Monarchies', in J.P. Sommerville (ed.), *King James VI and I: Political Writings* (Cambridge, UK: Cambridge University Press, 1994), 62–84.

[82] P. Zagorin, *Hobbes and the Law of Nature* (Princeton: Princeton University Press, 2009), 101 (see M. Oakeshott (ed.), *Leviathan* (Oxford: Blackwell, 1955), 219).

[83] F. Tönnies (ed.), *Behemoth or The Long Parliament: Thomas Hobbes* (Chicago: Chicago University Press, 1990), 116–17, as referenced in Poole, n. 66, 68–96, 71.

[84] M. Oakeshott, n. 82, 112. [85] Ibid. [86] Ibid., 219.

[87] Ibid., 466 (quoted in Zagorin, n. 82, 103). [88] Ibid., 219.

[89] R. Tuck and J. Barbeyrac (eds) and J Morrice (trans.), *Hugo Grotius: The Rights of War and Peace* (Indianapolis: Liberty Fund, 2005), 445 (II.2. XIV).

[90] Oakeshott (ed.), n. 82, 219; T. Sorell, 'Hobbes, Public Safety and Political Economy', in R. Prokhovnik and G. Slomp (eds), *International Political Theory After Hobbes* (Basingstoke, UK: Palgrave Macmillan, 2011), 42–55.

[91] Oakeshott (ed.), n. 82, 226.

us pause for thought because he wrote of 'taxes' in an absolutist context. Hobbes's attitude to prerogative was constitutive. The sovereign should 'choose law [rather than prerogative] in all but exceptional cases'.[92]

C. Absolutist Justifications

The impersonal allegiance of absolutism left wide scope for general levies. An absolutist order mandated political justifications. There was a political practice, even a natural law, relative to levying impositions, but still no public law of taxation.

Thinkers who had provided earlier theoretical bases for absolutist political orders, and the levies supporting them, had combined features of the feudal order with classical republicanism.[93] Niccolò Machiavelli (1469–1527), an out-of-favour public servant from Florence, a city-state carved out of the web of feudal allegiances on the Italian peninsula, turned not to Aristotle, as Aquinas had, but to Livy and to the history of ancient Rome.[94] Unlike Aquinas, Machiavelli did not take any natural law as an ethical yardstick, preferring instead to measure princes by their successes and failures and by their ability calculatingly to weigh means and ends in ensuring the safety of the people.[95] Consistent with this outlook, Machiavelli had been uninterested in the detail of taxation,[96] only in the skill or ineptitude with which levies were laid. In Catholic France, a Machiavellian impulse was embodied, though sublimated, in the work of various schools of absolutist theory,[97] the most famous of which has remained the work of Jean Bodin (1529–96), a significant adaptor of the image of taxes as 'the nerves of the state'.[98] It is to this world that the expedient dictum of Jean-Baptiste Colbert (1619–83) belongs, about taxation involving extracting the maximum number of goose feathers with the least hissing.[99]

It was possibly Thomas Cromwell (*c*.1485–1540)[100] who admitted Machiavelli's ideas to English government.[101] Cromwell's offices of Henry VIII's Principal Secretary and Chancellor of the Exchequer dominated 'the organs of English government more effectively and more creatively than any minister since de[s] Rivaux's day'.[102] Much later, a Kentish country squire, Sir Robert Filmer (1588–1653), wrote *Patriarcha*, a long-unpublished[103] theologico-political work clothing absolutism and the divine

[92] Poole, n. 66, 96.

[93] Ryan, n. 42, 233, 301–11.

[94] C. Vivanti, *Niccolò Machiavelli*, S. MacMichael (trans.) (Princeton: Princeton University Press, 2013), ch. 15.

[95] L. Strauss, *Thoughts on Machiavelli* (Chicago: University of Chicago Press, 1958), 216; P. Bobbitt, *The Garments of Court and Palace* (London: Atlantic, 2013), ch. 3.

[96] Nor in 'economic' matters generally (see A.O. Hirschman, *The Passions and the Interests*, 2nd edn (Princeton: Princeton University Press, 1997), 41).

[97] M. Koskenniemi, 'The Advantage of Treaties: International Law in the Enlightenment', 13(1) *Edinburgh Law Review* (2009) 27–67.

[98] C. Webber and A. Wildavsky, *A History of Taxation and Expenditure in the Western World* (New York: Simon and Schuster, 1986), 259.

[99] Quoted, e.g., in K. Ussher and I. Walford, *National Treasure* (London: Demos, 2011), 43.

[100] H. Leithead, 'Cromwell, Thomas, Earl of Essex', in *Oxford Dictionary of National Biography* (Oxford: Oxford University Press, 2004); online edn, May 2009, http://0-www.oxforddnb.com.pugwash.lib.warwick.ac.uk/view/article/6769 (accessed 17 March 2015).

[101] J.P. Coby, *Thomas Cromwell* (Lanham: Lexington, 2009), 31.

[102] H. Roseveare, *The Treasury* (London: Allen Lane, 1969), 37.

[103] Ryan, n. 42, 457.

right of kings with a mystic donation of the whole earth to Adam, the first king, and to all of Adam's firstborn ever since.[104] In relation to levies, the significance of Filmer's ideas was that they denied the possibility of private property in any resource—land or labour—out of which the subject would be free to grant taxation to a king.[105] Running through all of these ideas was 'reason of state', namely, 'a form of political reason driven by the need to ensure the survival and well-being of the state'.[106]

Absolutist monarchs tended to levy impositions in one of three ways. One was to impose general levies in reliance on the prerogative, as discussed above. A typical writ justified ship-money by the need 'to hasten the defence of the sea and kingdom with all expedition or speed that we can'.[107] Failing that, supply could be sought from Parliament on the basis already mentioned, namely to go along with parliamentary procedures only so far as expedient. Thirdly, the king might invoke what has been called 'fiscal feudalism'. In other words, as an absolute monarch, to rely on ancient feudal sources of revenue. This third possibility, 'feudalism kept alive for no other reason than to bring in revenue to the government' was also a matter simply of expedience.[108] Each was unlikely always to be equally prudent. An overarching enforceable justification for a levy was the essence of absolutist kingship, yet it did not exclude the presence of a private motive. Henry VIII's unsuccessful attempts to impose extra-parliamentary levies, together with Charles I's personal rule, show that absolutist levies in England were something of an aberration. The absolutist state was an example of what Oakeshott called *universitas*, an ideal type drawn from 'Roman private law',[109] with the state as an enterprise association,[110] its subjects promoting 'a common substantive purpose'.[111] *Universitas* was an implication of the divine right of kings.[112] Unlike in the feudal 'realm', however, the allegiance required of the subject was explicitly territorial. The whole country comprised 'the manor of England': all property was in the king. Absolutism was simply a matter of expedient rule. In the process, though, levies were beginning to change purpose, since there was a growing sense that they would be needed for purposes of the state ('*salus populi*'), as opposed to those of the prince himself. In fact, the British and Dutch republics provided a vivid contrast with absolutism. The British Instrument of Government of 1653[113] not only required, generally speaking, common consent to taxation, but it provided the eccentric James Harrington (1611–77) with the inspiration for *Oceana* (1656), an ideal republic constituted by the consent of freeholders.[114]

[104] J.P. Sommerville (ed.), '*Patriarcha*', in *Sir Robert Filmer: Patriarcha and Other Writings* (Cambridge, UK: Cambridge University Press, 1991), 1–68.

[105] R. Filmer, 'The Free-Holders Grand Inquest', in Ibid., 69–130, 128–9; C. Cuttica, *Sir Robert Filmer (1588-1653) and the Patriotic Monarch* (Manchester, UK: Manchester University Press, 2012), 148, 156.

[106] Loughlin, *Idea*, n. 26, 150.

[107] See S.R. Gardiner (ed.), *The Constitutional Documents of the Puritan Revolution, 1625–1660*, 3rd edn (Oxford: Clarendon, 1906), 105–8 (specimen writ), quoted in Morgan, n. 17, 282n.

[108] J. Hurstfield, 'The Profits of Fiscal Feudalism, 1541–1602', 8(1) *Economic History Review* (New Series) (1955) 53–61, 53, quoted in M.J. Braddick, *The Nerves of State: Taxation and the Financing of the English State, 1558-1714* (Manchester and New York: Manchester University Press, 1996), 72; Ryan, n. 42, 514–15.

[109] Oakeshott, n. 25, 199. [110] Ibid., 187. [111] Ibid., 205. [112] Ibid., 221.

[113] Recital 6; Art 30.

[114] J.G.A. Pocock (ed.), 'The Commonwealth of Oceana', in *James Harrington: The Commonwealth of Oceana and A System of Politics* (Cambridge, UK: Cambridge University Press, 1992), 1–266; Ryan, n. 42, 500–10.

Thus we have the third and fourth key components of the analysis. Though the absolutist state held no public law of taxation, it had a political practice of impositions. Moreover, as a political order, its levies attempted to override any pre-political, namely feudal, justifications for property rights.

IV. The Parliamentary State

The purposes of taxes in the parliamentary state were shaped by property rights and by consent. The reductive relationship of sovereign and subject, expressed or implied by absolutism, was transformed into the relationship of constituent and representative, its reach defined by reference to national borders. The status of levies as taxes, together with severe restrictions on prerogative, implied a circumscribed and understated public law of taxation. The characteristics of a parliamentary state's taxes were embodied, from 1787, in the taxes of the United States of America,[115] as well as in taxes of lands that remained colonized by the British until after World War I.

A. Parliamentary Ideals and Parliamentary Levies

Levies in the parliamentary state were justified by public purposes duly deliberated upon and negotiated between crown and Parliament.

In England, the parliamentary state has chiefly been associated with the limited monarchy of William III and Mary II (1689–1702), with Anne (1702–14), with the Hanoverian kings who followed,[116] and with the reign of Victoria (1837–1901). However, the parliamentary state took shape much earlier, in the reigns of Plantagenet, Lancastrian, and Yorkist kings. It is thus important to realize that, in England, the parliamentary state was no less a late medieval phenomenon than an eighteenth-century one. In France, during much of the eighteenth century, Anglophile philosophers, notably Montesquieu, looked wistfully across the Channel at what they perceived to be a society ordered according to law. Today, in the light of the ideological upheavals of the twentieth century, the parliamentary state has few if any analogues, although Kuwait,[117] certain principalities, and tiny offshore financial centres may yet be close to it. The parliamentary state, for Ryan, had both political and legal dimensions.[118] In political terms, it signified an order in which a prince governed subjects in furtherance of a public interest as to which he adjudicated to the greatest possible extent with the other estates of Parliament, namely the House of Commons and the House of Lords. In legal terms, a limited monarch was in no wise permitted to dispense with laws. The parliamentary state was principally concerned with persons and with the purposes of persons. The highest value appertaining to those persons was property, both in themselves and in their possessions, values protected by the subject's right to consent to taxation by Act of Parliament, as required by 'the fiscal constitution'.[119]

[115] D.J. Boorstin, *The Americans* (London: Weidenfeld & Nicolson, 1966), 393–400.

[116] P. Langford, *Public Life and the Propertied Englishman 1689–1798* (Oxford, Clarendon: 1991), 1–14, 35–51.

[117] Herb, n. 54, 82. [118] Ryan, n. 42, 462–3.

[119] J. Jaconelli, 'The "Bowles Act"—Cornerstone of the Fiscal Constitution', 69(3) *Cambridge Law Journal* (2010) 582–608; J. Locke, 'Of Civil Government. Book II: Second Treatise', in I. Shapiro et al. (eds)

The relationship between absolutist and parliamentary orders thus represented a partial transformation. What was at stake was twofold: the restriction of prerogative within a framework of public law or, as it was also called, 'political law', whose rationale was reason of state; and the reassertion of pre-political—or, feudal—property rights, as delineated in individual cases. Independent royal judges, the successors of their feudal counterparts, articulated the common law rules of property and contract as private law. Such a combination of laws formed the philosophical essence of tax law in the parliamentary state. The parliamentary state was, however, no monolithic conception any more than the absolutist had been. It was never completely secure, its intellectual limitations never conclusively tested as against absolutist tendencies.[120]

Unlike under absolutism or the English republic, no prerogatival rights to levies were retained in the parliamentary state. This followed from the priority accorded to a taxpayer's right to consent over his duty to the state. Parliamentary taxation took the form, successively, of: the subsidy (to 1640); the fifteenth and tenth (likewise, to 1640); customs duties (1340 onwards, with prerogatival interruptions);[121] the excise (1643, 1660 onwards); the hearth tax or 'chimney tax' (1662 to 1689); the land tax (1689 and thereafter); poll taxes (intermittently, from at least 1381 to 1699);[122] the window tax (1695 to 1851);[123] stamp duties (1694 onwards); and, most portentously, a relatively modest personal income tax (1799–1802, 1803–16, 1842 onwards).[124]

B. Parliamentary Relationships

With absolutist hiatuses, parliamentary government was the norm in England from around the end of the thirteenth century to the late nineteenth century. Royal, though independent, judges were crucial to its success.

The layered nature of parliamentary ties was expressed in 'the representative principle' and in 'the distribution of powers'.[125] These ideas were explored—differently—in the work of John Locke (1632–1704) and of Montesquieu.[126] The judges held the

Two Treatises of Government and *A Letter Concerning Toleration* (New Haven: Yale University Press, 2003), 161; A.J. Simmons, *On the Edge of Anarchy* (Princeton: Princeton University Press, 1993), 91, 96–8.

[120] P. Langford, *A Polite and Commercial People* (Oxford: Clarendon, 1989), 529. On public law as shaped by reason of state, see Loughlin, n. 26, 163. A similar anxiety is evident from current American tax controversies, in regard to which the pre-political and Lockeian picture of property rights (though not, of course, of feudal origin) remains ideologically important (see, e.g., the discussion in R.A. Epstein, *Design for Liberty: Private Property, Public Administration, and the Rule of Law* (Cambridge, MA, and London: Harvard University Press, 2011)).

[121] 14 Edw III (1340) c 1 (customs); 14 Edw III (1340) c 2 (customs) (see Morgan, n. 17, 176–9).

[122] M.J. Braddick, *Parliamentary Taxation in Seventeenth-Century England* (Woodbridge: Boydell, 1994).

[123] C. Stebbings, 'Public Health Imperatives and Taxation Policy: the Window Tax as an Early Paradigm in English Law', in J. Tiley (ed.), *Studies in the History of Tax Law*, vol. 5 (Oxford: Hart, 2012), 43–71.

[124] E.R.A. Seligman, *The Income Tax* (New York: Macmillan, 1911), 57–166.

[125] On this expression, rather than 'separation of powers', see C. Spector, *Montesquieu: Liberté, Droit, et Histoire* (Paris: Michalon, 2010), 178.

[126] A.M. Cohler et al. (eds), *Montesquieu: The Spirit of the Laws* (Cambridge, UK: Cambridge University Press, 1989), 156–66 (XI:6); Shapiro et al. (eds), n. 119, 164–71.

balance between crown and subject in two later eighteenth-century cases: *Entick v Carrington* in 1765;[127] and *City of Glasgow v Murdoch, Warren and Co* in 1783.[128] The levies of the parliamentary state were not tributary, nor were they appropriations. They were taxes *properly so called.*

It was a return to late thirteenth or early fourteenth century 'rights and liberties' that the 1689 Parliament sought to effect in the Bill of Rights:

> [T]he said lords spiritual and temporal, and commons … being now assembled in a full and free representative of this nation … do in the first place (as their ancestors in like case have usually done) for the vindicating and asserting their ancient rights and liberties, declare …
>
> …
>
> 4. That levying money for or to the use of the crown, by pretence of prerogative, without grant of parliament, for longer time, or in other manner than the same is or shall be granted, is illegal.[129]

This wording developed the substance of part of the eighth article of the Petition of Right of 1628, which in turn had been inspired by *Magna Carta*.[130] The Bill of Rights was a clear expression of the representative principle. It built on the 1660 Tenures Abolition Act and was dependent on a constituent elector being, at least in the shires, a freeholder with at least forty shillings a year.[131] There were many more such freeholders in 1689 than there had been in, say, 1489.[132] The 1688–1689 settlement was the adaptation of Hobbesian ideas to a sovereign as crown-in-parliament. Henceforth, as for most of the preceding four centuries, reasonably well-off freeholder Britons could be compelled to relinquish property in some or all of their possessions only if their elected representatives had consented on their behalf. Such freeholders rejected utterly the notion that the crown could be guided merely by expedient judgement. The anointed king's prudence had instead to be exercised with due regard to the just claim of the freeholder's ancient property right. It is this arrangement that Montesquieu detected as complementing the distribution of powers when he visited England in 1729–31.[133]

Both *Entick v Carrington* (a property and constitutional, rather than a tax, case as such) and *Glasgow v Murdoch, Warren and Co* illustrated the pervasiveness of Locke's ideas in eighteenth-century England, with a 'rule of law' mediated by an independent judiciary. In *Entick v Carrington*, after emphasizing that '[t]he Revolution restored this constitution to its first principles … and … neither widened nor contracted the foundation, but repaired, and perhaps added a buttress or two to the fabric',[134] Lord

[127] (1765) 19 St Tr col 1029, CP.

[128] (1782) 2 *Paton's Appeals* 615, http://solo.bodleian.ox.ac.uk/primo_library/libweb/action/dlDisplay.do?vid=OXVU1&docId=oxfaleph013034083 (accessed 1 October 2015).

[129] Bill of Rights 1689, 1 William & Mary (1688–1689) c 2, Art 4 (see also E.N. Williams, *The Eighteenth-Century Constitution 1688–1815* (Cambridge, UK: Cambridge University Press, 1970), 28).

[130] Kenyon, n. 52, 84.

[131] 8 Hen VI (1429) c 7 (electors).

[132] J. Leheny (ed.), *Joseph Addison: The Freeholder* (Oxford: Clarendon, 1979), 1.

[133] R. Shackleton, *Montesquieu* (Oxford: Oxford University Press, 1961), ch. 6.

[134] (1765) 19 St Tr col 1029, col 1068.

Camden CJCP trod a Lockeian path in defending the exclusivity of property rights against prerogatival search warrants of private houses:

> The great end, for which men entered into society, was to secure their property. That right is preserved sacred and incommunicable in all instances, where it has not be taken away or abridged by some public law for the good of the whole. The cases where this right of property is set aside by positive law, are various. Distresses, executions, forfeitures, taxes, &c. are all of this description; wherein every man, by common consent gives up that right, for the sake of justice and the general good.[135]

By man's entering into 'society', Lord Camden evidently had in mind some foundational moment for 'political society'. Perhaps also—and this is speculative—in speaking of men entering into society, he meant the election of the first knights of the shires to Parliament in the reign of Henry III. He spoke of the 1688–9 Revolution ('the Glorious Revolution') as repairing and reviving the ancient constitution. The Chief Justice acknowledged the public good as part of the reason for setting aside property rights by taxation. However, he also implied that the taxpayer consents, too, from a human impulse to distributive justice.[136]

The decision of the House of Lords in *City of Glasgow v Murdoch, Warren and Co* dates from twenty years later.[137] There, Lord Mansfield delineated the boundaries of parliamentary consent in relation to the construction of a taxation statute. The statute required a seller or brewer of beer 'living or carrying on his or her brewery, without the ... city of Glasgow' to give notice to Glasgow's magistrates, and hence to pay a duty of two Scots pence, on each pint that the seller or brewer imported into or sold in the city. To avoid the Act, Murdoch, Warren and Co. (the respondents) contracted to sell the quantity of beer previously sold in Glasgow to one Monro, who then supplied customers at the respondents' brewery premises in Anderston outside Glasgow. The Lords of Session had held that this 'device' enabled the respondents to avoid the duty. However, the House reversed the Lords of Session's interlocutor,[138] ordering that:

> the respondents, by selling beer and ale [to Monro], upon the express condition of his selling the whole in the town of Glasgow, and making discounts and allowances, is a manifest evasion of the act of the 28 Geo. II., and ought to be considered as selling within the town of Glasgow by the respondents themselves.[139]

The two cases illustrate the idea of the rule of law that E.P. Thompson described as an 'unqualified good': the idea that 'the essential precondition for the effectiveness of law, in its function as ideology, ... [is] that it shall display an independence from gross manipulation and shall seem to be just'.[140]

[135] Ibid., col 1066.

[136] S. Fleischacker, *A Short History of Distributive Justice* (Cambridge, MA: Harvard University Press, 2004), 23.

[137] I. Ferrier, 'The Meaning of the Statute: Mansfield on Tax Avoidance', *British Tax Review* [1981] 303–8.

[138] (1782) 2 Paton's Appeals 615, 617–18.

[139] Ibid., 618: see comments by Ferrier, n. 137, 305–6.

[140] E.P. Thompson, *Whigs and Hunters* (London: Penguin, 1990), 263, 267.

The commercial role of law in the parliamentary state was most fully explored in the work of Adam Smith (1723–90), university professor, independent scholar, and sometime customs officer.[141] Smith, a subtle and elusive moral philosopher, was the creator of a frustratingly incomplete philosophical system of law and government. That system yielded a conception of human nature[142] and of the historical effects of that nature in commercial relationships.[143] Fearful of the mischief engendered by extant theories of government and commerce, Smith concluded that the only solution was to be found in 'the natural system of perfect liberty and justice'.[144] Assuming something of Hobbes' mortal god, while softening elements of Hobbes' theory, Smith took aspects of contemporary taxation theory (especially from Montesquieu), supported them by minute detail, and formulated principles of taxation adapted to the eighteenth-century parliamentary state. Smith's teaching was encapsulated in his summary formulation of the four maxims of taxation:

> All nations have endeavoured, to the best of their judgment, to render their taxes as equal as they could contrive; as certain, as convenient to the contributor, both in the time and in the mode of payment, and, in proportion to the revenue which they brought to the prince, as little burdensome to the people.[145]

Like Hobbes's theory, this was an expedient and pragmatic view of taxation. Smith even allowed for a very small measure of redistribution.[146] To that extent, something of Aquinas was retained in Smith's philosophy. Taxes would be ineffective if these axioms were not heeded. The crucial point, though, was that the taxes so created were designed to institute government and government was there to protect property.[147] Indeed, it was the parliamentary protection of domestic manufacturers that anyway tended to frustrate the inauguration of 'the freedom of trade'.[148]

C. Parliamentary Justifications

Philosophers of the parliamentary state emphasized its Aristotelian origins, distancing themselves from the Machiavellianism of absolutism.

Writers who provided the philosophical basis of this propertied parliamentary order did so by combining features of the feudal law with new, more empirical, statements of natural law related to those exploited by Hobbes and Smith.[149] Machiavelli was present though understated in this new approach, possibly because he wanted to move beyond feudalism,[150] possibly because he did not mention natural law,[151]

[141] S. Fleischacker, *On Adam Smith's 'Wealth of Nations'* (Princeton: Princeton University Press, 2004).

[142] D.D. Raphael and A.L. Macfie (eds), *Adam Smith: The Theory of Moral Sentiments* (Indianapolis: Liberty Fund, 1982).

[143] R.H. Campbell et al. (eds), *Adam Smith: An Inquiry into the Nature and Causes of the Wealth of Nations*, 2 vols (Indianapolis: Liberty Fund, 1981).

[144] Ibid., II, 606 (IV.vii.c.44). [145] Ibid., II, 827 (V.ii.b.7). [146] Ibid., II, 842 (V.ii.e.6).

[147] Ibid., II, 715 (V.i.b.12). [148] Ibid., I, 471–2 (IV.ii.43–4).

[149] Ryan, n. 42, ch. 13. [150] Bobbitt n. 95, 121.

[151] I. Berlin, 'The Originality of Machiavelli', in H. Hardy (ed.), *Against the Current: Essays in the History of Ideas* (London: Hogarth, 1979), 25–79, 36.

possibly because in the parliamentary state his ideas had limited scope for operation. Sir Edward Coke (1552–1634), by contrast, promoted a return to medieval ideas of taxation and the even older ancient constitution.[152] In 1625, he told the House of Commons that, 'ordinary charges the Kinge should beare alone; but *ubi commune periculum, commune auxilium*'.[153] Coke would ultimately be one of the architects of the Petition of Right.[154] Filmer's arguments for the divine right of kings became the target for Locke's *First Treatise of Government* (1690),[155] one of the philosophical cornerstones of the parliamentary state. Locke denied the donation of the earth to kings as the first born of the first born of Adam.[156] Instead, in his *Second Treatise of Government* (1690),[157] Locke maintained the earth had been given at the creation to mankind in common, the holders of property rights in land today being the descendants by purchase of those who, in the state of nature, acquired property in land by mixing with the land the labour of their bodies.[158] Crucially, 'every man has a property in his own person: this nobody has any right to but himself. The labour of his body, and the work of his hands, we may say, are properly his'.[159] This 'bottom-up theory' articulates a conception of property rights as pre-dating the institution of the state.[160] The holder of such rights can grant part of them to the crown by way of taxation, although, for the grant to be valid, it must be made by the consent of the property-holder's elected representatives. Given the enormous expense of government, Locke wrote, all those who benefit from its protection should bear a proportion of the cost. However, this should only be with majoritarian consent. For it to be otherwise would 'subvert' the very purpose for which government was instituted: the protection of property.[161] It is with this conception of property and consent that Locke adapted Aquinas's theory of taxation to the institutions of representative government. With it, too, came a very thin version of the Aquinian ethical obligation of the holder of property rights to share the resource in which the rights subsist with those who lack the means to live.[162]

The consensual nature of the parliamentary state left even wider scope for general levies than did absolutism. This was because of the broadly based consent needed for taxes to be designed and implemented. The parliamentary order, however, mandated defence as essentially the sole justification for taxation. If he was not to borrow, the

[152] J.G.A. Pocock, *The Ancient Constitution and the Feudal Law*, 2nd edn (Cambridge, UK: Cambridge University Press, 1987), 39–40; P. Raffield, *Images and Cultures of Law in Early Modern England: Justice and Political Power, 1558-1660* (Cambridge, UK: Cambridge University Press, 2004), 199–208.

[153] S.R. Gardiner (ed.), *Debates in the House of Commons in 1625* (London: Camden Society, 1873), 32, quoted in G.L. Harriss, 'Thomas Cromwell's "New Principle" of Taxation', 93 *English Historical Review* (1978) 721–38, 738.

[154] Kenyon, n. 52, 82–5.

[155] J. Locke, 'Of Government. Book I: First Treatise', in Shapiro et al. (eds), n. 119, 7–99.

[156] Ibid., 14–18.

[157] J. Locke, 'Of Civil Government. Book II: Second Treatise', n. 119, 100–209.

[158] Ibid., 111–21. The invention of money was crucial for Locke (see J. Dunn, *Locke* (Oxford: Oxford University Press, 1984), 39–40).

[159] Ibid., 111. [160] Epstein, n. 120, 99.

[161] Shapiro et al. (eds), *Second Treatise*, n. 119, 163.

[162] J. Waldron, *God, Locke, and Equality* (Cambridge, UK: Cambridge University Press, 2002), 177n, noting Aquinas's *Summa Theologica*, II.q.66.

king had to ask Parliament for supply. Gradually, the parliamentary state dismantled the possibilities of prerogatival levies, though they were definitively removed only in 1689. Benevolences, for instance, were abolished in 1484, only to be reintroduced by prerogative in 1491.[163] This was the mixed, or limited, monarchy[164] so deplored by Hobbes, yet so essential to rights of property. There was a public law, as well as a natural law, of taxation.

In the parliamentary state, it was difficult for a king's private motives to prevail over public purposes. Henry VII provided an example of motives actually doing so.[165] Even Elizabeth I, though, had to negotiate with Parliament for supply.[166] Because the parliamentary state was in Oakeshott's terms a *societas*, however, the range of purposes for which taxes could be levied was necessarily restricted. *Societas*, the state as a 'civil association', is Oakeshott's contrasting ideal to the *universitas* referred to above. *Societas* was not an enterprise association but an association valuing loyalty, legality, and the rule of law.[167] *Societas* was the focus of allegiance rather than the vehicle for an overarching project.[168] Taxes raised for defence purposes thus became 'the sinews of power'[169] in a 'fiscal-military' state. Between 1689 and 1815, 'net expenditure' on the navy was rarely less than £1 million per annum.[170] Gerald Harriss mapped tax purposes over the period from *c.*1300 to 1625. He found barely a single case of parliament granting supply to the crown for a purpose other than defence.[171] Defence of the Protestant state was thus almost the exclusive justification for taxes, for centuries after Thomas Cromwell, with the brief interruption of Mary I's reign (1553–8). An Aquinian echo in a Machiavellian world was that parliamentary taxes were raised only at times of national emergency, notably income tax during the Napoleonic Wars.

So we come to the fifth and sixth building blocks of the analysis. The levies of the parliamentary state were not tributary, nor were they appropriations. They were taxes *properly so called*. They had two ingredients that levies under the other systems so far discussed did not have: legislative authority, that is, the authority of the people's representatives, rather than divine or royal will; and legal compulsion. Taxes were the subject of a relatively simple and understated public law, which complimented a strict private law of property of feudal origin. The design of tax legislation was informed by a branch of natural law increasingly thought of as 'political economy',[172] hinted at by Hobbes and brought to fruition by Smith.

163 1 Rich III c 2, 2 *Statutes of the Realm* 478.

164 G.L. Harriss, 'Medieval Doctrines in the Debates on Supply, 1610–1629', in K. Sharpe (ed.), *Faction and Parliament* (Oxford: Clarendon, 1978), 73–103, 100.

165 T. Penn, *Winter King* (London: Penguin, 2012), 160–3.

166 Harriss, n. 153, 733–4.

167 Oakeshott, n. 25, 201.

168 Ibid., 187.

169 J. Brewer, *The Sinews of Power* (Cambridge, MA: Harvard University Press, 1990).

170 N.A.M. Rodger, *The Command of the Ocean* (London: Penguin, 2006), 642–6.

171 Harriss, nn 153, 164. Especially after the foundation of the Bank of England in 1694, this purpose was likely to be satisfied by the use of land tax proceeds to service interest payments on government debt incurred to finance war (see P. Ackroyd, *The History of England Volume IV: Revolution* (London: Macmillan, 2016), 53).

172 Koskenniemi, n. 97, 66–7.

V. The Administrative State

The purposes of taxes in the administrative state have been to instantiate and prioritize rival, inconsistent, and ultimately irresolvable conceptions of fairness and, in so doing, to repair inefficiencies in the process of economic growth. While defence has necessarily remained a policy priority, all of this has shifted the emphasis away from the long-held eighteenth-century ideals of consent and property and towards effectiveness. The relationship of constituent and representative, characteristic of the parliamentary state, has been further mediated by a national administration whose discretions have revived something of the reductive characteristic of absolutism. And not only the national administration, a similar point applies to local levies, as well as to taxes in the current devolution arrangements with Scotland, and Northern Ireland and (as long as it remains relevant) with the European Union. The status of levies as taxes, together with a large administration, has created an all-embracing public law of taxation. The administrative state, as 'hollowed out' (and known as 'the regulatory state'), has formed the basis of the neoliberal regimes of Pinochet's Chile and Deng Xiaoping's China.[173]

A. Administrative Ideals and Administrative Levies

The imaginative tug of the parliamentary state has remained powerful, yet taxes in the *administrative* state have been justified by an ends-means approach characteristic of Oakeshott's *universitas*.

Although people feel nostalgia for the autonomy conferred by the parliamentary state, and although the personal ties of the feudal be increasingly absent, the absolutist virtue of obedience to the sovereign, as ascribed to the absolutist ideal, is nonetheless present in the administrative state. Absolutism's relationship of sovereign and subject becomes, in the administrative state, that of government and governed, often across and beyond national borders. The parliamentary state's layered relationship of enfranchised freeholders and crown-in-parliament was rendered the more complex, first by the heralding of mass democracy in 1928,[174] then by the embedding of business in government in the last quarter of the twentieth century. There developed international and regional organizations after World War I, which were designed to prevent jurisdictional double taxation and to facilitate enforcement of extrajurisdictional tax debts.

While parliamentary taxation is as central to the administrative state as to the parliamentary one, and while prerogatival levies continue to be unjustifiable, the discretion involved in the day-to-day administration of taxes in the administrative state is at times considerable.[175] While the constitutional norm of representative consent remains largely intact, the sphere of administrative action becomes ever greater. Taxation in

[173] D. Harvey, *A Brief History of Neoliberalism* (Oxford: Oxford University Press, 2005), chs 4 and 5.

[174] Representation of the People (Equal Franchise) Act 1928.

[175] National Audit Office and HM Revenue & Customs, *Settling Large Tax Disputes* (London: The Stationery Office, 2012–13), 188.

the administrative state is characterized by its sheer variety,[176] by its scope and by its changeability.[177] It has included, at various times: customs duties and excise duties on a wide range of commodities (e.g. on hydrocarbon oil); a more or less steeply progressive income tax (from 1910);[178] national insurance contributions (from 1911); capital gains tax (from 1965); estate duty, capital transfer tax, and inheritance tax (from 1894, 1974, and 1986); corporation tax (from 1965); value added tax (from 1973); new stamp taxes (from 1986 and 2003); and environmental taxes (1995 onwards). While the administrative state retains no rights to prerogatival taxation, taxpayer consent is perceived as apparently less important in this societal order than is the effectiveness of tax administration.

B. Administrative Relationships

The administrative state transforms the relationship between law and prerogative and highlights the differing logic of public law and economic theory. Administration is characterized by the enlisting of the distribution of powers in the enhancement of the executive in administration.

Although, like the parliamentary state, the administrative state justifies taxes through a political purpose, that purpose is considerably magnified, with Parliament's role apparently diminished, and property rights ever more shaped and qualified by legislation. The similarity of the administrative state to the absolutist state extends to the all-embracing nature of taxation as administrative law, especially with regard to the enforcement of liabilities to taxation. The significant difference with the absolutist state is that administration is subject to public law norms. Whereas in the parliamentary state, tax as public law negatively reinforced private laws of property, in the administrative state, with its enhanced executive, private law tends to be emasculated, if not undermined. The expedience of taxation law becomes its dominant characteristic, ideas of justice as betokened by property, as in the parliamentary state, becoming ever more remote. The administrative state is absolutism given legal form, its substance embodying the often inconsistent values of mass democracy and international business.

In the administrative state, the parliamentary state's allocation of competences as between executive, judiciary, and legislature is transformed, first, into a bureaucratically-enhanced executive, then into the business-enhanced regulatory state. The implications of the process were, as Loughlin has pointed out, recognized early on by Lord Denning,[179] who asserted that, '[p]roperly exercised the … powers of the executive lead to the welfare state; but abused they lead to a totalitarian state'.[180]

[176] See, e.g., the definition of 'tax' in the specimen 'Tax Deed of Covenant' in T. Sanders and P. Ridgway (eds), *Tax Indemnities and Warranties*, 3rd edn (Bloomsbury Professional: Haywards Heath, UK: 2009), 366. More generally, see Loutzenhiser (ed.), *Tiley's Revenue Law*, 8th edn (Oxford and Portland: Hart, 2016), 3–7.

[177] B.R. Cheffins and S.A. Bank, 'Corporate Ownership and Control in the UK: The Tax Dimension', 70(5) *Modern Law Review* (2007) 778.

[178] Seligman, n. 124, 207.

[179] Alfred Thompson Denning, *The Closing Chapter* (London: Butterworths, 1983), 117–19.

[180] Quoted in Loughlin, n. 4, 444n.

The implications of this in the tax context have been explored recently in a judicial review case involving tax settlements.[181] Considerable importance continues to be attached to, and controversy still surrounds, the judicial review of administrative action and of legislation.

Political law and natural law are different, one variant of the latter now being embodied in economic theory. The prescriptions of economics, in other words, are not unlike those of natural law. Commenting on Thomas Piketty's recent *Capital in the Twenty-First Century* (2013),[182] Martin Wolf inferred appropriately deterministic economic conclusions: 'there is no general tendency towards greater economic equality'; 'at least in normal times, capitalists save a sufficiently large share of their returns to ensure that their capital will grow at least as fast as the economy'; and '[t]he tendency for capital to grow faster than the economy is also more likely when the growth of the economy is relatively slow'.[183] All of this tends to pull against the idea that, irrespective of the economic justifications, tax policy should be based on political will. At the same time, the dominance of a public law of taxation, to the detriment of the private law of property, seems to align the administrative state with the absolutist one. Just as the characteristics of the parliamentary state were exported, so too have been those of the administrative state. At least initially, this was to the advantage of a 'global elite', but it is disadvantageous as evidence accumulates of dramatic economic disparities.

C. Administrative Justifications

While it certainly has other features, the administrative state is a Machiavellian one, close in spirit to absolutism. Aristotle's distributive justice, for instance, is not necessarily our idea of distributive justice, and reaching for 'a distribution of resources that meets everyone's needs'[184] requires a virtuosic reckoning of ends and means.

Thinkers who have provided the intellectual underpinning of the administrative state, as well as those who disparage it, focus upon the tax system's capacity for redistribution and regulation. Richard Henry Tawney (1880–1962) noted the dramatic economic disparities of industrial society and acknowledged the importance of redistributive taxation. In his *Equality* (1931),[185] Tawney wrote that reducing inequality could only be achieved:

> by means of taxation, and the use of the funds thus obtained to make accessible to all, irrespective of their income, occupation, or social position, the conditions of civilisation which, in the absence of such measures, can be enjoyed only by the rich.[186]

[181] *UK Uncut Legal Action Ltd v CRC* [2013] EWHC 1283 (Admin); (2013) 81 *Tax Cases* 890 (see de Cogan, *British Tax Review* [2013] 552–62).

[182] T. Piketty, *Capital in the Twenty-First Century*, A. Goldhammer (trans.) (Cambridge, MA: Harvard University Press, [2013] 2014).

[183] M. Wolf, 'Inequality Time', *Financial Times Life and Arts* (19–20 April 2014) 9.

[184] Fleischacker, n. 136, 2.

[185] R.H. Tawney, *Equality*, 5th edn (London: Allen & Unwin, [1931] 1964).

[186] Ibid., 122.

Contrariwise, the economist and political scientist, Friedrich von Hayek (1899–1992), denied the possibility of such objectivity. In *The Road to Serfdom* (1944),[187] Hayek declared that, 'of the problems of merit the planner must answer':

> the approach to greater equality answers practically none. Its content is hardly more definite than the phrases 'common good' or 'social welfare'. It does not free us from the necessity of deciding in every particular instance between the merits of particular individuals or groups, and gives us no help in that decision. All it tells us in effect is to take from the rich as much as we can. But when it comes to the distribution of the spoils, the problem is the same as if the formula of 'greater equality' had never been conceived.[188]

The Cambridge economist, Arthur Cecil Pigou (1877–1959), though he considered these issues, also contributed to the regulatory arguments. By focusing on the possibility of internalizing via taxation the externalities created by pollution,[189] Pigou laid the ground for the environmental taxes of the last two decades. More recently, Piketty (b.1971) has noted the declining capacity of individual states to mitigate massive inequalities of wealth. This is evidenced, he says, by tax revenues failing to keep pace with the ability of the wealthiest to consume and not to eat into capital. He has therefore called for a reexamination of the possibilities of high marginal income tax rates at the top end, together—more implausibly—with 'a global tax on capital'.[190] Critical attention has focused on the latter, but it is the former that is crucial. High marginal taxes at the top end, says Piketty, have actually been effective to reduce inequalities.[191] To say that the top rates do not raise revenue is, in a sense, to make a category mistake. Their essence is that they *dissuade*, say, corporate managers from negotiating unduly high remuneration packages. They are, in effect, a form of economic regulation.

These are not the only thinkers holding sway in the administrative state. Three others, in particular, continue to be important: Smith and Machiavelli, of course, but, much more significantly, Hobbes. The reason for this is that, in order to work, the administrative state needs to achieve a complete mastery both of the tax system and of the property rights with which taxation interacts. Hobbes' philosophy provides the intellectual framework for such a definitional dominance of the state over the individual in matters of tax and property.[192] Smith's philosophy, ethically influential though it has become, cannot accommodate the comprehensiveness of this structure. What is more, the natural law of Hobbes's philosophy is entirely compatible with the nostrums of economic theory in a way that Machiavelli, despite his apparent affinities to Hobbes, cannot directly address.

In Britain, in 2016, the range of public purposes for taxation expresses the prudential prioritization of ideologies as they interact with political realities. The public law that enacts this prioritization is Hobbes's 'civil science' in action, as political jurisprudence.[193] No employee who falls within the scope of the PAYE regulations can require

[187] F.A. Hayek, *The Road to Serfdom* (London: Routledge, [1944] 2001). [188] Ibid., 114.

[189] A.C. Pigou, *The Economics of Welfare*, 4th edn (London: Macmillan, [1920] 1952), Part II, chs 2, 3.

[190] Piketty, n. 182, chs 14, 15. [191] Ibid., 508–12.

[192] D. Jackson, 'Thomas Hobbes' Theory of Taxation', 21(2) *Political Studies* (1973) 175–82.

[193] M. Loughlin, 'The Political Jurisprudence of Thomas Hobbes', in D. Dyzenhaus and T. Poole (eds), *Hobbes and the Law* (Cambridge, UK: Cambridge University Press, 2012), 5–21.

to be paid her gross salary. No electricity can be supplied to larger businesses without charging climate change levy. Subsequent to its transfer, no property in land is fully recognized by the state until title to it has been registered. The administrative state mandates a wide range of tax policy purposes. Of these, by far the largest is welfare (at just under 25 per cent of public spending), closely followed by health (at around 19 per cent). Defence, the sole priority of the parliamentary state, is around five per cent of public spending in the administrative one.[194] The necessity of all of these is suggested by economistic notions of fairness and efficiency, outcrops of the Hobbesian (and perhaps also the Smithian) natural law.

The seventh and eighth elements of this analysis can thus be stated. The administrative state's taxes are, of course, taxes properly so called. Not only are they supported by legal compulsion, they are backed up by legislative authority. But this legislative authority, much greater in its ambition than that of the parliamentary state, furnishes a comprehensive public law. This public law even threatens to efface the private law of property. For all its ambition, this public law is grounded withal in economic theories with affinities to natural law.

VI. Conclusions

There are various possibilities for inquiring into the justifications for taxes and thus for drawing conclusions about the public law nature of contemporary tax law. The approach taken here has been to focus on the historical purposes behind levies.

Levies' purposes are intimately related to the ideals promoted by differing societal orders, the nature and scope of viable purposes being a function of the distinctiveness of these orders. The presence both of law and of distinctively political purposes is characteristic of tax law as public law. Thus, in a parliamentary state, the public law character of taxation is necessarily underemphasized. The fundamental component of such a political society is the pre-political—that is, feudal—private law of property, with tax law seeking both to consolidate that law and to modify it to only a minimal extent. Apologists for the parliamentary state, while implicitly recognizing the public law nature of tax legislation, tend to elide its relationship with property as private law. Instead, they tend to conceive of tax as civil law, emphasising its politico-societal basis by way of contrast with the basis of property law in a pre-political justice. The purpose of taxation is expressed mainly in maintaining the security of the state and the safety of its citizens or subjects. A contrast with this parliamentary way of thinking is provided by the feudal ideal on which it relies. Though a feudal realm was no political society, it did have a recognizable common law of property. Feudal levies were emblematic of a personal relationship between lord and vassal and the status of levies as the subject matter of public law was a question that did not arise.

[194] See *GOV.UK*, last updated 1 December 2015, http://www.gov.uk/annual-tax-summary (accessed 16 April 2015). For a detailed anatomization of the political history of taxation in the UK's evolving administrative state, see Martin Daunton's incomparable *Trusting Leviathan: The Politics of Taxation in Britain, 1799-1914* (Cambridge, UK: Cambridge University Press, 2001) and *Just Taxes: The Politics of Taxation in Britain, 1914-1979* (Cambridge, UK: Cambridge University Press, 2002).

If parliamentary and feudal ideals betoken similar attitudes towards the potentialities of property and the dangers of tax, absolutist and administrative ideals are in certain respects similar to each other too. What levies in the absolutist state have in common with taxes in the administrative state is denial of, or significant incursion on, property rights. Property rights are redefined in the administrative state, somewhat as they are denied in an absolutist one. The point of difference between absolutism and administration is that, with the latter, sovereignty is drawn down into the body of the people and its creations are subject to the supervision of public law.

The unifying theme of this chapter has been that the modern conception of tax law as public law is both historically contingent and philosophically contested.[195] The justifications proferred for taxation down the centuries vividly illuminate this central theme.

[195] The writer dedicates the chapter, with love, to Angela Kershaw. He has benefited from conversations with Dominic de Cogan (Cambridge), Miranda Fleischer (San Diego), Jane Frecknall-Hughes (Nottingham), Stuart P. Green (Rutgers), Theodore P. Seto (Loyola, Los Angeles), Chantal Stebbings (Exeter), and Henk Vording (Leiden). The writer is grateful to Mark Philp (Warwick), who valuably commented on, and discussed, an advanced draft, helping me thereby to clarify certain thoughts. Conclusions, mistakes, and omissions remain the writer's responsibility. He would also like to thank Helen Riley (University of Warwick Library) and Elizabeth Wells (Bodleian, Oxford) for tracking down an electronic version of *Paton's Appeals*.

2

Must We Pay for the British Museum? Taxation and the Harm Principle

*John Stanton-Ife**

'To force an unwilling person to contribute to the support of the British Museum is as distinct a violation of Mr Mill's principle as religious persecution.'[1] So wrote James Fitzjames Stephen in his *Liberty, Equality and Fraternity* on its first publication in 1873. The 'Mr Mill' in question is of course John Stuart Mill and the 'principle', Mill's harm principle: 'one very simple principle' as Mill called it,[2] though few of his readers have thought that it is very simple once one gets down to brass tacks—or that the argument of *On Liberty* as a whole proposes no more than a single principle. Mill had at least *stated* the nub of the principle pithily fourteen years previously in *On Liberty*: 'The only purpose for which power can be rightfully exercised over any member of a civilized society against his will is to prevent harm to others.'[3] Well then, said Stephen, taxing people to support the British Museum cannot be a 'rightful' exercise of state power, at least not consistently with Mill's principle. Stephen assumed that the compulsory raising of the tax triggers Mill's principle and then argued that it falls foul of it as the tax cannot be for the purpose of preventing harm to others. I will speak repeatedly below of 'Stephen's challenge to Mill' and of 'Stephen's incompatibility argument' and both locutions will refer to his quoted claim made in the opening sentence above, rather than any of the multitude of further arguments Stephen directed at Mill in his 1873 work.

Is Stephen right? Is taxing to support the arts and other expensive activities favoured by a sometimes esoteric minority of citizens a violation Mill's 'harm principle'? To this day the British Museum is significantly funded by the taxpayers of the UK and museum curators in many other countries similarly secure the necessary funding from the public purse.[4] I am here, as was Stephen, referring specifically to the funding of the British Museum partly because it is a good example of the general issue, but, more importantly, as a placeholder for any artistic, cultural, or esoteric educational purpose a state may choose to support financially from the pot of resources extracted from the taxpayer.

* I am grateful to all participants at the UCL seminar in 2015, to Grant Lamond for helpful comments, and, most of all, to Monica Bhandari and James Webb.

[1] J. Fitzjames Stephen, *Liberty, Equality, and Fraternity* (Indianapolis: Liberty Fund, 1993), 12.

[2] J.S. Mill, *On Liberty and Other Essays*, J. Gray (ed.), World's Classics Edition (Oxford: Oxford University Press, 1991), I, 9.

[3] Ibid.

[4] *British Museum*, Report and Accounts for the Year Ended 31 March 2015, https://www.britishmuseum.org/pdf/BM-report-and-accounts-2014-2015.pdf (last accessed 17 May 2016).

Philosophical Foundations of Tax Law. First Edition. Edited by Monica Bhandari.

On the face of it what Stephen says sounds plausible enough, but it is unlikely on reflection that the key notions of 'harm' or 'coercion' in Mill's principle are going to turn out to be at all straightforward. Perhaps, then, there is some compelling, if unobvious, way of showing that the tax in question is, *pace* Stephen, compatible with Mill's harm principle? Alternatively, perhaps a different version of the harm principle—for it is clear that there is by now more than one—is compatible with the tax and there is good reason to prefer it to Mill's version? Maybe one way or another the harm principle can survive Stephen's attack. We will look at these questions below.

If Stephen is right that the tax on the British Museum and Mill's harm principle are not compatible—to anticipate, I will conclude that he is right about this after examining some possible responses—what conclusion should then be drawn? At least two opposing lessons are possible, one that implies the tax in question has got to go, the other that it is the harm principle that ought to be dispensed with. In other words, first one might say: 'Stephen is right, so much the worse for taxation in support of the British Museum and related examples. The harm principle is a valid principle to apply to tax law and thus we have compelling reason to abandon taxes that violate the principle.' Thus the Millian harm principle could be deployed in support of those who oppose such cultural taxes today.[5] Secondly and alternatively, one might say: 'Stephen is right, so much the worse for Mill's (or some other) version of the harm principle. The harm principle is not a principle that should be used as a guide for the legitimate use of coercion by the law and government.' This was Stephen's own direction of travel in arguing as he did. While an admirer of Mill's utilitarian philosophy, Stephen sought in much of *Liberty, Equality and Fraternity*, to refute Mill's harm principle. Many liberal thinkers writing more recently have similarly assumed that the sort of cultural taxes under discussion must be legitimate and have sought ways of justifying that conclusion consistently with their liberal principles.[6]

My aim in this chapter is to consider certain aspects of the harm principle as a philosophical foundation of tax law. The question of state support via taxation for the arts—as well as for certain esoteric, expensive scientific, mathematical, or otherwise scholarly activities[7]—is one on which I will focus for a large part of the chapter. It is, I believe, a good route in to an examination of the harm principle in this context, displaying some of the problems in sharp relief, as well as being interesting and still controversial in its own right. The larger question, however, is what role, if any, the harm

[5] For example: P. Booth, 'Should the State Support the Arts?', IEA [web blog], 13 February 2015, https://iea.org.uk/blog/should-the-state-support-the-arts. J. Meadowcroft, 'From Big Macs to Big Brother: the Market and Culture', IEA [web blog], 10 September 2012, http://www.iea.org.uk/blog/from-big-macs-to-big-brother-the-market-and-culture. According to Meadowcroft 'it is surely morally wrong for people to be forced to pay for something that they do not want simply because a committee of the great and the good has deemed it culturally valuable.' Harry Brighouse, one suspects, is not unsympathetic to such taxes, but the tenor of his appraisal of the arguments is that they are formidably difficult to justify. See H. Brighouse, 'Neutrality, Publicity, and State Funding of the Arts', 24 *Philosophy and Public Affairs* (1995) 35.

[6] R. Dworkin, 'Can a Liberal State Support Art?', in *A Matter of Principle* (Cambridge, MA: Harvard University Press, 1985); J. Feinberg, 'Not with My Tax Money: The Problem of Justifying Government Subsidies for the Arts', in *Problems at the Roots of Law: Essays in Legal and Political Theory* (Oxford: Oxford University Press, 2003).

[7] Feinberg, n. 6, 103.

principle should play as a guiding and legitimating principle for taxation in general. The harm principle is one of the most famous ideas in the history of liberal thought. It is of course far from the only proposal made in the history of liberalism that could serve to gauge the legitimacy of taxation and other aspects of state activity.[8] 'Liberal' is not only the broad label we give to describe the form of government of many modern democracies, it also describes a long tradition of thought, made up of many ideas and thinkers, with many internal controversies and disagreements. The implications of 'Nozickian' or 'libertarian' thought on taxation, for example, will plainly be very different from the implications of 'Rawlsian' liberalism.[9] One important question in assessing the significance of the harm principle to taxation is how that principle relates to the other strands of liberalism just mentioned, a large issue I will not try to address here. What is especially striking about the part of liberal thought that goes by the name of the 'harm principle' is, in my view, how little exploration it has had in relation to tax law by way of comparison with the attention it has received in relation to criminal law. For the harm principle has loomed very large in the study of legitimating principles for criminalization. Most notably Joel Feinberg developed over four tightly argued monographs an account of the harm principle as applied to the criminal law in, as he himself put it, 'the motivating spirit of ... John Stuart Mill'.[10] More recently, Andrew Simester and Andreas von Hirsch have dedicated a monograph to defending a version of the harm principle as applied to the criminal law.[11] Why should the harm principle have received so much less attention in relation to the legitimacy of tax laws in their various guises?[12]

Interestingly for our purposes, however, Feinberg in the course of his volumes on the moral limits of the criminal law notes our problem, citing Stephen's challenge to Mill. He then observes, entirely properly, that, beyond the justification of the crime of tax evasion, it is not anything he needs to say anything about, as crime is his subject not tax. Despite that he goes on to attempt a reconciliation between the harm principle and his view that state support of the arts is legitimate. Subsequently, plainly piqued by the issue, he went on to write a paper on it, now freed from the constraints of his magnum opus on criminal law. Below we will take the way in which Feinberg wrestled with the issue as a point of departure. In particular we shall examine his conception

[8] For an excellent historical survey, see I. Carter, M. Kramer, and H. Steiner (eds), *Freedom: A Philosophical Anthology* (Malden: Blackwell, 2007), containing extracts from Mill as well as Kant, Locke, Berlin, Rawls, Nozick, Raz, and many more.

[9] Ibid., 79, 365, 407 (Rawls); 202, 261, 278 (Nozick). See also T. Nagel and L. Murphy, *The Myth of Ownership: Taxes and Justice* (Oxford: Oxford University Press, 2002).

[10] J. Feinberg, *The Moral Limits of the Criminal Law*. 4 volumes: *Harm to Others*, 1984; *Offense to Others*, 1985; *Harm to Self*, 1986; *Harmless Wrongdoing*, 1988. (Oxford: Oxford University Press, 1984–1988). The quotation in the text is from the last of these volumes, p. x.

[11] A.P. Simester and A. von Hirsch, *Crimes, Harms and Wrongs: On the Principles of Criminalisation* (Oxford: Hart, 2011).

[12] My claim is not that the issue of the relationship between tax law and the harm principle has been entirely ignored, merely that it has received much less attention than the relationship between crime and harm principle. Jethro Lieberman, for one, considers the implications of the harm principle for taxation in J.K. Lieberman, *Liberalism Undressed* (Oxford: Oxford University Press, 2012). According to Lieberman, 'the state necessarily may demand from citizens the means to pay for the discharge of its justified responsibilities under the harm principle', 102.

of harm as setback to interests in the light of his arguments against Stephen in relation to taxing in favour of arts and culture and so on.

I. Does Stephen's Incompatibility Argument Succeed?

Stephen's claim—that forcing an unwilling person to contribute to the support of the British Museum is incompatible with Mill's harm principle—is not spelled out by him in any great detail. He did, however, add a couple of elaborations to the bare assertion of the claim.

First, the argument, he said, applied to 'all taxation to which the taxed party did not consent' which cannot be understood on a rationale of 'prevention of harm to persons other than those coerced'.[13] This raises the question of which are the relevant cases of harm prevention. Among purposes that did, in his view, properly count as prevention of harm to such persons he named 'military or ... police purposes or ... the administration of justice'.[14] This already seems to suggest that Stephen was willing to see the Millian idea of harm as potentially quite wide: wider for instance than any simple notion of harm limited to the bodily and property interests of persons. Mill himself in *On Liberty* and in his other writings was—beyond the categories mentioned by Stephen—prepared to accept the legitimacy of coercion requiring a fair share of the costs of securing public goods; of redistributing wealth through taxes so as to ensure a decent minimum standard of living and equal opportunity; of regulating trade; and of making education compulsory, as well as various kinds of social welfare legislation, such as provision and maintenance of roads and sanitation, provision of some public education, and, interestingly for our purposes, state support of the arts.[15] We will not pause to consider whether Mill can successfully reconcile these commitments with his advocacy of the harm principle, save of course his endorsement of state support for the arts, the very commitment Stephen is calling into question as irreconcilable with the harm principle.

Secondly, and as far as the tax in support of the British Museum was concerned, Stephen further saw it as 'a case of coercion, for the sake of what the persons who exercise coercive power regard as the attainment of a *good object*'.[16] It is really quite simple to explain why we tax in support of the British Museum, he tells us: those officials who make the decision think, it is good to do so. That might be just as it should be, but it cannot, he stresses, be all right for Mill. As a basis for coercion, Mill's principle rules that out. Coercing people on the basis that one's aim is a good one is insufficient

[13] Stephen, n. 2, 12. [14] Ibid.

[15] J.S. Mill, *Principles of Political Economy*, J. Riley (ed.), World's Classics Edition (Oxford: Oxford University Press, 2008), V.xi.15. For discussion of these cases and full references to Mill's writings, see D.O. Brink, *Mill's Progressive Principles* (Oxford: Oxford University Press, 2013), 181.

[16] Stephen, n. 2, 12. (emphasis added). See also J.G. Murphy's support for the idea that 'society might support art, even the art of high culture that few people actually enjoy, simply because such art is judged (by the legislator) to be a good—not necessarily good for someone (in the paternalistic sense of improving character) but simply a good', in 'Freedom of Expression and the Arts', 29 *Arizona State Law Journal* (1997) 549, 564 (emphasis in the original).

justification for the coercion, whether it be seen as paternalistic, moralistic, aesthetic, or whatever, in the absence of any potential harm prevention.

Some commentators take the view that Mill's harm principle implies or is at least compatible with the value of neutrality and ought to be defended as such.[17] The neutrality constraint, as it applies most squarely to the present context, states that the principles justifying legislation, taxation, and other legal interventions must be 'neutral between competing conceptions of the good life'.[18] If we are to read Mill's harm principle as implying neutrality in this way, it will almost certainly condemn supporting the conception of the good life that values what the British Museum has to offer. What of the competing conceptions of the good life, a life spent honing videogaming techniques for example? No doubt it would in principle be possible to accommodate some other conceptions of the good life in the same way through taxation, but certainly not all. Even if Mill's principle does not imply the neutrality constraint—I suspect it does not, but take no position on that here—Stephen is pressing hard the argument that a defence of cultural taxes simply on the basis that they support what is good cannot be enough to avoid condemnation by Mill's harm principle. Stephen is in short pointing out that the real basis for cultural taxes such as that in support of the British Museum is a 'perfectionist' one, a point to which I will return.

A. Coercion

Here is a first response to Stephen's challenge. Mill's harm principle is only triggered where the state uses, plans, or contemplates using coercion.[19] If the tax raised in support of the British Museum and similar taxes is not coercive, or not coercive in the relevant sense, Stephen's challenge can be deflected. Mill's harm principle would not preclude the tax for the British Museum. It would neither support such a tax or, more pertinently for responding to Stephen, stand in its way. Let us now consider this response.

One might observe in support of this response that it is common for writers to *contrast* coercing certain conduct with taxing it. Robert Merrihew Adams, for example, in the course of expressing his view that it would be wrong to subject the possession and use of tobacco to serious criminal penalties gives as his reason 'the evils of coercion and punishment'.[20] Instead he recommends as entirely appropriate 'other government action to discourage (the possession and use of) tobacco *without coercion,* perhaps by raising taxes on tobacco products'.[21] Here, as do many others, Adams sees taxing as an essentially noncoercive alternative to criminalizing. Joseph Raz, whose own version of the harm principle we come to below, points to forms of state activity

[17] G.F. Gaus, 'State Neutrality and Controversial Values in On Liberty', in C.L. Ten (ed.), Mill *On Liberty* (Cambridge, UK: Cambridge University Press, 2008), 83.

[18] Ibid.

[19] Strictly speaking, Mill says the principle is triggered not only in relation to state coercion, but also in relation to 'the moral coercion of public opinion'. Mill, n. 2, [I, 9]. Since our concern is with the state activity of taxation, this is not a complication that needs to be addressed here.

[20] R.M. Adams, *Finite and Infinite Goods* (Oxford: Oxford University Press, 1999), 327.

[21] Ibid. Emphasis added.

aimed at promoting the good that do not involve 'a coercive imposition of a style of life'.[22] The state, rather than coerce people into or out of certain styles of life, can encourage or facilitate desired action, or discourage undesired behaviour. Raz gives as examples 'conferring honours on creative and performing artists, giving grants or loans to people who start community centres' and 'taxing one kind of leisure activity, e.g. hunting, more heavily than others'. This, he adds, is a far cry from 'the threatening popular image of imprisoning people who follow their religion, express their views in public, grow long hair, or consume harmless drugs'.[23] If writers like Adams and Raz are not conceiving the taxation, as opposed to the criminalization of specifically targeted conduct, as coercive, then surely the same can be said for the milder cultural taxes that concern us, or so the argument goes.

Perhaps we might build on this line of thought, by trying to imagine what it would be like if citizens were to be coerced into attending the British Museum or other cultural events. In a classic Italian comedy,[24] there is a scene in which the hero Fantozzi, an ordinary working man, who suffers constant bad luck and is perennially at the mercy of the whims of his bosses, has finished a hard day's work and is hoping to settle down to watch the football game between Italy and England at home on television. However, along with his fellow disgruntled workers, he is forced to return to his place of work in the evening for the sake of his cultural improvement. His employer insists the workers are to watch a screening of the Soviet 1920s silent film, *The Battleship Potemkin*. Not only that, they also must participate in a seminar after the screening and offer trenchant observations on the masterpiece they have beheld! Failure to comply may result in the sack. On entry, all the workers are frisked lest any has attempted to smuggle in a portable radio in order to listen to the football commentary on the sly (the employers were wise to that ploy: and many radios were confiscated!). This of course is the stuff of comedy; it is not presented as an accurate reflection of reality. It would be as absurd to coerce adults to attend the British Museum for their cultural improvement, as it is to coerce them into a heightened appreciation of the aesthetics of silent Soviet cinema.

This, however, only makes it clear that funding the British Museum out of tax revenue does not involve anything like the coercion that is involved when Mill's principle is usually invoked, such as where a threat of imprisonment is communicated via legislation to citizens should they attempt to murder or steal. Coercing people in these paradigm cases falling under the harm principle may in a sense be a coercive imposition of a style of life—a life without the freedom to murder or steal—but a clearly justified one, while coercing adult citizens into watching silent Soviet films or out of practising their religion would be unjustified uses of coercion. But the funding of the British Museum involves no coercive imposition of a style of life at all—no one need ever step inside the Museum if they do not want to—and those taxed are not prevented, at least not by their share of the cultural tax burden (if proportionately and

[22] J. Raz, *The Morality of Freedom* (Oxford: Oxford University Press, 1986), 161.

[23] Ibid. See also A.P. Simester, J.R. Spencer, G.R. Sullivan, and G.J. Virgo (eds), *Simester and Sullivan's Criminal Law*, 5th edn (Oxford: Hart, 2013), 658–9, who contrast criminalization with less restrictive forms of legal regulation including taxation.

[24] Luciano Salce, dir. *Il Secondo Tragico Fantozzi*. Italy, Rizzoli Films, 1976. [DVD, Medusa Video, 2003].

fairly distributed[25]), from adopting their own styles of life. Are we to conclude Stephen simply missed the mark in his attack on Mill, because we lack the sort of coercion to which the harm principle is supposed to relate? It has, moreover, been suggested that Mill's own understanding of coercion should be read as relying on something like the distinction implied here.[26]

In my view, while the above argument does point to a significant distinction, it is not an adequate way of seeing off Stephen's challenge to Mill. For the compulsory taxation on persons to fund the British Museum and similar cultural bodies remains coercive, even if it does not involve coercing anyone into, or out of, a style of life. It is no doubt less seriously coercive than that, but of course it does not follow that it is not coercive at all. Ultimately criminal penalties are as a matter of course threatened and enforced against tax evaders.[27] Under current arrangements what largely makes the maintenance and development of the British Museum and its free availability to the public possible is the funding raised through compulsory taxes. The action 'Maintain, develop and keep the British Museum open to the public' presupposes, as matters stand, the action: 'raise via taxation the revenues to do so'.[28] The object of evaluation in the case of the cultural taxes under consideration should be, as Gerald Gaus suggests, the 'complex act (raise revenues through taxation & spend them on X)'. This does, of course, assume, as is the case with many of the taxes of the sort, that the tax *is* raised compulsorily. There are, by way of contrast, other models possible and very much in existence that are not coercive in *either* of the senses we have just considered—for example in the case of state-franchised lotteries, such as The National Lottery in the United Kingdom. As its website breathlessly declares, much of the money raised by the National Lottery that is not set aside as prize money goes on supporting specific forms of life: players of the lottery help 'build local communities, power sports teams, save the environment, unleash creative talent, empower the elderly and unlock young potential. Each week 400 new projects are supported.'[29] But of course no one need play the lottery; opting out is as easy as refraining from buying a ticket. Not so with the taxes for the British Museum and manifold other taxes in support of various cultural activities and forms of life.

Hence we should reject the first response floated above to Stephen's claim against Mill. Taxing in support of the British Museum is sufficiently coercive to trigger Mill's

[25] The tax burden may not of course in reality be fairly and proportionately distributed in a given jurisdiction. The remedy, however, has to do with making such burdens fairer and more proportionate, rather than with the nature of the purposes for which the tax is raised. Or so the argument goes. I am here discounting the case of children and what might legitimately be involved in their education.

[26] See G.F. Gaus, 'The Moral Foundations of Liberal Neutrality', in T. Christiano and J. Christman (eds), *Contemporary Debates in Political Philosophy* (Oxford: Blackwell, 2009), 81, 91 and references therein.

[27] Cf. Feinberg, *Criminal Law*, vol. 4, *Harmless Wrongdoing*, 313: '[The crime of tax-evasion] is legitimately created on harm-principle grounds. If there were no crime of tax-evasion, then there would be no efficient way of raising revenue for public expenditure, at least some of which are needed by everyone (courts, police, defense forces, some social insurance schemes).' See also S. Green, 'Tax Evasion as Crime', in this volume.

[28] Here I am paraphrasing Gaus, n. 26, 91.

[29] 'About Us', *The National Lottery*, https://www.national-lottery.co.uk/about-us?icid=bsp:na:tx (last accesssed 22 May 2016).

harm principle properly understood. However, going forward, it is clear that attention is needed to the kind and degree of coercion that is involved: as we have seen, this can differ markedly from the coercive imposition of a style of life to the coercive raising of taxes in favour of styles of life that no one need participate in if they do not wish to. The harm principle in the context of taxation in short requires an understanding of what sort of coercion is involved. It is surely plausible to say that the extent to which justification under the harm principle is needed will vary according to what sort of coercion—and what degree of it—is involved. We should not think of coercion as merely as an 'all-or-nothing trigger' allowing us to say 'if it is (barely) present, then a harm principle justification is required, if it is not, no such justification is required'. Rather the extent of the necessary justification will surely be sensitive to the extent and kind of coercion in question.

B. Feinberg on Harm as Setback to Interests

As was mentioned above, Feinberg attempted to show that taxation in support of the arts is legitimate consistently with the harm principle. I will not use up the considerable space that would be needed to spell out in any detail the structure of Feinberg's version of the harm principle, but shall simply rely on his avowed aim to work in the spirit of Mill. I shall assume that Feinberg favours at least the view that state coercion is not legitimate if there is no justification available in terms of preventing harm (or offence) to others; in particular he wishes to rule out paternalistic and moralistic justifications.[30]

We can distinguish three separate arguments Feinberg makes in support of taxation for bodies such as the British Museum. First, *contra* Stephen, Feinberg suggests that some people may be harmed by a failure to support the British Museum. Secondly, as a question of 'rotational justice', taxpayers with no interest in the British Museum are likely to have other interests also supported by taxation levied, inter alia, from persons who do not share *those* interests. Thus we should look at such taxation in the round, not as a series of isolated instances. Thirdly, and rather surprisingly, he suggests that state support through taxation of the arts can be justified in terms of the creation or preservation of high intrinsic value. I will begin briefly by saying something about Feinberg's second and third arguments, but I will give much more attention to his first argument. As I will explain, his second and third arguments, in different ways, depend on or refer back to the first of the arguments. Detailed attention to the first argument will also focus attention on how the idea of 'harm' in the 'harm principle' is to be understood.

Feinberg's second argument—from rotational justice—assumes there are at least grounds already in existence for saying the terms of the harm principle are satisfied.

[30] In putting it this way, I am trying to adopt the widest possible interpretation of Feinberg. His official statement of the 'liberal' theory he favours asserts that 'the harm and offense principles, duly clarified and qualified, between them exhaust the class of morally relevant reasons for criminal prohibitions' (Feinberg, *Harmless Wrongdoing*, n. 10, X.) Although not a point I will deal with here, Feinberg takes offence prevention more seriously than Mill did, at least in the latter's canonical formulation of his harm principle.

The coercive taxation is raised in order to prevent some harm to others (we postpone examination of what that harm is said to be until our detailed consideration of Feinberg's first argument below). He follows this up, however, with a concern about fairness. Assuming tax money is spent on subsidizing the British Museum, what are we to say to those taxpayers who have no interest in the British Museum or benefit in no way from it? Feinberg's answer is that they might have relevant interests in *other* cultural, sporting, etc. activities which also receive state subsidies funded out of general taxation—and these activities may be of no interest or benefit to those who treasure the British Museum.

True enough, no doubt, in many cases. How far it is true will ultimately be an empirical matter, although the tendency of several disadvantages to 'cluster' together in the same persons (a number of whose earnings are presumably above a minimum threshold for taxation) might here give us considerable pause and some measure of pessimism that 'winning some' and 'losing some' will even themselves out tolerably well in relation to all taxpayers.[31]

Feinberg's third argument comes not as a detour in his major work on criminal law as do his other two arguments, but in the separate essay he wrote subsequently.[32] There he argued that the creation, maintenance, or preservation of things of high intrinsic value can be a legitimate basis in support of government subsidies paid for out of general taxation.[33] His major preoccupation in the essay is to defend the very idea of such intrinsic value in such a way that it is not reducible to benefits to specified persons. I am not myself disposed to question the existence of such intrinsic value and am happy to agree that the British Museum contains much of it within its walls, as does much other culture that many governments of the world subsidize. What is striking about the argument is that it appears to fly in the face of Feinberg's own commitment in his criminal law work to the harm principle. For in that work he argued *against* the possibility that the prevention of 'harmless wrongdoing' or 'free-floating evils'—intrinsically regrettable states of affairs that are evil for some reason other than that they harm or offend anyone[34]—could be a legitimate ground for criminalization. Now, by contrast, he is apparently arguing *in favour* of the view that there are 'free-floating values' and 'benefitless good things',[35] the support of which can be a legitimate ground for the state coercion involved in compulsory taxation. His only comment on this is uncharacteristically brusque. He claims to see no contradiction in this asymmetry: 'sometimes the truth comes in displeasingly untidy forms, and at any rate, we might expect some stark and asymmetric contrasts when comparing concepts as opposed as good and evil'.[36]

No doubt we should not be surprised if we encounter asymmetries now and again in our normative theories. But if the essential idea of the harm principle is (at least) that the state is not to coerce if there is no harm-prevention (or offence-prevention) in the offing, that seems to rule out both free-floating evils and free-floating values as justifications for coercion, be that criminalization or taxation. One might possibly argue that Feinberg is best read simply as requiring harm-prevention or offence-prevention

[31] J. Wolff and A. De-Shalit, *Disadvantage* (Oxford: Oxford University Press, 2007), 10.
[32] Feinberg, n. 6. [33] Ibid., 122. [34] Ibid., 108. [35] Ibid. [36] Ibid.

as a necessary condition for state coercion. As such that would not preclude other justifications (free-floating values, etc.) provided there is simultaneously some harm- or offence-prevention to be had as well. If so, the argument of course depends on there actually being some harm prevention implicit in continued support for the British Museum (I shall, to repeat, leave aside consideration of offence prevention). It is to that possibility that we now turn.

1. *Harm*

As we have seen, Stephen's understanding of 'harm', however it is to be understood, was not such that it allowed a harm-based justification of coercive taxation in favour of the British Museum. Is there a plausible way of understanding harm that would support such a harm-based justification in this context? Feinberg thought so. In the present section, I will aim both to evaluate Feinberg's specific argument to that effect and to look more generally at the Feinbergian notion of harm with a view to how it might eventually operate in the context of taxation, rather than crime.

One potential way of supporting taxation for the British Museum on the basis of the harm principle (that Feinberg rejects) would be to argue that 'harm' should be read so as to include 'failure to benefit'.[37] Put that way, it is clear that ceasing to support the British Museum would be to fail to benefit many of its users, or to fail to continue to do so. As it stands, however, failing to benefit cannot be sufficient for harm as Feinberg saw. For that would suggest that any undeserved financial windfall that might fall into someone's path—money that is not owed to the person in question or needed by her and so on—is something that the state would have a harm-based reason to supply, provided only that it has some capacity to benefit the recipient. Such a conclusion would be absurd.

Feinberg instead builds on his own well-known gloss on 'harm' as a 'setback to interests'.[38] By contrast with Mill's own relative neglect of the question of how 'harm' should be understood, Feinberg's suggestion has been influential, although plainly some specification of what is meant by 'setback to interests' in the present context will be necessary. In a passage which makes direct reference to Stephen's incompatibility argument, Feinberg writes:

> *Some* people would suffer setbacks to their interests if the British Museum were not supported, though perhaps most of those who are forced to pay taxes in its support would not be harmed on balance even if the British Museum were to disappear entirely. But for scholars who depend directly on the museum's resources, withdrawing those resources would be a serious setback to some of their most important personal interests. That fact by itself does not automatically justify taxing the others, but it shows that the bill of legislation supporting the British Museum can be classified as taxing some people to *prevent harm* to others, as well as taxing some people to provide a mere benefit to others.[39]

[37] Feinberg, *Harmless Wrongdoing*, n. 10, 312.
[38] Feinberg, *Harm to Others*, n.10, ch. 1.
[39] Feinberg, *Harmless Wrongdoing*, n. 10, 314. Emphases in the original.

Thus Feinberg rejects Stephen's claim that there is no harm to be prevented by ceasing state support of the British Museum, not because that would fail to benefit anyone, but because it may result in harm to 'vulnerable ulterior interests which are not widely shared'.[40]

One initial worry is that the triggering of the harm-based justification here supported seems not to be sensitive to *how many* ulterior interests may be at stake. Can it be sufficient to trigger the harm principle justification that there is only *one* scholar whose ulterior interests may depend on the British Museum in the way Feinberg suggests? It would seem so: if that one individual may actually be harmed, that would already be enough to establish that harm prevention is in the offing. On the face of it there need not be a dozen, a hundred, or a thousand.[41] It is true that the harm principle can be taken to suggest a necessary condition for state coercion, not a sufficient condition. Hence, even if harm to one person is sufficient to trigger the need for justification, one could still say that the fewer ulterior interests affected, the less likely the coercion in question will be justified, all things considered.

Be that as it may. Our main concern is with the question of whether Feinberg shows Stephen to be wrong by pointing to some genuine harm in this case. Feinberg's response harks back to the distinction he drew earlier in his four-volume work between 'ulterior interests' and 'welfare interests', two kinds of interest underlying his notion of harm.[42] The latter—welfare interests—are perhaps more obviously linked to harm. As Feinberg conceived them they are:

> the interests in the continuance for a foreseeable interval of one's life, and the interests in one's own physical health and vigor, the integrity and normal functioning of one's body, the absence of absorbing pain and suffering or grotesque disfigurement, minimal intellectual acuity, emotional stability, the absence of groundless anxieties and resentments, the capacity to engage normally in social intercourse and to enjoy and maintain friendships, at least minimal income and financial security, a tolerable social and physical environment, and a certain amount of freedom from interference and coercion.[43]

These are necessary means for more ultimate aims and must, generally, be jointly realized: 'deficiencies in one place are generally not to be compensated for by superiority in another'.[44]

As we saw above, Feinberg was not tempted to rest matters with welfare interests alone in accounting for which interests are set back in such a way as to be harmful. He is clear that his other category, 'ulterior interests', can be set back in such a way as to be harmful to the person whose interests they are. Examples he cites of such ulterior interests are:

> producing good novels or works of art, solving a crucial scientific problem, achieving high political office, successfully raising a family, achieving leisure for handicraft or

[40] Ibid., n. 10, 315.

[41] Cf. J. Gray, *Mill on Liberty: A Defence*, 2nd edn (London: Routledge, 1996), 136–7.

[42] Feinberg, *Harm to Others*, n. 10, 37–8. [43] Ibid., 37. [44] Ibid.

sport, building a dream house, advancing a social cause, ameliorating human suffering, achieving spiritual grace.[45]

In our context, he would, as we have also noted, add the example of certain scholars who depend on the British Museum's resources. While he accepts that without significant fulfilment of welfare interests a person is 'lost', welfare interests alone are 'grossly insufficient for a good life'.[46] If setbacks to 'ulterior interests' is a valid category of harm, it would indeed seem that it is a category that Stephen missed.

The issue of 'ulterior interests', having been identified early on by Feinberg in his work on the criminal law, was not one he needed to concern himself with to any great degree subsequently. For one thing, his 'welfare interest' category is plainly where the main concerns of the criminal law are going to lie. Moreover, as Feinberg convincingly demonstrated, the operation of the harm principle in the criminal law context must have built into it a wrongfulness constraint.[47] In essence, criminalizing conduct for the sake of harm prevention in the absence of wrongfulness is likely to be illegitimate in the criminal law context, as where one person's business drives another's into liquidation with devastating effects for the latter. Driving someone out of business may cause untold harm to those whose livelihoods and hopes depend on the business in question, but that in itself is no basis on which to render criminal the properly conducted business activities of the more successful operation. For the latter business has not acted wrongfully, unlike the murderer, kidnapper, or fraudster.

So much for the criminal law. Matters are different in the case of taxation and thus we see Feinberg resorting to his ulterior interests category in the British Museum case, as welfare interests are not in issue, nor can any wrongfulness constraint be relied upon to narrow down the category of ulterior interests.[48] We do not know what exactly Stephen would have made of Feinberg's welfare and ulterior interests. One suspects, however, from the tenor of his discussion that he would simply have refused to acknowledge the relevance of the latter, ulterior, category. Feinberg would have us accept as harmful to at least some (ulterior interests) a failure to continue support for the British Museum. Presumably, by parity of reasoning, failures to support his other examples of ulterior interests would also count as harmful. Taking one of Feinberg's

[45] Ibid., 37. [46] Ibid., 37. [47] Feinberg, *Harm to Others*, n. 10, ch. 3.

[48] As well as suggesting, as I do in the text, we should not begin by assuming that the harm principle in the context of taxation should be restricted by a wrongfulness constraint, as it plausibly is in the criminal law context, we also should not begin by assuming it should be restricted by a causation constraint. Lieberman suggests that the term 'harm' where deployed in the harm principle in the context of taxation should be used restrictively so that 'only harms people cause each other, not bad luck, may be redressed' (Lieberman, n. 12, 111). He proceeds to go to ingenious lengths to explain how it may yet be legitimate to tax in order to relieve the effects of natural disasters and calamities (111–13), pointing out for example that 'human activity, sometimes intentional ... always contributes to the turmoil that surrounds it, and may thus be the object of government intervention' (111).

Though too large an issue to explore in detail here, it may turn out (after reflecting on these and other cases) in the context of taxation, any harm principle analysis is best not hamstrung by either a wrongfulness or a causation constraint in the first place. Furthermore, in the context of the criminal law as well, I do not think that the harm principle is best read as limited only to 'harms people cause each other', but this is not the place to discuss that question (see R.A. Duff and S.E. Marshall, '"Remote Harms" and the Two Harm Principles', in A.P. Simester, A. Du Bois-Pedain, and U. Neumann (eds), *Liberal Criminal Theory: Essays for Andreas von Hirsch* (Oxford: Hart, 2014), 205.

other examples of such an ulterior interest, let us imagine that Paul can be decisively helped to 'build his dream house'. Imagine it is known that if Paul were to be paid the equivalent of half his annual salary, that would free up enough time for him to realize his ambition. Would he be harmed by the state if the money was not forthcoming? Even if we assume, to simplify matters, that the state believes it can afford to pay this regular money to Paul without compromising its other obligations, it is surely implausible to suggest that Paul is *harmed* if the money is not forthcoming. Feinberg, as we saw, plausibly rejected any interpretation of harm in terms merely of failing to benefit, for that implies that a failure to confer pure windfalls on persons would harm them. One wonders, however, if his own notion of 'ulterior interests' runs into a similar difficulty. For if he is in earnest that taxing for the British Museum prevents harm to some in virtue of the setback to those persons' ulterior interests, presumably the same can be said for what we might call 'qualified windfalls', that is windfalls that can only be used in support of ulterior interests and not, say, frittered away on inessentials that form no part of the beneficiary's ulterior interests. Take any of Feinberg's ulterior interests—successfully raising a family, achieving spiritual grace, and so on—and then ask whether any sum of money might genuinely and reliably support that interest—sending all members of the family in question on a holiday together, building a religious monument in someone's private garden—do we finally conclude that a failure to supply the requisite money constitutes a harm to the ulterior interest holder? This again is most implausible.

One might here respond with an observation that is often made about harm, namely that it has to do with *becoming worse off than one was*, while failing to obtain a benefit is more a matter of not becoming better off than before.[49] The British Museum is already supported, hence removing the support would make the relevant persons worse off and would thus harm them. The other examples, on the other hand, are all cases in which there is no current support, hence failing to supply the funding would not make anyone worse off than they previously were. Thus, the response concludes, the other examples would not harm anyone and Feinberg's response to Stephen stands. Now without suggesting that this answer would commend itself to Feinberg himself, it is in any case unsatisfactory. An alternative understanding conceives harm not only in terms of becoming worse off than one was, but also worse off than 'one is entitled to be in a way that affects [one's] future well-being'.[50] Of course such an understanding relies on an as-yet-unstated theory or account of entitlement. However, that seems a price worth paying to avoid the serious conservative bias that appears built into an understanding of harm as restricted simply to that which makes people worse off than they previously were.

In the background is a very deep issue about conceiving of harm in terms of a setback to interests, as Feinberg does. Feinberg is surely right that we have ulterior interests and that they are very important to our well-being, although it is starting to look as if the category might be impossible to contain within a workable harm principle. In

[49] H. Frankfurt, 'Necessity and Desire', in *The Importance of What We Care About* (Cambridge, UK: Cambridge University Press, 1988), 104, 109–10.

[50] Raz, n. 22, 414.

particular it looks as if the ulterior interests of Feinberg's British Museum scholars are not *qua* interests more compelling in terms of state support than Paul's dream house, or the family holiday, or religious monument of Feinberg's earlier examples (as we extended them). If these and so many other potential examples are really to be conceived in terms of harm in the ways we have considered, the idea of harm will surely have lost the purchase it would need in a workable harm principle.

2. *Harm and need*

Perhaps the solution is to abandon the category of ulterior interests and with it Feinberg's claim that anyone would be harmed by a cessation of state support for the British Museum. If so, that would seem also to be the end of Feinberg's harm-based defence of the state subsidy of the British Museum. One could attempt to work with Feinberg's welfare interests alone, without the ulterior interests. It is tempting here to invoke the idea of *need*, with the eventual application to tax in mind. Indeed, it is worth pausing to examine how need might relate to harm as it will help to make vivid what I think is a serious difficulty with Feinberg's understanding of harm as 'setback to interests'.

One might attempt to account for Feinberg's welfare interests in terms of need, in order to differentiate them from his ulterior interests and argue for the special normative salience of need. For such a move to be of any potential help, 'need' would have to be understood as having some specific substantive and categorical content. And that would rule out many accounts of need which assert that by its nature needing is always needing for a purpose, so that statements of need which do not mention relevant purposes are always shorthand for sentences that do mention them.[51] If that were the right understanding of need, any claim of need would only be as good as the purpose lying behind it, in which case one might as well forget needs and go straight to an evaluation of the various purposes lying behind each need claim. However, other accounts of need suggest not all needing is purely instrumental in this way. Interestingly such accounts often account for need in terms of harm or harm-avoidance. Indeed Feinberg himself in earlier work asserted 'in a general sense to say that S needs X is to say simply that if he doesn't have X he will be harmed'.[52]

One immediate problem, however, is that if we are attempting to elucidate the idea of harm and then suggest that some harming relates to needing, it is hardly helpful then to be told that needing is to be understood in terms of harming! Aristotle accounted for the cognate notion of 'necessity' thus:

> We call necessary that without which, as a joint cause, it is not possible to live, as for instance breathing and nourishment are necessary for an animal, because it is incapable of existing without them; and anything without which it is not possible for good to exist or come to be, or for bad to be discarded or got rid of, as for instance

[51] On such accounts (and why they should be rejected) see D. Wiggins, 'Claims of Need', in *Needs, Values, Truth*, 3rd edn (Oxford: Clarendon, 1998), 7.

[52] J. Feinberg, *Social Philosophy* (Englewood Cliffs: Prentice Hall, 1973), 111. For a detailed account relating need to harm, see Wiggins, n. 51.

> drinking medicine is necessary so as not to be ill, and sailing to Aegina so as to get money.[53]

There appear to be at least four senses of necessity in the passage, I believe, or at least discernible without much of a stretch:

(1) life and death necessity: a human (or other animal) will die without what is lacked.
(2) necessity for flourishing: necessity for the realization of some good.
(3) necessity to prevent matters getting worse than they would be according to some baseline; necessity for the avoidance of some bad.
(4) instrumental necessity.

The passage illustrates the range of possible uses of need and necessity and different ranges of normative force that may accompany the different uses. As we have already intimated sense (4)—purely instrumental needing—can be of no help if the idea of need is to help block out a sense of harm for a workable harm principle. If one is to get to Aegina from Athens—at least in Aristotle's day—one needs to sail. But one might go to Aegina for reasons good, bad, or indifferent. Aristotle imagines sailing to Aegina 'to get money'; this might involve selling something in the market or collecting a debt, as one is entitled to do, or to it might be attempted extortion, etc. Plainly such necessity is only as good (or bad) as that for which it is necessary. Accordingly needing in this sense cannot ground anything with, say, the force of a right. By contrast sense (1) plainly picks out something of crucial importance justifying, uncontroversially enough, spending through taxation on emergency services and so on. It is reasonable to be confident that this sense could ground something with the force of a right.

However, it is senses (2) and (3) that are particularly interesting in relation to our discussion. Sense (3) seems to fit naturally with the proposal that needing X is to be equated with harm as a consequence of not having X. Sense (2), by contrast, seems to fit with some other proposals of how needing should be understood, for example Anscombe's proposal that 'to say that [an organism] needs [a particular] environment is not to say, e.g. that you want it to have that environment, but this it won't flourish unless it has it'.[54] As an account of our ordinary sense of needing, it does not seem that either of senses (2) or (3) can be dispensed with. Both account for important aspects of our understanding of needs in particular and well-being in general. In other words, the hope that we can make the idea of 'harm' more precise for harm principle purposes by invoking the idea of need runs into the same difficulty I suggested Feinberg got into by claiming that there can be harm in ceasing to fund the British Museum through taxation. If this is needing, it is Anscombe's needing-for-flourishing; if it is harming, it is so by virtue of Feinberg's ulterior interests. However, it must again be remembered that the harm principle is supposed to operate as a robust protector of liberty or autonomy. I have been suggesting the notions just discussed—'that which is necessary for each of us to flourish' and 'all of our ulterior interests'—is too vast and

[53] Aristotle, *Metaphysics*, C. Kirwan (trans.) (Oxford: Clarendon, 1971), V 1015a20. Cf. Wiggins, n. 51, 25–6.

[54] G.E.M. Anscombe, 'Modern Moral Philosophy', 33(124) *Philosophy* (1958) 1, 7.

uncontrollable to work as the normative basis for something of the strength and normative role the harm principle is intended to have.

Feinberg himself accepted that invasions of welfare interests are 'more serious'[55] than invasions of ulterior interests pointing to the graver consequences of blocking or damaging the former as opposed to the latter. As far as welfare interests are concerned, he thought, 'a person's more ultimate aspirations are defeated too; whereas setbacks to a higher goal do not to the same degree inflict damage on the whole network of his interests.'[56] That said, Feinberg clearly sees ulterior interests as an important reason-giving component of the apparatus that makes up his version of the harm principle. So much is clear from his discussion of the British Museum case. This, I have been arguing, suggests a serious problem with the very notion of harm as 'setback to interests'. I do not think Feinberg is wrong to make the room he does for ulterior interests in accounting for interests in general. That is plausible. However, if such interests are to be a significant input into the harm principle itself, as Feinberg takes them to be, there simply appear to be too many of them.

My interim conclusion is that Stephen's incompatibility argument is essentially correct. Coercing through taxation for the sake of subsidizing the British Museum falls foul of the Millian harm principle. Feinberg's response, drawing on his own account of what harming is—setting back an interest, including setting back an ulterior interest—proves to be unsatisfactory, not because the account of interests is implausible, but because harming is understood by means of such a wide notion as human interests. Feinberg's two other arguments in favour of cultural subsidies—the argument from rotational justice and from supporting intrinsic values—remain available considerations in favour of such subsidies (the latter especially) but they are essentially arguments that stand or fall independently of the harm principle. I turn now to consider a different version of the harm principle, that contained in the so-called 'perfectionist liberal' theory of Joseph Raz.[57] Would the subsidies under consideration fare better on such an account or would they similarly fall foul of the harm principle?

II. Raz on Perfectionism and the Harm Principle

In order to get clear on Raz's 'perfectionist liberal' version of the harm principle, it is important to take his account in two stages. First, one must appreciate the perfectionist context of his account and, secondly, how the harm principle, which at first sight appears in tension with perfectionism, is nonetheless said by Raz to be derived from it.

Beginning with the perfectionist background, one should note that the label 'perfectionism' is itself an unsatisfactory one, not much liked even by proponents of the view, although it is too well embedded to dislodge. It might seem to conjure an image of a state seeking to 'perfect' persons through the compulsory imposition of a unitary system of values. That is light years from the views of those associated at least with the liberal strand of perfectionism, such as Raz himself, Thomas Hurka, George Sher, and

[55] Feinberg, *Harm to Others*, n. 10, 38. [56] Ibid., 37. [57] Raz, n. 22.

others.[58] One useful recent characterization of perfectionism has it that 'it is a proper function of government to encourage activities that are the most excellent, admirable, and fine; that this goal may be permissibly advanced by discouraging activities that are less than the most excellent, admirable and fine; and that the goal of human excellence justifies the government in discouraging these activities by limiting individual liberty'.[59] As far as I can see, Raz's perfectionism is consistent with this definition, though it is important to spell out how and where the limits of his account lie. In particular the limited extent to which liberty may permissibly be limited in this context is a matter to which he gives considerable attention.

Raz's emphasis is on the reasons that it is legitimate for governments to rely upon. There is, he says, 'no fundamental principled inhibition on governments acting for any valid moral reason'.[60] He thereby directly opposes the attempts of many fellow liberals to limit the range of reasons on which a government can legitimately rely to reasons that are 'public' in nature or to those that do not violate 'neutrality'.[61] He is adamant that it 'makes no sense to say of a state of affairs that it is good but that fact is no reason to do anything about it'.[62] Presumably he would say the same of the fact that a state of affairs is bad: that must similarly furnish a reason to do something about it. Thus in principle the reasons that apply generally are the reasons that apply to governments and none should in principle be excluded right from the start. Having a reason to do something is not of course the same as having a *conclusive* or all-things-considered reason to do that thing, an issue we come to below when we examine the second part of Raz's account. As he sees matters, then, it is the function of governments to promote the quality of life, including the moral quality of life, of those whose lives and actions the government can affect.[63] Governments as a matter of principle need not be neutral between competing conceptions of the good life; they should rather be sensitive to all the relevant reasons.

If the government can as a matter of principle have recourse to reasons based on a conception of the good life that many citizens may not share, might that not imply-exactly what I above suggested the liberal perfectionists reject: namely, that governments may purport to 'perfect' persons by means of the imposition of one supposedly correct view of the good life? Part of the answer to this will come below when we consider the second stage of Raz's account in which the harm principle is introduced. His perfectionism is also strongly value-pluralist and its leading idea is that of autonomy, notions which rule out such a dystopian possibility. There are, he says, 'many morally valuable forms of life which are incompatible with each other'.[64] That plurality

[58] T. Hurka, *Perfectionism* (Oxford: Oxford University Press, 1996); G. Sher, *Beyond Neutrality: Perfectionism and Politics* (Cambridge, UK: Cambridge University Press, 1997).

[59] P. de Marneffe, 'The Possibility and Desirability of Neutrality', in R. Merrill and D. Weinstock (eds), *Political Neutrality: A Re-Evaluation* (New York: Palgrave Macmillan, 2014), 44, 55.

[60] J. Raz, 'Facing Up: A Reply', 62 *Southern California Law Review* (1989) 1153, 1230.

[61] For examples of 'public reason' and 'neutrality' accounts, see respectively J. Rawls, *The Law of Peoples: With 'The Idea of Public Reason Revisited'*, Rev. edn (Cambridge, MA: Harvard University Press, 2001); and Gaus, n. 17 and n. 26.

[62] Raz, n. 60, 1230. [63] Raz, n. 22, 415. [64] Ibid., 161.

is something that governments (at least under modern conditions) must respect and foster. And crucially under the conditions of modern societies, governments should see to it that all persons are able to choose between an adequate range of valuable options.[65] In short, if the morality that is to be imposed is one that insists on choice for all between an adequate range of valuable options against a background of value pluralism, it is clear that the coercive imposition of a particular style of life is emphatically ruled out. The centrality of the requirement of an adequate range of valuable options for all also gives rise to autonomy-based duties on the part of all to support all others with the means necessary to choose such a valuable, autonomous life.

The complicating factor here is coercion. The use of coercion brings in to play the harm principle, at least for those authors who endorse such a constraint on legitimate government. As already noted, Raz is one such author. Notwithstanding his claim that all relevant reasons, including the moral and paternalist reasons Mill's and Feinberg's versions of the harm principle sought to rule out, are in principle available to governments, he too ends up arguing for a version of the harm principle. Raz's version is not a 'harm *to others* principle', as is Mill's and Feinberg's; it is a 'harm principle' shorn of the words 'to others'. Hence his version does not rule out paternalistic reasons as a matter of principle. Furthermore, he understands 'harm' in terms of setbacks to autonomy. He avoids entirely Feinberg's wider understanding of harm as 'setback to interests'. Earlier we had cause to cite Raz's understanding of the harm principle in terms not merely of refraining from making people worse off than they currently are, but of refraining from making them worse off than they are entitled to be:[66] 'the harm principle does not recognize only the duty of governments to prevent loss of autonomy. Sometimes failing to improve the situation of another is harming him.'[67] Harming, then, can involve failing in one's duty to another and one cannot necessarily avoid the charge that one has harmed another by pointing out (truly) that one has not left the other any worse off than she was before.

The harm principle should be interpreted in a particular way: as derived from the principle of autonomy:

> the principle is derivable from a morality which regards personal autonomy as an essential ingredient in the good life, and regards the principle of autonomy which imposes duties on people to secure for all the conditions of autonomy, as one of the most important moral principles.[68]

The use of compulsory taxation will be justified if 'the tax is raised to provide adequate opportunities, and is justified by the principle of autonomy in a way consistent with the harm principle'; and this must be done, Raz makes clear, in order to allow 'full scope to autonomy-based duties'.[69] If I fail to discharge my autonomy-based duties to others I harm them. I can legitimately be taxed on this basis, with the proviso that

[65] 'The government has an obligation to create an environment providing individuals with an adequate range of options and the opportunities to choose them.' Raz, n. 22, 418; 'the autonomy principle is a perfectionist principle. Autonomous life is valuable only if it is spent in the pursuit of acceptable and valuable projects and relationships.' Ibid., 417.

[66] Raz, n. 50. [67] Raz, n. 22, 415–16. [68] Ibid., 415. [69] Ibid.

the laws taxing me 'merely reflect and make concrete' my autonomy-based duties and those of the other citizens. In sum, 'coercion is used to ensure compliance with the law. If the law reflects autonomy-based duties then failure to comply harms others and the harm principle is satisfied.'[70] This, then, is 'the argument': justified taxation does not violate the harm principle and the harm principle is derived from the autonomy principle, which means that justified taxation must not be undertaken except in response to autonomy-based duties. If there is nothing in it, to put it crudely, for autonomy-based duties, taxation should not be raised.

As Raz himself summarizes the operation of his harm principle:

> the measures I [support] avoid direct coercion for perfectionist causes. The coercion that they involve can be fully justified on the grounds of protecting and promoting individual autonomy. The simplest example is that of taxation. Taxation is coercive. It is justified in my view only inasmuch as it is useful for the promotion and protection of autonomy for all.[71]

On the basis of this analysis it looks as if the way is clear for a government to reason as follows: 'we will support the British Museum on the basis of the valuable options to which it gives rise, options which, if chosen autonomously against a background of other valuable options, will give value to the lives of the choosers. In short we will support the autonomous lives of our citizens by helping foster this option (as well as a number of others).' This may be best achieved without government intervention of course, but if government *is* best placed to foster these options, there is no principled bar to their doing so. If so, moreover, it may do so by means of money raised from general taxation on the basis that the persons from whom the taxes are extracted have autonomy-based obligations to support others with the means necessary to choose between an adequate range of valuable options.

There are plainly large questions left open as to *which* valuable options should be fostered by the state, assuming the impossibility of fostering all such potentially valuable options. Raz himself says little about how governments should choose what to subsidize. What one apparently needs to establish is that the activity the government proposes to subsidize be a valuable one and that it can potentially engage the autonomous choices of people who also have other valuable options from which to choose. Presumably this account of autonomy would not support public spending on an option which, though a valuable one (as we can stipulate for the sake of argument), is one that there is no chance any of the current population would be minded to choose. Raz's claim that options a government can subsidize must be valuable gives his account a clear objectivist flavour. It also gives him the problem that objectivist moves in general face. As Ben Bradley puts it:

> objective theories face a worry about alienation: objective theories tell us that certain things are good for us whether we care about those things or not. But how could something be good for me if I did not care about it?[72]

[70] Ibid. [71] Raz, n. 60, 1232.

[72] B. Bradley, 'Objective Theories of Well-being', in B. Eggleston and D.E. Miller (eds), *Cambridge Companion to Utilitarianism* (Cambridge, UK: Cambridge University Press, 2014), 220–1.

Raz has a ready means of dealing with this alienation worry, by dint of the importance of choice to his account. The options indeed need to be valuable on his view (in a way that is independent of anyone's opinion on whether the option is valuable or not), but the option still needs to be chosen in preference to another available one. Individuals must of course choose for themselves, hence in a clear way the alienation worry is allayed.

A point touched on previously may also bear repeating. Disadvantage, as pointed out by Wolff and De-Shalit, can have a tendency to 'cluster'. One form of disadvantage suffered by a particular person may lead to another, which in turn leads to more and so on. This should be of particular concern for any standard demanding for all an adequate range of valuable options. Plainly a special priority should adhere to those who lack such an adequate range of valuable options and a possible remedy is the fostering of valuable options with which such persons are sufficiently likely to choose to engage. Just where support for the British Museum would stand in such an exercise is not immediately clear. Where a valuable option displays considerable continuity with the past and abandoning support for it risks the loss of the option forever, that is surely a highly pertinent consideration for a government in deciding how to distribute subsidies with the aim of creating or fostering valuable options from which people can choose. Matters like this will of course depend on the facts.

The upshot is that, in principle at least, subsidies drawn from general taxation in support of the British Museum are justifiable in accordance with Razian liberal perfectionism, constrained by the harm principle. The matter would ultimately depend on the application of the criteria just discussed against a background of complex practical data. In closing, however, it is important to state a reservation about the derivation of the Razian harm principle from its perfectionist background. We mentioned above that Raz claims that the harm principle can be derived from the principle of autonomy. But how is that to be done? And why do it? Why not shed the harm principle and work with an unrestricted perfectionism on the understanding that it is autonomy-based in the way Raz argues?

Raz's derivation of the harm principle from the autonomy principle is based on the perceived need to limit the *means* that can legitimately be adopted in promoting the well-being of people.[73] This takes us back to coercion. There is a special tension between coercion and autonomy. Coercion, Raz says, first of all, 'violates the condition of independence' and 'expresses a relation of domination and an attitude of disrespect for the coerced individual'. Secondly, he says, 'coercion by criminal penalties is a global and indiscriminate invasion of autonomy'.[74] We have seen that Raz assumes that taxation is coercive. But it is just as clear that it is not coercive in the sense of being a 'global and indiscriminate invasion of autonomy'. Now Raz applies these words specifically to criminal penalties but it is worth noting how different is the context of taxation that we are considering. Taxation made in order to yield the requisite sums to be passed on to the British Museum and so on is highly diffuse among those who pay and assuming a tax system that is appropriately progressive, it should leave no taxpayer

[73] Raz, n. 22, 420. [74] Ibid., 418.

without an adequate range of valuable options (assuming they had such an adequacy before the relevant proportion of the tax was demanded and paid). Hence this reason for deriving the harm principle from the principle of autonomy appears not to apply in the present context. The coercion is well short of 'global and indiscriminate'.

That leaves us with the argument that the harm principle is to be derived from the principle of autonomy on the basis that coercion expresses a domineering and disrespectful attitude to the person and her independence. However, it is hard to see how that consideration can have the effect of silencing a set of reasons that are *ex hypothesi* relevant, prior to any such silencing. The question is whether coercion is to be used and, if so, what justification is to be given, for justification there must be. That seems to tell us that the justification had better be strong enough, but it does not tell us anything about the kind of justification that would be required from the range of reasons the perfectionist initially judges relevant, reasons based, for example, on the repugnance of a certain option and so on. In short it is very hard to see how Raz can proceed from his starting point—rejecting the curtailing of available governmental reasons in various ways via neutrality or public reasons—to his harm principle—demanding via the harm principle the curtailing of reasons on which government can legitimately rely when using coercion.

If the derivation of the harm principle cannot be made to work on this account, we are left with the perfectionist (autonomy-supporting background) without the backup of the harm principle. How such an account could fare is an interesting question for another day.

III. Conclusion

As Feinberg observes, 'one of the functions of government is to *take*, as for example in taxation, and another is to *give*, as for example in subsidies'. 'Could', he goes on to ask, 'the ultimate theories of justification on both sides be the same?' And 'can a theory of governmental subsidies hope to proceed without a corresponding theory of political liberties?'[75] I have looked at the example of cultural subsidies made through compulsory taxation and have examined aspects of the liberal tradition of thought revolving around the harm principle in order to examine both sides of Feinberg's justificatory coin. I believe that Feinberg's vast work on the principled limits of the criminal law has been of great service to the study of the criminal law, both for those who agree with him and for those who oppose him. It has done much to frame issues for debate and to raise interesting new possibilities. One wonders what four Feinberg volumes on the principled limits of taxation would have looked like. I don't doubt that they would have had a similar impact to that his criminal law work has had.

I began with Stephen's claim that 'to force an unwilling person to contribute to the support of the British Museum' is incompatible with Mill's harm principle. Having examined the issue in detail I believe Stephen was right about that. I suggested that more attention than is usually given to the triggering condition of the harm principle,

[75] Feinberg, n. 6, vii.

namely the proposed use of coercion, is desirable. For the nature and degree of coercion can vary greatly. I proceeded to Feinberg's own response to Stephen's incompatibility argument. His response—that there is (ulterior) harm to be prevented by subsidising the British Museum—led, I suggested, to an account of 'harm' that is ultimately untenable, unable to play the normative role the harm principle is designed for. Feinberg did, however, leave other arguments in favour of subsidising the British Museum, notably his argument from intrinsic value, which essentially floated free of any argument based on the harm principle.

I went on to ask whether any other version of the harm principle, such as Raz's liberal perfectionist version, would similarly be incompatible with the subsidies for the British Museum. This account told what I took to be a more plausible story about how harm should be understood than Feinberg's did. I think in principle Raz's harm principle is not incompatible with the subsidies. However, the Razian account helps frame the question—one that requires attention to empirical matters—rather than to answer it definitively. While the furnishing or fostering of valuable options from which persons can potentially make autonomous choices is plausibly thought of as a legitimate government function, this does not tell us which options should be so supported. I considered some questions that might need to be considered in order to seek progress on this issue. I also suggested that it was not clear that the harm principle had been shown to have been successfully derived from the perfectionist premises of Raz's account. The question mark, I believe, over the perfectionist harm principle is whether it is adequately supported from within its own theory, rather than whether it is incompatible with the cultural subsidies under consideration.

I have only tried to examine one theoretical problem in taxation in relation to the harm principle. I am not confident that any version of the harm principle can be developed satisfactorily enough to serve as the sort of strong constraint on what makes for legitimate coercion that the harm principle is intended to deliver, in the taxation context as well as elsewhere. I do, however, believe that the engagement between this aspect of the liberal intellectual heritage, on the one hand, and taxation law and policy, on the other, can be a source of illumination on both sides.

3

Tax Evasion as Crime

*Stuart P. Green**

From the perspective of criminal law, tax evasion is a baffling and anomalous offence. It deviates from the traditional paradigm of crime in that the harms it causes are highly diffuse, significant only in the aggregate, and hard to identify with any certainty. It is also one of only a handful of crimes (at least under US law) that requires evidence of 'willfulness'— understood to mean a 'voluntary, intentional violation of a known legal duty'.[1] Such culpability is quite unusual in criminal law in that it allows mistake or ignorance of the law to be a defence.

Tax evasion also differs from other offences in terms of its incidence, which is probably higher than that of any other serious white-collar crime. According to one recent study, approximately 25 per cent of US taxpayers admitted to deliberately cheating on their taxes.[2] And the level of noncompliance is even higher outside the United States— in Europe, and especially in the developing world.[3] There are many reasons for such noncompliance, but one is certainly the fact that a significant percentage of people believe that cheating on their taxes is not morally wrong.[4] And it is striking as well that there is a long and fairly respectable tradition of tax resistance as a form of political protest, something that is hard to imagine in the case of crimes such as bribery, perjury, or fraud.[5]

* An earlier version of this chapter was presented to the Conference on 'Philosophical Foundations of Tax Law' at University College London (May 2015). For helpful questions and conversations, I am grateful to Monica Bhandari, Jennifer Bird-Pollan, Josh Blank, Cynthia Blum, Tony Dillof, Antony Duff, David Duff, Patrick Emerton, Miranda Fleischer, Judith Freedman, Ted Seto, Fadi Shaheen, Dan Shaviro, John Snape, and John Stanton-Ife.

[1] IRC §7201, interpreted in *United States v Pomponio*, 429 U.S. 10, 12 (1976); see also Mark C. Winings, 'Ignorance is Bliss, Especially for the Tax Evader', 84(3) *Journal of Criminal Law & Criminology* (1993) 575 (discussing the problems with allowing an ignorance of law defence for tax crimes).

[2] James A. Tackett et al., 'A Criminological Perspective of Tax Evasion', 110 *Tax Notes* (6 February 2006) 654, 654, available in *Tax Notes Today*, 2006 LEXIS TNT 25–73.

[3] See James Alm and Benno Torgler, 'Culture Differences and Tax Morale in the United States and Europe', 27(2) *Journal of Economic Psychology* (2006) 224; John Hasseldine and Zhuhong Li, 'More Tax Evasion Research in New Millennium', 31(2) *Crime, Law & Social Change* (1999) 91–104.

[4] See generally Leandra Lederman, 'The Interplay Between Norms and Enforcement in Tax Compliance', 64(6) *Ohio State Law Journal* (2003) 1453. In a recent Taxpayer Attitude Survey conducted by the IRS Oversight Board, 16 per cent of taxpayers disagreed with the statement that they should cheat 'not at all' on their taxes; 8 per cent said it was acceptable to cheat 'a little here and there', and 5 per cent said that people could cheat 'as much as possible'. See *IRS Oversight Board*, Taxpayer Attitude Survey 2007 (February 2008), http://www.treas.gov/irsob/reports/2008/2007_Taxpayer-Attitude-Survey.pdf.

For more on the complex psychology that underlies tax evasion, see Eric Kirchler, *The Economic Psychology of Tax Behaviour* (Cambridge, UK: Cambridge University Press, 2007).

[5] See generally David F. Burg, *A World History of Tax Rebellions* (New York: Routledge, 2004); Romain D. Huret, *American Tax Resisters* (Cambridge, MA: Harvard University Press, 2014).

Philosophical Foundations of Tax Law. First Edition. Edited by Monica Bhandari.

The laws concerning tax evasion are also enforced in a highly irregular manner (again, focusing particularly on the US context). For example, in 2009, the US government authorized the prosecution of only 1,210 criminal tax cases—representing a mere 0.00086 per cent of the 179.4 million individual tax returns filed in that year.[6] And, where prosecutions do occur, they are often brought in an uneven and highly selective manner.[7]

Despite, or perhaps because of, such anomalies, tax evasion is a crime that has tended to fall between the cracks of normative analysis. Criminal law theorists have largely avoided the subject altogether (perhaps because of tax law's reputation for being highly technical). Meanwhile, tax law theorists, though not avoiding the subject of tax evasion as such, have only rarely applied to it the basic tools of criminal law theory.

As a criminal law theorist myself, I am something of an exception here, having written about tax evasion twice before. On one occasion, I offered some preliminary thoughts on why it is wrong, from a moral perspective, to evade taxes.[8] On another occasion, I looked at what exactly is wrong with the *crime* of tax evasion: I considered why the rate of tax evasion is so high, why there is so much apparent scepticism about the wrongfulness of evading taxes, and why the enforcement of our laws against tax evasion is so irregular.[9]

In this chapter, I intend to take my analysis of tax evasion a bit further. First, I will argue that an understanding of how taxes differ from fees, fines, penalties, forfeitures, and other types of government assessments is crucial to an understanding of why tax evasion is morally wrong. Second, I will offer a more fully developed account of the moral content of tax evasion, explaining the role that the concepts of cheating, disobedience to the law, and what I call 'deceptive covering up' play in defining its moral content; and why, further, the concept of stealing is largely inapposite. Finally, I will consider the extent to which my analysis of tax evasion might be helpful in assessing the moral content of tax avoidance.

[6] Tax Division, US Department of Justice, FY 2011 Congressional Budget (2010), 25, http://www.justice.gov/jmd/2011justification/pdf/fy11-tax-justification.pdf. See *Individual Complete Report* (Publication 1304), Table 1.6, SOI Tax Stats—Individual Statistical Tables by Size of Adjusted Gross Income, IRS, https://www.irs.gov/uac/soi-tax-stats-individual-statistical-tables-by-size-of-adjusted-gross-income. See also Joshua D. Blank, 'In Defense of Individual Tax Privacy', 61(2) *Emory Law Journal* (2011) 265; Bruce Hochman and Steven Toscher, 'More Than Bad Luck: Differences in Civil and Criminal Fraud Sanctions under the Internal Revenue Code,' *taxlitigator.com* (2007), http://taxlitigator.com/more-than-bad-luck-differences-in-civil-and-criminal-fraud-sanctions-under-the-internal-revenue-code/.

[7] There are disparities both geographically and according to the type and wealth of the taxpayer. See David Cay Johnston, 'Audits Spread Unevenly Across U.S.', *New York Times* (12 April 1998), http://query.nytimes.com/gst/fullpage.html?res=9E0CE4D7133DF931A25757C0A96E958260&sec=&spon=&pagewanted=print; see also *TRACIRS*, Transactional Records Access Clearinghouse, District Enforcement (2010), http://trac.syr.edu/tracirs/findings/07/index.html; Michael Levi, 'Serious Tax Fraud and Noncompliance: A Review of Evidence on the Differential Impact of Criminal and Noncriminal Proceedings', 9(3) *Criminology & Public Policy* (2010) 493.

[8] Stuart P. Green, *Lying, Cheating, and Stealing: A Moral Theory of White-Collar Crime* (Oxford: Oxford University Press, 2006), 243–8.

[9] Stuart P. Green, 'What is Wrong with Tax Evasion?', 9 *Houston Business and Tax Law Journal* (2009) 221–36.

I. Defining Key Concepts

Before we can begin the normative analysis, it will be helpful to develop a definition of two key terms: *tax* and *tax evasion*. The account here is intended to reflect widespread, if not universal, usage, while at the same time extending the definitional analysis beyond where it has gone before.

A. What Is a Tax?

Although the 'what is a tax?' question has generated a good deal of litigation and court decisions, it seems to have attracted relatively little attention from theorists.[10] In the United States, the question arises primarily in the following contexts:

- Under the US Constitution, measures that constitute 'taxes' must originate in the House of Representatives, must be imposed 'uniformly' throughout the United States, may be used only 'to pay the Debts and provide for the common Defence and general Welfare of the United States', may not be levied on exports, and may not be imposed as a condition of the right to vote.[11] Other kinds of government fees lack such limitations. Similarly, many state constitutions require that tax legislation be enacted by a larger legislative majority than normal, or that they be passed by referendum. Thus, in order to determine if constitutional requirements have been complied with, courts at both the federal and state level have had to decide which assessments are properly understood as taxes and which constitute some other kind of assessment.[12]
- The federal and state constitutions also impose separate procedural requirements on other kinds of (non-tax) government assessment. For example, if a government assessment is determined to be a 'criminal fine', it must comply with a defendant's rights to confrontation, against double jeopardy, against self-incrimination, and to have his guilt decided beyond a reasonable doubt.[13] Similarly, if a government assessment is determined to be a 'taking', it will be prohibited under the Constitution's Takings Clause unless the government offers the property owner just compensation.[14] Courts have thus had to distinguish between measures that are really taxes and those that are in fact criminal fines or takings, as the case may be.

[10] Worth noting here is Bruno Peeters et al. (eds), 'The Relevance of a Concept of Tax', in *The Concept of Tax in EU Member States* (European Association of Tax Law Professors Congress, 2005), http://www.eatlp.org/uploads/public/part_I_concept_of_tax_in_eu_member_states_05_05_09.pdf.

[11] See generally Steve R. Johnson, 'Obamacare and the "What is a Tax?" Question', 63(2) *State Tax Notes* (9 January 2012) 155; Robert G. Natelson, 'What the Constitution Means by "Duties, Imposts, and Excises"—and "Taxes" (Direct or Otherwise)', 66(2) *Case Western Reserve Law Review* (2016) 297.

[12] See e.g. *Sinclair Paint Co. v State Board of Equalization*, 15 Cal. 4th 866 (1997) (upholding as a 'fee', rather than a tax, a California provision imposing a charge on persons selling products that contain lead).

[13] On taxes versus criminal fines, see e.g. *Department of Revenue v Kurth Ranch*, 511 U.S. 767 (1994) (invalidating Montana's so-called Dangerous Drug Tax, which imposed fees 'on the possession and storage of dangerous drugs', on the grounds that it was really a form of punishment and therefore required various procedural protections).

[14] On taxes versus takings, see Johnson, n. 11, 157 (pointing out that, if the government had to compensate citizens for money taken through revenue-raising tax measures, such measures would be self-defeating).

- The question of 'what is a tax?' also arises in a host of statutory contexts. For example, under the Internal Revenue Code itself, a taxpayer who paid foreign 'taxes' to a foreign country on foreign source income and is subject to US tax on the same income is often entitled to a credit or itemized deduction for those taxes.[15] Similarly, under US bankruptcy law, the claims of states for excise taxes owed by debtors have priority status and are non-dischargeable, but that treatment does not apply to measures that are called taxes but are determined in fact to be fines.[16]

Unfortunately, the cases that address the 'what is a tax?' issue tend to take an ad hoc approach, offering no clear, comprehensive definition or overarching set of criteria for distinguishing taxes from other kinds of payments to the government—whether they be 'user fees', 'criminal fines', 'forfeitures', 'takings', 'civil penalties', or other 'regulatory measures'. It is therefore worth trying to derive a more general definition of what should be regarded as a tax.

As a preliminary matter, I would suggest that the concept be defined as: (1) an exaction of money; (2) imposed and collected by a government authority; (3) on or from a private person or entity; where (4) such payment is compulsory; (5) imposed for non-punitive purposes; and (6) paid not in return for a specific service or privilege received from the government, but rather as a means to fund government operations more generally.[17]

Let us consider each element in turn: First, a tax involves the payment of money. Normally, taxes are assessed as a percentage of: the amount of money earned or received in some transaction (as in the case of income, gift, and inheritance taxes); the value of property owned (as in the case of real estate taxes); or the amount of money spent (as in the case of sales, excise, and *ad valorem* taxes). Some taxes are also assessed on a flat, per capita or per family unit (as in the case of poll and head taxes). When a taxpayer pays a tax, it is his choice which assets to liquidate or deplete in order to defray liability.[18] This is in contrast to government takings and forfeitures, which are directed at a particular asset or group of assets (such as a house, a car, or stocks and bonds.). Other kinds of compulsory, nonpunitive obligations should also avoid categorization as taxes. For example, conscription in the military would not be a tax, even if the conscript incurred opportunity costs, including loss of income, while fulfilling his service obligation.

Second, the requirement of payment must be imposed by a governmental entity. Thus membership fees paid to a private organization would not qualify as a tax. Nor would payments to a political candidate, political party, or individual government

[15] See Treas. Reg. 26 CFR §1.901–2(a)(2)(i) (2008) (payment made abroad is a 'tax' if it constitutes a 'compulsory payment pursuant to the authority of a foreign country to levy taxes'); see also Internal Revenue Service, 'What Foreign Taxes Qualify for the Foreign Tax Credit?' (updated 13 December 2014), https://www.irs.gov/individuals/international-taxpayers/what-foreign-taxes-qualify-for-the-foreign-tax-credit.

[16] See 11 USC §507(a)(8)E)(ii).

[17] For a similar, though slightly simpler, definition, see M. Barassi, 'The Notion of Tax and the Different Types of Taxes', in Peeters, n. 10, 33.

[18] Johnson, n. 11, 158.

official (whether legal or not). The government entities that assess taxes are typically legislative bodies, while the collection of taxes is normally performed by an administrative body (though this last feature seems to be a contingent rather than necessary condition of a tax scheme).

Third, the obligation to pay must be imposed on members of a class of private persons or entities. This means that a 'transfer' or 'forgiveness' payment made by one government entity to another—say, within a federal system—would not count as a tax. Nor would payments required of a particular individual only (as in the case of a forfeiture).

Fourth, the payment must be compulsory. Money given voluntarily to the government for the benefit of the public—say, to create a public park or refurbish a public museum—would not constitute a tax. Nor would (admittedly rare and, curiously, tax-deductible) gifts made to the US Department of Treasury's Bureau of Public Debt for the purpose of paying down the debt.[19] Also not qualifying as a tax would be money paid for the purchase of Treasury or municipal bonds, even if the proceeds of such bond offerings were used to fund public services.

Fifth, the payment must be nonpunitive. Therefore, money paid or property forfeited to a government as a fine or penalty imposed in response to a citizen's lawbreaking would not qualify as a tax, even if such money or property was used for general purposes. One question here is whether the assessment imposed for late payment of a tax should itself be regarded as a tax, or whether instead it should be thought of as a penalty. I would say that that part of the assessment meant to punish and deter late payment should properly be understood as a penalty or fine, rather than as a tax. On the other hand, to the extent that such penalty includes an interest payment meant to compensate the government for the present value of tax revenue lost, it could reasonably be characterized as part of the tax itself.[20]

Finally, and most complexly, to be a tax, a payment must be made not in return for a specific good or service or other economic benefit provided by the government to an individual or group of individuals, but rather for general purposes. Thus, money paid as tuition for attendance at a public university and tolls paid for the privilege of using a public bridge or tunnel should not be regarded as taxes. Both of these kinds of payment are properly viewed as fees which, in contrast to a tax, involve the payment of money for a particular good, service, or benefit not automatically conferred upon the general public. Payment of a fee can be avoided if one chooses not to take advantage of the benefit offered.[21] To say that fees are paid for a particular service, however, is not to suggest that tax revenues must always go into a general fund. For example, a sales tax on cigarettes, the proceeds of which were used exclusively to support public schools or

[19] Approximately 1.8 million dollars in gifts was given to the US Treasury during 2013. Gregory Korte, 'As National Debt Soars, Gifts to Pay it off Decline', *USA Today* (20 December 2013), http://www.usatoday.com/story/news/politics/2013/12/19/gifts-to-reduce-the-public-debt-decline/4059787/.

[20] In fact, the US federal tax system specifically distinguishes between tax penalties and interest. For example, Title 26 USC §6601 imposes interest on underpayments, while other sections impose penalties (called additions to tax) for things like failing to file (§6651) and accuracy issues (§6662). Thanks to Miranda Fleischer for bringing these provisions to my attention.

[21] See *Executive Aircraft Consulting, Inc. v City of Newton*, 252 Kan. 421, 427 (1993), quoted in Johnson, n. 11, 158.

health clinics, would still be a tax, so long as the tax liability was not directly tied to the taxpayer's receipt of services.

In practice, of course, the distinction between taxes and other kinds of government exactions is not always clear. For example, under the Federal Insurance Contributions Act (known as FICA), US wage earners are required to make payments which are used to support the federal Social Security and Medicare programmes. The amount one pays in FICA taxes throughout one's working life is partly, though not completely, correlated with the amount one is entitled to receive after one retires. The more one pays in, the more one is supposed to get back. It would therefore seem that FICA is a tax only in part, because it also functions as a government-funded annuity programme.[22]

Similarly, 'benefit taxes', such as those on motor fuels, are tied to the costs of providing public services, such as public roads. They also reflect a dual character: on the one hand, the heavier one's use of public roads, the more fuel one will likely have to buy, and the more money one will owe in gasoline tax. In that sense, gasoline taxes function as a fee: payment is correlated to use of government goods or services. On the other hand, the correlation is a loose one: a person can use streets and highways without paying gasoline tax (say, if she rides a bicycle or drives an electric car), and she can buy fuel without making use of the roads (say, if the fuel is being used in a tractor driven on her privately owned farm).

Given all of these complexities in trying to define the concept of 'tax', one might be tempted to take a different approach. Rather than thinking of 'tax' as a bright line category into which a given government exaction either falls or does not fall, we might think of it instead as a quality that a given exaction might reflect to one degree or another.[23] Under this approach, rather than saying that one exaction is a tax and another is not, we should instead say that a given exaction is more or less tax-like. For example, we might say that FICA is 'less tax-like' than income or sales tax because it benefits payers in a more direct manner than taxes of those sorts. While I have no objection in principle to such an approach (indeed, I follow a similar approach later in this chapter, when considering the distinction between *mala in se* and *mala prohibita*), it is worth recalling that, in practice, courts often will have to decide definitively whether or not a given exaction is a tax.

There is also another definitional issue that needs to be addressed. So far, we have been speaking of 'taxes' as if they always involved an obligation of a citizen to pay money to the government. But as many tax scholars have explained, although the principal goal of the tax law is to raise revenue, taxes are also used as an economic and social policy tool. The tax code does far more than just determine what constitutes 'income' to be taxed. It also decides what deductions and exemptions will be allowed,

[22] Cf. Kevin A. Hassett, 'Is the Payroll Tax a Tax?', *National Review Online* (29 March 2005), http://www.nationalreview.com/article/214027/payroll-tax-tax-kevin-hassett?target=author&tid=900912 (arguing that reduction in social security benefits is equivalent to increase in tax).

[23] See William Barker, 'The Relevance of a Concept of Tax', in Peeters, n. 10, 7 (arguing that we should think of taxes as 'charges on a sliding scale, which varies inversely with the degree of the private benefit and the significance of the public good'); Marc Bourgeois, 'Constitutional Framework of the Different Types of Income', in Peeters, n. 10, 100 ('there is a continuum, ranging from pure taxes where the taxpayer receives nothing, to fees for services whose value corresponds to what was previously paid by the government').

thereby encouraging supposedly socially beneficial conduct such as charitable giving, home ownership, and saving for retirement. And, these scholars argue, from an economic perspective, there is no real difference between encouraging some activity by reducing taxes owed and doing so by directly subsidizing that activity through government payments. From that perspective, as Dan Shaviro has explained, the distinction between taxes and spending is one of 'pure form'.[24] Indeed, this is the basic insight of 'tax expenditure' analysis.[25]

But the fact that tax breaks and government spending have similar economic effects does not imply that the concept of 'tax' must somehow include all government expenditures. The point of tax expenditure theory is not to expand the definition of tax, but rather to recognize that 'certain provisions of the tax laws are not really tax provisions, but are actually government spending programs disguised in tax language'.[26] If anything, the insights of tax expenditure theory should lead to a contraction in the definition of what constitutes a 'tax', not an expansion.

B. What Is Tax Evasion?

Having considered the meaning of *tax*, we can now consider the meaning of *tax evasion*. The concept is used in different ways in different criminal codes, and it will not be possible to find any universally applicable definition. However, I would like to consider three elements that appear in the definition of tax evasion used in many jurisdictions.

First is the idea of noncompliance. Tax evasion always involves a nonpayment or underpayment of taxes actually owed, whether by understating income, overstating deductions or exemptions, or simply failing to pay what is owed. Indeed, as we shall see below, the fact that a citizen has failed to pay the taxes he owes is what distinguishes tax evasion from mere tax avoidance. Both may cause similar harms and be motivated by similar motives, but only the first violates the law (assuming that tax avoidance has not been transformed into tax evasion through a taxpayer's defiance of a general anti-avoidance rule, or GAAR).[27]

[24] Daniel N. Shaviro, 'Rethinking Tax Expenditures and Fiscal Language', 57(2) *Tax Law Review* (2004) 187, 191. See also Miranda Perry Fleischer, 'Libertarianism and the Charitable Tax Subsidies', 56 *Boston College Law Review* (2015) 1345, 1349–51.

[25] As Stanley Surrey and Paul McDaniel put it in their seminal article:

> Whenever government decides to grant monetary assistance to an activity or group, it may elect from a wide range of methods in delivering that assistance. A direct government grant or subsidy may be made; a government loan may be made, perhaps at a special interest rate; a private loan may be guaranteed by the government; and so on. In contrast, the government may use the income tax system and reduce the tax otherwise applicable, by adopting a special exclusion, deduction or the like for the favored activity or group. Examples are investment credits, special depreciation deductions, deductions for special forms of consumption, low rates of tax for certain activities, and so on. These tax reductions, in effect, represent monetary assistance provided by the government.

Stanley S. Surrey and Paul R. McDaniel, 'The Tax Expenditure Concept and the Budget Reform Act of 1974', 17(5) *Boston College Industrial and Commercial Law Review* (1976) 689.

[26] Victor Thuronyi, 'Tax Expenditures: A Reassessment', *Duke Law Journal* (1988) 1155, 1155.

[27] In many jurisdictions, tax authorities have the power, through GAARs, to deny taxpayers the benefit of an arrangement they have entered into for an impermissible purpose. Where a taxpayer has engaged in

Second is the mental element. There is no tax evasion if *T*'s failure to pay taxes was inadvertent. In many jurisdictions, tax evasion requires not only an intent not to pay, but also actual knowledge of the legal duty owed. Tax evasion thus differs from most other crimes, which are governed by the rule of *ignorantia legis neminem excusat*.[28]

A third element appears in some tax evasion statutes, though it is less widely observed and seems less central from a conceptual standpoint. In at least a few countries (including the United States, Switzerland, the Philippines, and perhaps Nigeria), the crime of tax evasion (or tax fraud, as it is also known) requires not only that the evader purposefully avoid paying taxes owed, but also that he also take affirmative steps to avoid detection—say, by keeping a second set of books or fabricating records.[29] In the US context, at least, this distinction—between underpayment *simpliciter* and underpayment plus covering up—helps define the line between nonpayment of taxes as a misdemeanour or civil wrong and nonpayment of taxes as a serious felony offence. As we shall see below, this final element, when present, adds something significant to tax evasion's moral content.

Finally, as we saw above, under the tax expenditure approach, there is an argument that the tax system, broadly defined, should be understood to include not just payments by citizens to the government, but also payments by the government to citizens. If this were right, it would raise the question whether one can evade taxes not just by failing to pay taxes due but also by unlawfully claiming government entitlements above and beyond tax due, as under an earned income tax credit scheme. For reasons I'll explain below, I believe this would be a mistake. Simply because two transactions are economically equivalent does not necessarily mean that they are morally or legally equivalent.

II. The Moral Content of Tax Evasion

Under the hybrid theory of punishment that I have endorsed and articulated on previous occasions, moral blameworthiness is a necessary (though not sufficient) condition

such prohibited practice, and persists in claiming the tax benefit, it makes sense to say that *at that point* he is committing tax evasion.

[28] 'Ignorance of the law is no excuse.' See *Cheek v United States*, 498 U.S. 192 (1991).

[29] Under US law, wilful nonpayment of taxes *simpliciter* (including the failure to file a return) is generally treated as a misdemeanour offence under IRC §7203. Such noncompliance is contrasted to tax 'evasion' proper, which carries a penalty of five years in prison under §7201, and requires not only the wilful nonpayment of taxes but also some additional concealment of one's activities.

In Switzerland, failing to pay taxes and covering it up is known as 'tax fraud'. See Pietro Sansonetti, 'Tax Evasion: The Evolution of the Swiss Criminal Tax Law', *International Tax Review* (12 March 2013), http://www.internationaltaxreview.com/Article/3167155/Tax-evasion-The-evolution-of-the-Swiss-Criminal-Tax-Law.html.

In the Philippines, tax evasion can involve use of fictitious receipts, the keeping of double sets of books, false or fictitious entries in books, fictitious transactions in the name of dummy corporations, and the like. See Rosario G. Manason, 'Tax Evasion in the Philippines', 15(2) *Journal of Philippine Development* (1988) 167, http://dirp3.pids.gov.ph/ris/pjd/pidsjpd88-2tax.pdf.

For a discussion of what constitutes tax evasion in Nigeria, see Teju Somorin, 'Tax Evasion in Africa: Kinds of Evasion, How to Control it—The Nigerian Experience', *African Training and Research Centre in Administration for Development* (2010), http://unpan1.un.org/intradoc/groups/public/documents/cafrad/unpan043343.pdf.

for an act's being justly subject to criminal punishment.[30] Thus, if we want to know whether and why tax evasion should be a crime, we need to know the various ways in which it is morally blameworthy. One key element of any blameworthiness analysis is wrongfulness. As I have explained elsewhere, 'moral wrongfulness' reflects the extent to which a criminal act involves the violation of a freestanding moral norm, rule, right, or duty.[31] (This is in contrast to 'harmfulness', which reflects the degree to which a criminal act causes, or risks causing, what Joel Feinberg called a 'significant setback to another's interests'.[32]) Elsewhere, I have taken a preliminary look at the various ways in which tax evasion might be understood as wrongful.[33] Here, I want to modify, expand on, and correct some of that earlier analysis.

There are three alternative paradigms under which the moral wrong in tax evasion has traditionally been conceptualized: (1) as a form of 'stealing', (2) as a form of 'cheating', and (3) as a violation of the 'moral obligation to obey the law'. In what follows, I shall argue that while the concept of stealing proves, on inspection, to be mostly inapposite, cheating and disobedience to the law, as well as deceptive 'covering up', are all key to understanding why tax evasion is morally wrongful.

A. Tax Evasion as Stealing

Tax evasion has often been spoken of as a form of 'stealing'.[34] This view is problematic. In other work, I described the complex legal, moral, psychological, and cultural meanings that characterize the act of stealing and the crime of theft.[35] Stealing has traditionally involved the act of depriving another of a specific good or service without paying for it. It involves not just a temporary violation of the owner's right to exclude others from using the property, but also a more permanent violation of the owner's right to use or possess it himself.

Stealing, crucially, involves an involuntary transfer of property from victim/owner to thief. This transfer can be considered in terms of a common sense (if not strict economic) notion of zero sum-ness: what is the thief's gain must be the victim's loss.[36] Stealing thus represents a particularly significant assault on what has been called one's 'endowment' (as behavioural economists have explained, people ascribe more value to things they have in their possession, *ceteris paribus*, than they do to things owned or possessed by someone else).[37]

Evasion of taxes, as properly understood, fails to satisfy this stealing paradigm. To see why, contrast two cases, the first involving stealing, but no tax; the second involving

[30] Green, n. 8, 30–47. [31] Ibid.

[32] Joel Feinberg, *Harm to Others* (New York: Oxford University Press, 1984).

[33] Green, n. 8, 243–8.

[34] See e.g. Martin T. Crowe, *The Moral Obligation of Paying Just Taxes*, Studies in Sacred Theology 84 (Washington, DC: Catholic University of America Press, 1944), 42.

[35] Stuart P. Green, *Thirteen Ways to Steal a Bicycle: Theft Law in the Information Age* (Cambridge, MA: Harvard University Press, 2012), 91–114.

[36] Ibid., 210–11.

[37] The *locus classicus* is Daniel Kahneman and Amos Tversky, 'Choices, Values, and Frames', 39(4) *American Psychologist* (1984) 341; see also Maynard Smith, *Evolution and the Theory of Games* (New York: Cambridge University Press, 1992).

a tax, but no stealing. In the first case, homeowner *A* receives an assessment from his local municipality for the town-supplied water he uses. *A* could legally avoid paying the assessment by simply not using the town's water, and, say, using bottled water instead. But if *A* did in fact use the water, and then failed to pay the assessment, he would be depriving the municipality of a specific good without paying for it.[38] The zero sum paradigm would be satisfied; he would be committing theft.[39] He would not, however, have committed tax evasion, since the assessment that *A* failed to pay is not properly understood as a tax; rather, it's a fee. Moreover, we would normally expect the proceeds from the water assessment to be used specifically for system maintenance, rather than for general governmental purposes, though the use of the funds is not the decisive factor. The key point is that the fee charged is directly correlated with the good received.

The case in which *A* failed to pay his water bill can be contrasted to a second case in which homeowner *B* failed to pay the assessment imposed by his local municipality based on the value of his house. Here, *B* would not be paying for any *particular* good or service. The revenues from this tax would typically be used for general purposes: to support the public schools, the police, sanitation department, and other public works. And *B* would owe the same payment regardless of whether he actually made use of any of these services (e.g. he may choose to send his children to private school or to employ private security or sanitation services). Here, the zero sum paradigm would *not* be met. This would not be theft; rather, it would be tax evasion.

A person who intentionally failed to pay sales tax or VAT would also be committing tax evasion. While it is true that such taxes are tied directly to the *purchase* of goods, they are not tied to the *receipt* by the taxpayer of any particular benefit from the government. The tax is tied to the purchase of goods only as a means for determining the amount of tax owed, just as income tax is determined on the basis of income earned. In none of these cases would *B* have committed theft; rather, he would have failed to pay a debt that was owed. In such cases, we should say not that *B* was a thief, but rather that he was a debtor in default.

Consider other cases in which *B* fails to pay a debt he owes to *C*. For example, he might breach a contract, fail to pay child support, default on his mortgage, or fail to pay a tort judgment entered against him. In none of these cases would we normally say that *B* had stolen.[40] *B* would not have dispossessed another of property, and the zero

[38] Unfortunately, this is more than a law professor's hypothetical. Theft of water from municipal authorities has become an increasingly serious problem in the wake of recent drought conditions in California. See Kristin J. Bender, 'Water Thefts on Rise in Drought-Stricken California', *Salon* (23 February 2015), http://www.salon.com/2015/02/23/water_thefts_on_the_rise_in_drought_stricken_california.

[39] I have intentionally used a hypothetical involving an assessment for a 'tangible good' like water rather than for a 'public good' such as a road or bridge, because the zero-sumness of public good use is somewhat more complicated than in the case of tangible goods. The problem is that public services are, in economic terms, excludable, but not rivalrous. They are excludable because nonpaying consumers can ordinarily be excluded from use, but they are not necessarily rivalrous because the use of a bridge or road by *D* does not preclude simultaneous use by others, at least as long as there is no overcrowding. My point is simply that while *A*'s knowing use of water without payment constitutes a clear case of theft under the zero sum paradigm, his knowing use of a public bridge or road presents a more complicated case.

[40] The only exception is where *B* falsely agrees to honour the terms of a contract *at the time he entered into it*—that is, where he never intended to honour the contract in the first place; in that special case, we can say that *B* committed false pretences or fraud, both of which are properly understood as forms of

sum paradigm would not be satisfied. Such cases can be distinguished from ones in which *B* takes money from *C*'s wallet or bank account without his consent. Although the economic impact on *C* would be the same, from a moral (and legal) perspective, the cases would be distinguishable. Only in the second kind of case would we say that *B* had stolen from *C*.

This is not to say that one could never steal *in connection with* a tax scheme. Recall the previous discussion concerning tax expenditure theory. As we saw, the taxes people pay the government are part of a much larger and more complex system in which the government both gives tax breaks and makes direct expenditures to promote various social goals. For example, under the earned income tax credit programme, a working person with low income can have his taxes reduced, and in some cases may even receive a payment for an amount greater than that of any tax otherwise owed—meaning that the government essentially pays the wage earner money.[41] If *X* lied to the IRS about how much he earned or how much his business expenses were, and thereby avoided taxes he owed, that *would* be tax evasion. But if *X* lied to the IRS about his earned income tax status, and thereby obtained money *above and beyond any taxes owed*, he would on my view be committing theft or false claims.[42] And this distinction should hold even if the economic effect on the government would be the same in each case.

Another tax-related case in which theft is committed is where sales tax is collected by a seller from buyers at the point of purchase, and the seller then fails to turn over the proceeds, as required, to the state. Such cases *are* properly understood as theft, rather than as tax evasion. It was, after all, the buyer, not the seller, who had the obligation to pay the tax, and that obligation was discharged. The seller was simply holding the buyer's tax payment in a kind of trust, in the same way a bank or credit card company might hold money in trust for a customer. The seller who failed to turn over the sales tax proceeds would essentially be committing embezzlement.[43]

Yet another puzzle is raised by cases in which *A* pays no sales tax because he acquired a good through stealing rather than purchase. Could he be charged with evading sales tax? Sales tax typically applies to 'transfer[s] of title or possession, exchange, or barter ... *for a consideration*'.[44] Because thefts, by definition, involve no consideration, there is no sale, therefore no sales tax due, and therefore no evasion of sales tax. A more appropriate way to think about such cases is as an evasion not of sales tax but of *income* tax, analogous to cases in which defendants are prosecuted for evading tax on income earned from the sale of drugs, from bribes, or through racketeering activities (think of Al Capone). In those cases, the tax rules makes clear that income tax

stealing For further discussion of the differences between theft, fraud, and breach of contract, see Green, n. 35, 87–90.

[41] Jonathan Barry Forman, 'Earned Income Tax Credit', *Tax Policy Center*, http://www.urban.org/sites/default/files/alfresco/publication-pdfs/1000524-Earned-Income-Credit.PDF (accessed 20 October 2015).

[42] This view is also supported by the language of the basic tax evasion provision, which says that a person evades taxes if he 'willfully attempts in any manner to evade or defeat any tax imposed by this title or the payment thereof', 26 USC §7201.

[43] For an example of such reasoning, see *State v Chapman Dodge Center, Inc.*, 428 So.2d 413 (La. 1983).

[44] For example, California Revenue and Taxation Code §6606(a) (emphasis added).

must be paid regardless of whether income was earned legally or illegally, including through theft.[45]

There is one additional reason to reject the view that tax evasion should ordinarily be understood as a form of theft. In our system of law, almost all thefts are treated as crimes, even those that involve the stealing of low value items.[46] *Civil* theft, by contrast, is a fairly exotic cause of action.[47] In the case of tax evasion, the pattern is reversed; as noted above, only a tiny percentage of all cases of tax evasion are prosecuted criminally. The remainder are handled as civil violations, if at all. If tax evasion really were a species of theft, we would expect it to be treated much more consistently as a crime.[48]

B. Tax Evasion as Cheating

In previous work, I argued that, rather than thinking of tax evasion as a form of stealing, we would do better to think of it as a form of 'cheating', which I defined more generally as the: (1) violation of a (2) fair and (3) fairly enforced rule (4) with the intent to obtain an advantage over some party (5) with whom the rule-breaker is in a (6) cooperative, rule-governed relationship.[49] This account, I argued, had several advantages: it squared well with our common way of speaking of tax evasion as 'cheating on one's taxes'. It reflected the fact that evading taxes causes harm not just to the government but also to one's fellow citizens, who are forced to bear a heavier burden as a result of one's conduct. And it pointed to parallels between the moral content of tax evasion and other white-collar offenses such as insider trading, various kinds of fraud, and various regulatory crimes.[50]

It should be clear, however, that not all rule violations entail cheating. Consider a case in which a driver drives through a red light at 3:00 a.m. on a deserted rural road. The driver has violated the rule that requires drivers to stop at red lights, but he has not, in all likelihood, achieved an unfair advantage over anyone, and he has therefore not cheated. (This might not be true of every traffic offence: one can imagine a case in which a driver violates the rules of the road by, say, driving on the soft shoulder in order to get ahead of other drivers in a traffic jam. That would, on my account, be a form of cheating.)

[45] 26 USC §61 (Internal Revenue Code); IRS Publication 17, https://www.irs.gov/pub/irs-pdf/p17.pdf, 94, 96 ('other income' includes property obtained through stealing, bribes, and other illegal activities, such as selling drugs).

[46] See Green, n. 35, 161–5. [47] Ibid., 137–8.

[48] It is also worth pointing out that just because tax-evader *A cheats* his fellow citizens does not mean that he also *steals* from them. In theory, it is true that if *A* fails to pay the taxes he owes, other taxpayers somewhere down the line will presumably have to pick up the slack and pay more in taxes (either that, or the government will have to reduce expenditures). But, while such behaviour does constitute a form of cheating, it does not constitute stealing, since stealing requires that *A* deprive a property owner of his rights in property, and there is no indication that this has happened when *A* fails to pay his taxes.

[49] Green, n. 35, 247. For another work that emphasizes the significance of cheating, see Donald Morris, *Tax Cheating: Illegal—But is it Immoral?* (Albany: SUNY Press, 2012).

[50] Caron Beaton-Wells has also found the concept of cheating helpful in understanding the criminalization of price fixing. See 'Capturing the Criminality of Hard Core Cartels: The Australian Proposal', 31(3) *Melbourne University Law Review* (2007) 675.

Tax evasion, in contrast to the red light case, does potentially involve cheating: the tax evader violates the rule that requires citizens to pay the specific taxes they owe, and he normally does so for the purpose of obtaining an advantage over others. The tax evader is a free rider: he fails to pay his fair share of keeping our government running, while continuing to reap, or potentially reap, the benefits of being a citizen.

The point I am making about the centrality of cheating to our understanding of tax evasion bears some similarity to a point made by Herbert Morris, who argued that:

> [I]t is just to punish those who have violated the rules and caused the unfair distribution of benefits and burdens. A person who violates the rules has something others have—the benefits of the system—but by renouncing what others have assumed, the burdens of self-restraint, he has acquired an unfair advantage. Matters are not even until this advantage is in some way erased. Another way of putting it is that he owes something to others, for he has something that does not rightfully belong to him. Justice—that is punishing such individuals—restores the equilibrium of benefits and burdens by taking from the individual what he owes, that is, exacting the debt.[51]

Although he does not use the term, Morris does a good job of explaining the basic dynamic of what is, in essence, cheating: in violating a rule that others follow, and thereby breaching an obligation to restrict his liberty in the manner agreed, the cheater gains an unfair advantage.

A problem with Morris's theory, however, is that it puts more weight on the concept of cheating than it is capable of supporting. Morris was wrong to suggest that the idea of cheating underlies *all* crimes. As Jean Hampton explained, Morris's approach 'makes sense only if we believe that constraining ourselves so that we do not rape or murder or steal imposes a cost upon us. Yet that idea makes sense only if [we accept the absurd notion that] raping, murdering, and stealing are viewed by us as desirable and attractive.'[52]

Yet, while the idea that one's acts have created an 'unfair distribution of benefits and burdens' is insufficient to explain offences like rape and murder, it can play a significant role in defining offences such as tax evasion, since nonpayment of taxes is something that many people would find desirable and attractive, and since it does tend to create an unfair distribution of benefits and burdens.

C. Is There Tax Evasion That Does Not Constitute Cheating?

Under the account referred to above, *A* should properly be understood to have cheated if and only if (1) the rule that he violates is fair and enforced in an even-handed manner, and (2) he intends to obtain an unfair advantage over others. This would suggest that citizens who fail to pay taxes that are not fair, or who do not intend to obtain an advantage over others, have not cheated.

[51] Herbert Morris, 'Persons and Punishment', 502(4) *The Monist* (1968) 475. The argument in this and succeeding paragraphs is borrowed from Green, n. 35, 55–6.

[52] Jean Hampton, 'Correcting Harms Versus Righting Wrongs: The Goal of Retribution', 39 *UCLA Law Review* (1992) 1659, 1660.

Both possibilities need to be considered. Looking again at US law, we see a tax system that is less progressive than the tax systems of most other industrialized nations, and much less so than it was for most of the twentieth century. The top marginal rate in the United States is now only 39.6 per cent, compared to a rate of 94 per cent during World War II and about 70 per cent throughout the 1960s and 1970s. And the effective tax rate that many of the wealthiest individuals pay is actually considerably lower than 39.6 per cent.[53] Moreover, the US tax code contains countless provisions seemingly enacted for no reason other than to benefit special interest groups that have typically given large contributions to political candidates.[54] The code is also so complex that only the wealthy can afford the tax advice needed to take full advantage of the many devices it offers for lowering one's tax burden lawfully.[55] It is no surprise that a majority of Americans now say that the income tax system is unfair.[56]

The tax laws are also *enforced* in a manner that is arguably unfair (again, focusing on the US experience). As noted above, in 2007, the IRS examined less than 1 per cent of the approximately 179.4 million returns filed.[57] And the thoroughness of these audits has been dropping as well. According to the Independent Transactional Records Clearinghouse, the typical amount of time auditors spend on large corporate audits has decreased by twenty per cent in recent years.[58] There are also large disparities across districts, with residents in the New York metropolitan area, for

[53] According to economist Joseph Stiglitz, the richest 400 individual taxpayers in the United States, with an average income of more than $200 million, pay less than 20 per cent of their income in taxes—lower than mere millionaires, who pay about 25 per cent of their income in taxes, and about the same as those earning $200,000 to $500,000. And in 2009, 116 of the top 400 earners—almost a third—paid less than 15 per cent of their income in taxes. Joseph E. Stiglitz, 'A Tax System Stacked Against the 99 Percent', *New York Times* (14 April 2013), http://opinionator.blogs.nytimes.com/2013/04/14/a-tax-system-stacked-against-the-99-percent/?_r=0; see also Kim Parker, 'Yes, the Rich Are Different', *Pew Research Center Social and Demographic Trends* (27 August 2012), http://www.pewsocialtrends.org/2012/08/27/yes-the-rich-are-different/.

[54] These arguably include tax breaks for owners of vacation homes, racetracks, beer breweries, oil refineries, hedge funds, and movie studios, to name just a few beneficiaries of presumably unfair tax laws. See generally Stiglitz, n. 53; David Cay Johnston, 'Perfectly Legal: The Covert Campaign to Rig our Tax System to Benefit the Super Rich—and Cheat Everyone Else' (New York: Portfolio, 2003); Robert McIntyre, Citizens for Tax Justice, et al., 'The Sorry State of Corporate Taxes: What Fortune 500 Firms Pay (or Don't Pay) in the USA And What they Pay Abroad—2008 to 2012' (Washington, DC: Citizens for Tax Justice and the Institute on Taxation and Economic Policy, February 2014), http://www.ctj.org/corporatetaxdodgers/sorrystateofcorptaxes.pdf.

[55] These include deferring compensation, changing the timing of capital income to convert short-term gains into long-term gains, and converting ordinary income or losses to capital gains or losses. See US Senate Committee on Finance, 'How Tax Pros Make the Code Less Fair and Efficient: Several New Strategies and Solutions', *Report of the Senate Finance Committee Democratic Staff* (3 March 2015), http://www.finance.senate.gov/imo/media/doc/030215%20How%20Tax%20Pros%20Make%20the%20Code%20Less%20Fair%20and%20Efficient%20-%20Several%20New%20Strategies%20and%20Solutions_FINAL%20cover.pdf.

[56] Jeffrey M. Jones, 'Fewer Americans Now View Their Income Taxes as Fair', *Gallup.com* (15 April 2013), http://www.gallup.com/poll/161780/fewer-americans-view-income-taxes-fair.aspx.

[57] And the audit rate for the nation's largest corporations plunged to its lowest level in the last twenty years—approximately 26 per cent—less than half what it was in 1988. 'Audits of Largest Corporations Slide to All Time Low', *Transactional Records Access Clearinghouse/IRS*, http://trac.syr.edu/tracirs/newfindings/v13/.

[58] Ibid.

example, being subject to relatively low rates of audits and prosecution, and residents of California subject to much higher rates.[59]

Whether a given tax regime really is so unfair that people who evade it should not be regarded as cheating is, of course, an immensely difficult question, requiring both a sophisticated theory of economic and political justice as well as a deep familiarity with one or more tax codes, their legislative history, and their enforcement. Other contributions to this volume have touched on such issues.[60] For the moment, I think it is safe to assume that a tax code would have to achieve a fairly high level of unfairness before it could be said that an evader was not cheating.

And what about cases in which a tax evader does not intend to obtain an unfair advantage over others? Here, I have in mind the problem of tax resisters and tax protesters. Tax resisters object to paying taxes that will be used for government activities they oppose, such as waging supposedly unjust wars.[61] Tax protesters claim to believe that the tax law itself is unconstitutional or otherwise invalid. Both could conceivably argue that the reason they are not paying taxes is not that they wish to free ride on their fellow citizens, but rather that they have some more 'principled' reason for doing so.

This argument would be hard to sustain. The fact is that both tax resisters and tax protesters—whatever their motive—do free ride on their fellow citizens. Some tax resisters refuse to pay all or a portion of the taxes they owe, and instead make an equivalent donation to charity. But the fact that this money is given away, rather than kept, does not mean that the tax resister lacks an intent to obtain an unfair advantage over others. Almost everyone has *some* quarrel with the way their tax revenues are used, and would prefer to give their money to a handpicked charity instead. Tax resisters get both the benefit of taxes paid by others and the satisfaction of supporting a worthy charity. That sounds like cheating.

The case against tax protesters is even stronger. Like tax resisters, tax protesters also continue to reap the benefits of citizenship without paying their fair share. Unlike tax resisters, however, tax protesters do not typically maintain the pretence of giving their money to charity. Tax protesters might well believe that the tax laws are invalid, but they could presumably challenge these laws in ways that did not so directly benefit their own pocketbook.

Finally, what about a person who failed to pay the taxes he owed because he believed that 'everyone else' or 'most others' were doing the same? Would that still be cheating? So long as at least some people were following the rules and paying all the taxes they owed, there is an argument that *X* would be cheating, since he would still be gaining

[59] *Transactional Records Access Clearinghouse*, District Enforcement, http://trac.syr.edu/tracirs/findings/07/index.html (last visited 7 March 2009).

[60] See e.g. the contributions from Jennifer Bird-Pollan, Patrick Emerton and Kathryn James, Miranda Perry Fleischer, Theodore Seto, and Daniel Shaviro. See also, e.g., Liam Murphy and Thomas Nagel, *The Myth of Ownership: Taxes and Justice* (Oxford: Oxford University Press, 2002); Steven M. Sheffrin, *Tax Fairness and Folk Justice* (Cambridge, UK: Cambridge University Press, 2013); Alan M. Maslove (ed.), *Fairness in Taxation* (Toronto: University of Toronto Press, 1993); Louis Kaplow, *The Theory of Taxation and Public Economics* (Princeton: Princeton University Press, 2010).

[61] See, e.g., *Cheney v Conn* [1968] 1AER 779 (where a party objected to paying taxes that, in part, would be used to procure nuclear arms).

an unfair advantage over the honest taxpayers. On the other hand, recall that cheating requires that the rules be fair and that they be administered in an even-handed manner. In a society in which most people really were cheating on their taxes, and doing so with impunity, it seems unlikely that the tax laws would be being administered in an even-handed manner. In such a case, an argument could be made that *X* was not seeking an unfair 'advantage'; rather, he would merely be seeking to negate the 'unfair disadvantage' at which he had been placed. What is interesting here is that many people really do rationalize their failure to pay taxes on the fact that 'everyone else is doing it'.[62] In a sense, they are arguing that what they are doing is not cheating, and therefore not wrong.

D. Tax Evasion as Disobedience to the Law

So far, I have considered whether and to what extent the offence of tax evasion is informed by the moral wrongs of stealing and cheating. What remains to be considered is the extent to which tax evasion is defined by two other possible forms of moral wrongfulness—disobedience to the law (considered in this section) and deceptive covering up (discussed in the next).

The Catechism of the Catholic Church has long spoken of '[o]bedience to authority' as the principal ground upon which the obligation to pay taxes is grounded.[63] If that were true, it should therefore follow that the concept of *disobedience* would be a key to understanding why tax evasion is wrong. There are, however, several problems with this approach. First, there is a genuine debate about whether there really is a moral obligation to obey the law.[64] Second, every violation of a just law involves some form of disobedience. The disobedience approach, taken in isolation, therefore fails to explain how the moral content of tax evasion differs from (and is presumably more serious than), say, various trivial regulatory violations. Third, as we saw above, all cheating involves a rule violation. Since the rule at issue in tax evasion is a legal rule, it might seem that the analysis of tax-evasion-as-disobedience would be subsumed by the earlier analysis of tax-evasion-as-cheating.

Despite these objections, I believe that the concept of disobedience does add something of value to the analysis of the moral content of tax evasion. In contrast to the cheating analysis—which tends to highlight the wrong done, *horizontally*, to the taxpayer's fellow citizens—the disobedience analysis tends to highlight the *vertical*

[62] See generally Joel Slemrod, 'Cheating Ourselves: The Economics of Tax Evasion', 21(1) *Journal of Economic Perspectives* (2007) 25; Young-dahl Song and Tinsley E. Yarbrough, 'Tax Ethics and Taxpayer Attitudes: A Survey', 38(5) *Public Administration Review* (1978) 442.

[63] *Catechism of the Catholic Church* §2240 (Libreria Editrice Vatican, Provisional Draft, 1992). This paragraph draws on the discussion in Green, n. 35, 247. There is also empirical evidence to suggest that people who are 'rule followers' are more likely to comply with the tax laws. See Kelvin Law and Lillian Mills, 'CEO Characteristics and Corporate Taxes', *SSRN*, http://papers.ssrn.com/sol3/papers.cfm?abstract_id=2302329 (finding that corporate managers with military experience were less likely to pursue 'aggressive' tax planning than other managers).

[64] See, e.g., M.B.E. Smith, 'Is There a Prima Facie Obligation to Obey the Law?', 82(5) *Yale Law Journal* (1973) 950.

nature of the wrong (and harm) done to the government, which needs tax revenue to function.

Moreover, thinking about tax evasion as a form of disobedience also highlights its dual *malum in se*/*malum prohibitum* character. Crimes have traditionally been said to be *mala in se* if they involve conduct that is wrongful regardless of whether the conduct has been made illegal (murder and rape are good examples); and *mala prohibita* if they involve conduct that is wrong solely, or primarily, in virtue of their being illegal (the best examples here are certain regulatory offences, such as fishing without a licence). As I have argued elsewhere, however, there is no such thing as a pure *malum in se* or *malum prohibitum* offence.[65] Even those crimes that can most plausibly be considered *mala in se* are to some extent defined by law. Conversely, even conduct that is most clearly *malum prohibitum* has some nonlegal moral content. The point is that *malum in se* and *malum prohibitum* are better thought of as contrasting qualities along a continuum that, to one degree or another, characterize all criminal offences, rather than as precise categories into which specific offences either do or do not fit.

Tax evasion seems to fall somewhere near the middle of the continuum between *malum in se* and *malum prohibitum*.[66] One the one hand, the amount of money citizens owe to the government in taxes is determined entirely within a framework of legally defined rules. The wrong of tax evasion thus cannot be defined 'prior to and independent of law', as one commentator has claimed is characteristic of *mala in se* offences.[67] In that sense, tax evasion reflects a strong *malum prohibitum* character.

On the other hand, tax evasion also reflects significant attributes of *malum in se*-ness. No modern society could hope to function without a developed system of shared tax burdens. We do not need to know the particulars of a given tax code to know that evading those obligations, and thereby potentially free riding on others, is normally wrong. In that sense, tax evasion seems significantly more *malum in se* than regulatory offenses like buying pills without a prescription or practicing medicine (competently) without a licence.

E. Tax Evasion as Deceptive Covering Up

A final piece in the puzzle of tax evasion's moral content is supplied by the concept of deceptive covering up. As noted previously, in some countries, the crime of tax evasion requires not only that the evader purposefully avoid paying taxes owed, but also

[65] The concepts of *malum prohibitum* and *malum in se* are dealt with in detail in Stuart P. Green, 'Why It's a Crime to Tear the Tag Off a Mattress: Overcriminalization and the Moral Content of Regulatory Offenses', 46(4) *Emory Law Journal* (1997) 1533, 1570–80. I have written about the *malum in se*/*malum prohibitum* distinction more recently in Stuart P. Green, 'The Conceptual Utility of *Malum Prohibitum*', 55(1) *Dialogue: Canadian Philosophical Review* (2016) 33.

[66] For a similar argument, see Zoë Prebble and John Prebble, 'The Morality of Tax Avoidance', 43(3) *Creighton Law Review* (2010) 693, 736–7.

[67] Douglas Husak, *Overcriminalization: The Limits of the Criminal Law* (Oxford: Oxford University Press, 2008), 105.

that he conceal that activity—say, by hiding income, keeping a second set of books, or claiming personal expenses as business expenses.[68] This distinction—between underpayment *simpliciter* and underpayment plus covering up—marks the line between nonpayment of taxes as a misdemeanour or civil wrong and nonpayment of taxes as a serious felony offence.

Are we justified in punishing someone more for not only evading taxes but also covering it up? Elsewhere, I have discussed the role that covering up plays in defining such freestanding offences as perjury, false statements, obstruction of justice, criminal contempt, and misprision of felony.[69] Each offence allows for the prosecution of offenders who cover up a separate underlying crime. What makes tax evasion apparently unique is that the underlying wrong and its cover up are combined in a single offence. Imposing more serious penalties on tax evaders who try to conceal their wrongdoing thus seems a bit like imposing higher penalties on murderers who attempt to evade discovery, bank robbers who try to get away with their loot, and insider traders who seek to cover their tracks.

So what justification is there for combining the nonpayment of taxes and its cover-up in the same offence definition? The best answer I can offer is that *A*'s covering up his tax evasion will often offer strong evidence that *A* did understand what the law required and intended to violate it. Moreover, when nonpayment of taxes is covered up, it's generally more costly for the government to detect, and in that sense more harmful than mere nonpayment.

III. The Moral Content of Tax Avoidance

To this point, I have argued that tax evasion is wrong primarily because it involves a form of cheating (with disobedience to the law and deceptive covering up playing supporting roles). But what about tax *avoidance*—reducing one's taxes by means that, unlike tax evasion, do not involve a violation of the law? Is that wrong too? And assuming it is, is it wrong for the same reasons that tax evasion is wrong, or for different reasons? Strictly speaking, a work that seeks to explain the moral content of tax evasion need not address these issues. But they have puzzled so many commentators for so long that it is worth asking if there is anything in the foregoing analysis of tax evasion that might be helpful in assessing the moral content of tax avoidance as well.[70]

A. Distinguishing Reasonable from Unreasonable Tax Avoidance

Most citizens, whether law-abiding or not, wish to avoid paying the government the maximum amount the tax law might require. Tax evaders pay less by unlawfully failing to pay the taxes they owe. Tax avoiders try to lessen the amount of that obligation through legal means, using various tax avoidance devices such as deductions, credits,

[68] See discussion in n. 29. [69] See Green, n. 38, 133–47, 161–92.

[70] For a wide-ranging discussion of avoidance in the law, see Leo Katz, *Ill-Gotten Gains: Evasion, Blackmail, Fraud, and Kindred Puzzles of the Law* (Chicago: University of Chicago Press, 1996).

and exemptions. This attempt to lessen one's tax obligation through lawful means is referred to, in general, as 'tax avoidance'.[71]

But within this general category, a basic distinction emerges. Consider two contrasting cases: in one, *A* gives money to a recognized charity, and then claims a deduction on his tax return, thereby reducing the amount of his taxable income. In the other, *B* sells an asset solely for the purpose of taking a tax loss to be set off against ordinary income, and then repurchases it shortly thereafter. In the first case, *A* seems to have behaved in a manner that is consistent with the purpose of the legislation—namely, to encourage taxpayers to make charitable gifts. In the second case, by contrast, *B* seems to have behaved in a manner that is inconsistent with the purpose of the tax provision that allows taxpayers to set off losses against gains in calculating their tax base.

Many tax systems have sought to distinguish between such cases in their general avoidance rules. One formulation can be found in UK law. Under the so-called 'reasonableness test', tax arrangements are said to be 'abusive' if, 'they are arrangements the entering into or carrying out cannot reasonably be regarded as a reasonable course of action in relation to the relevant tax provisions, having regard to all the circumstances'.[72] These circumstances, in turn, include '(a) whether the substantive results of the arrangements are consistent with any principles on which those provisions are based (whether express or implied) and the policy objectives of those provisions, (b) whether the means of achieving those results involves one or more contrived or abnormal steps, and (c) whether the arrangements are intended to exploit any shortcomings in those provisions'.[73]

This distinction between reasonable and unreasonable tax avoidance seems to fit the two cases described above. The first transaction is consistent with the relevant provisions, is not contrived, and is not intended to exploit any shortcomings in the provisions. It therefore seems to satisfy the reasonableness test. By contrast, the second transaction cannot be regarded as a reasonable course of action in relation to the relevant tax provisions.[74] The substantive results achieved are inconsistent with the policy objectives of the applicable provisions, they involve contrived and abnormal steps, and they are intended to exploit shortcomings in those provisions.

B. Why Is 'Unreasonable' Tax Avoidance Morally Wrongful?

The distinction just drawn between reasonable and unreasonable tax avoidance seems useful as a descriptive matter, but it fails to explain why, or even if, the first should be viewed as morally neutral or even desirable, and the second as morally wrong. Unfortunately, the notion of cheating—though key to understanding the wrongfulness

[71] The literature on the difference between tax evasion and tax avoidance is immense. For a sampling, see Valerie Braithwaite (ed.), *Taxing Democracy: Understanding Tax Avoidance and Tax Evasion* (Burlington: Ashgate, 2003).

[72] Section 207(2) Finance Act 2013, http://www.legislation.gov.uk/ukpga/2013/29/section/207. For a useful discussion of the economic substance test in particular, see Robert McMechan, *Economic Substance and Tax Avoidance: An International Perspective* (Toronto: Carswell, 2013).

[73] Section 207(2) Finance Act 2013.

[74] Ibid.

of tax *evasion*—seems to have little immediate relevance here. By definition, tax avoidance, whether reasonable or not, involves no rule violation. And since there can be no cheating without a rule violation, it seems to follow that tax avoidance is not cheating.

Nevertheless, the idea that the tax law contains rules, and that rules can have significant normative force does point in the right direction. It has often been claimed that unreasonable tax avoidance violates the 'spirit' of the tax laws.[75] I think that is basically true. But more needs to be said about exactly why violating the spirit of such laws should be understood as morally wrongful.

Let us begin with two cases that I shall call 'tennis' and 'stock investing', respectively.

1. *Tennis*

Suppose that *A* and *B* head out to the club on Sunday morning for what *B* believes will be a friendly game of tennis. Ostensibly, they are playing for the normal, socially acceptable reasons that people play such games—to get some healthy exercise, enjoy the fun of competition, improve their skills, relish the sunny weather, perhaps even entertain onlookers. Now, imagine that *A*, defying *B*'s expectations and social convention, plays much more aggressively than *B* expected: he hits the ball as hard as possible during warm-ups; attempts to intimidate him into losing his cool; challenges every call made by the referee; makes loud, distracting noises when *B* is about to take his shot; aims shots directly at his head; deliberately stalls to slow the game down, and so forth. Is *A*'s conduct morally wrongful?

Because none of *A*'s behaviour (so far as I can tell—I am not a tennis player myself) violates the official rules of the game, we should conclude that he has not cheated.[76] However, he certainly seems to have violated the 'spirit' of the rules. Those rules play a role within, and help define, the larger practice of casual Sunday morning tennis games. Within this framework, winning is valued, of course, but only when it is consistent with the larger goals of practice. *A*'s behaviour seems at odds with the reasons that people ordinarily engage in such a cooperative venture: having fun, getting exercise, improving their skills. Indeed, it tends to directly undermine the achievement of such goals.

2. *Stock investing*

The basic purpose of the stock market is often said to be to provide fluid capital to companies that wish to expand their businesses. Individual traders hope to make

[75] See e.g. Judith Freedman, 'Is Tax Avoidance "Fair"?', in C. Wales (ed.), *Fair Tax: Towards a Modern Tax System* (London: Smith Institute, 2008); Hanna Filipczyk, 'Why is Tax Avoidance (Im)moral? Ethics, Metaethics, and Taxes', *SSRN* (27 October 2014), http://papers.ssrn.com/sol3/papers.cfm?abstract_id=2515557. The idea that unreasonable tax avoidance involves a violation of the 'spirit' of the tax laws is related to, though distinguishable from, an idea developed in John Braithwaite, *Markets in Vice, Markets in Virtue* (New York: Oxford University Press, 2005). Braithwaite argues that we can avoid the abusive loopholing that plagues tax rules by supplementing those rules with more general tax principles, such as a 'general anti-avoidance principle which states that schemes are illegal when their dominant purpose is a tax advantage, even if the scheme "works" as a shelter from detailed tax rules'. Ibid., 149.

[76] See *IFT.com*, International Tennis Federation (ITF) Rules of Tennis, http://www.itftennis.com/media/194067/194067.pdf.

money in the market by 'buying low' and 'selling high'. Like tennis, stock investing is a zero sum game: some players must lose for others to win. Traders, of course, must abide by certain rules of conduct. Most famously, they must refrain from trading on inside information. But imagine a case in which *C*, a professional stock trader, though never actually buying or selling on the basis of inside information, engages in so-called high frequency trading, using supercomputers and ultra-fast fibre-optic cables that allow him to make money from small discrepancies in short-term market gyrations, placing stock orders and cancelling them immediately if he doesn't see a gain.[77] Has *C* behaved wrongfully?

Once again, it seems likely that *C* has not violated the law (at least as it currently stands); and, therefore, it would be inaccurate to say that he has cheated. Yet, as in the tennis case, his conduct arguably does violate the 'spirit' of the rules regarding stock trading, which at some basic level are intended to 'level the playing field' by assuring investors that no one will have an unfair informational advantage. Without such a rule, it is possible that small investors would no longer want to invest in the market, and the market itself would suffer. Firms that engage in the sort of tactics that *C* has engaged in arguably undermine the basic purposes of the market. The more pervasive such conduct becomes, the less the cooperative ends of the practice will be served, and the more likely it is that the market will be viewed as so unfair that small investors will stop investing.

So what does all of this have to do with tax avoidance? Like tennis playing and stock trading, taxpaying is both a competitive and cooperative venture. It is competitive in the sense that almost everyone wants to minimize their own individual tax burden, inevitably at the expense of other taxpayers. It is cooperative in the sense that the tax laws are intended to raise revenue for the state that can ultimately be used to further community goals.

And, as in the case of tennis and stock trading, we need to consider the substantive ends that our tax system is intended to serve. A taxpayer who claims deductions and exemptions based on transactions that are consistent with the purpose of the provisions allowing such deductions and exemptions acts in accordance with tax law's purpose, and thereby does nothing wrong. Indeed, he has performed as the system wants him to do. He has given to charity, bought a house, or put money away for his retirement, and then claimed his deduction. From an ethical perspective, his behaviour is analogous to the tennis player who serves the ball hard or the investor who spends long hours poring over a corporation's fundamentals before deciding to buy or sell shares. None of this conduct is morally wrongful.

By contrast, when a taxpayer claims deductions based on transactions that are inconsistent with the purpose of the law, he disregards the basic rationale of the law, the substantive ends it is intended to serve, the mischief at which it is directed.[78] To understand a rule, as a normative demand, is, or should be, to understand its role within the relevant practice, the reasons that underpin it. To accept a rule as a normative guide must then be to accept it as serving that end, or playing that role—to accept it and

[77] For a popular account, see Michael Lewis, *Flash Boys* (New York: Norton, 2014).

[78] I am grateful to Antony Duff for his help in formulating the argument in this paragraph.

follow it in the spirit in which it was passed. That is how citizens in a tolerably just society *should* relate to the law: not as a set of imposed rules defining a game which they are trying to win—with tax authorities or fellow citizens viewed as opponents—but, rather, as a way of structuring their shared civic life and of ensuring that the resources needed are raised fairly. Therefore, if one accepts the view that there is a moral obligation to comply with the *letter* of tax laws that are passed in a just manner, it follows that there is also moral obligation to comply with the *spirit* of such laws. Tax avoidance that fails the business purpose test violates that obligation. For that reason, it should be viewed as morally wrong, even though not unlawful.

4

Kelsen, the Principle of Exclusion of Contradictions, and General Anti-Avoidance Rules in Tax Law

*John Prebble QC**

I. General Anti-Avoidance Rules

General anti-avoidance rules are found in increasing numbers of taxation statutes. They are often known as GAARs. Broadly speaking, GAARs impugn the fiscal planning of taxpayers who avoid taxes without breaking the law. GAARs address the case where taxpayers' transactions and investment structures comply with the law, and the terms of the law in question provide for tax to be levied in a favourable manner and at a favourable rate, but in effect the outcome is to avoid tax. In these circumstances, GAARs provide that the transactions and structures in question must be treated as void for tax purposes. The result is that tax applies not to the actual legal transactions that taxpayers have undertaken—that is, not to the avoidance transactions—but to notional transactions that are closer in legal form to the economic effect of what taxpayers have done.

We ordinarily use the term 'general anti-avoidance rules' to refer to legislated rules, but some jurisdictions develop judge-made rules that have a similar effect. A notable example is the substance-over-form rule of the United States of America, which Congress ultimately codified in March 2010 as §7701(o) of the United States Internal Revenue Code. In this chapter, 'GAAR' refers both to legislated and to judicially created general anti-avoidance rules.

The first statutory GAAR appears to have been section 29 of the New Zealand Property Assessment Act 1879, carried forward into section 40 of the Land and Income Assessment Act 1891.[1]

Many countries enacted GAARs during the twentieth century, but several major economies did so only in relatively recent years: China in 2007;[2] the United States in 2010,[3] as previously mentioned; the United Kingdom in 2013;[4] and India in 2013,[5] to come into force in 2016.

* The author is most grateful for the comments of Clemens Jabloner, Hanneke van Oeveren, and Zainab Radhi, who read earlier versions of this chapter. Mistakes are of the author's.

[1] Since 2007 the New Zealand GAAR has appeared as section BG 1 of the Income Tax Act 2007.

[2] Arts 47 and 120, Enterprise Income Tax Law of the People's Republic of China, Promulgation Order No. 63, 16 March 2007.

[3] 26 United States Internal Revenue Code §7701(o), enacted March 2010.

[4] Finance Act 2013 Part 5, General Anti-Abuse Rule, ss 206–15.

[5] Income Tax Act 1961 ss 123, 124, 125, 154, 291, enacted by the Finance Act 2012.

Philosophical Foundations of Tax Law. First Edition. Edited by Monica Bhandari.

In any discussion of tax avoidance it can be helpful to divide substantive provisions of income tax legislation into two categories, GAARs and everything else. In this context, 'everything else' includes both charging provisions and permissive or relieving provisions. Most tax legislation includes other kinds of law as well, such as rules about procedures for resolving disputes and rules governing administration, but such rules are not relevant to the present discussion.

An example of a charging provision is a rule that imposes tax on the profits of businesses.[6] An example of a relieving provision is a rule that permits taxpayers when they calculate business profits to deduct sums to allow for the depreciation of capital assets used in the business.[7] Some rules are hybrids, at the same time both charging provisions and relieving provisions, such as a rule that charges capital gains with tax, but at a rate lower than the rate that applies to income.[8] For conciseness, this chapter uses 'charging provisions' both in its literal sense and as a generic term that applies equally to all three categories: charging, relieving, and hybrid provisions. The chapter often has occasion to distinguish between charging provisions on one hand and GAARs on the other.

II. Example of Avoidance Using a Tax Shelter

Some of the most recognizable examples of tax avoidance involve structures known as 'tax shelters'. Tax shelters are designed to reduce the tax otherwise payable on other income that taxpayers derive. Commonly, they involve apparently business-like schemes that result in losses that for tax purposes can be set off against profits of other income, thus reducing the profits to be taxed and therefore the tax itself. Typically, the losses are losses for tax purposes only; taxpayers employing tax shelters do not ordinarily suffer economic costs or losses apart from transaction costs.[9] Other shelters operate by entitling taxpayers to claim a status that confers a reduction in tax. The structure that was the subject of the Australian High Court decision in *Cridland v Federal Commissioner of Taxation* (1977)[10] is an example.

Like many tax shelters, Cridland's scheme exploited a provision designed to mitigate certain unfairness in the tax system. The unfairness in question arose from the progression of the Australian income tax scale as the scale operates in the context of the sharp, climate-induced fluctuations typical in the income of many Australian farmers. Because of the structure of the rules for the taxation of trusts, this unfairness could bear particularly hard on beneficiaries of trusts that derived income from

[6] For example, Income Tax Act 2007 s CB 1(1) (NZ), 'An amount that a person derives from a business is income of the person.'

[7] For example, Article 101 of the Decree of the President of the Republic Italy of 22 December 1986, number 917 (The Italian Tax Code) (Art. 101, DPR 22 December 1986 n. 917).

[8] For example, Internal Revenue Code §1(h) (USA) (26 USC §1(h)); Income Tax Act; (*Einkommenssteuergesetz (EStG)*) §32d (Gesonderter Steuertarif für Einkünfte aus Kapitalvermögen) (Germany).

[9] Film production is a popular example. See, e.g., *Ensign Tankers (Leasing) Ltd v Stokes (Inspector of Taxes)* [1992] 1 AC 655, 64 TC 617 (HL) and *Peterson v Commissioner of Inland Revenue* [2006] 3 NZLR 433; (2005) 22 NZTC 19,098 (PC).

[10] *Cridland v Federal Commissioner of Taxation* (1977) 140 CLR 330 (HCA).

farming. A good year, where farming income had been taxed at a high rate on the progressive scale, might be followed by a poor year, with little or no income. But like most tax legislation, the Australian Income Tax Assessment Act 1936 had no provision to shift income from good years into bad years, either forwards or backwards. The result was that beneficiaries who derived farming income could well be taxed at a higher average rate than people with similar income that was spread evenly from year to year.

The Australian legislature addressed this unfairness by enacting section 157 of the Income Tax Assessment Act 1936 (Cth), which allowed beneficiaries of trusts that derived income from primary production to average their income over several years, and to pay tax on the averaged sums. Where taxpayers qualified for this treatment, averaging applied to all their income, not solely to farming income derived via trusts.

Cridland was in a position of having income that fluctuated, or that would fluctuate, in that he was a university student in the modest circumstances typical of a student, but he hoped to find a well-paying position after graduation. To qualify himself after graduation to average his income for tax purposes, Cridland purchased a unit (in effect, a share) in a unit trust that farmed cattle. The unit cost very little. The trust had been established to afford to students precisely such an opportunity. Its objective was to ensure that beneficiaries derived *some* income from primary production, albeit very little.

Armed with his unit, Cridland, now a salaried engineer, submitted his tax return with his salary spread back into his impecunious student years. The Commissioner declined to accept Cridland's calculations and taxed his salary according to the year when it was derived. The Commissioner relied on the Australian GAAR as it then stood, section 260 of the Income Tax Assessment Act 1936 (Cth), which read:

> Every contract, agreement, or arrangement made or entered into, orally or in writing, whether before or after the commencement of this Act, shall so far as it has or purports to have the purpose or effect of in any way, directly or indirectly —
> (a) altering the incidence of any income tax;
> (b) relieving any person from liability to pay any income tax or make any return;
> (c) defeating, evading or avoiding any duty or liability imposed on any person by this Act; or
> (d) preventing the operation of this Act in any respect, be absolutely void, as against the Commissioner, or in regard to any proceeding under this Act, but without prejudice to such validity as it may have in any other respect or for any other purpose.

Cridland objected. The case made its way to the High Court of Australia where, surprisingly, at least to a non-Australian, Cridland won, on the basis that he did in fact derive income from primary production. It did not matter that hardly any of Cridland's income was from farming, nor that his claim to be a farmer was based on nothing of substance. One would think it clear enough that under section 260 Cridland's scheme was void against the Commissioner as, inter alia, an

> arrangement [that had] ... the purpose or effect of in any way, directly or indirectly —
> (a) altering the incidence of any income tax; [or of] (b) relieving any person from liability to pay any income tax ...

In the submission of the present author, the *Cridland* case is so much an egregious example of a tax shelter that it is almost a caricature of tax avoidance, albeit that Cridland was in fact successful before the courts. One result was that the Federal Parliament replaced section 260 in 1980 with a much more complex GAAR.[11]

III. The Fundamental Problem of GAARs

The major difficulty posed by a GAAR is that on one hand a provision of a tax code permits the taxpayer to do whatever it is that he or she purports to do and to enjoy the fiscal benefits that the provision affords (or that the general structure affords). On the other hand, a GAAR in effect prohibits the taxpayer from relying on the provision in question. This position obtains even though (a) the GAAR's prohibition is expressed generally and (b) the permissive provision is specific. For instance, one rule may permit taxpayers to deduct certain expenses in calculating assessable income;[12] and another rule may permit taxpayers to rely on a defined status, being a status that confers tax benefits.[13] But a GAAR may purport to negate both those permissive rules, at least in the circumstances of the case in question. Worse, if the GAAR does override a permissive rule the overriding appears to breach the principle of statutory construction known as *generalia specialibus non derogant* (general provisions do not derogate from specific rules).

The *Cridland* case, discussed in Section II of this chapter, illustrates the problem. According to section 157 of the Australian Income Tax Assessment Act 1936, Cridland qualified to spread his income back into earlier years because he derived income from farming, albeit very little. On the other hand, it is obvious to the present author that Cridland's scheme had no purpose other than tax avoidance, and therefore should have been held to be void against the Federal Commissioner of Taxation.

The present author has argued elsewhere that, despite its apparent contradictory nature and other defects, a GAAR is a worthwhile, even a necessary, component of a tax code, at least of an income tax code.[14] But this necessity does not make GAARs easy to apply. A fundamental reason, probably the fundamental reason, is that GAARs may appear to breach, and, as a matter of substance, arguably do in fact breach, the logic behind the principle of exclusion of contradictions, often called the 'principle of non-contradiction'.

[11] Part IVA, Income Tax Assessment Act 1936 (Cth).

[12] For example, *Cecil Bros Pty Ltd v Federal Commissioner of Taxation* (1964) 111 CLR 430 (HCA, FC).

[13] For example, *Cridland v Federal Commissioner of Taxation* (1977) 140 CLR 330 (HCA, FC).

[14] For example John Prebble, Rebecca Prebble, and Catherine Vidler Smith, 'Retrospective Legislation: Reliance, the Public Interest, Principles of Interpretation and the Special Case of Anti-Avoidance Legislation', 22 *New Zealand Universities Law Review* (2006) 271–99; Zoë Prebble and John Prebble, 'The Morality of Tax Avoidance', 20 *Creighton Law Review* (Symposium Issue: Estate Planning, Moral, Religious, and Ethical Perspectives) (2010) 693–745; Rebecca Prebble and John Prebble 'Does the Use of General Anti-Avoidance Rules to Combat Tax Avoidance Breach Principles of the Rule of Law? A Comparative Study', 55 *St Louis University Law Journal* (Symposium Issue: Sanford E. Sarasohn Memorial Conference on Critical Theory in Taxation) (2011) 21–45. Amplified version in Susy Frankel (ed.), *Learning from the Past, Adapting for the Future: Regulatory Reform in New Zealand* (Wellington, NZ: LexisNexis, 2011), all available on the author's SSRN pages, http://papers.ssrn.com/sol3/cf_dev/AbsByAuth.cfm?per_id=115459.

IV. Aristotle

Aristotle explained the principle of non-contradiction in some detail, but for present purposes Gottlieb's simplified summary is sufficient:[15]

> According to Aristotle, first philosophy, or metaphysics, deals with ontology and first principles, of which the principle (or law) of non-contradiction is the firmest. Aristotle says that without the principle of non-contradiction we could not know anything that we do know. Presumably, we could not demarcate the subject matter of any of the special sciences, for example, biology or mathematics, and we would not be able to distinguish between what something is, for example a human being or a rabbit, and what it is like, for example pale or white. Aristotle's own distinction between essence and accident would be impossible to draw, and the inability to draw distinctions in general would make rational discussion impossible. According to Aristotle, the principle of non-contradiction is a principle of scientific inquiry, reasoning and communication that we cannot do without.

Gotlieb identifies three versions of the principle:[16]

1. It is impossible for the same thing to belong and not to belong at the same time to the same thing and in the same respect (with the appropriate qualifications) (*Metaph* IV 3 1005b19–20).
2. It is impossible to hold (suppose) the same thing to be and not to be (*Metaph* IV 3 1005b24 cf.1005b29–30).
3. Opposite assertions cannot be true at the same time (*Metaph* IV 6 1011b13–20).

We could usefully test the operation of a GAAR against any or all of the three versions, but the third seems to be the most apt. In the context of income tax law, the principle of non-contradiction seems to tell us that we cannot assert as true that a particular transaction is not taxable according to ordinary charging provisions of the statute but at the same time that the transaction is taxable according to the GAAR. And yet, on the face of it, that contradiction is precisely the effect of applying a GAAR.

We sense intuitively that the argument in the previous paragraph may not be the last word on the subject. Aristotle's principle of non-contradiction is tolerably compelling in the field of facts. One can accept that it is at least improbable that something can at the same time both be a rabbit and not be a rabbit. Expressing this thought in terms of Gotlieb's version 3, above, we would be reluctant to accept that both the following statements are correct: 'The animal in my hands is a rabbit' and 'The animal in my hands is not a rabbit'. But does the same reasoning necessarily apply to norms? There seems, somehow, more possibility that the norms 'you ought not to kill' and 'you may kill' could coexist than could the facts of rabbit and non-rabbit.

[15] Paula Gottlieb, 'Aristotle on Non-Contradiction', in Edward N. Zalta (ed.), *The Stanford Encyclopedia of Philosophy* (Spring 2013), http://plato.stanford.edu/archives/spr2013/entries/aristotle-noncontradiction/.

[16] Ibid.

Our intuition is correct. To a nonphilosopher, the following two norms appear to constitute a logical contradiction: 'The Commissioner ought to charge X tax on his income' and 'The Commissioner ought not to charge X tax on his income.' As Section V of this chapter explains, Kelsen tells us that this situation is not strictly speaking a contradiction. The reason is that the conflicting statements are 'ought' statements, not 'is' statements. Since neither statement claims that something 'is', the statements cannot contradict or be contradicted.[17]

While this may be the strict philosophical position there is more to say from a fiscal perspective. Take again the *Cridland* case, discussed in Section II. The claim seems unmeritorious on its face. But the taxpayer has at least a semblance of a grievance if on one hand the statute allows him to spread his income for tax purposes and on the other hand denies him that right. The contradiction may not be a true contradiction in philosophical terms, but taxpayers can be forgiven for thinking that it is a kind of a contradiction that merits study. Such study is the purpose of the sections of this chapter that follow.

V. Kelsen

The question that terminates the previous paragraph of this chapter is an example of the kind of question that Kelsen addressed in his book, *Pure Theory of Law*,[18] published in English in 1967. *Pure Theory of Law* was a translation of the second edition of Kelsen's *Reine Rechtslehre*, 1960, being a completely revised edition of the first edition of 1934. Professor Max Knight, the translator, explained Kelsen's mission in *Pure Theory of Law* in his 'Translator's Preface'. He said that Kelsen:[19]

> attempts to solve the fundamental problems of a general theory of law according to the principles of methodological purity of jurisprudential cognition and to determine to a greater extent than before the position of the science of law in the system of the sciences.

Considering these overall objectives, it is not surprising that in Kelsen's opinion the issue of whether the principle of non-contradiction applies as well to norms as to facts was a question worthy of consideration. Among other things, answering the question should help to place the science of law in relation to the system of sciences that addresses facts. Kelsen had already addressed the question in *General Theory of Law and State*,[20] where he concluded:

> The judgments 'A ought to be' and 'A ought not to be', for example, 'you ought to speak the truth' and 'you ought not to speak the truth' are just as incompatible with one another as 'A is' and 'A is not'. For the principle of contradiction is quite as valid

[17] Hans Kelsen, *General Theory of Norms*, Michael Hartney (trans.) (New York: Oxford University Press, 1991), 163–4, 213–14, 219.

[18] Hans Kelsen, *Pure Theory of Law*, Max Knight (trans.) (Berkeley: University of California Press, 1967), 73–4.

[19] Ibid., v.

[20] Hans Kelsen, *General Theory of Law and State*, Anders Wedberg (trans.) (Cambridge, MA: Harvard University Press, 1945), 408.

> for cognition in the sphere of normative validity as it is in that of empirical reality. [Kelsen wrote of the 'principle of contradiction', but it is clear that he used this expression to mean what others mean by the 'principle of non-contradiction'. When he came to *Pure Theory of Law* Kelsen used the more informative label, the 'Principle of Exclusion of Contradictions'.[21]]

By 1960 it seems that Kelsen had realized that this passage was an oversimplification and that logically he could not argue that the principle of non-contradiction applied in the same manner to norms as it does to facts. Although still writing in the magisterial tone that characterizes *Pure Theory of Law* Kelsen refined and diluted his conclusion.[22]

In *Pure Theory of Law*, Kelsen started from the proposition that the canonical form of a legal norm is an ought statement in the form of, 'If somebody steals he ought to be punished.'[23] Kelsen resiled from the broad proposition quoted from *General Theory of Law and State*,[24] above, and conceded that:[25]

> Since legal norms, being prescriptions (that is, commands, permissions, authorizations), can neither be true nor false, the question arises: how can logical principles, especially the Principle of the Exclusion of Contradiction[26] ... be applied to the relation between legal norms, if, according to traditional views these principles are applicable only to assertions that can be true or false? The answer is: logical principles are applicable, *indirectly*, to legal norms to the extent that they are applicable to the *rules of law which describe the legal norms* and which can be true or false. Two legal norms are contradictory and can therefore not both be valid at the same time, if the two rules of law that describe them are contradictory.

Two clues to the import of this passage are the words 'indirectly' and the meaning that Kelsen gives to the expression 'rules of law' (both italicized above). In using 'indirectly', Kelsen admits that, logically, he must concede that he cannot apply the principle of non-contradiction to legal norms. The meaning that Kelsen gives to the expression a 'rule of law' amplifies the reason. Kelsen explains that by 'rule of law', he means

[21] Kelsen used lower case initial letters for 'principle of contradiction' in *General Theory of Law and State* (text accompanying previous footnote) but there are initial capitals for 'Principle of Exclusion of Contradictions' in *Pure Theory of Law* (text at n. 26). It seems probable that it was Kelsen's idea to keep the capital letters in the style of the German language. Max Knight, the translator, was conscious that the style of *Pure Theory of Law* wears its origin on its sleeve. Knight wrote, 'This translation, carefully checked by [Kelsen], represents a compromise between a contents-conscious author and a form-conscious translator. Kelsen's immense experience with misinterpretations of his works as a result of "elegant" translations had to be the deciding factor when seemingly repetitious or Germanic-sounding passages, expunged from or rephrased in an earlier draft of the translation as too literally mirroring the original, were restored.' See 'Translator's Preface', in Kelsen, n. 18, vi.

[22] In discussing the principle of non-contradiction, Kelsen did not mention Aristotle in either *General Theory of Law and State* or *Pure Theory of Law*, though the index to the former contains six references to Aristotle in other contexts. No doubt Kelsen thought that he was writing for erudite readers for whom references to Aristotle's role in the development of Western philosophy would be supererogatory.

[23] Kelsen, n. 18, 75.

[24] Though *Pure Theory of Law* does not mention *General Theory of Law and State* in the context under discussion here.

[25] Kelsen, n. 18, 74, emphasis added.

[26] In *Pure Theory of Law*, Kelsen adopted this more expansive label for what he had called simply 'the principle of contradiction' in *General Theory of Law and State*. See passage quoted at n. 21 of this chapter.

not a norm, such as a law promulgated by a legislator, but a 'statement formulated by the science of law ... describing [the] norm',[27] such as a description of the norm that a scholar might write. For example, a legislator might promulgate a norm 'prescribing execution against a person who does not fulfil a marriage promise and does not compensate for the damage',[28] whereas a scholar's description of this norm might say, 'that execution [that is, civil execution, such as a bailiff's seizure and sale of the goods of the defendant] ought to be carried out against a person who does not fulfil a marriage promise and does not compensate for the damage'.[29]

The discussion just described occurs on pages 73 and 74 of *Pure Theory of Law*. Kelsen returns to the Principle of Exclusion of Contradictions with more confidence later in the same book, and asserts that:[30]

> [L]ogical principles in general and, and the Principle of the Exclusion of Contradictions in particular, are applicable to rules of law describing legal norms and therefore indirectly also to legal norms. Hence it is by no means absurd to say that two legal norms 'contradict' each other. And therefore only one of the two can be regarded as objectively valid. To say that *a* ought to be done and at the same time ought not to be done is just as meaningless as to say at the same time that *a* is and at the same time that it is not. A conflict of norms is just as meaningless as a logical contradiction.

For Kelsen, a conflict of norms within a single legal system was a serious matter. One norm, or the other, or perhaps both, must be invalid.[31] It behooves us therefore to resolve the conflict if at all possible, either by applying the principle of statutory interpretation *lex posterior derogate priori*[32] or by construing the two apparently conflicting norms, to understand that they are in fact separate, with one norm creating an exception to the other.[33] Nevertheless:[34]

> If neither the one nor the other interpretation is possible, then the legislator creates something meaningless; we have then a meaningless act of norm creation and therefore no act at all [that is, nothing that can be called a norm] whose subjective meaning can be interpreted as its objective meaning; no objectively valid legal norm is present.

Troubling though this outcome may be in theory, is it a matter for serious concern in practice? One bears in mind that Kelsen's argument reaches this outcome, by his own admission, only 'indirectly', and only by almost redefining his terms from 'legal norms' to a special meaning of 'legal rules' that Kelsen seems to invent for the occasion. Furthermore, while they are logically correct, the examples that Kelsen gives are not particularly realistic—for instance a statute that stipulates both that 'adultery is punishable and adultery is not punishable'.[35] One suspects that if there are examples of true contradictions between legal norms they are most likely to have occurred by mistake. It is not surprising that later in life Kelsen changed his mind about his belief expressed in *Pure Theory of Law* that if legal norms contradict each other there is a

[27] Kelsen, n. 18, 73. [28] Ibid. [29] Ibid. [30] Ibid., 206.
[31] The present author's deduction by implication from Kelsen, n. 18, 206.
[32] A later [inconsistent] law overrides an earlier law. [33] Kelsen, n. 18, 206–7.
[34] Ibid., 207. [35] Ibid., 206.

breach of the Principle of the Exclusion of Contradictions, which breach results in invalidity of the norms in question.[36]

Nevertheless, there was more utility in the discussion of the Principle of Exclusion of Contradictions in *Pure Theory of Law* than Kelsen eventually claimed. The discussion might shed limited light on law in general, but the discussion contributes substantially to our understanding of general anti-avoidance rules in tax statutes.

VI. GAARs and the Principle of Exclusion of Contradictions

The world has increasing numbers of statutory GAARs, each duly enacted by its legislature, and each recognized as law by courts that have jurisdiction in tax cases. GAARs are rarely attacked as unconstitutional, and such attacks generally fail.[37] Nevertheless, it is undeniable that at least at some level GAARs contradict charging or relieving provisions in income tax legislation. That is their purpose.

Return to *Cridland v Federal Commissioner of Taxation*,[38] the example discussed in Section II of this chapter. The taxpayer, Cridland, was undeniably a beneficiary of a trust and he undeniably derived income from primary production via that trust. In the words of section 157 of the Income Tax Assessment Act 1936 (Cth), Cridland was therefore entitled to spread his income backwards from the current year to earlier years in order to take advantage of the lower rate thresholds of those years, lower rates that Cridland had not exhausted at the time because as a nonsalaried student he then derived a lower income. On the one hand, the High Court of Australia vindicated Cridland, holding that he was entitled to benefit from his tax minimization scheme.

On the other hand, the GAAR, section 260 of the same statute, quoted in full in Section II of this chapter, said:

> Every ... arrangement ... shall so far as it has ... the purpose or effect of in any way, directly or indirectly ...
>
> (b) relieving any person from liability to pay any income tax ... be absolutely void, as against the Commissioner.

It is hard to think of any purpose that the arrangement had apart from relieving Cridland of liability to pay income tax. Cridland owned only one unit in the farming trust in question, so the arrangement was certainly not a business or investment proposition on his part. On the facts of the case, there was no other conceivable purpose for the arrangement.

As applied to the facts of the *Cridland* case, sections 157 and 260 of the Income Tax Assessment Act do appear to be in conflict, especially if we frame the conflict in terms of Kelsen's explanation of scholars' descriptions of rules of law, discussed in the previous section of this chapter. One rule, derived from section 157, provides

[36] See Section XI of this chapter.

[37] A leading example is *National Federation of Independent Business v Sebelius*, 567 U.S. ___(2012), 132 S.Ct 2566, 183 L. Ed. 2d 450. Even this attack was flanking rather than head-on, in that the taxpayer's primary argument was that the Obama health reforms, adopted in the same statute as the American GAAR, namely The Patient Protection and Affordable Care Act 2010, were unconstitutional.

[38] *Cridland*, n. 10.

that in calculating his income tax liability Cridland may claim the status of primary producer, together with the reduction in tax that this status confers. The other rule, derived from section 260, provides that Cridland ought not to claim this status and reduction in taxation. In 1977 the Australian High Court resolved the conflict by holding that section 157 prevailed, at least on the facts of that case.

It is not likely that the High Court would reach the same conclusion today, but what the *Cridland* case illustrates is more general than the court's actual conclusion. First, the case reminds us that, whatever the facts, a court must come to a conclusion in GAAR cases; courts are bound to decide GAAR cases just as they are bound to decide all cases. In this light, talk of conflict of norms somehow misses the point. No matter how conflicting two relevant norms seem to be, the court must resolve the conflict. But this conclusion is formal, even superficial. The problems with GAARs are much deeper.

In the context of a discussion about the Principle of Exclusion of Contradictions one such problem stands out: what is the relationship between the charging and relieving provisions of a taxing statute on one hand, and the statute's GAAR on the other? As McCarthy P said, a GAAR that avoids arrangements that have the purpose of avoiding tax or of simply relieving a taxpayer from tax 'cannot be given a literal application, for that would … result in the avoidance of transactions which were obviously not aimed at by the [GAAR]'.[39] For instance, the GAAR would avoid a gift to charity made with a purpose of qualifying for a charitable deduction, which presumably cannot be the purpose of the GAAR. Lord Wilberforce made the same point, in more detail. Speaking of the then New Zealand GAAR, he said in 1971:[40]

> It fails to specify the relation between the section and other provisions in the Income Tax legislation under which tax reliefs, or exemptions, may be obtained. Is it legitimate to take advantage of these so as to avoid or reduce tax? What if the only purpose is to use them? Is there a distinction between 'proper' tax avoidance and 'improper' tax avoidance? By what sense is this distinction to be perceived?

In the *Cridland* case, the conflict between the relieving section 157 of the Australian statute and section 260, the statute's GAAR, is instructive in answering Lord Wilberforce's questions. The sections are norms; it follows that logically they cannot constitute the two sides of a factual contradiction. But, as explained, when we re-cast sections 157 and 260 and describe their effect as one describes rules of law, they do appear to contradict one another. From this perspective, there appears to be a true logical contradiction. As Kelsen points out, the existence of such logical contradictions in legal systems are at least a theoretical possibility. But apparently, unable to find practical examples Kelsen advanced only hypothetical possibilities, such as the example mentioned, of rules that do, and that do not, punish adultery. Also as mentioned, if such contradictions occur they will probably be the result of mistakes.

[39] *Commisioner of Inland Revenue v Gerard* [1974] 2 NZLR 279, 280 (CA).

[40] *Mangin v Commissioner of Inland Revenue* [1971] NZLR 591, 602 per Lord Wilberforce (dissenting) (PC).

In sharp contrast, the tension between GAARs and relieving provisions is an everyday conflict with which tax scholars, taxpayers, tax officials, and tax judges struggle daily, in many jurisdictions. The conflict between a GAAR and a relieving provision is far from a mistake; legislatures enact GAARs specifically to nullify transactions that would otherwise be unexceptionable.

Like most legal philosophers, Kelsen wrote, and probably knew, little about tax law. It is unlikely that it occurred to Kelsen that tax law might be different in kind from most other areas of law[41] and unlikely that he ever made the acquaintance of a GAAR, that unusual species of law that is designed with a built-in contradiction. This is our loss. Legal science would most certainly have benefited from Kelsen's thoughts. Nevertheless, although we cannot profit from thoughts that Kelsen undoubtedly would have had about GAARs specifically, his general, if somewhat hypothetical, thoughts about contradictory norms and about the Principle of Exclusion of Contradictions shed welcome light on this complex area of law. To summarize, GAARs and relieving provisions do contradict one another. Courts must struggle to resolve that contradiction. It helps, as a start, at least to recognize the nature of the problem.

A good example of mischaracterization of the problem occurred in the New Zealand Supreme Court case of *Ben Nevis Forestry Ventures Ltd & Ors v Commissioner of Inland Revenue* (2009),[42] a case about a tax shelter. The New Zealand Supreme Court was inaugurated in 2004 to replace the Judicial Committee of the Privy Council as New Zealand's final court of appeal. *Ben Nevis* was the Court's first tax avoidance case. Speaking for the majority, McGrath J explained that it was desirable to settle the approach to be applied to resolve the:[43]

> continuing uncertainty about the inter-relationship of the general anti-avoidance provision with specific [taxing and relieving] provisions. [He continued:[44]]
>
> It is accordingly the task of the Courts to apply a principled approach which gives proper overall effect to statutory language that expresses different legislative policies. It has long been recognised those policies require reconciliation.[45]

McGrath J's words are a candid judicial statement that explicitly recognizes a general category of contradictions between legal norms, being contradictions that are explained by contradictory policies (taxation or relief from tax on one hand, and the frustration of avoidance on the other). But can we agree with his Honour's attempt at reconciliation of the inconsistency? McGrath J adopted the metaphor of a tandem bicycle and said:[46]

[41] See papers cited at nn 14 and 69.

[42] *Ben Nevis Forestry Ventures Ltd & Ors v Commissioner of Inland Revenue* [2008] NZSC 115; [2009] 2 NZLR 289 (SC).

[43] Ibid., [100] per McGrath J.

[44] Ibid., [102] per McGrath J.

[45] *Commisioner of Inland Revenue v Gerard* [1974] 2 NZLR 279, 280 (CA), per McCarthy P and *Challenge Corporation Ltd v Commissioner of Inland Revenue* [1986] 2 NZLR 513, 549 (CA and PC), per Richardson J,also reported as *Commissioner of Inland Revenue v Challenge Corporation Ltd* [1987] AC 155 (PC). (Court's footnote amplified.)

[46] *Ben Nevis Forestry Ventures Ltd & Ors*, n. 42, [103] per McGrath J.

> We consider Parliament's overall purpose is best served by construing specific tax provisions and the general anti-avoidance provision so as to give appropriate effect to each. They are meant to work in tandem. Each provides a context which assists in determining the meaning and, in particular, the scope of the other. Neither should be regarded as overriding. Rather they work together.

One is reduced to repeating 'tandem' without managing to illuminate McGrath J's meaning. To unpick the metaphor of a tandem bicycle, assume that the front wheel and rider represent a charging or relieving provision, or an investment structure, relied upon by a scheme of minimization of tax (using 'minimization' as a neutral term that may or may not entail the avoidance that is the target of a GAAR). The rear wheel and rider represent the GAAR. Assume further, that in the case at bar the correct conclusion is that the GAAR annihilates the scheme of tax minimization as an arrangement that has a purpose of tax avoidance. What has happened to the bicycle? Have the rear rider and wheel overtaken the front rider and wheel? Where a scheme for tax minimization has fallen to a GAAR as an arrangement to avoid tax it is stretching things to say that the GAAR and the provisions on which the scheme to minimize tax work 'together'. On the contrary, the GAAR switches off the benefit-conferring rule on which the tax planner relied.

The discussion of *Ben Nevis Forestry Ventures Ltd & Ors v Commissioner of Inland Revenue* reveals that even though GAARs do not give rise to breaches of the Principle of Exclusion of Contradictions in the sense to which logicians refer, that is, in the sense of the exclusion of factual contradictions, the tension between legal rules derived from GAARs and legal rules derived from relieving or other tax laws presents courts with contradictions that are in respects that are relevant for legal reasoning the same as true logical contradictions. As Kelsen describes such contradictions they are rare within legal systems, to the extent of being almost hypothetical. But they are not rare when we take into account the operation of GAARs, operations that are both practical and frequent. *Ben Nevis* demonstrates that resolving the problem of GAARs is a problem worthy of Kelsen himself.

VII. Resolving Conflicts Between GAARs and Other Rules of Tax Law

As explained in the previous section of this chapter, the problem of resolving contradictions between GAARs and other rules of tax law does not map precisely onto the problem of repairing a breach of the Principle of Exclusion of Contradictions. Since strictly speaking that principle refers to contradictions of fact, a true contradiction may be resoloved only by deciding that one or both elements of the contradiction is incorrect. But contradictions in law must be solved. Kelsen does not explain what is to be done about such contradictions, apart from recommending endeavours to interpret rules so as to avoid them.[47] The reader infers that if there is a breach that cannot be

[47] Kelsen, n. 18, 206.

resolved by turning to principles of statutory interpretation, it is probably necessary to resort to extra-legal remedies. In a curious way, the same thing happens with GAARs.

A court of final appeal may possibly resolve an issue of a contradiction between norms with a response that can hardly be called 'law'. The decision will be binding on the parties, but it may not solve a deep conflict between norms. Such a result is indeed often the position for cases that turn on GAARs, cases that are notoriously inconsistent.[48]

The reason is that conflict between a charging or relieving provision of tax law and a GAAR logically cannot be resolved by reasoning that is strictly legalistic; if there are contradictory provisions of law of similar status the contradiction can be resolved, if at all, only by reference to criteria that are outside the conflicting provisions. By definition, in the case that this chapter considers there are no legal provisions superior in the hierarchy of norms of the state in question to which the contradiction can be referred for resolution. (If there were such superior norms we could not speak in terms of a contradiction of rules of law.) Ultimately, it turns out that the criteria that have been mentioned—that is, criteria that are outside the conflicting provisions—are not criteria of law but criteria of economic substance, or sometimes of morality, as will be explained.

All this is not to say that courts do not try to resolve conflicts between charging provisions and GAARs by reference to rules of law. Indeed, the judicial history of GAARs is largely a history of just that phenomenon. Courts are forever thinking of rules to resolve these conflicts. A good example is the so-called doctrine of choice, which the High Court of Australia invented in *W.P. Keighery Pty Ltd v Federal Commissioner of Taxation*.[49] Their Honours explained the doctrine thus:[50]

> Whatever difficulties there may be in interpreting s. 260, [the then Australian GAAR] one thing at least is clear: the section intends only to protect the general provisions of the Act from frustration, and not to deny to taxpayers any right of choice between alternatives which the Act itself lays open to them.

On its face, this passage is entirely plausible. But a moment's thought shows that if the doctrine of choice is indeed a rule of law, then, at least in principle, a GAAR could have no effect. The reason is that wherever a GAAR is relevant to a transaction, it must be because there are at least two ways in which the legal structure of the transaction can be arranged, one attracting less tax than the other.

This situation is not a matter of cause and effect. The existence of a GAAR is not caused by, nor does it cause, a transaction to be able to take more than one possible legal form. Rather, the only cases where authorities may need to call on a GAAR

[48] For example, Canadian Supreme Court cases on the Canadian GAAR cannot be reconciled in any satisfactory manner. Compare, for example, *Canada Trustco Mortgage Company v Canada* 2005 SCC 54 with *Mathew v Canada* 2005 SCC 55. In the respectful view of the author, the reasoning of the Supreme Court of Canada is inconsistent between the two cases. For an excellent analysis of the cases, albeit an analysis that is more charitable to the Court, see David G. Duff, 'The Supreme Court of Canada and the General Anti-Avoidance Rule', 60 *Bulletin of International Taxation* (February 2006) 54.

[49] *W.P. Keighery Pty Ltd v Federal Commissioner of Taxation* [1957] 100 CLR 66 (HCA, FC).

[50] Ibid., [20] 86, per Dixon CJ, Kitto and Fullagar JJ. McTiernan J agreed, 96.

are cases of transactions that permit two or more legal forms. For instance, in the *Cridland*[51] case, discussed in Section II of this chapter, the taxpayer could have earned his salary in the same guise of employee as other salary earners, or he could have pretended (as he did) to be an earner of farming income. If there is only one possible legal form for a transaction then employing that form cannot be stigmatized as tax avoidance. But where there are two possible forms, the doctrine of choice would say that the taxpayer may choose the option that is fiscally cheaper without triggering the GAAR.

Broadly speaking, a GAAR may apply if (a) the taxpayer chooses the option that is fiscally cheaper and if (b) that option has some quality or other that may be impugned and that may thereby attract the GAAR: undue complexity, artificial valuations, and so on. In short, when a case is such that the GAAR may apply then that will be a case where the doctrine of choice potentially applies; that is, the doctrine of choice maps onto the cases where a GAAR applies. The two have the same preconditions. But where the preconditions apply, and where, therefore, potentially both the GAAR and the doctrine of choice apply, then the doctrine ousts the GAAR. *Ex hypothesi*, a GAAR is ousted by the same conditions that are necessary for it to operate at all. It is perhaps for this reason that countries with mature GAARs have rarely seen courts applying the doctrine of choice since about 1990. Not that the doctrine is dead: in what looks suspiciously like agency capture, a GAAR in a Draft Directive for a Common Consolidated Corporate Tax Base for the European Community (2011) made the doctrine of choice a central element:

> *Article 80 General anti-abuse rule*
>
> Artificial transactions carried out for the main [sole] purpose of avoiding taxation shall be ignored for the purposes of calculating the tax base.
>
> The first paragraph shall not apply to genuine commercial activities where the taxpayer is able to choose between two or more possible transactions which have the same commercial result but which produce different taxable amounts.

It seems that someone spotted the problem, and in 2012 the Danish Presidency proposed that the second paragraph should be changed to:

> The first paragraph shall not apply to genuine commercial activities carried out for valid commercial reasons.

VIII. Principles of Economic Substance

The preceding paragraphs of this chapter have considered the doctrine of choice not because it is important in the jurisprudence of GAARs (though it is significant in that context) but in order to illustrate by example that one cannot reconcile a conflict of norms between a GAAR and a charging provision by referring to legal norms.

Except when they operate what may be called a 'candid' GAAR, judges seldom expressly articulate the point, but, being unable to refer to legal rules to resolve cases

[51] *Cridland*, n. 10.

of avoidance and GAARs, courts turn instead to principles of economic substance. In this chapter, a 'candid' GAAR means a GAAR that explicitly directs the court, or sometimes tax inspectors, to determine avoidance cases by reference to economic substance. Candid GAARs may be compared with standard GAARs, which generally have much the same effect in the end, but which are framed in terms such as, for example: 'A tax avoidance arrangement is void as against the Commissioner for income tax purposes.'[52]

A recent candid GAAR, enacted in 2014, is Article 556-1 of the Tax Code of Kazakhstan. Unusually from a Western perspective, Article 556-1 is directed to tax authorities rather than to courts or to taxpayers, but this difference of drafting does not appear to lead to any substantial difference in effect. The article reads:[53]

> Tax authorities conducting taxation audits shall ignore any act or failure to act on the part of a taxpayer or group of taxpayers, including all business or other transactions, where such act or failure to act (a) lacks economic substance and (b) causes a decrease in tax liability; and the tax authorities shall ignore such act or failure to act in determining the liability of such taxpayers. For the purposes of this article 'taxpayer' includes 'tax agent'.

Probably the most famous candid GAAR is §7701(o) of the United States Internal Revenue Code, which Congress inserted in March 2010. The core provisions of §7701(o) are:

> (o) Clarification of economic substance doctrine
> (1) Application of doctrine
> In the case of any transaction to which the economic substance doctrine is relevant, such transaction shall be treated as having economic substance only if—
> (A) the transaction changes in a meaningful way (apart from Federal income tax effects) the taxpayer's economic position, and
> (B) the taxpayer has a substantial purpose (apart from Federal income tax effects) for entering into such transaction ....
> (5)(A) The term 'economic substance doctrine' means the common law doctrine under which tax benefits under subtitle A with respect to a transaction are not allowable if the transaction does not have economic substance or lacks a business purpose.

The author quotes the Kazakh and American GAARs at some length to make the point that when judges are faced with reconciling conflicting norms—that is, charging rules and GAARs—they have no choice but to step outside the law and to test the facts of the case according to principles of economic and business substance.

[52] Income Tax Act 2007, s BG 1 (New Zealand).

[53] Translation by Мария Джаембаева, Almaty, edited by the author; '(a)' and '(b)' added for clarity. The original Russian reads:

> При выявлении в ходе налогового контроля случаев совершения налогоплательщиком (налоговым агентом) или группой налогоплательщиков (налоговых агентов) действия (бездействия), сделки, хозяйственной операции, в которых не содержится экономический смысл, повлекших уменьшение налогового обязательства, органы налоговой службы определяют налоговое обязательство таких налогоплательщиков (налоговых агентов) без учета указанных действия, сделки, хозяйственной операции.

Judgments in cases where standard GAARs are in play are much less explicit, but, particularly in jurisdictions that have had relatively long experience with GAARs, one often finds references to criteria of economic substance. For instance, in *Federal Commissioner of Taxation v Purcell*, Knox CJ said[54] that the provisions of the then Australian GAAR:[55]

> are intended to and do extend to cover cases in which the transaction in question, if recognised as valid, would enable the taxpayer to avoid payment of income tax on what is really and in truth his income.

By these words, his Honour meant that the income in question was income of the taxpayer in a substantive, economic, sense, even though legally he did not derive or own the income himself.

Sometimes courts illogically cling to the illusion of deciding a GAAR case according to legal rules, while at the same time determining the case according to economic substance. For instance, in the New Zealand case of *Ben Nevis Forestry Ventures Ltd & Ors v Commissioner of Inland Revenue*,[56] discussed in Section VI of this chapter, the Supreme Court embarked on a 'principled approach'[57] without in the end identifying any relevant principle of law, apart from that of giving 'proper effect'[58] to relevant statutory language, something that we expect of a court as a matter of course. Ultimately, the case appears to have turned on questions of economic reality. The courts should:[59]

> consider the use made of the [charging provision in question] in the light of the commercial reality and the economic effect of that use. The ultimate question is whether the impugned arrangement, viewed in a commercially and economically realistic way, makes use of the specific provision in a manner that is consistent with Parliament's purpose. If that is so, the arrangement will not, by reason of that use, be a tax avoidance arrangement. If the use of the specific provision is beyond Parliamentary contemplation, its use in that way will result in the arrangement being a tax avoidance arrangement.

It is instructive to consider this kind of argument in the more general terms that Kelsen employed. A good example is his subchapter, 'Causal and Normative Social Science'.[60] What happens, as he explains there, is that without specific recognition by legal scientists (or by judges, as in the passage just quoted from the *Ben Nevis* case) arguments like the argument set out in the passage quoted from *Ben Nevis* move from 'ought' to 'is'. There is no superior rule in the hierarchy of norms to resolve the conflict; in other words, the 'ought' of positive, man-made norms is exhausted. The court turns instead to the 'is' of the science of economics, a science that attempts to explain human behaviour causally, operating in the same manner as natural sciences

[54] *Federal Commissioner of Taxation v Purcell* (1921) 29 CLR 464, 466 (HCA, FC).

[55] Commonwealth of Australia Income Tax and Social Services Contribution Assessment Act 1936–1951, s 260.

[56] *Ben Nevis Forestry Ventures Ltd & Ors*, n. 42. [57] Ibid., [13]. [58] Ibid., [102].

[59] Ibid., [109].

[60] Hans Kelsen, 'Causative and Normative Social Science', in Max Knight (trans.), n. 18, 85 ff.

and other social sciences. This invocation of 'is', of fact, is of course anathema to the fundamental thesis of Kelsen's pure theory of law.[61]

IX. Principles of Morality

As explained, when together the need to resolve conflicts between charging rules and GAARs and the mandates of logic require a departure from strictly legal rules, courts generally turn to economic reality, but occasionally they resort instead or as well to norms of morality. For instance, in *Elmiger v Commissioner of Inland Revenue*[62] Woodhouse J adopted the following passage from the United States Supreme Court case of *Higgins v Smith*:[63]

> Each tax according to a legislative plan raises funds to carry on government. The purpose here is to tax earnings and profits less expenses and losses. If one or the other factor in any calculation is unreal it distorts the liability of the particular taxpayer to the detriment of the entire tax-paying group.

Occasionally, a court will explain the operation of a GAAR in terms that appear to call on both morality and economic reality at the same time. Thus, in *Gregory v Helvering*, which turned on the American judge-made GAAR, the Supreme Court said:[64]

> The whole undertaking, though conducted according to the terms of [a particular provision of the United States tax code], was in fact an elaborate and devious form of conveyance masquerading as a corporate reorganization, and nothing else. The rule which excludes from consideration the motive of tax avoidance is not pertinent to the situation, because the transaction upon its face lies outside the plain intent of the statute. To hold otherwise would be to exalt artifice above reality and to deprive the statutory provision in question of all serious purpose.[65]

Analytically, the shift from law to morality is a different kind of move from the shift from law to criteria of economic substance. As explained, the latter involves a move from law to fact. In contrast, going from law to morality is a shorter journey, from one normative system (law) to another (morals). Nevertheless, the pure theory of law sets its face against that journey just as resolutely as it does against moving from law to fact.

[61] Kelsen, n. 18, 4–10, 193, and *passim*.

[62] *Elmiger v Commissioner of Inland Revenue* [1966] 683, 687 (Woodhouse J), affd [1967] NZLR 161 (CA).

[63] *Higgins v Smith*, 308 U.S. 473 (1940), 476–7.

[64] *Gregory v Helvering*, 293 U.S. 465 (1935), 469–70.

[65] Despite such observations, common law courts are adamant that morality has no place in judging whether tax avoidance has taken place. See, for example, *Ben Nevis Forestry Ventures Ltd & Ors*, n. 42, [15]: '[The judicial process of determining whether tax avoidance has occurred] must enable decisions to be made on individual cases through the application of a process of statutory construction focusing objectively on features of the arrangements involved, without being distracted by intuitive subjective impressions of the morality of what taxation advisers have set up.'

X. Economic Substance, Morality, and the Pure Theory of Law

The mode of reasoning in applying GAARs described in the previous section of this chapter, deferring to criteria of economic substance or of morality, is wholly incompatible with Kelsen's pure theory of law.[66] Nevertheless, when it comes to GAARs the law has reached its boundaries. In order to resolve a conflict of norms where one norm is a GAAR, courts must abandon the hierarchical climb towards the Grundnorm[67] and, bursting the bubble of law, must turn instead to norms that are outside law. Practice thus inevitably departs from Kelsen's theory and, where the norm is tested by reference to economic substance, practice departs from Kelsen's principle, 'The reason for the validity of a norm is always another norm, never a fact.'[68]

(There is an interesting parallel with Luhman's theory of autopoiesis, which posits that law is self-creating and autonomous, not part of other social systems and barely influenced by them.[69] Like Kelsen's pure theory of law, Luhman's theory of autopoiesis also breaks down when it tries to account for GAARs, and breaks down for similar reasons.[70])

These conclusions lead to several reflections. First, although it fails to account for GAARs, Kelsen's pure theory is nevertheless a powerful explanatory tool, a tool that for the most part depicts the nature of law accurately. At the same time, the failure of the pure theory when it comes to GAARs contains a lesson: that we cannot expect a GAAR to yield to standard legal reasoning, isolated from considerations of economic substance and even of morality. In turn, this lesson shows that from the perspective of Kelsenian analysis (more precisely, the mirror image of Kelsenian analysis) fundamental theory did not support the turn that scholars observed[71] in United States avoidance jurisprudence towards formality and literalism, occurring from approximately 2001. In Kelsenian terms, that turn seemed to respond to the pure theory of law, but it was mistaken to do so. The courts should have hewed to the economic substance approach of earlier years.[72] This mistake took on even greater significance in 2010, when Congress codified the economic substance doctrine as a candid statutory GAAR.[73]

[66] Kelsen, n. 18, 195–278 and *passim*.

[67] The Grundnorm, translated in *Pure Theory of Law* as the 'basic norm', is a norm presumed by the pure theory of law as the ultimate authority for the norms of a legal system. Kelsen, n. 18, 4–10, 193, and *passim*.

[68] Hans Kelsen, *What is Justice*? (Berkeley: University of California Press, 1957), 219. See also M.P. Golding, 'Kelsen and the Concept of "Legal System"', in Robert S. Summers (ed.), *More Essays in Legal Philosophy* (Oxford: Basil Blackwell, 1971), 69, 77.

[69] See generally, Geraldine Hikaka and John Prebble, 'Autopoiesis and General Anti-Avoidance Rules', 21 *Critical Perspectives on Accounting* (Symposium Issue: Critical Perspectives on Taxation) (2010) 545–59.

[70] Ibid.

[71] For example, Philip Postlewaite, 'United States: the Judicial Sham Doctrine', in Zoe Prebble and John Prebble (eds), 'Comparing the General Anti-Avoidance Rule of Income Tax Law with the Civil Law Doctrine of Abuse of Law', *Bulletin for International Taxation* [2008] 151, 165, §9.3 ff. A notable example is *Compaq Computer Corp v Commissioner*, 277 F.3d 778 (5th Cir. 2001), discussed in that work.

[72] Described in Postlewaite, above n. 71, 165.

[73] See Section VIII, 'Principles of Economic Substance', in this chapter.

Secondly, does the failure of the pure theory to account for GAARs shed any light on Kelsen's change of mind late in his career on the principle of non-contradiction when applied to norms? The following section addresses that question.

XI. Validity of Conflicting Norms

From the 1960s, Kelsen took a different view on the application of the principle of non-contradiction to conflicts between norms. His last word on the subject was in *General Theory of Norms*, which appeared in 1991, eighteen years after his death. In that book, Kelsen wrote:[74]

> As far as conflicts between general norms are concerned, it is not the case–as I claimed in my *Pure Theory of Law*–that a conflict of norms which cannot be resolved by the principle *lex posterior derogate legi priori* makes no sense and that both norms are therefore invalid. Each of the two general norms makes sense and both are valid.

This new and opposite approach attracted criticism.[75] In favour of Kelsen's later opinion is that, broadly speaking, according to the pure theory of law the validity of a norm depends not on its content but on whether it is authorized by a norm that is superior in the hierarchy to which it belongs.[76] Against that approach is the consideration that even if two norms are properly authorized, together they make no sense if they contradict each other.

This chapter is not the place to resolve that conflict. But what can be said is that the case of a GAAR and a conflicting charging provision may be advanced as an example of two norms that are both undeniably valid but that conflict with one another. That is, the norms conflict with one another in the sense that to resolve the conflict we must go outside the law and resort to considerations of economic substance and possibly of morality, as explained in Section X of this chapter. Would Kelsen have taken comfort from this example? It is hard to say. As explained in footnote 41 of this chapter, Kelsen gave very little attention to tax law[77] and it seems unlikely that he ever turned his mind to, or even heard of, a general anti-avoidance rule. The best that we can say is that as a true scholar Kelsen would have been glad to encounter a legal norm of a kind that he had not previously met. But would his pleasure have been alloyed when he appreciated that it is in the core nature of GAARs that their conflict with charging provisions of taxation law is in the end resolved by resort to the extra-legal principles of economic substance and even of morality?[78] From this perspective, one is almost relieved on Kelsen's behalf that he never knowingly encountered a GAAR, a species of law that calls into question two fundamental foundations of the pure theory.

[74] Hans Kelsen, *General Theory of Norms*, M. Hartney (trans.) (Oxford: Oxford University Press, 1991), 214, discussed in Neil Duxbury, 'The Basic Norm: An Unsolved Murder Mystery', LSE Law, Society and Economy Working Papers 17/2007, http://eprints.lse.ac.uk/24614/, 2.

[75] For example, J. Raz, 'Critical Study: Kelsen's General Theory of Norms', 6 *Philosophia* (1976) 495.

[76] For example, Kelsen, n. 18, 193 ff.

[77] There is an isolated example of Kelsen's thoughts on taxation in H.L.A. Hart, 'Kelsen Visited', 10 *UCLA Law Review* (1963) 709, 717–22.

[78] Sections VIII and IX above.

XII. Conclusion

On the face of it, the implications of these considerations are of no more than scholarly interest. But there is in fact more. These implications are important to the modern world. The author has argued elsewhere that although GAARs are odd as a form of law, and that although GAARs appear to breach a number of the requirements that we generally insist on as criteria of good law, GAARs are at worst a necessary evil, necessary to counteract the shortcomings that are inherent in income tax law. The modern state relies a good deal on income tax law and cannot afford the luxury of permitting taxpayers to avoid paying their share by exploiting income tax law's inherent weaknesses.[79]

[79] See e.g. the papers cited above at note 14, and see generally John Prebble, 'Ectopia, Formalism, and Anti-Avoidance Rules in Income Tax Law', in W. Krawietz, N. MacCormick, and G.H. von Wright (eds), *Prescriptive Formality and Normative Rationality in Modern Legal Systems, Festschrift for Robert S. Summers* (Berlin: Duncker and Humblot, 1994), 367–83; John Prebble, 'Philosophical and Design Problems That Arise from the Ectopic Nature of Income Tax Law and Their Impact on the Taxation of International Trade and Investment', 13 *Chinese Yearbook of International Law and Affairs* (1995) 111–39, reprinted as John Prebble, 'Ectopia, Tax Law, and International Taxation', *British Tax Review* [1997] 383; John Prebble, 'Can Income Tax Law Be Simplified?', 2 *New Zealand Journal of Taxation Law and Policy* (1996) 187; John Prebble, 'Should Tax Legislation Be Written from a Principles and Purpose Point of View of a Precise and Detailed Point of View?', *British Tax Review* [1998] 112; see also John Prebble, 'Why Is Tax Law Incomprehensible?', *British Tax Review* [1994] 380–93.

PART II

DESIGN AND MECHANICS OF THE TAX SYSTEM

GENERAL PRINCIPLES

5

Michael Oakeshott and the Conservative Disposition in Tax Law

*Dominic de Cogan**

I. Introduction

It is commonplace to claim that one's tax system is excessively complex and incoherent, but in the United Kingdom we seem to have more justification than most.[1] Work performed by the Office of Tax Simplification (OTS) between 2010 and 2013 revealed that we have 6,102 pages of primary tax legislation, 1,042 reliefs and allowances, and 639 numerical thresholds for the imposition of particular types of tax treatment.[2] This sense of overwhelming detail is reinforced by subtler indications of complexity such as the proliferation of definitions in tax legislation,[3] and of course this is before we even get to the content of the law or its administration.

The obvious response to this predicament is to argue that 'something must be done' and in particular that tax law ought to be reformed so that it is simpler and more coherent. Unfortunately, this has been said for many years[4] but remains to be fulfilled. The enormous intellectual influence of the most ambitious reviews of taxation, the Income Tax Codification Committee report of 1936[5] and the Meade Report of 1978,[6] has not translated into direct impact upon practical law reform, and a similar

* Thanks to Graham Gee for introducing me to Oakeshott; to the Leverhulme Trust and Birmingham Law School for support during the early stages of this work; to Sean Coyle, David Feldman, John Snape, Caroline Turnbull-Hall, and John Whiting for invaluable comments on earlier drafts; and to the participants in the UCL conference 'Philosophical Foundations of Tax Law' for a fascinating discussion. The opinions expressed in this chapter are nevertheless those of the author, as are any remaining inaccuracies.

[1] P. Harris, 'A 200-page Income Tax Constitution for the UK?', Centre for Tax Law Conference, 'Celebrating the End of the Rewrite', London, October 2010, http://resources.law.cam.ac.uk/ctl/A%20200-page%20Income%20Tax%20Constitution%20for%20the%20UK.doc (accessed 29 June 2016).

[2] See generally Office of Tax Simplification, 'Tax Complexity', https://www.gov.uk/government/collections/tax-complexity (accessed 18 June 2016).

[3] Office of Tax Simplification, 'Review of Definitions in Tax Legislation', September 2013, https://www.gov.uk/government/publications/definitions-in-tax-legislation-and-their-contribution-to-complexity (accessed 18 June 2016).

[4] See for example the comments in the draft report of Mr Lowe in the *Report from the Select Committee on Income and Property Tax*, 1861 (C 503), xxiv; for further discussion of this speech, see Edwin R.A. Seligman, *The Income Tax: A Study of the History, Theory and Practice of Income Taxation at Home and Abroad* (New York: Macmillan, 1911), 162.

[5] See Income Tax Codification Committee, Report, Vol. I, 1935–6 (Cmd. 5131), discussed in John Pearce, 'The Income Tax Law Rewrite Projects: 1907–56', in John Tiley (ed.), *Studies in the History of Tax Law*, vol. 6 (Oxford: Hart, 2013).

[6] J.E. Meade and Institute for Fiscal Studies, *The Structure and Reform of Direct Taxation* (London: Allen & Unwin, 1978).

Philosophical Foundations of Tax Law. First Edition. Edited by Monica Bhandari.

fate seems likely to await the Mirrlees Review volumes of 2010 and 2011.[7] In contrast to the effective mothballing of these rational and internally consistent proposals, much more profound practical changes have proceeded from the sprawling and multi-faceted Royal Commission reports of 1920[8] and 1953–5,[9] as well as the more limited but critically important Departmental and Select Committee reports of 1905 and 1906.[10] Even in these instances the process of implementation took place incompletely and over many years, and represented not a radical rationalization of the law but rather 'a new patchwork taking the place of an old one'.[11] It is also noteworthy that the Royal Commissions enjoyed significant buy-in from the government and revenue authorities.[12] In broad terms, it seems that tax reform proposals have been more successful in prompting practical change where their recommendations are resilient to piecemeal acceptance and are capable of implementation in the particular time and place of publication.

There has been no Royal Commission relating exclusively to tax since 1955,[13] and it is noteworthy that the most substantial reform endeavour in recent years has been the Tax Law Rewrite Project. The ambitions of this initiative were much more limited and consisted of the reworking of existing tax legislation into more readily comprehensible language, with changes to the substantive law ruled out of scope except in some insignificant respects. An Office of Tax Simplification ('OTS') was established in 2010 as an independent[14] office of HM Treasury, with a remit to study specified areas of taxation law and to make recommendations to the government. This represents a very tentative step back towards the tradition of the Royal Commissions[15] in the sense of institutionalizing research into practicable tax reform; evidently, the OTS operates on a much smaller scale in terms of personnel, funding, and scope.

[7] James A. Mirrlees and IFS, *Dimensions of Tax Design: The Mirrlees Review* (Oxford: Oxford University Press, 2010); James A. Mirrlees and IFS, *Tax by Design; The Mirrlees Review* (Oxford: Oxford University Press, 2011).

[8] *Report of the Royal Commission on the Income Tax*, 1920 (Cmd. 618). It is instructive to read at p. 2 that 'complexity … must inevitably be present in any system devised for the purpose of dealing effectively with an almost infinite variety of taxable capacity on the part of individual taxpayers, a variety which is sure to be found in any modern commercial and industrial community.'

[9] See *Royal Commission on the Taxation of Profits and Income, Final Report*, 1955–6 (Cmd. 9474), including the memorandum of dissent by Nicholas Kaldor and others.

[10] *Report of the Departmental Committee on Income Tax*, 1905 (Cd. 2575); *Report from the Select Committee on Income Tax*, 1906 (Cd. 365).

[11] Élie Halévy, 'Before 1835', in Harold Laski, Ivor Jennings, and William Robson (eds), *A Century of Municipal Progress: 1835–1935* (London: Allen & Unwin, 1935), 35, cited in Martin Loughlin, *Legality and Locality* (Oxford: Clarendon, 1996), 36.

[12] For example, the 1920 report lists amongst its contributors not only Arthur Cecil Pigou, Professor of Political Economy at Cambridge, but also Josiah Stamp, Assistant Secretary to the Board of Inland Revenue and perhaps the most famous tax administrator in British history; see further John Harry Jones, *Josiah Stamp, Public Servant* (London: Isaac Pitman, 1964).

[13] Taxation has, of course, been discussed in the course of Royal Commissions dealing primarily with other subjects; see, for example *Royal Commission on Local Government in England*, 1968–9 (Cmnd. 4040), 131.

[14] *Office of Tax Simplification Framework Document*, July 2010, https://www.gov.uk/government/uploads/system/uploads/attachment_data/file/193545/ots_framework_document_jul10.pdf (accessed 21 June 2016). Note that this document has since been superseded.

[15] The possibility of a return to this tradition of Royal Commissions was prompted by a conversation with Professor Peter Harris and Dr Alexis Brassey.

The next question is why the UK tax system has reached such a state of complexity and incoherence, and why theoretically informed reform proposals have done so little to alter this position. This is too broad a question to be addressed in a single chapter, but the word 'conservatism' captures the spirit of a number of the conventional explanations. The first of these is the simple observation that the experience of revolutionary political change is more distant in the United Kingdom than in most other jurisdictions, which has contributed to a tendency to amend old forms rather than starting anew. A variation on this argument is that the basic structure of the UK income tax was determined in the early nineteenth century, long before most other jurisdictions.[16] As with British industry,[17] this resulted in a 'first-mover' disadvantage whereby certain structural features became entrenched that later proved to be inconvenient.[18] A third explanation is that control over tax policy has become concentrated in the executive,[19] despite a history of independent local administration and of conflicts relating to the Parliamentary control of taxation.[20] This has sustained a suspicion that central government tends to stifle innovation, instead domesticating pressures for change into forms that are readily practicable within existing structures.[21] Any prospect that the consolidation of tax policy functions into HM Treasury following the O'Donnell Review of 2004[22] might have made the policy-making process more permeable to radical ideas from outside government seems to have been disappointed.[23] Fourthly, it is possible that elements of shared background[24] or at least

[16] The modern UK income tax is usually said to derive from the Income and Property Taxes Act 1803, despite some important earlier developments and a hiatus from 1816 to 1842.

[17] See, for example, Donard de Cogan and Trevor Baldwin, 'Innovazione technologica e stagnazione finanziaria. Lo sviluppo della telegrafia internazionale tra il 1866 il 1900', *Memoria e Ricerca* 5 [2000] 25–43.

[18] One example is the non-taxation of capital gains and the non-deductibility of capital expenses, which had to be worked around in various ways: see Dominic de Cogan, 'Purposive Interpretation in the Age of Horse Trams', *British Tax Review* [2015] 80–92. Another example is the emergence of modern corporate taxation (1803) before modern corporate law (1844): see John Avery Jones, 'Defining and Taxing Companies 1799 to 1965', in John Tiley (ed.), *Studies in the History of Tax Law*, vol. 5 (Oxford: Hart, 2012).

[19] James Alt, Ian Preston, and Luke Sibieta, 'The Political Economy of Tax Policy', in IFS, n. 7, 1210.

[20] See generally Chantal Stebbings, *The Victorian Taxpayer and the Law* (Cambridge, UK: Cambridge University Press, 2009). Even 'local' taxes such as rates have been subject to similar pressures: see Loughlin, n. 11, 94.

[21] See generally Richard Rose and Terence Karran, *Taxation by Political Inertia: Financing the Growth of Government in Britain* (London: Allen & Unwin, 1987).

[22] HM Treasury and Gus O'Donnell, *Financing Britain's Future: Review of the Revenue Departments*, March 2004, http://webarchive.nationalarchives.gov.uk/+/http:/www.hm-treasury.gov.uk/media/FBAA7/odonnell_fore_ch1_245.pdf. In broad terms this led to the amalgamation into a single department of direct and indirect taxes formerly under the purview of the Inland Revenue and Customs & Excise respectively. It also resulted in a shift of tax policy capability from the revenue departments to HM Treasury.

[23] See generally Christopher J. Wales, 'The Implications of the O'Donnell Review for the Making of Tax Policy in the UK', *British Tax Review* [2004] 543–65, 543; Christopher J. Wales, 'The Making of Tax Policy in the Post-O'Donnell World: Can the HMT-HMRC "Policy Partnership" Meet the Challenge?', *British Tax Review* [2009] 245–9. Equally, it is widely accepted that the formalization of consultation arrangements has improved the detailed implementation of policy: see HM Treasury and HM Revenue and Customs, *Tax Policy Making: A New Approach* (London: HM Treasury, 2010); Tony Prosser, *The Economic Constitution* (Oxford: Oxford University Press, 2014), 98.

[24] For a recent commentary on social background in the law, see Michael Blackwell, 'Old Boys' Networks, Family Connections and the English Legal Profession', *Public Law* 3 [2012] 426–44.

shared professional language[25] within the relatively small tax policy community tend to encourage the pursuit of desired policy outcomes through the incremental modification of existing concepts rather than through sudden structural change.

Whatever our explanation, it is clear that there is a strong tendency within UK tax policy that may fairly be described as 'conservatism'. This chapter aims to understand this tendency more fully, its refusal to disappear, and its place within the tax legal system, as well as to start a conversation on how meaningful tax reform might be achieved by 'working with the grain' of conservatism instead of wishing that it did not exist. There are many ways in which these questions might be addressed; the approach of the present chapter is to explore the work of one of the pre-eminent theorists of British conservatism, Michael Oakeshott. What is particularly striking about Oakeshott's writing is that he raises deceptively simple questions about law and politics but then proceeds to address them not by recourse to a simple answer, but instead by exposing the underlying tensions that are involved. The most famous example of this is the distinction that he draws between civil association and enterprise association,[26] but this chapter also focuses on a similar although less fully explored tension between conservatism and the attainment of a body of rules that corresponds to the rule of law.[27] In the present context, the question is how conservatism might influence our ability to reform tax rules so that they correspond more fully to the rule of law.

The sense that the work of Oakeshott might help us to understand the role of conservatism in tax law is reinforced by the volume and lucidity of his writing on the nature of law, conservatism, the importance of tradition, and indeed the role of taxation in political history. This said, his views on law cannot be said to fall effortlessly into place.[28] In his introductory essay to *Leviathan*, Oakeshott observes that 'any account worth giving' of Thomas Hobbes's book 'must be an interpretation' and is 'not a substitute for the text'.[29] The same is eminently the case for Oakeshott's own work, and in particular it seems fruitful to look not only for logical consistency in his writing but also for what might be termed temperamental continuities. This approach draws support from Oakeshott's frequent reference to 'disposition',[30] in the sense of *how* one goes about things as opposed to *what* one thinks. It may also be particularly relevant to those instances in which he appears to express a concrete preference for ideas that he has previously sought to isolate from practical concerns.

This point highlights a further challenge with the present endeavour, which is that ideally the notion of small 'c' conservatism would be isolated from the UK

[25] Dominic de Cogan, 'A Changing Role for the Administrative Law of Taxation', 24(2) *Social & Legal Studies* (2015) 251–70.

[26] In broad terms, this is a distinction between individualist and collectivist conceptions of political society, but see further discussion at n. 48.

[27] This tension is discussed in Steven Gerencser, 'Oakeshott on Law', in Paul Franco and Leslie Marsh (eds), *A Companion to Michael Oakeshott* (University Park, PA: Pennsylvania State University Press, 2012), 313–14.

[28] Gerencser, n. 27, 313.

[29] Michael Oakeshott, 'Introduction to *Leviathan*', in *Rationalism in Politics* (Indianapolis: Liberty Fund, 1991), 248.

[30] Michael Oakeshott, 'On Being Conservative', in n. 29, 407.

Conservative Party and also from the particular political preferences of author and reader. This is certainly one of the ambitions of the present chapter. However, it is instructive that Michael Oakeshott himself evidently found these boundaries difficult to sustain,[31] which serves as a warning that the role of conservatism may be incapable of discussion in a manner that is politically neutral in every respect.[32]

The remainder of this chapter concentrates on a single problem that has already been stated, but which brings into focus the questions raised throughout this Introduction. This is how Michael Oakeshott's theory of the rule of law as a coherent system of rules conforming to certain formal requirements might behave in a context where a conservative approach to legal change is considered inevitable or even desirable. Oakeshott addressed this matter rather obliquely; he also varied widely in his response, from qualified support of Jeremy Bentham's radical programme of legislative reform,[33] to strikingly extreme expressions of gradualism,[34] to the presentation of the rule of law as an intellectual construct rather than a direct commentary on concrete arrangements.[35] Nevertheless, it is possible to tease out the idea that the rule of law is indeed a worthwhile guide to practical reform, but is incapable of being implemented in a pure form.[36] If this interpretation of Oakeshott's thought is supportable, it demonstrates clear parallels with the relative successes of the Royal Commissions—and to a lesser extent the Office of Tax Simplification—in achieving concrete changes to the tax system.

The argument is expounded in three stages. First, Michael Oakeshott's conception of the rule of law is expounded and then imagined in the context of UK taxation. Second, his ideas relating to tradition and conservatism are explored, together with the challenges that they raise for the practical achievement of a tax system corresponding to the rule of law. The chapter concludes with some thoughts on how high ambitions for tax reform can be reconciled with a greater degree of concrete action.

[31] See Andrew Gamble, 'Oakeshott's Ideological Politics: Conservative or Liberal', in Efraim Podoksik (ed.), *The Cambridge Companion to Oakeshott* (Cambridge, UK: Cambridge University Press, 2012), 153–77; Jesse Norman, 'Michael Oakeshott, Conservative Thinker Who Went Beyond Politics', *New Statesman*, 17 April 2014, http://www.newstatesman.com/politics/2014/04/michael-oakeshott-conservative-thinker-who-went-beyond-politics. For a (much) more critical perspective, see Perry Anderson, 'The Intransigent Right at the End of the Century', 14(18) *London Review of Books* (1992) 7–11, discussed in Duncan Kelly, 'Reconfiguring Reason of State in Response to Political Crisis', in David Dyzenhaus and Tom Poole (eds), *Law, Liberty and State: Oakeshott, Hayek and Schmitt on the Rule of Law* (Cambridge: Cambridge University Press, 2015), 188.

[32] This is a more general problem; even matters of detail may be difficult to separate entirely from political ideology: see generally John Snape, *The Political Economy of Corporation Tax* (Oxford: Hart, 2011).

[33] Oakeshott, n. 29, 133, 141.

[34] Refer to text at n. 154.

[35] As Poole puts it, 'a world of pure *lex* seems more like a theoretical postulate, a kind of philosophical glass bead game, than a remotely viable constitutional idea': see Tom Poole, 'The Mystery of Lawlessness: War, Law and the Modern State', in Dyzenhaus and Poole (eds), n. 31, 180. Oakeshott himself acknowledges that the way in which he conceptualizes the mode of political association that supports the rule of law (civil association or *societas*) is an abstraction from rather than a simple description of political history: Michael Oakeshott, *On Human Conduct* (Oxford: Clarendon, 1975), 200–1.

[36] Refer to text at nn 82, 136.

II. The Rule of Law

Michael Oakeshott's conception of the rule of law could be summarized in terms that would differ little from more familiar accounts such as that of Lon Fuller.[37] More significant is the route by which he arrives at this understanding, and in particular the background political and legal theory within which he situates the rule of law. This necessitates a brief excursus into his explanation of where law comes from, what it should be used for, and its relationship with a particular mode of political association that he terms 'civil association' or *societas*, before we proceed to the particular question of taxation under the rule of law. Oakeshott's ideas on these matters are deeply interconnected, and should accordingly become clearer as the following paragraphs progress.

A. The Source of Law

Oakeshott's account of the source of law is similar, although not identical, to that of Thomas Hobbes. Hobbesian sovereignty is premised on the consent of the governed; the authority of a civil association for Oakeshott depends on the acknowledgment by those subject to it that it is authoritative. This may in turn rest more on historical contingency than on any more conscious form of agreement.[38] In keeping with Hobbes, Oakeshott's account of the source of law is highly centralized. The 'maker and custodian of the law' is a 'legislative office … following a recognized procedure'.[39] This is most obvious in respect of primary legislation but also holds for other types of law. Accordingly, the force of a customary or common law rule 'cannot lie in its antiquity … its traditional acceptance or in the recognition of the desirability of what it prescribes; its authenticity derives from a presumption, namely, that it cannot resist appropriation, rejection, or emendation in a legislative enactment'.[40]

The role of the courts is correspondingly rather circumscribed, the task of a judge being 'to relate a general statement of conditional obligation to an occurrence' not to 'regard itself as the custodian of a public policy or interest in favour of which … to resolve the disputed obligation'.[41] This leaves Oakeshott decidedly lukewarm on the development of legal principle through the common law:[42] 'although it may belong to the procedure of … a court to take account of decisions in earlier allegedly similar cases, it will not recognize them as precedents to be followed: its concern will be with the analogical force of the distinctions they invoked.'[43]

[37] Refer to text at n. 60.

[38] See Oakeshott, n. 35, 149–54; Nehal Bhuta, 'The Mystery of the State', in Dyzenhaus and Poole (eds), n. 31, 19–22.

[39] Michael Oakeshott (ed.), 'The Rule of Law', in *On History and Other Essays* (Indianapolis: Liberty Fund, 1999), 150.

[40] Ibid., 151. [41] Ibid., 158.

[42] Compare Friedrich Hayek, *Law, Legislation and Liberty*, vol. 1 (London: Routledge, 1973), ch. 5; Edwin Simpson, 'The *Ramsay* Principle: A Curious Incident of Judicial Reticence?', *British Tax Review* [2004] 358–74; Prosser, n. 23, 103.

[43] Oakeshott, n. 39, 159. Oakeshott states further that judicial reasoning might have the effect of contracting or expanding 'the range of meaning the rule will tolerate' and in this sense influence subsequent decisions: see Oakeshott, n. 35, 136.

Thus far the legal force of a rule does not depend on any deliberation of its quality, but simply on the authorship or custodianship of the legislative office in the context of procedures that demonstrate that it is a legal rule.[44] Without more, we might classify Oakeshott's theory as a fairly unremarkable exercise in mid-twentieth-century positivism, albeit with a different focus from Hart's rule of recognition.[45] Nevertheless, we might already find much to welcome from a UK tax perspective. The deeply ingrained tradition of demanding the assent of the House of Commons to the imposition of tax burdens finds a close parallel in Oakeshott's formal theory of source. Admittedly there is little explicit support in Oakeshott for interpretative literalism of the type that once dominated the judicial approach to taxing statutes,[46] but his hesitance on common law development is much closer to the dominant position in taxation than in many other fields of law.[47] The idea that tax law has force primarily because the 'legislative office' says so is hardly controversial, however much we might quibble about other matters such as the composition and procedures of that office.

B. The Use of Law; Civil Association

It is when we examine how law is used that the consequences of the analysis in terms of civil association become clearer. As for Hobbes, legal rules do not lose authority simply because they are applied to purposes of which we disapprove. Yet civil association denotes much more than following prescribed legislative procedures. It is, rather, a way of relating to other people which is distinguished by those procedures but also by the absence of any common substantive purpose.[48] More broadly, it reflects a characteristically conservative preoccupation with 'the existence of protected domains in which a person remains free from the will of others'.[49] In 'The Rule of Law' Oakeshott begins the explanation by referring to the rules of a game such as cricket. The player will certainly wish to win, but it would be a misunderstanding to conceive of the rules

[44] This procedural aspect helps Oakeshott to separate the rule of law in a civil association from other types of noninstrumental 'moral associations': see Oakeshott, n. 35, 161, discussed in Paul Franco, *Michael Oakeshott: An Introduction* (New Haven: Yale University Press, 2004), 159. The self-reinforcing character of Oakeshottian law is discussed at greater length in Gerencser, n. 27.

[45] For Oakeshott, rules can certainly specify the conditions whereby other rules will be recognized. The ultimate authority, however, is that of the civil association itself rather than 'a single ultimate rule of recognition, an unconditional and unquestionable norm from which all others derive their authority': Oakeshott, n. 35, 151.

[46] That is because the judicial task is to relate general rules to particular facts, which does not postulate literal interpretation. For the old position in UK taxation law, see *Partington v Attorney General* (1869–70) LR 4 HL 100 and the critical discussion thereof in Hubert Monroe, *Intolerable Inquisition? Reflections on the Law of Tax* (London: Stevens, 1981).

[47] Of the two most striking examples of judge-made tax law in the UK, the recognition of accounting principles in cases such as *Odeon Associated Theatres v Jones* [1971] 2 All ER 407 has been incorporated into various statutory provisions, whereas the anti-avoidance doctrines developed in *Ramsay v IRC* [1982] AC 300 and subsequent cases have now been recharacterized as the application of orthodox principles of statutory interpretation: see *Barclays Mercantile v Mawson* [2004] UKHL 51; [2005] 1 AC 684.

[48] The reference to interpersonal relations here is deliberate. Oakeshott believes that the mode of association reflects the temperament of its members, with civil association suiting a character that could crudely be described as 'individualistic': see Oakeshott, n. 35, 236–7.

[49] Sean Coyle, *Dimensions of Politics and English Jurisprudence* (Cambridge, UK: Cambridge University Press, 2013), 102.

as 'guides to the effective use of power' or as awarding 'advantages or disadvantages to the competitors'.[50] Rather they are conditions to be observed by all players regardless of outcome: 'Subscription to these rules is not itself a possible substantive action; it is the observance of adverbial qualifications imposed upon … actions'. These 'non-instrumental' rules 'exist and are known in advance of any occasion of play and they subsist independently of any such occasion'.[51]

The discussion of games conveys the important idea that some activities are worth pursuing regardless of outcome, although doubtless it is also pleasant to win games.[52] However, this is only a starting point and the rules of a civil association 'are not the rules of a game the jurisdiction of which is settled in terms of an engagement (like a cricket match) which itself constitutes a relationship'.[53] They certainly seek to influence how we do things but do not presuppose that we shall do anything in particular. More importantly, they do not express loyalty to a commonly held purpose such as one might discern in 'an army, a "village community", a sect, a fellowship, a party, a fraternity, a sodality, a *collegium* or a guild'.[54] To this list Oakeshott adds the obvious example of a corporation and, somewhat less obviously, 'a productive undertaking (a bassoon factory)'. These cases of 'enterprise association' are 'chosen' relationships 'from which an agent may extricate himself by a choice of his own',[55] but of course a state operated on a similar basis would have much more coercive implications.

The notions of civil and enterprise association 'are ideal characters'[56] by which Oakeshott seeks to isolate and explain certain conflicting tendencies in European political history, and accordingly we should not expect either to be visible in pure form amongst existing jurisdictions.[57] Yet the discussion of associations certainly influences our conception of a legal system, to the extent that it is not too misleading to describe Oakeshott's version of the rule of law as a working through of the implications of civil association. Might it follow, then, that rules applied contrarily to Oakeshott's understanding of civil association are not law (or '*lex*') in the full sense? On the whole Oakeshott steers away from this conclusion,[58] but there is an exception. If a rule is not merely objectionable in content but cannot even logically operate as an adverbial condition of human action—for example if it is secret, retrospective, or contemplates outlawry—then it cannot be '*lex*' as understood within the context of a civil association.[59]

[50] Oakeshott, n. 39, 137. [51] Oakeshott, n. 39, 137.

[52] The theme of 'stochastic rationality' running through much of Oakeshott's work is explained in Erika Kiss, 'The Rules of the Game', in Dyzenhaus and Poole (eds), n. 31, 214–33. As Kiss explains (at 224–9), noninstrumentality assures success in the sense of playing for the sake of it, which is of the essence, but also offers a chance of success in the sense of winning the game, which is a by-product.

[53] Oakeshott, n. 35, 128.

[54] Ibid., 114. Note that this lends a certain stability to civil association in that one may disapprove of the purposes pursued by others without questioning the authority of the association itself.

[55] Ibid., 114. [56] Ibid., 109.

[57] This point is reinforced throughout the third essay of *On Human Conduct* (n. 35).

[58] Yet there remains a sense in which the coexistence of civil and enterprise association within modern European states might force us to accept (potentially significant) limitations on Oakeshott's rule of law.

[59] Oakeshott, n. 39, 152–3; Oakeshott, n. 35, 153; see also Thomas Hobbes, *Leviathan*, C.B. Macpherson (ed.) (Harmondsworth: Penguin, 1968), 339 (Part 2, ch. 27, 'Of Crimes, Excuses, and Extenuations').

The proximity to Lon Fuller's account of the rule of law is evident, although Covell argues that, 'Oakeshott did not go on to draw the conclusion that attention to the logic of judicial deliberation called into question the dualism of law and society presupposed in the model of law which the legal positivists inherited from Hobbes.'[60] What Oakeshott does concede is that his account of the rule of law is compatible with the evaluation of validly promulgated *lex* in terms of justice and injustice (*jus* and *injus*). This type of deliberation cannot prevent *lex* from having formal authority, nor does it encompass every form of possible criticism,[61] but it does involve 'the negative and limited consideration that the prescriptions of the law should not conflict with a prevailing educated moral sensibility capable of distinguishing between the conditions of ' "virtue," ... "good conduct" ... and those which are of such a kind that they should be imposed by law ("justice")'.[62]

This is significant because it leads our attention to the awkward question of whether civil association (and hence the rule of law) is something more than a radical abstraction 'from the contingency and ambiguity of historical reality'[63] and indeed something to which we should aspire in our practical arrangements. On the one hand this step is discouraged by Oakeshott himself,[64] sometimes in rather strong terms. On the other hand, Oakeshott's own educated moral sensibility evidently smarts at the use of law to coerce individuals into state-sanctioned ends, not least in the rather extreme expression of the article 'The Tower of Babel' that follows 'The Rule of Law' in the collection *On History*.[65] Boucher remarks that Oakeshott did offer prescriptions, despite his protestations to the contrary, at least 'in so far as he is questioning the desirability not of any particular law but of all laws that are instrumental'.[66] The point is given greater force by Oakeshott's observation in *On Human Conduct* that the history of European states disclosed 'an unresolved tension between two irreconcilable dispositions' corresponding to civil and enterprise associations.[67] One or other disposition might be prioritized within the context of a particular state, with Oakeshott's own

[60] Charles Covell, *The Defence of Natural Law: A Study of the Ideas of Law and Justice in the Writings of Lon L. Fuller, Michael Oakeshott, F.A. Hayek, Ronald Dworkin, and John Finnis* (Basingstoke: Macmillan, 1992), 84–5. This perhaps understates the extent to which Oakeshott regards the rule of law as dependent on political association and in turn on the character of the members of that association. For example, he stresses that 'the emergent states of modern Europe ... were not manifestly the stuff of which *universitates* [i.e. enterprise associations] are easily composed', partly on account of their religious diversity: Oakeshott, n. 35, 234.

[61] Oakeshott, n. 39, 153.

[62] Ibid., 174. This is a famously vague formulation, but seems consistent with the disinclination to perfectionism that Oakeshott exhibits elsewhere: see further n. 65.

[63] Franco, n. 44, 181. [64] See Michael Oakeshott, 'Political Education', in n. 29, 65–6.

[65] Michael Oakeshott, 'The Tower of Babel', in n. 39. To summarize brutally, the entire resources of a fictional community are dedicated to the single project of building a tower. This breeds enthusiasm but also increasing material hardship and personal resentment, and culminates in the collapse of the tower and the death of every single inhabitant.

[66] David Boucher, 'Schmitt, Oakeshott and the Hobbesian Legacy in the Crisis of Our Times', in Dyzenhaus and Poole (eds), n. 31, 145–6.

[67] Oakeshott, n. 35, 200–1. Characteristically Oakeshott proliferates terminology, with *societas* denoting civil association and *universitas* enterprise association.

preference suggested by his comment on the rule of law that it 'remains the most civilized and least burdensome conception of a state yet to be devised'.[68]

It is therefore not unreasonable to consider whether civil association gives us an attractive account of taxation law. The secondary Oakeshottian problem of whether we should reform our existing arrangements in favour of such an account is postponed to further below.

C. The Rule of Tax Law

What sort of arrangements, then, might the rule of tax law imply? The first difficulty is that even a night-watchman state requires revenues, yet those liable for taxes tend to regard them as more than a merely adverbial constraint upon behaviour, but rather a substantive transfer of their property to the ruler.[69] As Oakeshott puts it, 'the belief ... that no man should be deprived without his consent of what was his own ... made taxation difficult to convert from a bargain to a legal obligation'.[70] From this perspective, the insistence in Article 4 of the Bill of Rights 1689 'That levying Money for or to the Use of the Crowne by pretence of Prerogative without Grant of Parlyament ... is Illegall' can be seen as a final recognition not only of constitutional taxation but of tax as authentically legal at all.[71]

Assuming that the expression of consent through the formal procedures of the legislative office allows tax to be regarded as *lex* despite the substantive element of providing money, the requirements of civil association might otherwise be applied in their full rigour. Tax rules would be expected to be noninstrumental in two senses. First, they would be 'neutral', neither encouraging nor discouraging particular substantive decisions on the part of taxpayers. As is well known to economists, this is likely to involve not only a desistance from 'sin taxes' but also the removal of both intended and unintended tax incentives. Second, the revenues would be applied to the very limited task of administering the civil association and nothing more. In particular, they would not be used to fund common benefits,[72] although of course there would be nothing to stop *cives* from contributing to enterprises of their own choosing. This very restrained understanding of a tax system would be reflected in law by rules of general application, and in the event of a dispute, the task of applying the general rules to the particular factual context would fall to the courts. This might involve a difficult exercise of reasoning but would not require the court to consider questions of *jus* and would not in itself create new law.[73]

The problem with this account is that taxation is one of the most important instruments of modern government; indeed, the emergence of efficient techniques of tax collection over a period of several centuries enabled the pursuit of 'public sector' activities of an ambition and scale that would previously have been unthinkable.[74]

[68] Oakeshott, n. 39, 178. Poole argues that a civil association unmixed with the characteristics of an enterprise association would be undesirable, but that we might still cherish the former tendency whilst regarding the latter as a necessary evil: Poole, n. 35, 178–82.

[69] Oakeshott, n. 35, 255, drawing on Bodin.

[70] Ibid., 211.

[71] Refer to Snape's contribution in the present volume.

[72] See Snape, n. 32, 41.

[73] Refer to text at nn 40–3.

[74] See Kelly, n. 31, 209.

This process, Oakeshott notes, was associated with a 'modification of the idea of taxation'[75] according to which the products of a modern European state were 'recognized as corporate income, and the manner in which it was to be shared among its members ... recognized as no less a corporate concern than the manner in which it was produced'.[76] Incidentally, this historical perspective brings a new complexion to the argument of Murphy and Nagel[77] (discussed in more depth elsewhere in this volume[78]) that property rights owe their existence to government and are therefore subsequent to the extraction of taxes by that government. Oakeshott acknowledges this line of argument[79] but inverts it by claiming that such all-encompassing conceptions of political association are only possible if efficient techniques of ruling already exist, including predictable tax collection.

Whilst some commentators have suggested that civil association might be consistent with at least some of the trappings of the modern welfare state,[80] the transformation of 'taxation ... into a means of acquiring direct control over a large part of "national income" to be expended in favoured projects or distributed in the form of "truck" '[81] is decidedly not what Oakeshott means by the rule of law. He acknowledges explicitly in *On Human Conduct*[82] that modern European states differ to a greater or lesser degree from the ideal of civil association, and this observation undoubtedly applies to taxation.

This divergence from undiluted civil association extends also to the detailed provisions of UK tax law. In many instances the law functions conspicuously poorly as an adverbial framework for taxpayer behaviour, either because it provides little instruction on matters of importance[83] or, conversely, because there is a profusion of rules without any obvious means of navigation. An example of the latter is the disorganized patchwork of statutory and common law rules relating to the taxation of employee benefits, which incidentally support a range of more or less trivial policy aims.[84] Added to this is a constant temptation on government to intervene in order to ensure 'correct' tax outcomes rather than waiting for disputes to be resolved formally

[75] Oakeshott, n. 35, 277.

[76] Ibid., 293, 301. Note in particular the reference to distributive justice on page 293.

[77] See generally Liam Murphy and Thomas Nagel, *The Myth of Ownership: Taxes and Justice* (Oxford: Oxford University Press, 2002).

[78] See J. Snape, 'The "Sinews of the State": Historical Justifications for Taxes and Tax Law'; and J. Stanton-Ife, 'Must We Pay for the British Museum? Taxation and the Harm Principle', in this volume.

[79] Although note that Murphy and Nagel's famous exposition of the argument was published almost three decades after *On Human Conduct* (n. 35).

[80] See David Dyzenhaus, 'Dreaming the Rule of Law', in Dyzenhaus and Poole (eds), n. 31, 258–9. Even those of us unpersuaded by this reading of civil association will notice that Oakeshott does not appear to fetishize private property to the extent of certain other conservative theorists. The institution of private property can certainly promote freedom, but Oakeshott's emphasis is not on protecting wealth as such but on preventing the concentration of power by 'government, great business and industrial corporations and by trade unions': see Michael Oakeshott, 'The Political Economy of Freedom', in n. 29, 393–4; Gamble, n. 31, 172.

[81] Oakeshott, n. 35, 301.

[82] See generally Oakeshott, n. 35, ch. 3.

[83] The legal framework relating to UK tax residence was, if not silent, noticeably quiet prior to the enactment of the Statutory Residence Test in the Finance Act 2013.

[84] The problems in this field of law have been surveyed in *Office of Tax Simplification*, 'Review of Employee Benefits and Expenses: Final Report', July 2014, https://www.gov.uk/government/uploads/system/uploads/attachment_data/file/339496/OTS_review_of_employee_benefits_and_expenses_final_report.pdf (accessed 18 April 2015).

through the courts.[85] As Snape observes, this may involve the widespread use of 'detailed non-statutory technical material',[86] not to mention forms of administrative coercion that seem quite out of harmony with the idea of a civil association.[87]

Leaving aside macro-political questions such as whether welfare state provision is justified in principle, is the rule of tax law within a civil association something to which we might aspire? Intuitively, there is much to welcome. Instead of the present mass of detailed statutory and subordinate rules, the proliferating and often unnecessary common pursuits, and the surprising paucity of guidance in certain areas, we could substitute a much simpler and more general framework of rules. Moreover, this would not need to be characterized as a trade-off between 'simplicity' and 'legal certainty'; for Oakeshott, uncertainty is an ineliminable feature of the application of general rules to particular facts.[88] An attempt to circumvent the problem by increasing the specificity of rules is at best a 'fruitless attempt to spell out what cannot be spelled out in advance of the event' and at worst an abandonment of general rules in favour of 'continuous managerial decisions'.[89] The latter is characteristic, not of the rule of law but of the managed pursuit of a purpose under an enterprise association.

The rule of tax law might therefore look something like the system proposed by Avery Jones,[90] at least to the extent that statutory detail would be reduced and the ensuing general rules applied by judges to concrete disputes. Yet there are limits on the extent to which uncertainty could be minimized by appealing to 'abstract principles corresponding to those found in the E.C. Treaty'.[91] With or without such a guide the court is faced with the same essential challenge of applying a general rule to a specific situation.

It might be objected that the function of noninstrumental rules in providing a framework, within which taxpayers can pursue their own self-chosen activities, sits uneasily with Oakeshott's preference that those rules be general in nature. Surely a certain degree of specificity is needed in order to help individuals plan their tax affairs with confidence, yet Oakeshott's theory gives no guidance on where the line should be drawn. Admittedly, Oakeshott lived and worked at a time when the volume of UK tax legislation was significantly smaller than at present. So it is a fair assumption that he would have been shocked by the level of detail in modern taxing statutes. In any case, the idea that detail is necessarily helpful to taxpayers is not itself without difficulty. As Hobbes said, 'The written Laws, if they be short, are easily misinterpreted, from the divers significations of a word, or two; if long, they be more obscure by the diverse significations of many words.'[92] Oakeshott's omission to specify what level of generality we should look for in *lex* is therefore conspicuous but hardly surprising.

[85] This may well be understandable given the characteristic delay of courts and the ingenuity of tax advisors. The point is that it is not the mark of a civil association as described by Oakeshott.

[86] Snape, n. 32, 41.

[87] A notorious recent example is the 'accelerated payment' regime under which taxpayers may be required to pay disputed tax liabilities upfront and then pursue repayment later: Finance Act 2014, Part 4, ch. 3.

[88] Oakeshott, n. 35, 135. [89] Ibid., 135.

[90] John Avery Jones, 'Tax Law: Rules or Principles', *British Tax Review* [1996] 580–600.

[91] Ibid., 593. [92] Hobbes, n. 59, 322 (Part 2, ch. 26, 'All Laws Need Interpretation').

highlights the difference by reference to cookery and fine arts.[97] A cookery book may be helpful but it does not displace the need for practical skill in cooking, any more than 'a high degree of technical knowledge, even where it is both subtle and ready' in itself provides 'the ability to create a work of art'.[98]

It is worth pausing to observe that a similar attitude towards tax law might place an unusually strong emphasis on the accumulated experience of officials, advisors, and taxpayers. It is also likely to discourage the search for an intellectually complete scheme of tax reform, the success of which would be judged according to its faithful implementation of technical knowledge.[99] Instead we might concentrate our efforts on developing a coherent account of how the various concrete arrangements of our tax system 'hang together as a whole but not as a logical system.'[100] Given that such an account is inextricable from the finer detail[101] it is not reasonable to expect that all of its elements would necessarily point in the same direction or even remain constant beyond a certain overall sense of continuity.[102]

This conception of a coherent system that is nevertheless not referable to a complete and deliberate intellectual plan is expressed by Oakeshott in the language of 'tradition' although, perhaps fittingly, not with total consistency.[103] It is important to note that political tradition suggests a more substantial range of activities than John Major's picturesque 'cricket and warm beer' stereotype but also something less overbearing than the modern notion that we should exhibit an appropriate degree of 'Britishness' in our individual lives.[104] What we are talking about here is not social homogeneity but a 'legally organized society and ... the manner in which its legal structure ... is reformed'.[105]

Consisting as it does of a complex patchwork of behaviours, a political tradition is not something that can be learned in a classroom or from a book:

> our political education ... begins in the enjoyment of a tradition, in the observation and imitation of the behaviour of our elders, and there is little or nothing in the world which comes before us as we open our eyes which does not contribute to it.[106]

As always Oakeshott's argument is attractive and lucid. However, we might be excused for wondering whether political tradition is valuable in its own right or merely

[97] Ibid., 11–17. [98] Ibid., 13.

[99] In particular, it would entail a 'rejection of the view that politics is a shadow thrown by economics' (Oakeshott, n. 30, 431), although not necessarily of the more moderate view that economics could be used as the starting point or even as an integral part of a sophisticated political analysis: see Snape, n. 32, 116–17.

[100] Stephen Smith, 'Practical Life and the Critique of Rationalism', in Podoksik (ed.), n. 31, 141. Note that this process is still very much 'rational' in normal usage, although not 'Rationalist' in the specific sense discussed in the text at n. 93.

[101] Oakeshott, n. 64, 55, 62. [102] Ibid., 62. [103] Franco, n. 44, 96–7.

[104] Franco points out that Oakeshott's substitution of 'practice' for 'tradition' in *On Human Conduct* 'avoids the misleading substantive and communitarian connotation in the latter' and 'brings out more explicitly than before the procedural and non-instrumental character which lay behind the notion of tradition in *Rationalism in Politics*.'; see Paul Franco, *The Political Philosophy of Michael Oakeshott* (New Haven: Yale University Press, 1990), 8. See also the discussion of Oakeshott's attitude towards social unity in Bhuta, n. 38, 16–17.

[105] Oakeshott, n. 64, 69. [106] Ibid., 62.

something of which we ought to be aware as a potential obstacle to beneficial change. After all, given the resemblance between civil association and Hobbesian sovereignty, it would be extremely surprising if Oakeshott's criticism of rationalism left no room for law reform. His somewhat grudging admission that 'The significance of Bentham as a reformer of the law … is immense'[107] would also caution against such a conclusion. Yet if Oakeshott disapproves of the unnecessary disturbance of traditions, as seems probable from the rather poetic tone of 'Political Education', this might suggest a much more restricted conception of legal change than is often advocated. Indeed, the prevalent view amongst tax policy specialists is that reform should be rather more ambitious and deliberate than it is at present. Is tradition so important that we should abandon any such aspirations?

D. A Conservative Temperament

One way of dealing with this is to accept that Oakeshott put forward a variety of complex arguments over a long career and could not be expected to achieve exact consistency, despite strong continuities throughout his *oeuvre*. This view might gain encouragement from the following comments concerning the ideology of the French Revolution:

> here … are disclosed, abstracted and abridged, the common law rights of Englishmen, the gift not of independent premeditation or divine munificence, but of centuries of the day-to-day attending to the arrangements of an historic society.[108]

We might conclude from this that common law precedent provides a neat way of developing law whilst respecting Oakeshottian tradition. The law would not be changed precipitately but grow[109] through a pursuit of the intimations of existing arrangements.[110] Yet this suggestion is difficult to reconcile with the function of the legislative and judicial offices under a civil association,[111] and with Oakeshott's restrictive attitude towards legal precedent.

Another option is to recall the distinction that Oakeshott draws between *lex* and *jus*.[112] It might be *injus* to impose new *lex* in a manner unnecessarily destructive of existing traditions or practices, but that would not in itself deprive the relevant rules of legal force. To provide an example from UK taxation, it might be thought *injus* to repeal the familiar retirement relief for capital gains tax and to replace it with a 'taper' relief devised on the back of an envelope and targeted at an array of common social ends.[113] Our evaluation of this rationalist scheme might be all the more critical given that it had to be abandoned after a decade and replaced with a close variant of the original retirement relief. Yet this unnecessary and disruptive interference with tax practice in no sense prevented taper relief from being *lex* during its formal period of operation.

[107] Oakeshott, n. 33, 150. [108] Oakeshott, n. 64, 53. [109] See Oakeshott, n. 30, 411.
[110] See Oakeshott, n. 64, 57. [111] See Gerencser, n. 27, 313. [112] Refer to text at nn 57–62.
[113] See Natalie Lee and Rupert Seal, 'Capital Gains Tax Relief on the Disposal of Business Assets: A Clear Strategy for Encouraging Entrepreneurs?', *Journal of Business Law* [2013] 723–46.

A sharper sense of the relationship between tradition and legal change is to be found in Oakeshott's account of conservatism.[114] Conservatism in this sense is not to be understood as a set of fixed beliefs but as a disposition.

> To be conservative ... is to prefer the familiar to the unknown, to prefer the tried to the untried, fact to mystery, the actual to the possible, the limited to the unbounded, the near to the distant, the sufficient to the superabundant, the convenient to the perfect, present laughter to utopian bliss. Familiar relationships and loyalties will be preferred to the allure of more profitable attachments; to acquire and to enlarge will be less important than to keep, to cultivate and to enjoy; the grief of loss will be more acute than the excitement of novelty or promise.[115]

A conservative disposition implies a certain ambivalence to change, which 'can be welcomed indiscriminately only by those who esteem nothing [and] whose attachments are fleeting'. By contrast, 'the inclination to enjoy what is present and available is the opposite of ignorance and apathy and it breeds attachment and affection'.[116] This is strong stuff, but a conservative cannot be expected to resist change altogether[117] (which is impossible) but to emphasize continuity and perhaps to presume against reform on the grounds that 'innovation entails certain loss and possible gain'.[118]

This understanding of conservatism is potentially just as inimical to attempts to 'roll back the frontiers of the state'[119] as to post–World War II collectivism. In turn this has led John Gray to argue that the cultural foundations of traditional conservatism have been destroyed by precisely the 'neoliberal' policies favoured by Margaret Thatcher and others.[120] Whether this argument has overall force is beyond the scope of the present chapter, except to note that even highly technical and recently invented activities are susceptible to a conservative disposition in the sense described by Oakeshott. The protocols of computer programmers may be no less traditional than the old-fashioned yet still tenacious practice of attending an Anglican church every Sunday.

In any case, Oakeshott recognizes that the conservative temperament is hardly dominant in modern society and does not expect any given person to exhibit it in all areas of life. 'A servant ill-recompensed for his service, asks for a rise; and one dissatisfied with his conditions of work, seeks a change.'[121] Nevertheless there remain certain areas of our life where such an attitude is to be welcomed. The most obvious is friendship, but closer to the technical sense of tradition is what we might call tools of the trade: 'When the plumber goes to fetch his tools he would be away even longer than is usually the case if his purpose were to invent new or improve old ones.'[122] A yet more

[114] Franco identifies this as the point of 'displacement in Oakeshott's critique of Rationalism away from epistemological considerations to more recognizably moral and political ones': Franco, n. 44, 102.

[115] Oakeshott, n. 30, 409. [116] Ibid.

[117] Coyle observes that Oakeshott's conservative 'attitude of mind is defined not by the denial of change or refusal to submit to it, but by a particular manner of accommodating to change': Coyle, n. 49, 101.

[118] Oakeshott, n. 30, 411. This reasoning might be likened to the precautionary principle: see Gamble, n. 31, 163.

[119] See Gamble, n. 31, 167.

[120] John Gray, 'The Undoing of Conservatism', in *Enlightenment's Wake* (Abingdon: Routledge, 1995), in which Oakeshott is discussed at 158–65.

[121] Oakeshott, n. 30, 416. [122] Ibid., 420.

relevant example is the solicitor who 'can use his own (annotated) copy of Pollock on *Partnership* or Jarman on *Wills* more readily than any other'.[123]

Oakeshott now comes to the point with regard to law. He reiterates his vision of law as 'general rules of conduct' which enable 'individuals to pursue the activities of their own choice' but do not impose 'substantive activities'.[124] A conservative disposition is not only consistent with this conception of law but positively supports it, on two grounds. First, whilst law is not in Oakeshott's view an instrument of state-defined common ends, it is so of privately decided purposes and is therefore analogous to the tools of a trade. Second, a conservative approach to legal change acts as something of an antidote to the 'the nuisance of those who spend their energy and their wealth in the service of some pet indignation, endeavouring to impose it upon everybody'[125] and thus helps to protect law from being diverted into the service of a common enterprise. It may along the same lines restrain the over-hasty transplant of arrangements that operate successfully in the context of one political tradition to another in which they are entirely untested.[126]

If Oakeshott's approach to conservatism is relevant to law generally, it must also be relevant to the law that imposes taxes, in fact *a fortiori* as so few substantive ends can be pursued without engaging it. The point is that whilst an individual wishing to carry out a perfectly ordinary activity (such as employing a child-carer or working overseas for a few months) might be met with terrifically complicated tax rules, she can also draw on widespread practical experience amongst officials, professionals, and other taxpayers in dealing with such rules. In this way, what initially seemed obstructive to her plans can rapidly become a matter of routine. To change this routine in favour even of 'simplified' or 'neutral' rules is inevitably disruptive and potentially damaging,[127] that is, exchanging a certain loss and the risk of a greater loss for a merely putative gain.[128]

This line of reasoning throws up some interesting possibilities. Perhaps stability is most important in respect of the everyday procedural rules and practices that are peculiarly apt to be described as 'tools of the trade'. A conservative approach to these matters, it might be argued, is what allows the system to tolerate the frequent and detailed changes to substantive tax rules of which an Oakeshottian observer would also disapprove. For example, the recent requirement on employers to provide 'real time

[123] Ibid., 419. [124] Ibid., 424. [125] Ibid., 428.

[126] Oakeshott's reference to 'eyes focused upon distant horizons and minds clouded with foreign claptrap' in 'The Political Economy of Freedom', n. 80, 397, may be uncharacteristically clumsy but is balanced by corresponding doubts as to the successful export of English political traditions: see 'Political Education', n. 64, 55. There is also an obvious resonance with some of the questions raised by comparative lawyers and legal pluralists: see, for example, Gordon Woodman, 'The Development "Problem" of Legal Pluralism: An Analysis and Steps Towards Solutions', in Brian Tamanaha, Caroline Sage, and Michael Woolcock (eds), *Legal Pluralism and Development: Scholars and Practitioners in Dialogue* (Cambridge, UK: Cambridge University Press, 2012).

[127] Such as the introduction in the Finance Act 2013 of a cash basis of calculating trading profits for small business, which has the consequence for some taxpayers of requiring an additional set of strategic decisions around which basis should be adopted.

[128] As is discussed further in the text to n. 130, it is unhelpful to consider this as a blanket disapproval either of change or of the application of reason to legal problems. The preferable view is that rational reform should be considered carefully and pursued if the attendant risks are acceptable.

information' to the revenue authorities[129] may not be amongst the most exciting topics for tax research, but has consequences for the day-to-day continuance of business which might be rather profound for small enterprises in particular. It is quite right, therefore, that this change has received such close scrutiny in the professional press despite lacking the headline potential of, say, an additional penny on the income tax.

Perhaps more controversially, we might question the assumption that the Tax Law Rewrite of 1997 to 2010 adopted a conservative approach by focussing on the wording of tax legislation as opposed to its content. The old wording, after all, constituted the day-to-day working materials of the tax professional. The ability of many older tax experts to reel off section numbers of the Income and Corporation Taxes Act 1988 may have perplexed the more junior amongst us, yet it gave professionals a speed and security with the legislation that one suspects was undervalued in the Rewrite process.

E. The Limits of Conservatism

Whilst Oakeshott highlights the 'present enjoyment' that is sought by those of a conservative disposition,[130] he accepts that the arguments for change may outweigh those of inaction. The most pertinent example is his observation that 'a variety of inventions and considerable changes in the conduct of business, seem now to have made the current law of copyright inadequate'.[131] A conservative would not resist change in such a circumstance, but will:

> prefer to enforce a rule he has got rather than invent a new one … delay a modification of the rules until it is clear that the change of circumstances it is designed to reflect has come to stay for a while … be suspicious of proposals for change in excess of what the situation calls for, of rulers who demand extra-ordinary powers in order to make great changes … think it proper to consider the occasion of the innovation with care.[132]

There is much to welcome here from a tax legal perspective. Indeed, it is hardly unknown amongst tax specialists to wish that governments would produce less legislation, restrict themselves to what is necessary, and give greater consideration to this smaller output. Nevertheless, it might be suggested that Oakeshottian conservatism is simply overtolerant of the deficiencies of existing arrangements. Some things are beyond repair.

This criticism might even be expressed by reengaging with Oakeshott's concept of a civil association. As matters stand, the tax system is distant from the framework of adverbial rules described in 'The Rule of Law' and *On Human Conduct*. Not only do the taxing statutes routinely lay down common endeavours with authoritarian implications of varying severity, but the pursuit of these endeavours is often so poorly expressed in the legislation that taxpayers are liable to be 'tripped up' even while

[129] *GOV.UK, HM Revenue & Customs*, 'Real Time Information: Improving the Operation of Pay As You Earn' (17 December 2014), https://www.gov.uk/government/publications/real-time-information-improving-the-operation-of-pay-as-you-earn (accessed 17 September 2015).

[130] Oakeshott, n. 30, 415. [131] Ibid., 430. [132] Ibid., 431.

pursuing ends deemed legitimate by the government. This is one thing for the well-resourced, who can draw upon expert advice and previous experience in order to navigate the rules safely or even advantageously, but quite another for those who lack such resources.

The problem is sharpened further when taxpayers seek to manipulate the rules in order to reduce their liabilities to counter-intuitively low levels. In principle, in a civil association, such activities would be governed by judicial determinations as to the concrete application of general rules. If a judge determines that a rule requires a person to pay tax, then she pays tax but not otherwise. In practice, though, the litigation of tax cases is both slow and selective, which can provide irresistible opportunities to profit from 'tax avoidance' either in the interim or absolutely. As this could be extremely destructive of the formal equality that is characteristic of Oakeshott's *lex*,[133] reliance is placed on more responsive forms of administrative control[134] in order to ensure that the legislative framework is not subverted.

The irony of this method of defending civil association is that it shifts the emphasis decisively from general adverbial rules towards the use of frequent and detailed administrative interventions for the purpose of 'preventing avoidance'. The closeness of such techniques to Oakeshott's descriptions of enterprise association is unmistakable, especially when accompanied with rhetoric to the effect that tax avoiders are appropriating to themselves the corporate income of the state.[135] This in turn could lead us in two directions. First, we might conclude that the realization of civil association and the rule of tax law is for practical purposes impossible without changes so drastic that some of the Thatcherite reforms would seem timid in comparison. Proposals for 'flat' or proportionate taxes with low rates and limited reliefs come close to this position, as they are typically designed to remove many of the tax incentives, disincentives, and special regimes that create opportunities for avoidance and consequently the need for administrative controls. The second approach is to follow the tenor of the third chapter of *On Human Conduct*[136] and to accept that our tax system is likely for the foreseeable future to contain a rather uneasy cohabitation of elements of civil and enterprise association. On this basis we might try to encourage the former but without attempting to eradicate the latter with a zeal entirely at odds with Oakeshott's writings on conservatism.[137]

IV. Conservatism and Reform

The first of these approaches doubtless has its attractions, but also abandons any serious attempt to reconcile Oakeshott's ideas on civil association with his defence of conservatism. The second suggestion requires more thought. The point

[133] See Oakeshott, n. 39, 152–3.

[134] See Adrian Vermeule, 'Local and Global Knowledge in the Administrative State', in Dyzenhaus and Poole (eds), n. 31, p. 312.

[135] See text at nn 54–5 and 73–6.

[136] Oakeshott, n. 35.

[137] Pertinently, it may be possible to temper the tendency towards enterprise association by insisting that tax administration adheres to certain principles of administrative law. This possibility is discussed in more depth in de Cogan, n. 25, 251–70.

is that as soon as we abandon the notion that either civil or enterprise association could be implemented in full—in present terms, that the success of a tax rule could be assessed either by reference to the final achievement or the austere disavowal of specified social objectives—the idea of a realizable destination for tax reform starts to lose force.[138] We are instead faced with a perpetual work in progress. That this predicament might pervade even the most essential elements of our tax system can be seen by returning to Oakeshott's comment that taxpayers tend to disparage the removal without consent of what they consider to be their own property.[139] Whilst consent to taxation has long been institutionalized under Article 4 of the Bill of Rights 1689,[140] the widespread resistance to high marginal income tax rates in the 1970s (which *inter alia* precipitated the *Ramsay* line of jurisprudence[141]) suggests that it would be a mistake to treat this consent as entirely open-ended.[142]

If tax reform is something that cannot be settled once and for all, even in some of the most fundamental respects, it does not follow that certain visions for its future cannot be furthered. Naturally, this requires not only technical expertise but also the political skill and judgement that Snape describes in *The Political Economy of Corporation Tax*.[143] Put in a different way, reformers must have an intellectual command over the law and its conceptual underpinnings (itself no small feat given the sheer accumulation of detail in UK taxation law) but must also possess a keen instinct for what is possible from both a political and practical standpoint. In turn this implies a capacity to draw on professional experience and historical knowledge in a manner that is consistent, to say the least, with Oakeshott's writing's on conservatism.[144]

This retreat from higher hopes may seem to be an intellectual surrender and a shirking of any serious attempt to improve the law, perhaps borne of an excessive fear of revenue volatility.[145] Oakeshott cautions us against overstating the matter:

> Some ... people are apt to exaggerate the current disorder; the absence of plan is so conspicuous that the small adjustments, and even the more massive arrangements, which restrain the chaos seem to them nugatory. ... They feel that there ought to be something that ought to be done to convert this so-called chaos into order, for this is no way for rational human beings to be spending their lives. Like Apollo when he saw Daphne with her hair hung carelessly about her neck, they sigh and say to themselves: 'What if it were properly arranged.'[146]

[138] The ideas of George Osborne might, nevertheless, be interpreted as moving the UK tax system towards something resembling civil association. The following article is instructive, although the author does not discuss Oakeshott or civil association specifically: John Snape, 'Stability and its Significance in UK Tax Policy and Legislation', *British Tax Review* [2015] 561–79.

[139] Refer to text at n. 70.

[140] Refer to text at n. 71.

[141] See *Ramsay v IRC* [1982] AC 300.

[142] This episode is discussed colourfully in Nigel Tutt, *The Tax Raiders: The Rossminster Affair* (London: Financial Training, 1985).

[143] See e.g. Snape, n. 32, 218 ff ('The virtuosity of prudent corporation tax reform').

[144] Refer to text at n. 114.

[145] In any case, who could seriously argue that this is an unworthy concern?

[146] Oakeshott, n. 30, 425–6.

This rather accords with the conspicuous failure of attempts to impose rationalist schemes of taxation upon advanced Western democracies,[147] yet even in Oakeshott's traditionalist vein of writing, politics is depicted as something more sophisticated than 'merely doing what was done "last time"'.[148] That this accolade has been earned by at least some of our tax reforming endeavours is apparent from the Royal Commission reports discussed in the introduction to this chapter, but we might also note the influence of models that are designed to be taken into account but not implemented precisely. The OECD and UN Model Tax Conventions, for example, have limited legal force[149] but have had profound implications for the structure and content of many tax systems. Along similar lines, it might be possible to construct a model tax constitution that covers both domestic and international aspects of UK income tax law, and which could be used as a point of departure for real tax reforms.[150] Attention might also be paid to the *Corporate Tax Roadmap* of 2010,[151] which announced the UK government's medium-term intentions on a number of linked topics. This was welcomed widely and in retrospect provided quite a reasonable summary of the reforms actually carried out by the government over its term from 2010 to 2015. It is not surprising that there has been enthusiasm, not only for a reprise of the idea but for an extension to all business taxes and even personal taxes.[152]

A connected point is that, to a degree, change can be subsumed within existing legal concepts. In a different context Oakeshott makes the arresting claim that even crises such as the Norman Conquest and the Bolshevik revolution took place within existing political traditions rather than obliterating them, at least if by tradition we mean a 'flow of sympathy' rather than 'a fixed and inflexible manner of doing things'.[153] Whether this description is apposite to those events is beyond the scope of this chapter, but it certainly fits important elements of the UK tax system. For example, the apparently revolutionary imposition of a corporation tax in 1965 was prefigured not only by the profits tax of 1947, the corporation profits tax of 1920, and the excess profits duty of 1915, but a much older history of imposing income tax on corporations.[154] There is, moreover, some anecdotal evidence that reforms benefit from such historical continuity. For instance, there are obvious parallels between the loan relationships

[147] In addition to the examples given in the introduction to this chapter, see the *Report of the Royal Commission on Taxation* (Ottawa: Queen's Printer, 1966), known more widely as the Carter report; the prospects for more recent endeavours such as the Mirrlees Review, the string of Australian reform projects, and even the EU's Common Consolidated Corporate Tax Base look shaky: refer *inter alia* to Richard Vann, 'Corporate Tax Reform in Australia: Lucky Escape for Lucky Country?', *British Tax Review* [2013] 59.

[148] Oakeshott, n. 80, 396, cited in Kevin Williams, 'Education as Conversation', in Podoksik (ed.), n. 31, 121.

[149] There are, however, sophisticated arguments as to the legal and interpretative status of the Model Tax Conventions and their associated commentaries: see, for example, Reuven Avi-Yonah, *International Tax as International Law* (Cambridge, UK: Cambridge University Press, 2007).

[150] This would be an adaptation (it might be said 'watering-down') of the proposal in Harris, n. 1.

[151] *GOV. UK, HM Treasury and David Gauke MP*, 'Corporate Tax Roadmap', 29 November 2010, https://www.gov.uk/government/publications/the-corporation-tax-road-map (accessed 29 March 2015). See also Snape, n. 32, 40.

[152] References could be proliferated but a typical example is Paul Stainforth, 'Tax Journal Report: Views from Business: Tax Policies and Priorities for the Government', *Tax Journal*, 1267 (2015) 8.

[153] Oakeshott, n. 64, 59.

[154] Avery Jones, n. 18, 1.

regime that eliminated the distinction between capital and revenue within defined boundaries, and the annual investment allowance that allows a 100 per cent deduction of capital expenditure of up to £500,000 per year.[155] The latter has been enacted much more recently but has strong roots in the previous law stretching back at least to Sir John Anderson's Budget of 25 April 1944,[156] whereas the latter still has the semblance of artificiality. Tax legal concepts are not preserved in aspic and existing categories may well be beyond repair, yet perhaps it is an underrated legislative skill to express new rules in terms that are already widely understood.

F. Inchoate Reform and the OTS

Another method of seeking concrete reform at the expense of theoretical ambition is to limit the scope of reforms to particular areas of importance. Tax reformers would be expected to have a thorough appreciation of the possible knock-on consequences of their work for contiguous areas of law and practice, but would not seek to solve the structural problems of taxation in one go. This is of course the style of reform that has been institutionalized with the establishment of the Office of Tax Simplification (OTS) in 2010. The OTS has been subject to a number of criticisms, which, however, seem questionable if the perspective adopted in this chapter is accepted. For instance, it is often argued that the recommendations of the OTS are insufficiently radical,[157] but it might be answered that the depth of change is less important than whether it is necessary and outweighs its disadvantages. As taxation is not only critically important for the maintenance of public revenues but forms a prominent part of the framework within which private ends are chosen, a particularly cautious style of law reform might be merited in this field.

It might also be objected that the activities of the OTS are insufficiently independent of central government.[158] Its officials work in the same buildings as HM Treasury (HMT) and HM Revenue & Customs (HMRC);[159] welcome secondees from these departments as well as from the private sector;[160] agree terms of reference with Ministers;[161] and gain technical assistance from HMRC.[162] The OTS develops its own recommendations based on detailed evidence,[163] the ultimate decision whether to proceed resting with Ministers. It is said that a more visibly independent body might

[155] Capital Allowances Act 2001, s. 51A(5). This is the correct figure at the time of writing but may be liable to change.

[156] Dominic de Cogan, 'Law and Administration in Capital Allowances Doctrine: 1878–1950', in Tiley (ed.), n. 5, 193–5.

[157] These views are noted in Adrian Sawyer, 'Moving on from the Tax Legislation Rewrite Projects: A Comparison of the New Zealand Tax Working Group/Generic Tax Policy Process and the United Kingdom Office of Tax Simplification', *British Tax Review* [2013] 321–44, 338; Judith Freedman, 'Editorial: Creating New UK Institutions for Tax Governance and Policy Making: Progress or Confusion?', *British Tax Review* [2013] 373–81, 375; Tracey Bowler, *The Office of Tax Simplification: Looking Back and Looking Forward*, Tax Law Review Committee Discussion Paper no. 11 (London: IFS, 2014), 1, http://www.ifs.org.uk/uploads/publications/TLRC/TLRC_OTS_DP_11.pdf (accessed 30 March 2015).

[158] This point is anticipated by John Whiting, the Tax Director of the OTS, in 'Analysis—Introducing the Office of Tax Simplification', *Tax Journal*, 1040 (2010) 7.

[159] Freedman, n. 157, 375; Whiting, n. 158.

[160] Bowler, n. 157, 4.

[161] *OTS Framework Document*, n. 15.

[162] Bowler, n. 157, 4.

[163] Ibid., 15.

provide greater impetus for radical reform,[164] but there is surely something to be said for a working relationship between the OTS and the revenue departments which produces proposals that are usable rather than merely interesting.[165] If the idea is instead that the legislative office should choose to exercise its power in favour of comprehensive schemes that prioritize intellectual prowess over practicability or continuity, then our discussion returns directly to Oakeshott's portrayal of rationalism.

The most convincing criticism of the OTS is that it has simply lacked the necessary resources to operate in the most fulfilling way.[166] This point is largely uncontested but concerns the extent of the institution's activities rather than the scope and direction thereof. In fact, for a highly regarded group of experts to embark on limited examinations of important questions, to draw on established practical traditions, to make a range of feasible recommendations, but to leave the ultimate decisions to government, is about as close as a programme of tax reform could approach to our Oakeshottian story. Indeed at the present time it is difficult to envisage how the Law Commission could navigate the pitfalls of tax reform more expertly, except that its resources would allow it to achieve a greater depth and breadth of research.

G. Concluding Comments: Stating the Obvious?

This chapter has travelled through a wide range of concepts used by Michael Oakeshott, such as civil and enterprise association, rationalism, tradition, and conservatism. The outcome of the discussion is hardly unfamiliar. We desire low rates of tax under clear rules that interfere minimally with our lives, yet which fund a wide range of useful common enterprises. We pay less attention to the possible incongruity in our wishes, and we are unprepared to tolerate the disruption that a serious attempt to implement them might occasion. These tensions may well be obvious to us on reflection, but are brought into much clearer focus by Oakeshott's lucid and enjoyable writings. Most importantly, he encourages us to take conservatism seriously whether or not it happens to appeal to our own sensibilities. This seems good advice even—perhaps especially—in these rather turbulent times.

164 Freedman, n. 157, 375–6.

165 Refer to Bowler, n. 157, 23; Christopher J. Wales and Christopher P. Wales, *Structures, Processes and Governance in Tax Policy-Making: An Initial Report* (Oxford: Centre for Business Taxation, 2012), 64, http://www.sbs.ox.ac.uk/sites/default/files/Business_Taxation/Docs/Publications/Reports/structures-and-processes-in-tax-policy-making.pdf.

166 Refer to Committee of Public Accounts, *Tax Avoidance: The Role of Large Accountancy Firms: Forty-Fourth Report of Session 2012–13* (HC 870, 26 April 2013), referenced in note 4 of Freedman, n. 157, 374; Wales and Wales, n. 165, 64; Sawyer, n. 157, 333; Bowler, n. 157, 24.

6

The Justice of the Tax Base and the Case for Income Tax

*Patrick Emerton and Kathryn James**

This chapter is a response to Liam Murphy and Tom Nagel's *The Myth of Ownership*.[1] It takes as its point of departure that book's claim that 'the choice of tax base has only instrumental significance for economic justice',[2] being simply a tool for achieving welfare outcomes.[3] We will contest this claim.

Decisions relating to the design of a tax system involve choices with respect to a finite number of parts: what to tax (i.e. the tax base), who to tax (i.e. the taxpaying unit), and how to tax (i.e. choices relating to rates, credits and deductions, and special provisions such as exemptions).[4] The choice of tax base is foundational to the other components. We readily accept that distributive considerations are important to economic justice, that choices of who and how to tax are important mechanisms of distribution, and hence that the choice of tax base must be sensitive to distributive considerations. We argue, however, that distributive justice depends upon more than merely considerations of individual welfare outcomes. Thus there can be reasons for favouring one choice of tax base over another that are independent of the use of taxation for the pursuit of welfare.

Murphy and Nagel present their claim that the choice of tax base is of only instrumental significance to economic justice as following from their 'conviction ... that there are no property rights antecedent to the tax structure. Property rights are the product of a set of laws and conventions, of which the tax system forms a part.'[5] We

* The authors would like to thank David Duff, Stuart Green, Matthew Harding, Miranda Perry Fleischer, Marilyn Pittard, Janice Richardson, Ian Roxan, Kristen Rundle, and Dale Smith for helpful discussions on some of the ideas and arguments in this chapter.

[1] Liam Murphy and Tom Nagel, *The Myth of Ownership* (Oxford: Oxford University Press, 2002).

[2] Ibid., 98.

[3] Murphy and Nagel's account of economic justice focuses primarily on the provision of public goods—a topic not dealt with in this chapter—and on the provision of a decent social minimum by way of either transfers or the public provision of services: Murphy and Nagel, n. 1, 74, 94–5. Although they also make reference to equality of opportunity (Ibid., 74, 95) as we discuss in more detail below their conception of equality of opportunity is rather modest, and does not inform their account of the justice of the tax base: see text to n. 8.

[4] Walter Hettich and Stanley L. Winer, *Democratic Choice and Taxation: A Theoretical and Empirical Analysis* (Cambridge, UK: Cambridge University Press, 1999), 42.

[5] Murphy and Nagel, n. 1, 74; see also 8.

Philosophical Foundations of Tax Law. First Edition. Edited by Monica Bhandari.

accept the second of these two sentences but do not fully accept the first. We do not argue that justice *requires* that there be property rights antecedent to the tax structure (although in some circumstances the existence of property rights antecedent to the tax structure may be compatible with justice). Rather, our argument is that justice typically requires that there be principles that are prior to the tax structure and that bear upon questions of property rights and other private law rights, and hence that the tax structure, including the choice of tax base, must be sensitive to such principles. We further argue that there are such reasons of principle to favour the taxation of private wealth, and that in practice this means the taxation of income.

Our argument to this conclusion is roughly Rawlsian in character. We think this is broadly consistent with the approach to economic justice adopted by Murphy and Nagel, but it is not identical. As we will explain in more detail in Section I below, our approach differs from Murphy and Nagel's in two main respects. The first we think is primarily a difference of technical detail: unlike Murphy and Nagel, we deploy the Rawlsian idea that the political principles that give effect to ideals of justice are articulated and implemented in *stages*: first abstract political philosophy, then the formulation of a constitution consistent with the dictates of philosophy, then the enactment of legislation under that constitution, etc. We contend that principles concerning private law rights that arise at the constitutional stage, and hence that constrain (or ought to constrain) legislative choices, can thereby constrain the choice of the tax base. Because this conclusion follows from a difference of technical detail, we believe that it might be seen as broadly consistent with Murphy and Nagel's approach to the relationship between the tax base and economic justice, although we will argue that our technical gloss, if it is merely that, is nevertheless an important one.

The second respect in which we differ from Murphy and Nagel is our emphasis upon the importance of equality: equal worth of the political liberties, fair equality of opportunity, and the relationship between these forms of equality and the distribution of property holdings in a society. Although Murphy and Nagel are sensitive to the connection between property holdings and political power,[6] they do not connect this directly to the tax structure; rather, they present reform of the role of money in politics as one desirable prior condition for serious reform of taxation.[7] In respect of equality of opportunity, they favour a weaker constraint than Rawls's fair equality of opportunity, regarding it as sufficient that 'people have an adequate degree of control over their own prospects' and that 'justice in outcomes is secure'.[8] We favour a more Rawlsian approach, on which both the fair worth of the political liberties and fair equality of opportunity are regarded as important components (via procedural justice) of justice in outcomes. Our difference from Murphy and Nagel on this point leads us to reach different conclusions about the relationship between taxation and outcomes, which in turn lead us to reject the claim that the principle connection between economic justice and the tax base is a purely instrumental one.

[6] See, e.g., their call for campaign finance reform: Murphy and Nagel, n. 1, 187–8.

[7] Ibid., 187.

[8] Ibid., 158. See also 119, 157–8, 186–7.

I. The Basic Argument

As Pogge explains in *Realizing Rawls*, the Rawlsian account of justice is *semi-consequentialist*: that is to say, it is essentially forward-looking, and determines the justice of a society's institutional scheme (what Rawls calls the *basic structure*) by reference to the outcomes it will tend to bring about,[9] and in particular, by reference to the outcome it will bring about for the worst-off social grouping: this outcome is to be maximized, relative to the position of the worst-off grouping in other feasible schemes.[10]

As this brief statement brings out, the Rawlsian account of justice requires the making of two distinct sorts of counterfactual (or, at least, projective) judgment. First, there is the need to ascertain the consequences that an institutional scheme would (or will) bring about; second, there is the need to ascertain the consequences that other feasible schemes would bring about. The second of these has been criticized on the grounds that it makes social and political criticism very difficult in practice. Because determining the justice (by Rawlsian lights) of an existing institutional scheme requires undertaking a very complex counterfactual investigation, in order to work out how much better or worse off the worst-off social group would be under feasible alternative institutional schemes, it is very hard to show that any actual given institutional scheme is unjust. This difficulty is particularly marked in comparison to an egalitarian conception of justice, which simply requires making an actual comparison of the worst-off social group to other social groups in the actual world.[11]

This chapter will not address these objections, and will remain noncommittal on the precise criteria of distributive justice. It will follow Murphy and Nagel, however, in accepting that distributive justice (1) is primarily a question about the justice of institutional schemes, and (2) is to be ascertained in a forward-looking fashion. This feature of Murphy and Nagel's position is made clear when they state that:

> All the normative questions about what taxes are justified and what taxes are unjustified should be interpreted instead as questions about how the system should define those property rights that arise through various transactions—employment, bequest, contract, investment, buying and selling—that are subject to taxation....
>
> [C]onsiderations ... will be applied to the evaluation of the entire system of rules *and its results* ...
>
> The right answer will depend on what system *best serves the legitimate aims of society* with legitimate means and without imposing illegitimate costs.[12]

[9] Thomas Pogge, *Realizing Rawls* (Ithaca: Cornell University Press, 1989), 44–7. The Rawlsian account is not fully consequentialist, because it focuses only on benefits and burdens brought about by the basic structure, and not upon natural goods and ills: see 46.

[10] Ibid., 43–4 (§3.4), 66–70 (§§5.2–5.4).

[11] Ted Honderich, *After the Terror* (Edinburgh: Edinburgh University Press, 2001), 50–1; Raymond Geuss, 'Liberalism and its Discontents' (2002) and 'Neither History nor Praxis' (2003) in *Outside Ethics* (Princeton: Princeton University Press, 2005), 22–3, 33.

[12] Murphy and Nagel, n. 1, 74–5 (emphasis added). Pogge suggests, as a necessary condition of a conception of justice being deontological rather than semi- (or fully) consequentialist, that it treat as a relevant consideration only those outcomes that are *established* by an institutional scheme—that is, those outcomes that the schemes rules and procedures expressly call for—and not those outcomes that are

Any forward-looking conception of justice will require projective judgments of the first sort described above, that is, determining what will be the consequences of the actual institutional scheme of a society.

A. Institutions as the Object of Projective Judgments of Justice

One distinctive feature of Rawls's account of justice is that it incorporates the need for, and the making of, these sorts of projective judgments in a particular structured way. The basic idea is set out in Rawls's early paper 'Two Concepts of Rules': Rawls distinguishes between (1) the justification of a *practice*—that is to say, the roles that it creates and the 'moves' that it permits—and (2) the justification of *a particular action performed pursuant to that practice*.[13] A practice is justified to the extent that its existence and operation serves (or will serve) desirable social ends; whereas a person acting pursuant to a practice justifies her particular action by reference to the role that she occupies and the rules that govern that role. Projective judgments of the sort we are considering play a crucial role in justifying the inauguration and maintenance of practices. Typically, however, they are not elements of the practices themselves.[14]

Although not all practices involve, give rise to, or arise within the context of institutional schemes,[15] institutions and the roles to which they give rise are one important class of practices. Hence, the distinction drawn by Rawls applies to institutional schemes and to the decision-making that takes place within them, such as decisions to tax a particular base. A just institutional scheme is one in which, if the holders of institutional roles within that scheme follow the rules that constitute and govern the operation of those roles, then just outcomes will result. In designing such an institutional scheme, projective judgments about the likely outcome of adopting such-and-such a scheme for this particular society will of course be crucial to judging whether or not the scheme is just. But there is no reason to think that the roles that are created within the institutional scheme will generally require their occupants to make decisions by reference to such projective judgments. For instance, a just institutional scheme will have to specify the power of officials within a taxation office to issue notices of assessment; but it is unlikely that the rules which set out the powers and duties of such officials will require them, in deciding whether or not to issue an assessment notice, to consider the overall implications for economic justice of issuing such a notice. There

merely engendered by the scheme; this is analogous to a deontological conception of personal morality's greater concern with what agents *intended* to be the effects of their actions, rather than with effects that they did not intend but merely foresaw: Pogge, n. 9, 38, 44–7. It seems that Murphy and Nagel's view is not deontological in this sense, as their concern is not with the abstract category of entitlements established by an institutional scheme, but its practical results.

[13] John Rawls, 'Two Concepts of Rules', in Samuel Freeman (ed.), *John Rawls: Collected Papers* (Cambridge, MA: Harvard University Press, [1955] 1999).

[14] Rawls discusses two practices in detail: punishment and promising. Projective judgments are an element of the practice of punishment as it takes place in some criminal justice systems, because sentencing depends upon making a judgment as to the prospects of the offender's rehabilitation; but these are not projective judgments about the contribution of that system of punishment to social justice or well-being. Projective judgments are not generally an element of promising at all, except for the role they might play in generating excuses for promise-breaking.

[15] Examples include the practices of promising, courtesy, and etiquette.

is certainly no reason to think that a tax system would *better* contribute to economic justice by requiring those officials to make such judgments, and given the complexity of such judgments there is good reason to think that it would be *worse* to build the need for such judgments into the relevant rules.[16] Rather, we expect that a system that sets out more practical and workable rules for issuing notices of assessment, and also includes well-designed rules establishing the incidence and extent of taxation, will better contribute to achieving economic justice.

There is an unresolved tension in 'Two Concepts of Rules', however, and we need to explain how the same tension does not arise in respect of our account. In this early paper, Rawls is assuming a broadly utilitarian conception of social well-being, and it is this assumption which gives rise to the tension. As Pogge points out, the division of labour in respect of projective judgments between drawing upon such judgment to design practices, but not necessarily calling upon the participants within such practices to make such judgments, is not stable when the conception of social well-being in play is a utilitarian one. This is because the utilitarian cannot explain why a person should honour the requirements of the role in which she finds herself acting, if breaching those requirements will maximize utility.[17] To return to our example of our tax official: suppose she knows that a particular taxpayer, if his tax obligations are understated in a notice of assessment, will spend the money that otherwise he would have paid in tax on some valuable social project, which will contribute more to overall welfare than would the receipt and public expenditure of that money; and suppose that utilitarianism is a sound theory of justice. The tax official then has a reason to break the rules of her office and issue an assessment that understates the taxpayer's tax liability. Generalizing the example, we can see that within a utilitarian conception of justice the institutional scheme is not stable, even if optimally designed to maximize utility, because those who occupy the roles that it creates can have, on occasion, reasons of justice to break the rules that define their roles. Once justice is characterized in the semi-consequentialist way described above, however, this instability cannot emerge: if a society is just precisely in virtue of the outcomes that are engendered by its institutional scheme *being engendered by that scheme*, then a person who occupies a role within that scheme can have no reason of justice to act contrary to the requirements of the role. Personal efforts, including breaking the rules of one's office, can change the effects that an institutional scheme brings about, but they cannot make the scheme itself more or less just, because the justice of the scheme is determined by the outcomes that it itself tends to bring about.[18] And, indeed, if the institutional scheme

[16] Scheffler notes that the complexity of the judgments necessary to achieve justice provides a reason to vest institutions rather than individuals with the job of achieving justice: Samuel Scheffler, 'Distributive Justice, the Basic Structure and the Place of Private Law', 35(2) *Oxford Journal of Legal Studies* (2015) 213, 220. The point made in the text is that the same consideration can warrant delimiting the matters to which an institutional actor may have regard in carrying out her function.

[17] Pogge, n. 9, 40. Rawls's own treatment of this tension in 'Two Concepts of Rules' seems to beg the question by assuming that if a practice is justified on utilitarian grounds then a person occupying a role within that practice cannot have any reason grounded in utilitarian considerations for acting contrary to the requirements of that role on a given occasion: see Rawls, n. 13, 40, note 25.

[18] This is Pogge's analysis: Pogge, n. 9, 40–1. Rawls emphasizes that this institutionally oriented conception of justice is an impersonal one; it is not concerned with which particular individual gets what,

really is just, then the better that officials understand this forward-looking justification of the scheme, the more reason they have to adhere to the requirements of the roles that it defines.[19]

In the ideal case this would be an instance of what Rawls calls *perfect procedural justice*:[20] to the extent that the institutional scheme was in fact just, by acting within the parameters of her role a person would help ensure a just outcome without herself having to have that just outcome in mind (assuming that the rules that governed her role did not require her to do so). When it comes to some institutions, however, this sort of perfection is not attainable: however well designed the rules are, and however faithfully they are followed, there simply can be no guarantee that they will deliver the right outcome. Rawls labels such institutions instances of *imperfect procedural justice*, and gives the criminal trial as an example: 'The desired outcome is that the defendant should be declared guilty if and only if he has committed the offense with which he is charged.... But it seems impossible to design the legal rules so that they always lead to the correct result.'[21]

The next subsection develops these ideas about the ways in which institutions can instantiate procedural justice.

B. The Stages of Institutional Construction

Rawls describes a four-stage sequence for thinking about the justice of a society's institutional scheme; the first three stages are relevant to this chapter. The *first stage*, as noted in the Introduction above, is to determine general principles of justice; this is a philosophical task, and as we have already noted this chapter does not attempt to specify such principles in any detail. The *second stage* is to settle upon a constitution that will give effect to the principles of justice within a particular society, given its particular circumstances, history, political culture, etc.[22] Rawls is particularly concerned with the question of how a constitution will protect basic liberties,[23] but it is obvious that a just constitution must also be designed to ensure, to the extent that is possible, that decisions taken under it will produce outcomes that conform to the requirements of justice, including distributive justice.[24]

but rather with the patterns of outcomes generated by institutional arrangements: see John Rawls, *A Theory of Justice* (Cambridge, MA: Harvard University Press, 1971), 64.

[19] Pogge, n. 9, 40–2. Cohen puts pressure on this claim by pointing to the dependence of institutions upon individual actions. He notes that individual action itself tends to reinforce the character of the roles and rules that make up an institution and thereby contribute to the outcomes engendered by an institutional scheme: see G.A. Cohen, *If You're an Egalitarian, How Come You're So Rich?* (Cambridge, MA: Harvard University Press, 2001), ch. 9. Cohen makes this argument in the context of attacking the Rawlsian focus upon justice as an ideal for institutional structures rather than as an ideal for individuals; but the argument also seems to imply that the occupant of some particular role can have reasons of justice to act in a way that will tend to transform the character of those roles and rules, and thereby make new (and better) outcomes possible that otherwise would not have been. This is a challenging objection to the Rawlsian approach to justice, and we are unable to fully address it within the scope of this chapter, although in Section II we say some things in defence of focusing upon institutions rather than individual action in theorizing about justice.

[20] Rawls, n. 18, 85. [21] Ibid., 85. [22] Ibid., 196–7, 200, 357. [23] Ibid., 199.

[24] See the discussion in Pogge, n. 9, 153–60.

Rawls argues, we think correctly, that a constitution can at best be an instance of *imperfect procedural justice*: there is no way of drafting and implementing a constitution which will guarantee that every political decision taken pursuant to it will be consistent with the demands of justice.[25] As we will now explain in some detail, this unavoidable feature of any feasible constitution is of great importance at the *third stage*, which is the enactment of legislation under the constitution.[26]

Rawls identifies two reasons why a constitution cannot be an instrument of perfect procedural justice. The first is that the role of legislator cannot be defined in such a way as to fully exclude the need to make projective judgments of justice. As he puts it, 'A just constitution must rely to some extent on citizens and legislators adopting a wider view [i.e. wider than "a narrow or group-interested standpoint"] and exercising good judgment in applying the principles of justice.'[27] This creates the possibility of error, even if intentions are good. The second is that '[T]he question whether legislation is just or unjust, especially in connection with economic and social policies, is commonly subject to reasonable differences of opinion.'[28] The reason for this is that such judgment 'depends upon speculative political and economic doctrines and upon social theory generally' and that the application of principles of distributive justice 'in a precise way normally requires more information than we can expect to have'.[29] Furthermore, the 'nature of the principles themselves may leave open a range of options rather than singling out any particular alternative'.[30] These points are familiar ones in discussions of tax policy and of economic policy more generally. In the context of reflections upon the justice of an institutional scheme, it is challenging to establish a fully adequate grasp of what would count as the right outcome, even if we could design a constitution which would always deliver it (which, for the first reason identified above, we cannot).

These reasons lead Rawls to conclude that much legislation will be an instance of (what he calls) *quasi-pure procedural justice*.[31] Unfortunately Rawls does not define this notion, nor its relation to the notion of imperfect procedural justice. He does, however, define the notion of *pure procedural justice*. A procedure secures pure procedural justice when (1) there is no *independent* criterion for assessing whether or not the outcome of the procedure is just, but (2) the procedure itself ensures that, whatever the outcome happens to be, it is just.[32] A simple—perhaps simplistic—example is the distributive outcome that results from a series of fair bets between two parties: there is no independent criterion for judging the justice of that outcome, but whatever it is, if the bets were truly fair then the outcome is consistent with the requirements of justice.[33] Furthermore, as Pogge points out, the difference between *imperfect procedural justice* and *pure procedural justice* is a matter of degree rather than of fundamental kind. First, 'as the space of possible outcomes grows too large or too dense for any

[25] Rawls, n. 18, 197–8, 221, 353–60. See also John Rawls, *Political Liberalism*, rev. edn (New York: Columbia University Press, 1996), 336–7, 339.

[26] The fourth stage is adjudication, that is, the application of rules to particular cases, whether by judges or by administrators: Rawls, n. 18, 199.

[27] Ibid., 360. See also 357. [28] Ibid., 198–9. [29] Ibid., 199. See also Rawls, n. 25, 229–30.

[30] Rawls, n. 18, 362. [31] The phrase occurs in Rawls, n. 18, 362. [32] Rawls, n. 18, 85.

[33] The example is from Rawls, n. 18, 86.

outcome to be precisely connectible to the ... independent criteria' for a just outcome, imperfect procedural justice 'shades into pure procedural justice'.[34] That is to say, as we lose our epistemic grasp on the details of the outcomes, we lose our ability to judge them against the independent criteria for just outcomes, and become more reliant upon the procedure itself being a reliable, if not perfect, generator of just outcomes *in virtue of those outcomes being the result of the procedure*. Second, if the necessarily imperfect constitution is to actually perform its function of establishing an institutional scheme for a society, then members of the society must accept its outcomes even when convinced that it has produced an outcome that does not satisfy the (independently known) requirements of justice. In other words, an imperfect procedure, if it is to work at all, 'must, in general, be regarded *as if it were pure*'.[35] If the procedure is part of a just institutional scheme, then the alternative to treating it as if it were pure is to overthrow the scheme; but if the scheme is truly the best, in respect of the social outcomes it generates, then there can be no reason of justice for overthrowing it.

It seems to be these features of the legislative process that lead Rawls to label it quasi-pure procedural justice. '[F]or these situations,' says Rawls, if the enacted law is 'within the range of those that could reasonably be favoured by rational legislators trying to conscientiously follow the principles of justice, then ... [t]he situation is one of quasi-pure procedural justice. We must rely on the actual course of discussion at the legislative stage to select a policy within the allowed bounds.'[36] Pogge, however, makes the point that this sort of case is different from a case of pure procedural justice in the strict sense; hence, we suggest, the use of the qualifier 'quasi'. While legislation may in many cases be an instance of pure procedural justice *from the perspective of those whom it governs*, this does not mean that *legislators* are entitled to treat legislating in this fashion. In cases of (unqualified) pure procedural justice, such as the rolling of the dice to determine the outcome of a fair bet, there are no independent principles concerning the outcome to which the one performing the procedure must pay regard. Legislators, however 'must try in good faith and to the best of their abilities' to achieve an outcome that conforms to the requirements of justice.[37]

We will now explain how the character of legislation as quasi-pure procedural justice contributes to an understanding of the force of constitutional principles, and their relationship to the requirements of justice.

C. Constitutional Constraints Upon Projective Judgments of Justice

With the above understanding of the second and third stages in mind, we can see that distinct projective judgments are required at these two distinct stages. First, in determining the constitution, a judgment must be made that *this* rather than *that* constitution is most likely, for the society in question, to bring about and secure the requirements of justice. The only constraints on the decision at this stage are the general requirements of justice, as determined by political philosophy.

[34] Pogge, n. 9, 152. [35] Ibid., 152 (emphasis in original). [36] Rawls, n. 18, 362.

[37] Pogge, n. 9, 153. (Pogge is talking here of adjudicators rather than legislators, but the difference of role makes no difference to the point about what performing the role requires.)

Second, in legislating, a judgment must be made by the legislator(s) that *this* piece of law, enacted in *this* form rather than *that* form, is most likely to bring about and secure the requirements of justice in virtue of the obligations it creates, the transactions that it permits or prohibits, etc. However, at this point additional constraints apply: in particular, legislation must conform to the requirements of the constitution.[38] There are two reasons why this is so.

The first reason is that set out above in our discussion of 'Two Concepts of Rules': the legislator is participating in an institutional practice established under the constitution. Hence she can only justify her legislative decisions by reference to the rules that constitute and govern that practice, which include the ones set out in the constitution. (Those rules do not *exhaust* the relevant considerations for proper exercise of the office; as we have seen, the legislator must also make projective judgments.)

This reason would not apply if the sort of instability that we saw above, in respect of a utilitarian framework of justification, threatened to arise in the legislative context we are now considering. However, the second reason answers this concern. As we have seen, legislation will frequently be a matter of quasi-pure procedural justice. But this claim can only be maintained if those who are governed by the constitution have a reason to treat it in this manner, and this will only be the case if, in fact, the constitution has been established on the basis set out above—namely, as being the constitution most likely to secure the requirements of justice for the particular society in question. The decisions of a legislator who departs from the requirements of the constitution therefore lose any such claim to be the products of quasi-pure procedural justice, and hence lose whatever claim they might have had to be the outcome of a just institutional scheme. Hence a legislator cannot have reasons of justice for departing from the constitution, if the constitution itself has been determined in the right way.[39]

There are two main ways that a constitution can constrain the decision-making of a legislator. One is by setting out legally enforceable rules for valid legislation. This is the manner in which Rawls envisages a constitution protecting basic liberties,[40] and Pogge envisages extending this to protecting certain aspects of distributive justice.[41] The other is by shaping the parameters of public reason. By *public reason*, Rawls means political argumentation that takes place in the public sphere, and hence

[38] Rawls, n. 18, 198; Rawls, n. 25, 340. Rawls does not, however, fully spell out the reasons given in the text that follows, above. Rather, he emphasizes the reason set out below in n. 39.

[39] A third reason is given by both Rawls and Pogge, but it depends upon a particular understanding of the requirements of justice and the way in which a constitution should give effect to them. In Rawls's theory, upholding and respecting fundamental liberties (including political liberties, such as the right to vote and to stand for office) has 'lexical priority' over any gains in distributive justice that might be secured by unconstitutional legislation: see Rawls, n. 18, 302. Hence, because a just constitution will give effect to and protect these fundamental liberties, departing from its requirements in pursuit of distributive justice would violate lexically prior requirements of justice, and hence could not be justified by an appeal to the requirements of justice: Ibid., 87, 199; Pogge, n. 9, 157–8.

[40] See e.g. the discussion of 'constitutional restrictions' on legislative freedom, and the ensuing lengthy discussion of judicial review in relation to free speech, in Rawls, n. 25, 337–9, 342–56, 359–63.

[41] He argues that fair equality of opportunity and a decent social minimum should be constitutionally protected in the same way as basic liberties, and hence similarly constraining on what is permissible by way of legislation: Pogge, n. 9, 158–60. In later work Rawls appears to accept this argument in respect of the social minimum (but not fair equality of opportunity): see Rawls, n. 25, 228–9.

is committed to calling upon (and only upon) principles and ideals that are shared in that public sphere.[42] In *A Theory of Justice*, Rawls presents the constitutional role of public reason in negative terms, helping to explain how legislation is an instance of quasi-pure procedural justice by pointing to the *absence* of certain resources within public reason: 'those who disagree with the [legislative] decision made cannot convincingly establish their point within the framework of the public conception of justice.'[43] In *Political Liberalism*, public reason is seen also as an active source of constitutional constraints upon legislative decision-making: 'at each stage the reasonable frames and subordinates the rational',[44] which is to say that legislators, in pursuing the ends to which they are committed, recognize that in doing so they must put forward fair terms of social cooperation, as expressed in the constitution which itself has been adopted on the grounds that it will best secure the outcomes that justice requires.[45]

D. Constitutional Constraints Applied to the Choice of Tax Base

We can now see how the choice of the tax base can come to have more than purely instrumental significance for justice. In some cases, the constitution may contain express prohibitions or mandates which bear upon the tax base, in which case—at the legislative stage, when the details of tax policy come to be worked out—legislators will have reasons of justice, flowing from the constitution, to prefer one choice of tax base over another.[46] In circumstances where, under a constitution, the raising of taxes depends upon the exercise of an express power to do so,[47] interesting questions of characterization may also arise,[48] particularly if there are relevant constitutional limitations that operate alongside the taxing power, such as in relation to the compulsory acquisition of property.[49]

[42] Hence public reason excludes appeals to principles or ideals that belong to a particular religious or moral viewpoint and are not common to the whole (and varied) range of such viewpoints that members of a society might subscribe to: see Rawls, n. 25, 10. For a fuller discussion of the idea of public reason, see John Rawls, 'The Idea of Public Reason Revisited', in *The Law of Peoples with 'The Idea of Public Reason Revisited'* (Cambridge, MA: Harvard University Press, 1999).

[43] Rawls, n. 18, 362. The notion of public reason does not appear in its fully developed form in this work, but as the quoted passage indicates, it is present in a prototypical fashion.

[44] Rawls, n. 25, 349. On the contrast between the reasonable and the rational, see also 48–54.

[45] Rawls does not always make this role of constitutional principle clear, however. For instance, he says that 'With the two principles of justice on hand, we have a possible common court of appeal for settling the question of property as it arises in the light of current and foreseeable social circumstances': Rawls, n. 25, 339. The reference to a 'common court of appeal' is an allusion to the notion of public reason; but in linking public reason directly to abstract principles of political philosophy, Rawls neglects the mediating role of constitutional principles which he himself sets out ten pages later.

[46] See e.g. *Constitution of the Italian Republic*, Art. 53: 'Every person shall contribute to public expenditure in accordance with their capability. The tax system shall be progressive', https://www.senato.it/documenti/repository/istituzione/costituzione_inglese.pdf; *Spanish Constitution*, s 31: 'Everyone shall contribute to sustain public expenditure according to their economic capacity, through a fair tax system based on the principles of equality and progressive taxation, which in no case shall be of a confiscatory scope', https://www.constituteproject.org/constitution/Spain_2011.pdf.

[47] See e.g. *Australian Constitution*, s 51(ii); *US Constitution*, Art. I, Section 8, Clause 1.

[48] See e.g. *National Federation of Independent Business v Sebelius* 567 US___(2012), 132 S.Ct 2566.

[49] See e.g. *Australian Constitution*, s 51(xxxi); *United States Constitution*, Amendment V.

The cases which will be the principal focus of the remainder of this chapter, however, are those cases where the constitution establishes principles that affect the content of the public reason of a particular society, and thereby shape the reasons that can be given in favour of, or against, some particular choice of tax base.

A simple example to illustrate this possibility would be a political debate about resource taxation, taking place within a society whose constitution contains a patrimony clause providing that the natural resources of the nation are the property of the nation (and/or its people).[50] The existence of such a clause and the principle it establishes would mean that, within the public reason of that society, some arguments about the suitability of resource taxation as a component of the tax base have greater weight, providing stronger reasons of justice in favour of a particular choice of tax base.

Consider, for instance, two arguments made in the *Australia's future tax system* report (known as the 'Henry Review', after its lead author) for favouring a resource rent tax over an output-based royalty. One argument is that output-based royalties discourage investment because they do not permit deduction of the costs of production.[51] This argument appeals solely to economic efficiency, treating the question of tax policy as a purely instrumental one. Hence it would not be apt to draw support from constitutional principles. A second argument is that Australian governments, 'as owners of natural resources on behalf of the community … should seek to obtain an appropriate return from resource exploitation',[52] and that output-based royalties 'collect a greater share of the returns to non-renewable resources when profitability is low or negative and collect a smaller share of returns when profitability is high', and hence have tended to systematically underprice Australia's nonrenewable resources.[53] In the context of a patrimony clause, this second argument in favour of a particular tax instrument would draw force from constitutionally grounded considerations of public reasons. (Although Australia does not have such a clause in its constitution, the reference to Australian governments being the 'owners of natural resources on behalf of the community' is a clear attempt to appeal to a principle of this sort.)

[50] See e.g. *Constitution of the Republic of the Philippines* (1987), Art. XII (2): 'All lands of the public domain, waters, minerals, coal, petroleum, and other mineral oils, all forces of potential energy, fisheries, forests or timber, wildlife, flora and fauna, and other natural resources are owned by the State.… The exploration, development, and utilization of natural resources shall be under the full control and supervision of the State', http://www.gov.ph/constitutions/the-1987-constitution-of-the-republic-of-the-philippines/the-1987-constitution-of-the-republic-of-the-philippines-article-xii/; *Constitution of the Republic of Indonesia* (1945), Art. 33(3) 'The land, the waters and the natural resources within shall be under the powers of the State and shall be used to the greatest benefit of the people', http://www.parliament.am/library/sahmanadrutyunner/indonesia.pdf; *Constitution of the Kingdom of Norway* (1814), Art. 110b: 'Every person has a right to an environment that is conducive to health and to natural surroundings whose productivity and diversity are preserved. Natural resources should be made use of on the basis of comprehensive longterm considerations whereby this right will be safeguarded for future generations as well. In order to safeguard their right in accordance with the foregoing paragraph, citizens are entitled to be informed of the state of the natural environment and of the effects of any encroachments on nature that are planned or commenced', http://www.constitution.org/cons/norway/dok-bn.html.

[51] Commonwealth of Australia Treasury, Australia's Future Tax System Review Panel, *Australia's Future Tax System: Report to the Treasurer*, The Treasury (Canberra: Australia's Future Tax System Review Panel, 2009) (hereafter '*Henry Review*'), Part 2, 222.

[52] *Henry Review*, n. 51, Part 2, 219.

[53] Ibid., 226.

E. Do Murphy and Nagel Disagree with This Analysis?

It might seem that the foregoing argument and analysis is consistent with Murphy and Nagel's claim that the choice of tax base is a purely instrumental matter: on the account that we have given, the tax base is being chosen within an institutional context that is itself conventionally determined on the basis of considerations of justice. The possibility that we are pointing to, of the choice of tax base being something on which noninstrumental principles have some bearing because of their place within the public reason of a society, itself can arise only within such an institutional context.

Although this is true, we think that the point we have made is an important one. Because of the impossibility of authoring a constitution as a system of perfect procedural justice, with the resultant need to treat a just constitution *as if* it was a mechanism of pure procedural justice, the constraints that the constitution imposes upon the content of public reason, and the contributions that it makes to that content, are of great practical importance to arguments about the justice of legislation. After all, the presence of those principles in the constitution, and the resulting shaping of public reason, is part of what makes the constitution a just one. From an Archimedean perspective we can (in principle) observe that such principles have no independent moral force beyond their contribution to the realization of just outcomes; but in the practice of politics no legislator has, or is in a position to assert that she has, access to such an Archimedean perspective. She is obliged to make her case by appealing to the considerations of justice as shaped by the constitution. And in so far as constitutional principles bear upon the choice of tax base, these are considerations of justice which are, from the perspective of the legislator, not merely instrumental. As in the model of 'Two Concepts of Rules', she cannot step out of her role, and disregard the principles that constitute and give content to that role, yet also claim to be acting for reasons of justice (given that justice is to be understood in terms of the outcomes of the workings of the institutional scheme of which the legislator's role is an element).

II. Private Rights, Equality and Justice

As we indicated in the introduction, there is another point on which we differ from Murphy and Nagel—namely, the relationship between equality and justice. In the remainder of this chapter we will explain this difference, and how—in light of the analysis above—it provides a further reason to think that the choice of tax base is a matter of more than instrumental significance for justice. Our focus is upon Murphy and Nagel's claim that *there are no property rights antecedent to the tax structure*. In this section we first consider how private rights should be conceived of within the Rawlsian framework, and will then argue that there is good reason to think that, in a just constitution, at least some aspects or elements of private rights will be subject to constitutional principles. In Section III we will consider the implications of such principles for the choice of tax base.

A. The Place of Private Legal Rights Within a Just Institutional Scheme

Rawls clearly regards private rights as an important element of a just society. As well as the right to own personal property (but not necessarily economically productive property), which he includes among the basic liberties that any just institutional scheme must honour,[54] Rawls regards the 'substantial use of a system of free competitive markets' as the best way to satisfy the requirements of justice.[55] A system of free markets depends upon private rights in relation to the ownership and exchange of assets, as well as rights against various forms of fraud, coercion, and the like.[56] In the preceding section we have ourselves assumed that a constitution which is the best that can be achieved from the point of view of justice (yet nevertheless, and inevitably, imperfect) might establish principles relating to private rights, such as provisions relating to the compulsory acquisition of property, or a patrimony clause vesting ownership of natural resources in the nation or its people.

What is not clear is the basis of private rights within a broadly Rawlsian approach to justice. Rawls writes that 'all legal rights and liberties other than … [those] protected by the various constitutional provisions … are to be specified at the legislative stage in the light of the two principles of justice and other relevant principles.'[57] This shows that Rawls simply takes for granted that there will be rights and liberties specified by law, presumably including private rights. (It also reinforces our point, made above, that constitutional principles contribute importantly to the content of public reason.)

It seems that, as component parts of the overall institutional scheme of a just society, private rights must be permitted and shaped only in ways that serve the ends of justice.[58] In a recent article Scheffler expresses the concern that this means that there is no basis for an autonomous or quasi-autonomous domain of private law within such a framework:

> If contract law and other areas of private law belong to the basic structure, and if the basic structure is regulated by … principles of justice, then how do those principles guide or constrain the design of private law, if not by requiring that these areas of law be tailored in such a way as to maximize [distributive justice]?[59]

One possible answer to this concern would be to identify other, non-economic, principles of justice that might support the existence, in a just society, of an institutional scheme of private rights. Rawls suggests that the importance of self-respect might

[54] Rawls, n. 18, 61; Rawls, n. 25, 298. [55] Rawls, n. 25, 364; see also Rawls, n. 18, 87, 282.

[56] For discussion of the latter class of rules, see Rawls, n. 25, 268. [57] Ibid., 338.

[58] A passage in Rawls's essay 'The Basic Structure as Subject', reprinted in n. 25, 268–9, has sometimes been interpreted as suggesting that Rawls took the opposite view: see e.g. Pogge, n. 9, 23; Liam Murphy, 'Institutions and the Demands of Justice', 27(4) *Philosophy & Public Affairs* (1999) 251, 258; Kevin A. Kordana and David H. Blankfein Tabachnick, 'The Rawlsian View of Private Ordering', 25 *Social Philosophy and Policy* (2008) 288, 295–8. We favour the view that the best interpretation of Rawls, or at least of the notion of 'basic structure' that he deploys, is that it includes the rules of private law. We share this conclusion with Pogge, n. 9, 23–4; Murphy, n. 58, 261; Kordana and Tabachnick, n. 58, 297–8; Scheffler, n. 16, 218–20.

[59] Scheffler, n. 16, 225; and see also the discussion at 227–9, 232.

provide such a basis, at least to some extent.[60] In this chapter we will not pursue this suggestion, however. Rather, we wish to consider a second way of understanding the place of private law within a broadly Rawlsian approach to justice.

This alternative way once again begins from the basic idea of 'Two Concepts of Rules'. In a just institutional scheme, the framework of private law rules will be justified because they contribute, overall, to just outcomes. But this does not mean that the private law rules, themselves, require those who deploy them to have regard to the justice of the outcomes they are pursuing. Rawls puts the point in terms of the practicalities of legal rules:

> [T]he conditions necessary for background justice can be undermined, even though nobody acts unfairly or is aware of how the overall result of many separate exchanges affects the opportunities of others. There are no feasible rules that it is practicable to require economic agents to follow in their day-to-day transactions that can prevent these undesirable consequences. … [For instance, i]t is obviously not sensible to impose on parents … the duty to adjust their own bequests to what they estimate the effects of the totality of actual bequests will be on the next generation, much less beyond.[61]

Rather, there is to be 'an institutional division of labor between the basic structure and the rules applying directly to individuals … and to be followed by them in particular transactions'.[62] We think the point Rawls is making here is very similar to the point we made above in relation to the tax official: the best way to achieve just outcomes is not to oblige economic actors, in making their decisions, to have direct regard to considerations of economic justice (which, apart from anything else, they are not well-placed to assess). Rather, it is to devise a system of rules that can be effectively followed by those actors and which, when followed across society, will contribute to just outcomes.[63] This is how private law comes to enjoy a relative degree of autonomy from direct considerations of justice. That degree of autonomy will, in practical terms, only

[60] Rawls, n. 25, 298 ('the right to hold and have exclusive use of personal property … [so as] to allow a sufficient material basis for a sense of personal independence and self-respect'), 318 ('Self-respect is rooted in our self-confidence as a fully cooperating member of society capable of pursuing a worthwhile conception of the good'). Somewhat curiously, in *The Law of Peoples* Rawls defends the essentially territorial character of peoples as the subjects of international justice, *and* compares national territory to property, *and* identifies peoples as each enjoying a legitimate sense of self-respect grounded in an awareness of shared culture and history, but does *not* appeal to the value of self-respect to ground this territoriality. Rather, Rawls says that both property (at the personal level) and territoriality (at the collective level) are institutions justified by the need to ensure that some definite agent (individual or collective) has responsibility for ensuring the non-deterioration of that asset: Rawls, n. 42, 8, 29, 34–5, 38–9, 47–8, 61–2. For suggestions that certain sorts of property claims might be grounded in the contribution that they make to communal self-respect, see Lael K. Weis, 'Resources and the Property Rights Curse', 28(1) *Canadian Journal of Law & Jurisprudence* (2015) 209, 233; Patrick Emerton, 'International Economic Justice: Is A Principle Liberalism Possible?', in Sarah Joseph, David Kiley, and Jeff Waincymer (eds), *The World Trade Organization and Human Rights: Interdisciplinary Perspectives* (Cheltenham: Edward Elgar, 2009), 160, note 129. For a (non-Rawlsian) discussion of the importance to individual self-respect of entering private legal transactions, see Patricia J. Williams, 'The Pain of Word Bondage (a tale with two stories)', in *The Alchemy of Race and Rights* (Cambridge, MA: Harvard University Press, 1991), 146, esp. 146–51.

[61] Rawls, n. 25, 266, 268. [62] Ibid., 268–9.

[63] Scheffler makes much the same point, but while noticing that the 'division of labor' Rawls has in mind is not the same as a technical analytic distinction that Rawls draws in 'Two Concepts of Rules' he does not point out that it relies on the distinction drawn in that paper between justifying a practice, and justifying action undertaken pursuant to a practice: Scheffler, n. 16, 220, note 10. Kronman does

be increased by the fact that most legislation promulgating rules of private law will be an instance of quasi-pure procedural justice.

Liam Murphy criticizes this 'division of labor' argument that private law enjoys (relative) autonomy from considerations of justice: 'It would be possible, for example, to enact a positive law requiring citizens to aim at justice continually in their daily lives.'[64] Murphy goes on to say that such a law 'may be a thoroughly unappealing idea, practically and normatively, but it is perfectly possible'.[65] We do not agree that such a law would be perfectly possible. No doubt we can conceive of a legislature enacting a legal text proclaiming such an obligation,[66] but that does not establish that such a law is genuinely feasible in any contemporary society characterized by an industrial economy, participation in global markets, massive and heterogeneous urban populations, etc. These sorts of societies depend upon bureaucratic administrative structures, and divisions of roles and responsibilities more generally, in order to function.[67] When we focus on private rights, this is particularly evident: most assets are owned by artificial entities (companies) that cannot exist outside an institutionally defined set of roles, obligations, and entitlements, and take the form of intangibles of various sorts (contractual rights, bank accounts, shares and other choses in action), such that the idea of pursuing justice in respect of these things outside the institutional framework is very hard to grasp (for instance, in making a choice to withdraw money from one's bank account so as to make a charitable donation to some cause, one is already implicated in a whole range of proprietary and regulatory structures that have very significant implications for justice).[68]

articulate the point, making reference to 'Two Concepts of Rules', but with particular reference to the role of adjudicators:

> There is no reason to think that judges or anyone else can correctly assess the distributional consequences of particular transactions ... [but] even if one agrees ... that in particular cases judges and others charged with responsibility for policing individual transactions should apply established legal rules regardless of their distributional consequences, it does not follow that distributional effects should also be ignored in the initial design of a system of transactional rules or in the choice of new rules....

Anthony T. Kronman, 'Contract Law and Distributive Justice', 89 *Yale Law Journal* (1980) 472, 501, note 64.

64 Murphy, n. 58, 262. Murphy goes on to agree with Cohen's criticism (n. 19) of the Rawlsian focus upon justice as an ideal for institutional structures rather than as an ideal for individuals: see 264–5, 267, 285.

65 Murphy, n. 58, 262.

66 Although identifying *conceivability* with genuine *possibility* is contentious: see, for instance, Scott Soames, *Reference and Description: The Case against Two-Dimensionalism* (Princeton: Princeton University Press, 2005), ch. 9.

67 In this chapter we take no view on whether this is a good or bad thing (as in Weber's characterization of the modern economic order as an 'iron cage'): Max Weber, *The Protestant Ethic and the Spirit of Capitalism*, Talcott Parsons (trans.) (London: Allen & Unwin, 1930), 181; for an argument that the system of institutionally defined roles that characterizes that order is a systematic source of *injustice*, see Scott Veitch, *Law and Irresponsibility: On the Legitimation of Human Suffering* (Milton Park: Routledge-Cavendish, 2007), esp. chs 2 and 3. Unlike Pogge, who suggests that institutions are, per se, 'a central factor in determining the conditions prevailing in some social system' (Pogge, n. 9, 33), we think that institutions as the focus of considerations of justice take on a particular salience in the sorts of societies we have described.

68 Murphy may not disagree with the point made in the text: after posing the question 'If people have a duty to promote just institutions, why do they lack a duty to promote whatever it is that just institutions are *for*', he replies 'A bad answer will be that the most effective way to promote equality or well-being is

In these circumstances, it *is* the function of legislators to have regard to the requirements of justice in *their* day-to-day decision-making. As explained in Section I, this is a distinctive feature of their role under a just constitution. The next subsection will consider the extent to which just lawmaking, in respect of private law, ought to be constrained by constitutional principles.

B. Constitutional Principles and Private Law

As Rawls points out, large concentrations of private wealth are a threat to political liberty. In particular, the degree of power and influence to which this gives rise threatens to undermine the worth of others' rights to vote, to stand for office, and to take part in political debate, tending to render such rights purely formal. Hence, systematic steps must be taken to prevent such concentrations of wealth from building up, and to break them up when they do arise.[69] Fair equality of opportunity, which requires that positions and offices are open to all regardless of social origins, is also threatened by large concentrations of private wealth.[70]

This threat posed by private wealth to equality suggests two ways in which the principles of a just constitution will bear upon the details of private law rights. First, we can expect a just constitution to contain express principles that bear upon these various aspects of equality,[71] and which thereby provide support within public reasons for elements of private law (property, contracts, artificial entities, and the regulation around them) that prevent or at least reduce the emergence of these sorts of concentrations of private wealth. Second, if the political system is reasonably to be treated as an instance of quasi-pure procedural justice then it must be protected from oligarchic capture. So the very need to maintain the justice of the constitution itself provides support, within public reason, for shaping private law so as to help establish and maintain equality.

The details of any express constitutional principles, and the ways in which the need to maintain the political system as an instance of quasi-pure procedural justice play out in the public reason of a given society, will naturally vary across societies, reflecting their distinctive histories and practices. We might also expect a just constitution to contain further principles bearing upon matters of private law that systematically affect the welfare of large numbers of people, the details once again varying across societies. There is no reason to expect the relevance and operation of such principles to be confined to tax policy and legislation. For instance, the legal rules that govern employment contracts are likely to be another recurrent example. Thus, if a constitution

to promote just institutions. This is a bad answer because when it is correct it is the answer that anyone should give', and hence does not give any reason to think of institutions as having a *special* status as the subject matter of justice: see Murphy, n. 58, 280, and see also 271. A better answer may be that just institutions are the *only*, or the only *practical*, way of promoting what just institutions are for.

69 Rawls, n. 18, 224–6, 277–9; Rawls, n. 25, 326–8.

70 Rawls, n. 18, 73, 87, 278; Rawls, n. 25, 266.

71 When Rawls denies that fair equality of opportunity is a 'constitutional essential' (Rawls, n. 25, 228–30) he seems to have in mind the first sort of constitutional function identified above (namely, establishing rules that determine the validity of legislation) rather than the second (namely, establishing principles that inform the public reason of a society).

expresses, or contains provisions which give rise to, a principle around the entitlements of wage earners to a decent wage, or to share in the fruits of industry, this will provide support within the public reason of that society for legislation mandating a minimum wage.[72] The same or similar principles might also support legislation governing other aspects of employment contracts, such as rules regulating unfair dismissals.[73]

C. The Contributions of Taxation to Justice

The reason we mention these other possible ways in which constitutional principles might bear upon the content and limits of private rights is to reinforce our point that the choice of tax base is of noninstrumental importance to justice. The instrumental purpose of ensuring revenue for distributive purposes, thereby ensuring just welfare outcomes, can be pursued at least in part by other means. But as Section III will argue, taxation—and particularly income taxation—is essential to preventing excessive concentrations of private wealth.

We think that Murphy and Nagel's failure to explore these sorts of interactions between constitutional principles and private rights, and hence to note the principled reasons that can then arise in favour of one or another approach to tax design, results from two weaknesses in their analysis.

The first of these is their suggestion that campaign finance reform, rather than taxation, is a preferable solution to the problem of political inequality resulting from excessive concentrations of private wealth.[74] Regulation of campaign finance can take two forms, however. If it is enacted via legislation, then its claim to be just is in part dependent upon having emerged from a just constitution via quasi-pure procedural justice; and, as we have argued, this depends upon limiting concentrations of private wealth. And taxation is one way to achieve this. Alternatively, if campaign financing is itself regulated by the constitution, or at least guided by principles that are contained within the constitution, then we have an instance of constitutional principles bearing upon the regime of private law (e.g. advertising contracts, the giving of gifts, etc.). And it is at least conceivable that such principles might also bear upon questions of tax design, for instance by providing considerations, as part of the public reason of such a society, for taxing or exempting certain donations to political organizations.

The second is their tendency to favour transfers as the means for ensuring justice in welfare outcomes. This preference can be seen in the favouring of transfers over social provision of services,[75] and also in their preference for transfers over a minimum

[72] See e.g. *Constitution of the Kingdom of Norway* (1814), Art. 110: 'It is the responsibility of the authorities of the State to create conditions enabling every person capable of work to earn a living by his work'; the *Australian Constitution* (1901), s. 51(xxxv), which deals with 'Conciliation and arbitration for the prevention of industrial disputes' and thereby established a constitutional basis for the system of fixing minimum just wages that operated from the time of the famous *Harvester* judgment (*Ex parte HV McKay* (1907) 2 CAR 1) until other mechanisms for setting the minimum wage in Australia began to be adopted from 1996 onwards.

[73] For a discussion of these sorts of examples, and of the use of private law to achieve Rawlsian justice, see Kronman, n. 63.

[74] Murphy and Nagel, n. 1, 115.

[75] Ibid., 90–2.

wage.[76] This tendency leads them to see one important function of taxation—the generation of revenue—as its sole function, and then to see one possible function of revenue—to enable transfers—as *its* sole function.

Murphy and Nagel state, quite plausibly, that 'the most effective way of improving the condition of people below the average would be ... to substantially increase their disposable income'.[77] One available means to improve disposal incomes is through the provision of a minimum wage, but Murphy and Nagel cite the 'perennial debate [in the United States] about rises in the minimum wage' and conclude that 'it seems likely that this is a measure that could achieve only modest improvement in the income of those with the least marketable skills, because large increases would be too damaging economically'.[78] Elsewhere in their book, however, they state that similar concerns about the economic effects of taxes and transfers 'can provide arguments about tax justice only by reference to some standard of what makes one result more just than another'.[79] We think that the same reply can be made in defence of the minimum wage, particularly when its possible grounding in constitutional principles is noted. Murphy and Nagel seem to adopt the same flawed approach of the critics of the income tax (i.e. assuming a natural pre-governmental state which is distorted by government intervention, this time in the form of the setting of minimum wages). In any event, there is no clear consensus on the interaction of the minimum wage and economic growth. Twenty-one of thirty OECD countries have statutory minimum wages.[80] The countries with the highest minimum wages in the OECD in 2013 include: Luxembourg, Netherlands, Belgium, Australia, France, Ireland, New Zealand, the United Kingdom, Canada, and the United States.[81] The research shows that if the minimum wage is not set too high it is not necessarily an impediment to growth and employment.[82]

The framing of the minimum wage as an alternative to transfers funded by taxation can also create a false impression as to how these two mechanisms of justice interact. For instance, the existence of a robust minimum wage does not mean that taxation is not needed just because the problem of welfare justice has been solved in another way. Taxation may have other important work to do in addition to underpinning transfers. Besides the contribution to political and civic equality made by the taxation of wealth, taxation can provide revenue for the social provision of services. Recent research suggests that, even more so than increasing disposable income, it is 'pre-market distribution' (i.e. education and health policies) that appears most conducive to fostering

[76] Ibid., 182–4. Rawls expresses the same preference: Rawls, n. 18, 277, 308–9.

[77] Murphy and Nagel, n. 1, 182.

[78] Ibid. See also Murphy, n. 58, 260–1, where Murphy expresses scepticism that the pursuit of justice via regulating what sorts of contracts are permissible could be as efficient or unobtrusive as taxes and transfers.

[79] Murphy and Nagel, n. 1, 92.

[80] John Martin and Herwig Immervoll, 'The Minimum Wage: Making it Pay', 261 *OECD Observer* (May 2007), 11, 12.

[81] *OECD*, 'StatExtracts—Real Minimum Wages' (26 March 2015), http://stats.oecd.org/Index.aspx?DataSetCode=RMW.

[82] Martin and Immervoll, n. 80, 12. Research also shows that it is not simply a matter of setting the minimum wage rate but considering the interaction with the tax and transfer system. For instance, inflation and taxation coupled with the withdrawal of social security benefits can take away many of the gains of a minimum wage.

growth and reducing inequality, because in this way the potential of a population's human capital is best realized.[83] Cingano contends that:

> Government transfers have an important role to play in guaranteeing that low-income households do not fall further back in the income distribution. This is not only restricted to cash transfers. Other important elements of this pillar are policies to promote and increase access to public services. This concerns services such as high-quality education or access to health. Such measures smooth inequality stemming from cash incomes immediately, but they furthermore constitute a longer-term social investment to foster upward mobility and create greater equality of opportunities in the long run.[84]

Cingano concludes that 'policies that help [to] limit ... or—ideally—revers[e] the long-run rise in inequality would not only make societies less unfair, but also richer'.[85]

III. The Justice of the Tax Base

The options for choices over the tax base have been relatively constant for centuries, the main contenders being wealth and resources, consumption, and income. The emphases placed by different regimes and societies have changed over time, with early systems favouring the taxation of resources and wealth (mainly in the form of land), then transactions (consumption) and then income as a mainstay of taxation in the twentieth century in many developed economies. Most modern tax systems involve a mix of all three bases, and as the following discussion reveals there is a degree of overlap between each base.

We agree with Murphy and Nagel that what ultimately justifies taxation is its contribution to just outcomes, both redistributively and more broadly. But, as we have argued, considerations of justice, particularly as mediated through constitutional principles and their role in the public reason of a society, mean that the choice of tax base is not purely instrumental. In the previous section we argued that the likely presence in a just constitution of a principle of political equality and fair equality of opportunity, in conjunction with the need to maintain the constitution as just (and thereby to uphold legislation as quasi-pure procedural justice), supports arguments in favour of wealth as an object of taxation. The use of mass-revenue-raising taxation to provide social services is a further important mechanism for dealing with the threat that inequality poses to justice. There are, therefore, reasons of principle for favouring a mass-revenue-raising tax that also taxes wealth. As we will now argue, as a practical matter that means taxing income.

[83] Jonathan D. Ostry, Andrew Berg, and Charalambos G. Tsangarides, 'Redistribution Inequality and Growth', *IMF Staff Discussion Note* SDN 14/02 (April 2014), https://www.imf.org/external/pubs/ft/sdn/2014/sdn1402.pdf, 5.

[84] Frederico Cingano, 'Trends in Income Inequality and its Impact on Economic Growth', *OECD Social, Employment and Migration Working Papers* 163 (OECD Publishing, December 2014), http://dx.doi.org/10.1787/5jxrjncwxv6j-en, 29.

[85] Ibid., 28. Ostry et al. refer to these policies as 'win-win' policies, that is policies that are both good for economic growth and equality rather than a trade-off between the two: Ostry, Berg, and Tsangarides, n. 83, 5.

For developed economies no tax has surpassed the income tax for over a century in doing so well at raising revenue. The rest of this section explains the superior capacity of the income tax to raise revenue and to tax wealth when compared to alternative tax bases, using the Haig-Simons definition of income as the entry point for the analysis. Section IV then addresses the prospects for the income tax in a globalized economy, resulting from taxpayers attempting to minimize or avoid their income tax liability through activities such as tax avoidance and evasion, base erosion, and profit-shifting.

A. Taxing Wealth by Taxing Income

The classic Haig-Simons definition states that *income* is equal to *consumption* plus *savings* (i.e. increases in net wealth) over a period of time.[86] To put it simply, if we assume that inputs must equal outputs then all wealth or income can either be spent or saved.[87] One can see immediately from this formulation that income incorporates the other main bases of wealth and consumption.

If we flip the equation we can say that consumption is equal to income minus saving (over a period of time).[88] This reveals a key difference between the income tax and consumption tax that has divided the respective supporters and detractors of each base: a consumption tax, in failing to tax wealth, is prima facie to the advantage of those who control and accrue economic resources. It may be argued, however, that this difference between income and consumption as alternative tax bases is overstated, and is mostly a matter of timing.[89] A consumption tax will tax wealth that has enabled consumption. If taxation is measured over a lifetime, a consumption base and an income base will be prima facie identical for those who consume what they earn in a lifetime.[90] However, as with most things in fiscal policy, this claimed 'lifetime equivalence' of income and consumption bases is contestable.

[86] Robert Murray Haig, 'The Concept of Income—Economic and Legal Aspects', in Robert Murray Haig (ed.), *The Federal Income Tax* (New York: Columbia University Press, 1921); Henry Simons, *Personal Income Taxation: The Definition of Income as a Problem of Fiscal Policy* (Chicago: University of Chicago Press, 1938), 49.

[87] Edward J. McCaffery, 'Three Views of Tax', 18(1) *Canadian Journal of Law & Jurisprudence* (2005) 153, 155. As we elaborate later in this section, wealth which is saved rather than spent consists of assets which can be used in various ways and have value beyond the potential market consumption they represent. It should also be noted that from the point of view of justice, one important way of 'spending' wealth is to pass it on by way of gift or inheritance.

[88] John R. King, 'The Concept of Income', in Parthasarathi Shome (ed.), *Tax Policy Handbook* (Washington, DC: IMF, 1995), 117. This definition of consumption can be contested, with consumption being understood in terms of extraction of an asset from the 'social pool' rather than in terms of the utility resulting from the relinquishing of economic power: Harry Grubert and Richard Krever, 'VAT and Financial Services: Competing Perspectives on What Should be Taxed', 65(2) *Tax Law Review* (2012) 199, 199–204.

[89] As the Haig-Simons definition reveals, time is crucial to the calculation of income. 'The measurement of income implies allocation of consumption and accumulation to specified periods': Philip Burgess Simons, Graeme S Cooper, Richard J Vann, Miranda Stewart, and Richard E Krever, *Cooper, Krever & Vann's Income Taxation: Commentary and Materials*, 7th edn (Pyrmont, NSW: Thomson Reuters, 2012), 7.

[90] The IMF contends that '[t]axing consumption is equivalent to taxing accumulated assets and labor income': IMF, *Fiscal Exit: From Strategy to Implementation, Fiscal Monitor November 2010* (Washington, DC: IMF, 2010), 80.

We assume that the reader is familiar with the well-known concern that income taxation falls unevenly upon these notionally common bases, depending upon the timing of consumption: because it taxes savings twice—once when earned, and again when those earnings are invested and realize a return—it favours current over future consumption, and in virtue of this 'nonneutrality', distorts decisions relating to production, work, saving, and consumption. A consumption tax, on the other hand, only distorts choices relating to work (because by increasing the cost of goods it discourages consumption and therefore work), but is neutral in relation to choices over saving and production (because it ignores all income until spent/consumed). Indeed, the purported neutrality of consumption taxes in relation to the timing of consumption choices is one of the key features that underpin support for consumption taxation, on the basis that an individual is not penalized for choosing to consume later (by saving now) as they are under the income tax.[91] The double taxation of savings is broadly considered anathema to good tax design, not only inefficient (because of the distortions to which it gives rise) but unfair (because it penalizes taxpayers in equal positions regarding their lifetime earnings based solely on the timing of their consumption decisions). However, we do not accept this consensus.

1. *The alleged unfairness of the income tax*

The objection to the income tax as unfair rests on the claimed superiority of a lifetime measure of income and the permanent income hypothesis. The *Henry Review* provides an example of this:[92]

> The essential reason for treating lifetime, long-term savings more favourably is that income taxation creates a bias against savings, particularly long-term savings. Taxes on savings income, including *the taxation of inflationary gains*, can discriminate against taxpayers who choose to defer consumption and save. The longer the person saves and reinvests, the greater the implicit tax on future consumption ...

[91] For the classic summary of the divide between income and consumption taxation see, e.g., William Andrews, 'A Consumption-Type or Cash Flow Personal Income Tax', 87(6) *Harvard Law Review* (1974) 1113; Alvin Warren, 'Would a Consumption Tax be Fairer Than an Income Tax?', 89(6) *Yale Law Journal* (1980) 1081. Blumkin et al. note that 'wage taxes can be thought as prepaid consumption taxes, while consumption taxes like the VAT and retail sales taxes are viewed as post-paid consumption taxes' and reject the income taxation of savings on grounds that it 'distorts the taxpayer's inter-temporal consumption allocation'; they then go on to contest the equivalence of the wage tax with the VAT on empirical grounds: Tomer Blumkin, Bradley J Ruffle, and Yosef Ganun, 'Are Income and Consumption Taxes Ever Really Equivalent? Evidence from a Real-Effort Experiment with Real Goods', 56(6) *European Economic Review* (2012) 1200, 1201. There is also a well-known debate on whether income or consumption is a more or less reliable measure of welfare, which we will not address here: Alvin Warren, 'Would a Consumption Tax Be Fairer Than an Income Tax?', 89(6) *Yale Law Journal* (1980) 1095–7.

[92] *Henry Review*, n. 51, Part 1, 32 (emphasis added). In relation to the taxation of inflationary gains, it is generally accepted in the public finance literature that both an income tax and a consumption tax in theory do not tax inflationary gains: Daniel N. Shaviro, 'Replacing the Income Tax with a Progressive Consumption Tax', 103, *Tax Notes* (5 April 2004) 91, 101. The taxation of inflationary gains under the income tax only occurs because of a failure to index income tax rates in Australia which occurs mostly for reasons of administrative or political expediency that enable revenue gains based on increases in nominal rather than real incomes.

> These individuals pay a higher lifetime tax bill than people with similar earnings who choose to save less.

Underpinning this objection is Milton Friedman's *permanent income hypothesis*, which proposes that people's current consumption choices are based on their expected lifetime earnings rather than what they earn in a given period, and that saving is therefore merely a means of smoothing one's consumption over a lifetime; for example, by saving in middle age so as to maintain consumption during retirement.[93]

Shaviro explains how insights from optimal commodity taxation literature reinforce the lifetime measure/permanent income hypothesis. Optimal commodity taxation holds that it is more efficient to impose a uniform commodity tax (one that applies at the same rate across all market goods) than one that varies according to the price elasticity of different commodities.[94] If we assume that present and future consumption are just two different commodities, and that '[s]avings decisions merely reflect commodity choice within [a] budget line' that is determined by lifetime earnings, then it makes no more sense to discriminate between future and current consumption than it does to discriminate between different types of goods at the same time.[95]

If an income tax penalizes individuals with equal lifetime earning capacities purely on the basis of the timing of consumption choices (because one decides to save more during periods of high earnings so as to spend more later while the other decides to spend all they have) then one can see, by extension, the horizontal equity imperative for a consumption tax. Indeed, Shaviro draws further on optimal taxation and welfare economics analysis to show that:[96]

> [T]he cases for income averaging and for consumption taxation are closely linked ... [B]oth follow from viewing lifetime budget lines as the key attribute in discerning total and marginal utility, a stance that relies on the permanent income hypothesis to establish that all equivalent lifetime budget lines are indeed effectively the same.

[93] Daniel Shaviro, 'Beyond the Pro-Consumption Tax Consensus', 60(3) *Stanford Law Review* (2007) 745, 750, 763–6; Milton Friedman, *A Theory of the Consumption Function* (Princeton: Princeton University Press, 1957), 20–37; Franco Modigliani and Richard Brumberg, 'Utility Analysis and the Consumption Function: An Interpretation of Cross-Section Data', in Kenneth K. Kurihara (ed.), *Post Keynesian Economics* (New Brunswick: Rutgers University Press, 1954), 338.

[94] *Price elasticity* refers to the extent to which the supply and demand of a good is responsive to changes in price, and therefore to taxation that is incorporated into that price. Ramsey had argued that it was most efficient to apply a commodity tax at differential rates according to the relevant price elasticity of the good (e.g. high rates for goods with inelastic demand, such as bread, and low rates for goods with elastic demand, such as fairy floss): F.P. Ramsey, 'A Contribution to the Theory of Taxation', 37(145) *Economic Journal* (1927) 47. Atkinson and Stiglitz showed that this is not the case, and that subject to reasonable assumptions it is better to tax commodities equally: A.B. Atkinson and J.E. Stiglitz, 'The Design of Tax Structure: Direct Versus Indirect Taxation', 6 *Journal of Public Economics* (1976) 55, 56–9, 73–4; Shaviro, n. 93, 760.

[95] Shaviro, n. 93, 781, 783. This leaves aside goods that might act as substitute for leisure—for example, golf clubs—for which there might remain efficiency arguments to tax at higher rates: Ibid., 759–60, notes 51, 53; W.J. Corlett and D.C. Hague, 'Complementarity and the Excess Burden of Taxation', 21(1) *Review of Economic Studies* (1953) 21.

[96] Shaviro, n. 93, 780–1. See also Daniel Shaviro, 'The Economics of Tax Law', *Public Law & Legal Theory Research Paper Series Working Paper* No. 14-04, *Law & Economics Research Paper Series Working Paper* No. 14-06 (2014), 20–1.

However, they are then vulnerable to the same objections, three of which are explored here.[97] First, the approach excludes (or at least struggles to incorporate) uncertainty and risk. One does not know at the start of one's working life what one's overall earnings will be, and a person who guesses wrong cannot cross the space-time divide and retrospectively alter consumption behaviour to match later earnings.[98] Second, even if one could accurately project into the future, for the models to hold in practice one would require complete capital markets that enable people to borrow and lend across time so as to (1) invest current earnings for future consumption, (2) borrow against future earnings for current consumption, and (3) adjust fully and immediately to changes in current earnings, whether anticipated or not. Only the first is fully available.[99] Third, individuals do not act rationally, especially when it comes to assessments about time. For example, individuals can be myopic and apply a much higher discount rate in favour of the present over future periods. What therefore matters most to current well-being is not necessarily lifetime earnings but currently available resources.[100] As the US Treasury succinctly put it:

> [I]t is the current year's income that in large part determines the current living standard and the sum out of which most taxes are paid. Moreover, the current year's income is usually regarded as the most practical basis for the comparison of ... tax burdens at various income levels.[101]

The lifetime measure model is also open to an objection similar to that advanced by Murphy and Nagel against analyses of the burden of taxation that ignore the location of both taxation and property rights within a larger institutional scheme. The lifetime measure model takes for granted a whole host of institutional arrangements, such as undertaking training so as to generate income potential (and hence temporarily depressing income), and retirement,[102] which are themselves part and parcel of the same economic and social system to which the tax system belongs.[103] Hence, the treatment of these as if they were noninstitutional considerations that can be used to ground fairness constraints on taxation arrangements is incoherent.

There are further grounds for not regarding the double taxation of savings as an objection to the income tax. If one accepts that wealth and its yield represents more than simply the ability to fund future consumption, then one might support an income tax on this very basis.[104] Furthermore, there are intergenerational transfers of wealth,

[97] For a comprehensive critique see Shaviro, n. 93, 762–6, 770–7, 781. [98] Ibid., 772.

[99] Ibid., 749, 770–7. [100] Ibid., 775.

[101] US Department of the Treasury, *Tax Reform for Fairness, Simplicity, and Economic Growth*, vol. 3 (Washington, DC: Office of the Secretary, Department of the Treasury, 1984), ch. 8, 90.

[102] In setting out the lifetime measure approach to taxation, Shaviro takes for granted that people retire (and hence lose their labour income), and also considers the circumstances of people borrowing to finance their education: Shaviro, n. 93, 766, 770. See also Edward J. McCaffery, 'A New Understanding of Tax', 103(5) *Michigan Law Review* (2005) 807, 815.

[103] For instance, hunter-gatherers do not undertake formal education which they must finance by borrowing. Nor do they *retire*, as opposed to simply growing old.

[104] McCaffery, for example, points out that it was precisely the double taxation of savings that generated initial support for the introduction of the income tax in the United States: McCaffery, n. 102, 809–10; Edward J. McCaffery and James R. Hines, Jr, 'The Last Best Hope for Progressivity in Tax', *University of Southern California Law School Law and Economics Working Paper Series* No. 92 (2009), 82.

which remind us that not all wealth is spent or consumed in a lifetime. We share the concerns of Murphy and Nagel that this unspent wealth is not captured under a consumption tax.[105]

Shaviro argues that even a consumption tax that is permanently deferred (because wealth/income is never spent/consumed) offers value to the government (the present liability can be borrowed against to fund government services) and a corresponding burden to the saver (because the present value of future consumption is reduced by the present, though not yet payable, tax liability).[106] We reject this argument for two reasons. First, it is hard to observe or quantify the actual value of the deferred tax liability if there is little to no chance the tax will ever be levied. A presently enforced and paid tax liability might be worth much more than a future potential liability which might never be enforced or not at the same rate. Second, the argument in part depends on a claim that unspent wealth has no benefit beyond future market consumption:

> [S]avings and wealth are ... subsidiary to consumption in that they derive their value entirely from that potential use, whether its use is proximate or not. That ability to buy things is, after all, the difference between real money and play money from board games such as Monopoly and Life.[107]

Contrary to Shaviro, we believe that wealth yields more than consumption power.[108] We are particularly interested in its capacity to yield political power. As Rawls notes, such greater political influence is not only itself a threat to justice (because it is contrary to political equality) but it also enables high wealth individuals to manipulate future rules so as to conceal future consumption or reduce the effective tax rate, thereby entrenching and exacerbating this injustice.[109] More generally, political power stems from more than just the ability to consume. Much of it lies in the ability to invest, and thereby to control the use of society's productive assets.[110]

[105] Murphy and Nagel, n. 1, 115. [106] Shaviro, n. 92, 103–5. [107] Ibid., 106.

[108] Groenewegen also argues that retained wealth generates utility even if not consumed, and hence should be liable to taxation on the same basis as consumption:

> Wealth ownership, after all, provides more than just income. Its returns generally have greater permanence, therefore provide more security, and are obtained without much sacrifice of leisure while wealth ownership also confers social status and perhaps more importantly, access to credit on better terms. From a slightly different perspective ... many important personal wealth items can be said to yield a regular stream of psychic income not easily assessable as income for income tax purposes ... A regular tax on the ownership of wealth irrespective of its yield can capture the psychic income from assets like housing, cars and pleasure boats, furniture, clothing, and jewellery as well as from collections of art, antiques, books, and so on.

Peter Groenewegen, 'Options for the Taxation of Wealth', 2 *Australian Tax Forum* (1985) 305, 306–7. The same point is made in Murphy and Nagel, n. 1, 114–16, 149–50. For criticism of their analysis of wealth, see Kevin A. Kordana and David H. Tabachnick, 'Tax and the Philosopher's Stone', 89(3) *Virginia Law Review* (2003) 647, 673–6.

[109] Rawls, n. 18, 86–7, 224–6, 277–8.

[110] The idea that assets are nothing but a source of consumption power seems to fit with a general tendency in some theoretical tax policy analysis to treat all assets as purely financial and not real. Curiously, in a discussion of the benefits of wealth Bankman and Weisbach do not consider that wielding power generates any significant consequences beyond contributing to the welfare of the individual who wields the power: Joseph Bankman and David A. Weisbach, 'The Superiority of an Ideal Consumption Tax Over an Ideal Income Tax', 58(5) *Stanford Law Review* (2006) 1413, 1449, 1450.

2. *The alleged inefficiency of the income tax*

As was noted above, criticism of the double taxation of savings is directed at purported efficiency consequences as well as purported unfairness. The premise that informs the efficiency critique of the income tax is that economic growth (and therefore overall welfare) is best achieved when markets are left to operate without governmental interference, and hence that tax policy should, as much as possible, be neutral towards the operation of the market. The point of course has always been contentious, but has been the dominant strand in public finance since at least the 1970s.[111] However, recent empirical work has begun to challenge this consensus. This work suggests that inequality may in fact impede economic growth, especially when there is a large gap between low-income households and the rest of the population.[112] Moreover, the research suggests that not only is inequality in disposable incomes bad for growth, but that redistribution (in the form of taxation and transfers) is, at worst, neutral to growth.[113]

Recent contributions have also emphasized the efficiency benefits of taxing realized gains (because high savings can dampen work effort),[114] of taxing income at progressive rates[115] and even of taxing capital income.[116] In essence, this new research shows that it is economically efficient to tax realized earnings because they are a more reliable measure of welfare/ability to pay. As Shaviro summarizes it, the fact that an income tax uses more information than a consumption tax (because it makes net lifetime tax liability depend on savings decisions and therefore on the timing of consumption relative to earnings) is a reason in favour of the efficiency of the income tax.[117]

Even to the extent that the distortion complaint retains any plausibility, we agree with Murphy and Nagel that private rights 'are the product of a set of laws and conventions, of which the tax system forms a part', and hence cannot be erected in opposition

[111] See, e.g., Institute for Fiscal Studies, *The Structure and Reform of Direct Taxation (Report of a Committee chaired by Professor J.E. Meade)* (London: Allen & Unwin, 1978); Jonathon Gruber, *Public Finance and Public Policy*, 3rd edn (New York: Worth, 2011), 754–6; *Consumption Tax Trends 2012: VAT/GST and Excise Rates, Trends and Administration Issues* (Paris: OECD, 2012), 11–13.

[112] Cingano, n. 84, 20–2.

[113] Ibid., 19; Ostry, Berg, and Tsangarides, n. 83, 4. Piketty notes that the decrease in the top marginal income tax rate between 1980 and today is closely related to the increase in the top centile's share of national income over the same period, but not to the rate of productivity growth, which remained the same. On this basis he opines that reduced top marginal rates simply incentivized executives to bargain for higher wages without any corresponding rise in productivity: Thomas Piketty, *Capital in the Twenty First Century* (Cambridge, MA: Harvard University Press, 2014), 509–10.

[114] Shaviro, n. 93, 778, 785. For more generally on the work of dynamic public finance theory, see: Narayana R. Kocherlakota, *The New Dynamic Public Finance* (Princeton: Princeton University Press, 2010). See also Piketty, n. 113, 527. Piketty runs a related argument that a tax on capital would incentivize capital holders getting a greater return on capital stock (so as to pay the tax liability). Those who did not would have to realize assets to pay taxes with the assets going to those who should put them to more productive use. This argument should not be overstated, however, because (according to Piketty) the returns to capital are in many respects a product of luck based on the timing of market cycles and not solely based on the talent of the capitalist.

[115] Peter Diamond and Emmanuel Saez, 'The Case for a Progressive Tax: From Basic Research to Policy Recommendations', 25(4) *Journal of Economic Perspectives* (2011) 165, 167–83.

[116] Ibid., 167–83; Mikhail Golosiv, Narayana Kocherlakota, and Aleh Tsyvinski, 'Optimal Indirect and Capital Taxation', 70 *Review of Economic Studies* (2003) 569, 580.

[117] Shaviro, n. 93, 785–6. Shaviro further notes that this casts doubt on the attempt to extend the conclusions of optimal commodity taxation from the case where the commodities are simultaneously available to a treatment of present and future consumption periods as simply two different commodities.

to the outcomes of a just tax system.[118] To the extent that the complaint of 'distortion' is a complaint about the effect of the income tax upon economic growth and aggregate welfare, then we emphasize the priority of justice over aggregate welfare. Given that, as we have argued, the income tax is not merely about raising revenue but about contributing to a just society, the question should then be: even though the income tax distorts in comparison to a no tax world, is it justified by principles of justice, including the principles underlying or expressed by a just constitution? We have argued that it is.[119] Murphy and Nagel also affirm the priority of justice over marginal increases in welfare, although they state the requirements of justice simply in terms of the availability of revenue for redistribution, rather than the concerns of equality that we have emphasized.[120]

3. *Taxing returns upon investment*

It is argued that an income tax cannot effectively capture the bulk of returns upon investment, because these returns are attributable to risk rather than the risk-free rate of return, and sophisticated investors can always adjust their portfolio to increase their risk, and hence their return on risk, relying upon the tax deductibility of losses to offset the increased risk of loss that corresponds to the increased return.[121] It is therefore claimed that the incidence of the income tax differs from that of the consumption tax only in capturing the risk-free return to waiting, and the general consensus is that this is only a very modest component of returns to savings.[122] (Although Shaviro makes the point that when it comes to the super-rich—enormous fortunes that are held over long periods of time—there might be a revenue and equity imperative for taxing this return to waiting.[123])

[118] Murphy and Nagel, n. 1, 74. That is not to deny, as we have argued above, that considerations of justice in relation to private rights may themselves play a role in shaping a just tax system.

[119] Even Blumkin et al., in arguing for the benefits of consumption over income taxes, concede that 'distributive goals might justify the distortive effects of the income tax': T. Blumkin, B. Ruffle, and Y. Ganun, n. 91, 1201.

[120] Murphy and Nagel, n. 1, 140–1.

[121] Joseph Bankman and Thomas Griffith, 'Is the Debate Between an Income Tax and a Consumption Tax a Debate About Risk? Does it Matter?', 47 *Tax Law Review* (1992) 377; Noel B. Cunningham, 'The Taxation of Capital and the Choice of Tax Base', 52 *Tax Law Review* (1996) 17; Joseph Bankman and Barbara H. Fried, 'Winners and Losers in the Shift to a Consumption Tax', 86 *Georgetown Law Journal* (1998) 539; and see also the discussion in Murphy and Nagel, n. 1, 117–18; Shaviro, n. 96, 18; Shaviro, n. 92, 100–3. Shaviro makes the point that, if these arguments are correct, then the distortion introduced by the income tax's double taxation of savings is attributable solely to its treatment of the return to waiting, which would not be taxed by a consumption tax: Shaviro, n. 96, 18.

[122] Writing in 1992, Bankman and Griffith state that 'Over the past sixty years, the real, riskless rate of return has been near zero', while Shaviro, writing in 2004, states that 'historically the real riskless return ... has been less than 1% per year': Bankman and Griffith, n. 121, 377; Shaviro, n. 92, 101. Bankman and Griffith state that 'during the years 1926–1989, the average riskless, real rate of return was just .5%', while Cunningham states the real risk-free return to waiting to have averaged 0.6 per cent from 1926 to 1996, and 1.74 per cent from 1990 to 1996: Bankman and Griffith, n. 121, 387; Cunningham, n. 121, 21. Writing in 1998, Bankman and Fried state that 'Over the years, the annual riskless return has been about 5%': Bankman and Fried, n. 121, 542, note 10. However, this figure has not been adjusted for inflation.

[123] Daniel N. Shaviro, n. 92, 103.

We cannot adequately discuss these arguments within the scope of this chapter, but do note that they rest on certain assumptions that may not hold true in the real world: (1) that all investment losses are fully deductible;[124] (2) that investors are able to change their portfolios at little or no cost;[125] and (3) that investors are able to purchase additional investments at a given level of risk at the same price as they would be able to in the absence of an income tax.[126]

One striking feature of these arguments, which seems directly related to assumption (3), is that in the worked examples provided by way of illustration, the total expected return is less in the 'no tax' world than in the tax world.[127] Where does the extra money come from? It arises from the assumption that productive but risky assets are available for exploitation, which the taxpayer (given her risk profile) will not exploit unless the government joins her as (in effect) an insurer against some of the potential losses (by way of the tax deductibility of those losses).[128] We might doubt whether, in the real world, these additional productive investments, and hence these additional revenues, are actually available.[129]

[124] Bankman and Griffith, n. 121, 398–400; Bankman and Fried, n. 121, 543.

[125] Bankman and Griffith, n. 121, 397; Bankman and Fried, n. 121, 543–4.

[126] Bankman and Griffith, n. 121, 397–8; Bankman and Fried, n. 121, 543; Cunningham does not expressly address this point, but does assume that an investor can increase her exposure to a particular risky investment without affecting the rate of return on that investment: Cunningham, n. 121, 30–1, note 54.

[127] Thus, in Bankman and Griffith's example (n. 121, 393–5), in the no-tax world $100 is invested half in a risk-free, no-return investment, and half in an investment with equal chances of delivering a 100 per cent return or a 50 per cent loss, for expected outcomes of either $150 or $75 (with equal chances) and hence an expected return of $12.50. In the world with a 30 per cent income tax the same $100 is invested at $28.57 and $71.43 across the risk-free and the risky investments respectively, likewise generating expected outcomes of either $150 or $75 (with equal chances) and hence an expected return of $12.50; but tax obligations are also generated and discharged, either a $21.43 liability or a $10.71½ entitlement to a deduction (in equal chances), which is an expected return to the government of $5.35¾. Similarly, in Cunningham's example (n. 121, 32–4), in the no-tax world $1,000 is invested half in a risk-free investment returning 0.6 per cent, and half in an investment with equal chances of delivering a 30 per cent return or a 6 per cent loss, for expected outcomes of either $1,153 or $973 (with equal chances) and hence an expected return of $63. In the world with a 33⅓ per cent income tax the same $1,000 is invested at $250 and $750 across the risk-free and the risky investments respectively, generating expected outcomes of either $1,151 or $971 (with equal chances) and hence an expected return of $61 (the $2 reduction in expected return corresponds to a 33⅓ per cent tax on the 0.6 per cent risk-free rate of return); but tax obligations are also generated and discharged, either a $75.50 liability or a $14.50 entitlement to a deduction (in equal chances), which is an expected return to the government of $30.50.

[128] Bankman and Griffith describe this using the metaphor of the government becoming a 'partner' in the taxpayer's investment: Bankman and Griffith, n. 121, 394. That it is the extra investment in the risky opportunity that generates the additional returns that flow to the government as tax revenue can easily be seen by noting that, in both examples, the following two ratios are equal: the ratio of the expected return to the government (by way of tax revenue) to the taxpayer's expected return in the income tax world; and the ratio of the additional money invested in the risky investment (in the income tax world) to the original investment (in the no-tax world). An exception in Cunningham's example is the $2 that results from the income tax operating upon the risk-free rate of return.

[129] Cunningham touches on this economic hypothesis, of the effectively unlimited availability of investments at a given level of risk and return, in a discussion of some similar properties of an idealized cash-flow tax. He contrasts, as potentially relevant to a proper understanding of whether the yield on investment is burdened by the tax, circumstances in which an investor's investment opportunities at a given rate of return are or are not limited: Cunningham, n. 121, 26–9. He characterizes the issue as 'primarily semantic' (27), and while noting that 'the limited investment situation may be an important one' expresses preference for the view on which an investor's opportunities are not limited on the ground that it 'is both simple to understand and to apply' (28). We think that, in understanding the scope for taxation

Assumption (2) might hold true if all investments were readily substitutable, such as financial assets, but appears less so if investments are in less fungible, tangible assets. Although the substitutability of the former for the latter increases in a modern economy (where mechanisms such as hedging allows for the ability to transform real assets into financial ones, and therefore more readily allow for the changing of portfolios), events such as the global financial crisis suggest that the ability to turn all real assets into financial assets might not be unlimited.

B. The Role of Wealth Taxation

The taxation of wealth need not be addressed by an income tax alone. Wealth taxes should, in principle, be able to play an important role.[130] The problem is that, in practice, the effective implementation and administration of wealth taxes has proved elusive.

In theory there are a number of options available to tax wealth. Most options in practice are variations on wealth transfer taxes, requiring some specific transfer from donor to recipient. These include bequest taxes, either estate taxes levied on the estate of the deceased or inheritance taxes levied on the inheritance of individual recipients. Such taxes generally require complementary gift taxation to avoid inter vivos transfers defeating the operation of the taxes.[131] An alternative is an accessions tax, which applies on a cumulative basis to gifts or inheritances received by an individual throughout their life.[132] Much less popular alternatives include attempts to impose annual net wealth levies. The most recent and high profile example of such a proposal comes from Thomas Piketty's proposal to adopt a new tax on global capital, levied annually on all classes of asset valued at market rates and applied at progressive rates. Although such an idea might have merit in principle, in practice individual countries have struggled to implement anything like an effective annual wealth levy let alone one that requires global or at least a degree of regional coordination (e.g. the automatic sharing of banking information to identify assets held and the individuals who hold them).[133] A combined progressive annual wealth and accessions tax was proposed by the Meade Committee. Its aim is to tax, at the time of transfer, the unearned benefit from a transfer of wealth by gift or bequest not only at that time but for the remainder of the donee's lifetime (such a tax tries to capture the lifetime value of an asset gifted to a donee by multiplying its present value by an annuity multiplier reflecting the expected lifetime of a donee plus a discount rate).[134]

of wealth by means of an income tax, addressing empirical questions of the sort raised in Bankman and Griffith (n. 121, 397–8) and Bankman and Fried (n. 121, 543–4) must take priority over simplifying assumptions.

[130] For instance, the *Henry Review* noted that a well-designed bequest tax would improve equity by helping to distribute opportunities more evenly across the community: *Henry Review*, n. 51, Part 2, 141.

[131] Ibid., Part 2, 141, 144.

[132] Ireland has such a tax: Ibid., Part 2, 144.

[133] Piketty, n. 113, 516–18. France has an annual wealth levy which, according to Piketty, is riddled with exemptions and based on the flawed method of self-declared asset holdings. Germany suspended a similar tax in 1997 and Sweden abandoned theirs in 2005: Ibid., 645, note 37.

[134] For a sympathetic presentation, see Groenewegen, n. 108, 319–21, 323–4. For criticisms, see Murphy and Nagel, n. 1, 156–7. Their principal criticism of the 'PAWAT' is that it discriminates between wealth consumed and wealth given away within a lifetime (under the PAWAT only the latter attracts

All such taxes are beset by valuation and administrative difficulties.[135] Furthermore, many wealth transfer taxes are not effective at breaking up concentrated holdings of wealth.[136] In part this is a product of the design and implementation of such taxes in practice. The political unpopularity of these taxes manifests in poor design with exemptions leaving a large bulk of assets untaxed. This is also reflected in a relatively low generation of revenue by wealth transfer taxes: about 0.41 per cent of total tax revenue across OECD.[137] It has been argued that this may be a sign of the *success* of wealth taxation in reducing concentrations of wealth, if it is a result of holdings being broken up so as to fall below taxation thresholds.[138] While extreme disparities of wealth continue to exist, however, so does the need to break up large holdings of wealth, as well as the need to generate revenue to provide social services. Given the practical experience and outcomes of wealth taxation, we suggest that this means choosing income as the primary tax base.[139]

This is not to deny that the same forces that undermine the capacity of wealth taxation as an effective means of breaking up concentrations of wealth affect the income tax. Piketty demonstrates how many modern tax systems have or will become regressive at the top of the income hierarchy.[140] High wealth individuals are able to engage in lawful tax minimization (and unlawful tax evasion) to pay effective tax rates far below one per cent of their economic incomes.[141] The results would be even more markedly regressive if individuals were classified according to centile of total resources accrued (from both earned income and capitalized inheritance).[142] We nevertheless contend that the income tax is the preferred vehicle for breaking up concentrated wealth, for

a rebate of the tax paid). However, if the principal function of the PAWAT is to ensure fair equality of opportunity—as they accept it to be (155)—then the discrimination does not seem unreasonable, as consumption provides opportunities that giving away (typically) does not. (It might seem that Murphy and Nagel are simply objecting to the PAWAT's discrimination between consumption choices, but at another point in their discussion of wealth taxation they reject the 'implausible idea that taxes should be neutral among consumption choices' in accepting as unobjectionable the possibility of 'double taxation' of gifts in circumstances where the donee is taxed, the donor is not entitled to a deduction, and the donor meets the cost of the donee's tax as part of the gift (154).)

135 See e.g. the discussion in Groenewegen, n. 108, 311–13, 320. Piketty rejects one-off levies on transfers because the fluctuation in the returns to capital make the value of the gift to the donor difficult to measure at the time of the transfer: Piketty, n. 113, 527.

136 Groenewegen, n. 108, 313–14; Willard H. Pedrick, 'Oh to Die Down Under! Abolition of Death and Gift Duties in Australia', 14(4) *University of Western Australia Law Review* (1982) 438, 453. Pedrick argues that the mere symbolic presence of estate taxes is nevertheless important: see 454.

Australia adopted a graduated land tax in 1910 to promote the breakup of large holdings, but this was repealed in 1952 'on the ground that significant redistribution of land ownership had taken place': Pedrick, n. 136, 460–1.

137 *Henry Review*, n. 51, Part 2, 143. Groenewegen notes that Australia generated higher than OECD-average revenues via estate duties during the 1960s: Groenewegen, n. 108, 308. Pedrick, writing in the early 1980s, suggests that estate duties can raise from 1 to 3 per cent of government revenue: Pedrick, n. 136, 454.

138 See, e.g. David Duff, 'Taxing Inherited Wealth: A Philosophical Argument', 6(1) *Canadian Journal of Law & Jurisprudence* (1993) 3, 8.

139 Rawls favours a consumption tax as a means of raising revenue for redistributive purposes, and identifies the function of progressivity, and of wealth taxes, as being not to raise revenue but rather to ensure that property is widely distributed, rather than concentrated, for reasons of equality: Rawls, n. 18, 277–9. The political and administrative challenges of wealth taxation lead us to favour income taxation instead.

140 Piketty, n. 113, 496–7. 141 Ibid., 525. 142 Ibid., 497.

the following reasons. First, the income tax has proved itself capable of breaking up concentrations of wealth in the past, as Piketty himself observes:[143]

> [T]he evidence suggests that progressive taxation of very high incomes and very large estates partly explains why the concentration of wealth never regained its astronomic Belle Epoque levels after the shocks of 1914–1945.

Second, one cannot overestimate the importance of institutionalization in taxation. The fact that the income tax has been implemented in modern democracies and remains so more than a century later points to its durability. Moreover, the tax contains the solutions to the issue (just as its current implementation contains the seeds of its destruction); as Piketty himself argues, one solution to restore progressivity would be to 'tax all of a person's income, including the part that accumulates in trusts, holding companies and partnerships'.[144] Piketty thinks it simpler to introduce an untried tax, but we disagree. The history of taxation in the twentieth century shows that it is far easier to build on existing institutions (however flawed) than to attempt a new proposal on a grand scale.

Ultimately, it need not be an either/or option. Piketty's co-ordinated tax on global capital is proposed as an addendum to the progressive income tax and estate taxes, and 'the primary purpose of the capital tax is not to finance the social state but to regulate capitalism.'[145] While adopting all three might result in accusations of double or triple taxation, each might in its own imperfect way find a means to actually tax the resources of the extremely rich. Piketty himself stresses the importance of progressivity as a matter of justice:[146]

> If the modern social state is to continue to exist, it is therefore essential that the underlying tax system retains a minimum of progressivity, or at any rate that it not become overly regressive at the top.

Murphy and Nagel, while describing the choice between an income tax or a consumption tax coupled with a wealth tax as 'purely pragmatic',[147] also favour the income tax, on the grounds that:

> that's where the money is. Increases in wealth … are a very important part of the income of the upper segments of the economic distribution, and income taxes rather than wealth or accessions taxes seem the most politically practicable means of taxing them.[148]

[143] Ibid., 495. [144] Ibid., 526.

[145] Ibid., 518. Piketty's research shows the value of taxation as a data collection tool: at present we know little of the real fortunes of the super-rich, let alone how to go about regulating them, because we simply do not have the information available. His proposed capital tax would be one way to attempt to identify and categorize the relevant assets in question.

[146] Ibid., 497. Piketty sees progressive taxation as serving two functions: first, to break up indecent and useless compensation through confiscatory rates of between 80 and 90 per cent on extremely high incomes (the top 0.5 to 1 per cent of the distribution); and second, to fund the social state (i.e., to provide health, education, social support) by applying high rates (of between 50 and 60 per cent) on the top 5 to 10 per cent. He claims this would not have a negative impact on growth rates in developed economies: Ibid., 513, 640, note 51.

[147] Murphy and Nagel, n. 1, 116–17, and see also 112, 186. [148] Ibid., 186.

Their reason for favouring income tax over consumption plus wealth taxes is therefore the same as ours: feasibility. But their reason for insisting on the taxation of wealth is different from ours. As the quote indicates, for them wealth 'is where the money is': it is part of generating revenue for redistributive purposes. This suggests that if sufficient revenue could be generated without needing to tax wealth (for example, by the 'money machine'[149] of a VAT), then consumption as the principal tax base would be acceptable. We contend that the importance of equality as an element of justice, and the role of wealth taxation in helping to reduce inequality, gives a reason of principle to favour the income tax.

IV. Taxation in a Globalized Economy

This final section of the chapter discusses contemporary challenges to the income tax base. Increasingly, the threat to the income tax arises at the global level.

At the domestic level, there are the usual avoidance and evasion issues that beset any national tax, including schemes specific to the income tax. Under a pure Haig-Simons income tax, any (net) gain over a given period would be taxed whether realized or not. However, no system resembles this in practice because 'administrative difficulties do not permit full implementation of this principle';[150] for example, taxpayers need liquidity to pay current tax liabilities. Hence, in practice, income tax is subject to a realization requirement. This gives rise to an inordinate number of problems and numerous tax planning opportunities, through sheltering income by deferring the realization of gains and/or inflating or bringing forward currently deductible losses. This departure from the Haig-Simons ideal leads some to reject the income tax altogether.[151] While we concede that these are serious issues, exacerbated by poor laws, we contend that they are not insurmountable. Furthermore, as Section IV.B shows, consumption taxes face their own compliance, administrative, and enforcement challenges.[152]

At the global level, the increasing globalization of capital markets has further encouraged the relatively long-standing practice of harmful tax competition, whereby nation states under-cut corporate income tax rates and/or the corporate tax base so as to attract mobile capital. Beyond the list of jurisdictions renowned for being tax havens and/or for their financial secrecy laws (e.g. the Cayman Islands, Barbados, Bermuda, British Virgin Islands, Luxembourg, and Switzerland[153]), a visible instance

[149] The President's Advisory Panel on Federal Tax Reform, *Simple, Fair, and Pro-Growth: Proposals to Fix America's Tax System* (Washington, DC: US Government, 2005), 192; Michael Keen and Ben Lockwood, 'Is the VAT a Money Machine?', 59(4) *National Tax Journal* (2006) 905, 905; Michael Keen and Ben Lockwood, 'The Value Added Tax: Its Causes and Consequences', 92(4) *Journal of Development Economics* (2010) 138, 139.

[150] Richard Musgrave, 'In Defence of an Income Concept', 81(1) *Harvard Law Review* (1967) 44, 59.

[151] See the thoughtful treatment of the issue in Shaviro, n. 93, 787. See further Andrews, n. 91, 1113.

[152] Shaviro, n. 96, 21. For the problems with the VAT see Kathryn James, *The Rise of the Value Added Tax* (New York: Cambridge University Press, 2015), chs 3, 6.

[153] Tax Justice Network-Australia, *Who Pays for Our Common Wealth: Tax Practices of the ASX 200* (Tax Justice Network-Australia and United Voice, 2014), 40–1, http://www.unitedvoice.org.au/news/who-pays-our-common-wealth.

of harmful tax competition might be seen in the setting of corporate income tax rates. Corporate tax rates in the OECD fell from an unweighted average of 47.5 per cent in 1981 to 25.5 per cent in 2013.[154] Although accompanying base-broadening (such as the introduction of capital gains taxation in countries like Australia) has meant that the rate reductions have not resulted in a significant decline in corporate tax to GDP ratios,[155] evidence shows that the base broadening has not fully compensated the rate reductions as effective marginal and average company tax rates have fallen across the OECD.[156]

In any event, the problem is much more serious than simply headline tax rates, because if all companies were in fact paying 25 per cent income tax then perhaps many states would not be in fiscal crises. As Devereux and Vella contend, the international tax system, prone as it is to competition between individual governments, 'has led to progressively reduced rates and is increasingly leading to progressively reduced tax bases as well'.[157] As the next subsection shows, it is not just 'pariah' tax states that have facilitated the harmful tax practices that enable many multinational enterprises (MNEs) to pay minimal to no tax in any jurisdiction.[158]

A. Harmful Tax Practices

In recent years much attention has focused on multinational enterprises (MNEs) engaging in harmful tax practices, such as base erosion and profit shifting (BEPS). In essence, MNEs arrange their affairs to take advantage of a combination of disparate tax rules in different jurisdictions, and the concepts that underlie them.[159]

The income tax is levied on an origin basis (i.e. the tax is imposed where production occurs). It therefore requires that income generated across multiple jurisdictions be allocated among those jurisdictions for taxing purposes. In an ideal world this would be a true reflection of the value added by real economic activity within those respective jurisdictions. However, the taxation of cross-border income is far from ideal. Rather than one single overarching legal framework for the determination of tax liability of cross-border income, the taxation of cross-border income is based on a combination of domestic tax laws, bilateral tax treaties, some multilateral treaties (such as EU Regulations and Directives), as well as various soft law such as the OECD Model

[154] OECD, 'Corporate and Capital Income Taxes', *OECD Tax Database* (2015), Table 11.1, Historic Table 11.1, http://www.oecd.org/tax/tax-policy/tax-database.htm#C_CorporateCaptial.

[155] Alan J. Auerbach, Michael P. Devereux, and Helen Simpson, 'Taxing Corporate Income', in James Mirrlees, Stuart Adam, Timothy Besley et al. (eds), *Dimensions of Tax Design: The Mirrlees Review* (Oxford: Oxford University Press, 2010), 846–50; *Henry Review*, n. 51, Part 2, 161. OECD corporate tax to GDP ratios were 2.3 per cent in 1981 and 2.9 per cent in 2012; see Revenue Statistics—Comparative Tables, *OECD* (30 October 2015), http://stats.oecd.org/index.aspx?DataSetCode=REV.

[156] *Henry Review*, n. 51, Part 2, 162.

[157] Michael P. Devereux and John Vella, 'Are We Heading Towards a Corporate Tax System Fit for rhe 21st Century?', 35(4) *Fiscal Studies* (2014) 449, 453.

[158] For a discussion of recent changes to tax laws in the United Kingdom and the United States having the explicit intent of introducing tax shelters, and thereby retaining domestic capital and attracting foreign capital, see Devereux and Vella, n. 157, 457–9 (UK), 459–60 (US).

[159] For a discussion of how some aspects of multinational tax avoidance stem from the realization requirement, see Shaviro, n. 96, 21–4.

Tax Treaty (highly influential as a basis for structuring these other laws, such as bilateral tax treaties).[160] Rules govern who gets to tax (which requires determinations of taxpayer residency and income source, among other things);[161] who pays tax (based on the residency status of the taxpayer and determined at the level of individual entity rather than corporate group); what is taxed (raising issues such as the treatment of active income and passive income;[162] mismatching of income and deductions; and the disparate treatment of debt and equity under the income tax); when taxation occurs (raising issues around realization); and, how much is liable to be taxed in each jurisdiction (determined through transfer pricing rules built around the arms-length principle). BEPS exploit every component of these rules, as well as the inconsistencies in these rules between jurisdictions, to dramatically reduce or eliminate taxation of MNEs. In essence, they exploit a lack of inclination among nation states to ensure, according to the guiding principle that ostensibly informs international taxation, that income is taxed at least 'once, and once only'.[163]

The strength of MNEs is their ability to exercise centralized control over geographically dispersed functions. MNEs are well positioned to take advantage of the growth of intangible, mobile wealth-producing assets, such as intellectual property, as well as flexible supply chains and growing global markets. Although the 'efficiencies of common control pose significant economic advantages',[164] the structures of MNEs have also provided a perfect vehicle for tax arbitrage. There are myriad schemes ranging in complexity. The exact details are not necessary to canvass here, but an overview of some of the issues is illustrative of the dimension of the problem.[165]

[160] 'Model Tax Convention with respect to Taxes on Income and Capital', *OECD* (2014), http://www.oecd.org/ctp/treaties/2014-model-tax-convention-articles.pdf. See also the alternative model convention proposed by the United Nations: United Nations, *Model Double Taxation Convention between Developed and Developing Countries* (2011), http://www.un.org/esa/ffd/documents/UN_Model_2011_Update.pdf.

[161] National tax systems notionally divide into territorial systems (which tax residents and nonresidents only on income derived from sources located domestically) and worldwide systems (which tax residents on their worldwide income, including income earned through foreign subsidiaries, and tax nonresidents on income derived from sources located domestically). In practice most national tax systems are a combination of the two. Determining jurisdiction to tax therefore depends on definitions of residency (where a person who has the right to receive the profits of the activity resides) and source (where the economic activity giving rise to the income takes place). See generally: Devereux and Vella, n. 157, 450; *OECD*, 'Addressing Base Erosion and Profit Shifting' (Paris: OECD Publishing, 2013), 33–6, http://dx.doi.org/10.1787/9789264192744-en. For a discussion of how these concepts are becoming obsolete, see Devereux and Vella, n. 157, 453–4; OECD, n. 161, 33–6.

[162] The general compromise arising from the League of Nations negotiations that led to the establishment of a framework for international taxation was that source countries were allocated primary taxing rights over the active income of a business and residence countries allocated primary rights over passive income such as dividends, royalties, and interest (subject to a circumscribed right for the source country to impose a withholding tax on certain types of income such as dividends and interest). The concept of 'permanent establishment' is the basic nexus for determining whether a jurisdiction has taxing rights in relation to the business profits of a non-resident taxpayer: Devereux and Vella, n. 157, 450–1; OECD, n. 161, 33–6; and see, e.g., *OECD*, n. 160, Arts 7, 10, 11, 12.

[163] 'Draft of a Bilateral Convention on Administrative Assistance in Matters of Taxation', in *Report Presented by the Committee of Technical Experts on Double Taxation and Tax Evasion* (League of Nations Publications, 1927), 23, http://biblio-archive.unog.ch/Dateien/CouncilMSD/C-216-M-85-1927-II_EN.pdf.

[164] Reuven S. Avi-Yonah and Ilan Benshalom, 'Formulary Apportionment—Myths and Prospects', 3(3) *World Tax Journal* (2011) 371, 377.

[165] The literature on harmful tax practices by multinational corporations is enormous. For an outline of common techniques, see, e.g., OECD, n. 161, 39–46, 73–81; Tax Justice Network-Australia, n. 153,

MNEs are able to mobilize laws that facilitate corporate groupings (that give rise to the efficiencies just mentioned) but exploit tax rules which generally apply at an entity level (enabling tax-effective artificial arrangements within such groupings). Common techniques involve the use of intra-group or related party dealings to transfer profits to low or no tax jurisdictions (where there is little or no economic activity) and/or expenses to high tax jurisdictions. Whereas a domestic tax system should in theory respond to such activity through adopting a matching principle (to ensure that a payment deductible by the payer is generally taxed in the hands of the recipient), there is no equivalent coherence or coordination at the international level. Given the differing approaches between nation states there is potential for the different tax rules of different jurisdictions to result in either double taxation or nontaxation/double non-taxation. Most of the work on international tax has been to develop a framework of rules to avoid double taxation (e.g. through bilateral tax treaties based on the OECD Model Convention). However, as the OECD notes '[c]orporations have urged bilateral and multilateral cooperation among countries to address differences in tax rules that result in double taxation, while simultaneously exploiting difference (*sic*) that result in double non-taxation.'[166]

A significant number of schemes exploit the distinction drawn by the income tax laws of most jurisdictions between debt (generally treated as deductible for tax purposes) and equity (non- deductible for tax purposes).[167] This might include the use of debt-financing among corporate groups (e.g. a subsidiary in a low tax jurisdiction will lend money to a parent in a high tax jurisdiction so that the former pays little to no tax on interest received but the latter can claim significant deductions on those same interest payments). More sophisticated schemes employ hybrid entities or hybrid financial instruments that exploit the differential treatment of debt and equity under the income tax laws of different jurisdictions. For example, a financial instrument might exhibit enough features to be treated as debt in a (high tax) jurisdiction so that payments are deductible by the putative borrower but enough features to be treated as specific types of equity, such as tax exempt dividends, in the jurisdiction of the putative lender.[168]

Much tax planning also occurs in relation to transfer pricing rules designed to allocate the share of income attributable to different jurisdictions. Much criticism is levelled at the Arm's Length Standard (ALS) that informs transfer-pricing rules.[169] The ALS requires that for tax purposes related parties must allocate income as it would be allocated between unrelated entities in the same or similar circumstances. This assessment is undertaken through a 'comparability analysis' where the 'controlled transaction' is compared against a 'comparable uncontrolled transaction', taking into account such factors as the property or services transferred, the functions performed by the

39–42; UK HL Select Committee on Economic Affairs, 'Tackling Corporate Tax Avoidance in a Global Economy: Is a New Approach Needed?', 1st Report of Session 2013-14 (HL Paper (2013-14) No. 48); Yariv Brauner, 'What the BEPS?', 16 *Florida Tax Review* (2014) 55; Antony Ting, 'iTax—Apple's International Tax Structure and the Double Non-Taxation Issue', 1 *British Tax Review* (2014) 40; Edward Kleinbard, 'Stateless Income', 11 *Florida Tax Review* (2011) 699; Devereux and Vella, n. 157.

[166] OECD, n. 161, 34. [167] Ibid., 37. [168] Ibid., 39–41, 43.

[169] OECD, n. 160, Art. 9.

parties (having regard to assets used and risks assumed), the contractual terms, the economic circumstances of the parties, and the business strategies pursued by the parties.[170] Avi-Yonah and Benshalom identify the 'fallacy that lies at the system's central core' as 'the belief that transactions among unrelated parties can be found and that they can be used as meaningful benchmarks for tax compliance and enforcement.'[171] Whereas members of MNEs might once have essentially operated as independent entities and so benchmarking incomes against uncontrolled comparables made sense, due to advances in communications and transportation technology this is no longer the case.[172] Indeed, in those markets for which it makes sense to have common control it is unlikely that a reasonably close uncontrolled comparable can be found.[173] Market forces generally influence the behaviour of unrelated parties,[174] but this is not the case for transactions between related entities and attempts to artificially apply market-related factors, such as comparing risk for which there is no true comparator, are liable to fail. One of the underlying assumptions of the ALS, for example, is that the more extensive the functions, assets and/or risks, the greater should be the remuneration attributed to the entity that performs those functions, holds those assets, and/or bears those risks.[175] To the extent that these factors are mobile and tax-elastic, such as risk or intangible assets, then there is an incentive to shift these factors to subsidiaries in low-tax jurisdictions. For example, when an MNE develops a product, such as a patent, the real risk is borne by the whole group. However, because transfer pricing rules operate at the entity level, an MNE might transfer the patent to subsidiaries in low or no tax jurisdictions so that they bear the 'risk' of the patent's failure. The subsidiary might then receive significant income (in the form of royalty payments from other members of the group) but pay little to no tax on the income. While intangible assets have enabled the easy proliferation of these schemes, transfer pricing arrangements designed to artificially diminish income can occur across any class of assets, tangible or otherwise (as the Starbucks example below demonstrates assets).[176] The crucial point here is that regardless of the specific means employed to achieve the outcome, the current system encourages the use of 'economically equivalent but legally different transactions'[177] so that increasingly MNEs have significant discretion over where taxable income is declared and how much is paid (if at all).[178]

Given the nature of the activity, the full extent of BEPS is difficult to quantify, but the amounts involved are staggering. For example, it is estimated that one US company alone, Apple, adopted such techniques to shelter US$44 billion of income from 2009 to 2012.[179] The OECD and IMF data on foreign direct investment further hints

[170] The OECD refers to the comparability analysis as 'at the heart of the application of the arm's length principle': *OECD Library*, 'Transfer Pricing Guidelines for Multinational Enterprises and Tax Administrations' (2010), 33 [1.6], and see also 41–3 [1.33]–[1.36], http://www.oecd-ilibrary.org/taxation/oecd-transfer-pricing-guidelines-for-multinational-enterprises-and-tax-administrations-2010_tpg-2010-en; OECD, n. 161, 36.

[171] Avi-Yonah and Benshalom, n. 164, 376. [172] Ibid., 376. [173] Ibid., 377.

[174] OECD, n. 170, 31, [1.2]. [175] OECD, n. 161, 36, 42; and see also OECD, n. 160, Arts 7, 9.

[176] Avi-Yonah and Benshalom, n. 164, 384. [177] Ibid., 385.

[178] Auerbach, Devereux, and Simpson, n. 155, 854.

[179] *US Senate Committee on Homeland Security and Governmental Affairs, Permanent Subcommittee on Investigations*, 'Offshore Profit Shifting and the U.S. Tax Code—Part 2 (Apple Inc.)' (21 May 2013),

at the magnitude of the issue. In 2010 Barbados, Bermuda, and the British Virgin Islands received more foreign direct investment (FDIs) (a combined 5.11 per cent of global FDIs) than Germany (4.77 per cent) or Japan (3.76 per cent). Similarly, in 2010 these same three jurisdictions made more investments into the world (combined 4.54 per cent) than Germany (4.28 per cent).[180] All the anecdotal data suggest such practices are widespread among a large number of companies across a range of sectors.[181]

The consequences of such activities are profound. Perhaps most serious is that they undermine the capacity of nation states to provide the revenue necessary to function (and which in turn provide much of the infrastructure necessary for these companies to operate (and profit), such as markets in which to sell their products, courts to recognize and enforce their property rights, and so on). This discussion has largely focused on developed economies, but in many ways the impact on developing and transitional economies is far worse. As a recent report highlights, '[m]oney lost by developing countries in tax dodging and other illicit losses far outweighs global spending on foreign aid.'[182] In addition, the behaviour disadvantages domestic taxpayers in the jurisdiction where profits were derived, because they have to pay more to bolster falling revenues, and also disadvantages domestic businesses who might be unable to avail themselves of the same avoidance techniques and are therefore at a comparative disadvantage to the MNEs who do not pay tax or who do so at an extremely low level.[183] Others highlight that this rent-seeking behaviour results in a suboptimal allocation of resources, driven by tax rather than economic considerations.[184]

There has been increasing public exposure of such activities,[185] but while the behaviour might temporarily harm the reputation of the culprits, as was demonstrated with the reaction to the avoidance activity of Starbucks in the United Kingdom,[186] public

17 (testimony of Stephen E Shay), http://www.hsgac.senate.gov/subcommittees/investigations/hearings/offshore-profit-shifting-and-the-us-tax-code_-part-2; Ting, n. 165, 40.

[180] OECD, n. 161, 17–18.

[181] For a summary of recent studies in the area, see: OECD, n. 161, Appendix B. See also Edward Kleinbard, 'Through a Latte, Darkly: Starbucks's Stateless Income Planning', *Tax Notes* (24 June 2013) 1515, 1516; OECD, n. 161, 5–7, ch. 2; and see below, n. 184.

[182] Tax Justice Network-Australia, n. 153, 7.

[183] For example, the effective tax rate paid by ASX 200 companies is 26 per cent (the statutory rate is 30 per cent): Tax Justice Network-Australia, n. 153, 13; see also Australian Taxation Office, 'Companies', in *Taxation Statistics 2012–2013: Detailed Tables*, Table 5, https://data.gov.au/dataset/taxation-statistics-2012-13/resource/06326fed-41e9-47d4-ae4f-00d2f6b19d44.

[184] See e.g. Edward Kleinbard, n. 181, 750–70. Kleinbard highlights an obvious instance of this distortion in the failure of US parent companies to repatriate billions of dollars in profits to the United States so as to avoid payment of tax: p. 720. A 2014 report by Audit Analytics estimated that in 2014 the total amount of indefinitely reinvested earnings of the Russell 1000 index (of the top 1000 equity firms in US markets) was $2.119 trillion, an increase of 93 per cent from 2008: *Audit Analytics*, 'Overseas Earnings of Russell 1000 Tops $2 Trillion in 2013' (1 April 2014), http://www.auditanalytics.com/blog/overseas-earnings-of-russell-1000-tops-2-trillion-in-2013/.

[185] See e.g. *Bloomberg*, 'The Great Corporate Tax Dodge' (2015), http://topics.bloomberg.com/the-great-corporate-tax-dodge/; 'But Nobody Pays That', *The New York Times*, Special Series (2015), http://topics.nytimes.com/top/features/timestopics/series/but_nobody_pays_that/index.html; 'Tax Gap', *The Guardian*, Special Series (2015), http://www.theguardian.com/business/series/tax-gap; Tim Dickinson, 'The Biggest Tax Scam Ever', *Rolling Stone* (27 August 2014), http://www.rollingstone.com/politics/news/the-biggest-tax-scam-ever-20140827?page=2.

[186] After public revelations that Starbucks paid no corporate tax in the United Kingdom in the three years until 2012 (and only £8.6 M in fifteen years on sales of £3 billion), Starbucks in the United Kingdm announced that the company would voluntarily make payments of $10 M per year for the fiscal year from

shame alone is not something that has produced any significant behavioural change. Despite the activity generating much condemnation from lawmakers,[187] the media, and the public, the condemnation has not resulted in substantive action that will fix the problem, even though there has been much work in this area. The reality is that the practices are enduring (if not unchanging) and widespread.[188]

Many of the companies are resident in the United States, which in theory taxes on a worldwide basis (i.e. tax should be paid on income derived anywhere in the world), and some commentators highlight as a major impediment to reform the United States' adoption of rules that not only prevent double taxation but in fact encourage double non-taxation.[189] These selfsame companies have not been shy in lobbying to maintain and extend the benefits that accrue from the US government's reluctance to act to change this situation.[190]

While some countries are attempting to go it alone,[191] all agree that the problem requires a globally coordinated solution. For example, the OECD (in conjunction with

2013 to 2014 (by not claiming deductions for the intra-group dealings that had enabled the company to repeatedly report losses in the United Kingdom, for instance by making payments for various products (coffee beans) and services (roasting) to subsidiaries in low/no tax jurisdictions): Terry Macalister, 'Starbucks Makes £5m Voluntary Tax Payment', *The Guardian* (24 June 2013), http://www.theguardian.com/business/2013/jun/23/starbucks-pays-corporation-tax; Simon Neville and Jill Treanor, 'Starbucks to Pay £20m in Tax Over Next Two Years After Customer Revolt', *The Guardian* (7 December 2012), https://www.theguardian.com/business/2012/dec/06/starbucks-to-pay-10m-corporation-tax.

[187] *UK HC Committee of Public Accounts*, 'Tax Avoidance—Google', 9th Report, Session 2013-14 (HC Paper (2013-14) No. 112); *UK HC Committee of Public Accounts*, 'HM Revenue and Customs: Annual Report and Accounts', 19th Report, Session 2012-13 (HC Paper (2013-14) No. 716), 7–11; *US Senate Committee on Homeland Security and Governmental Affairs, Permanent Subcommittee on Investigations*, 'Offshore Profit Shifting and the US Tax Code—Part 1' *(Microsoft & Hewlett-Packard)* (20 September 2013), 1–9, http://www.hsgac.senate.gov/subcommittees/investigations/hearings/offshore-profit-shifting-and-the-us-tax-code); *US Senate Committee on Homeland Security and Governmental Affairs, Permanent Subcommittee on Investigations*,n. 179, 1–10; *Parliament of Australia, Senate Economic References Committee*, 'Corporate Tax Avoidance (2014–2015)', http://www.aph.gov.au/Parliamentary_Business/Committees/Senate/Economics/Corporate_Tax_Avoidance/Terms_of_Reference.

[188] The US Government Accountability Office reports that from 1998 to 2005, 24 per cent of US-controlled corporations and 34 per cent of foreign-controlled corporations reported zero tax liabilities: US Government Accountability Office, *Tax Administration: Comparison of the Reported Tax Liabilities of Foreign- and U.S.-Controlled Corporations, 1998–2005*, GAO-04-358 (Washington, DC: Government Accountability Office, 2008), 8. Wittendorff highlights that the first federal US Regulation addressing transfer pricing was in the War Revenue Act of 1917: Jens Wittendorff, *Transfer Pricing and the Arm's Length Principle in International Tax Law* (Alphen aan den Rijn, The Netherlands: Kluwer Law International, 2010), 31–2.

[189] Ting, n. 165, 41; Hugh J. Ault, 'Some Reflections on the OECD and the Sources of International Tax Principles', *Tax Notes International* (17 June 2013), 1195, 1198; Devereux and Vella, n. 157, 460.

[190] See e.g. Simon Bowers, 'US Tech Giants Launch Fierce Fightback Against Global Tax Avoidance Crackdown', *The Guardian* (22 January 2015), https://www.theguardian.com/business/2015/jan/21/us-tech-tax-avoidance-google-amazon-apple.

[191] The UK Government confirmed that it would introduce a Diverted Profits Tax to apply at a rate of 25 per cent on profits that have been diverted off-shore to take effect on 1 April 2015. It will apply to both UK and foreign multinational companies: HR Revenue & Customs and HM Treasury, *Overview of Tax Legislation and Rates*, 11, [1.46] (18 March 2015), https://www.gov.uk/government/uploads/system/uploads/attachment_data/file/418689/OOTLAR_v8.1.pdf; HM Revenue & Customs, 'Diverted Profits Tax—Consultation Draft' (2014–2015), https://www.gov.uk/government/uploads/system/uploads/attachment_data/file/385741/Diverted_Profits_Tax.pdf. The Australian Government has adopted a different approach, proposing amendment of the current general anti-avoidance provision to try to prevent the diversion of business profits by MNEs whose annual global revenue exceeds AUD$1 billion. An exposure draft bill has received public comments but at the time of writing a final version is yet to be

A more fundamental problem is that law reform is potentially very disruptive to precisely the type of autonomy that is protected within a civil association. How can an individual go about selecting long-term ends without a very substantial degree of continuity in the legal framework, in the tax field or otherwise? To put the same point in a different way: if we are to recast our tax legal arrangements according to a series of books and articles, even those of Oakeshott himself, are we not then using the law to obtrude our own intellectual enthusiasms into the plans of others? It is to this problem that we now turn.

III. Conservatism and Tax Law

One of the most celebrated and distinctive elements of Oakeshott's thought is his attack on the application of 'rationalist' techniques to politics. The problem is summarized lucidly by Gee and Webber:

> Distinguishing the rationalistic propensity is an unshakeable faith in the power of reason to identify exact, complete, and orderly solutions to the practical problems that arise in the real world. Reasoning by reference to and in terms of a set of abstract principles, the Rationalist prioritises well-reasoned and well ordered, even if untried, solutions over the tried and tested, but often untidy established ways of doing things. ... The Rationalist's error is not that he recognises the authority of reason, but that he recognises no authority except that of reason and, even then ... only by equating reason with a special kind of technique.[93]

What Oakeshott takes issue with is not only the imposition on political life of intellectual schemes designed by reference to a type of reasoning most closely associated with natural science.[94] It is the belief that abstract reason can provide a shortcut to good outcomes in a manner that is inconceivable even in the natural sciences. Indeed Oakeshott observes that 'the coherence of scientific activity' lies not 'in a body of principles or rules to be observed by the scientist, a "scientific method"' although 'such principles and rules no doubt exist' but rather in 'the way the scientist goes about his investigation, in the traditions of scientific inquiry'.[95] The manner of reasoning observable in scientific hypotheses therefore presupposes the existence of people who have already been inculcated into the practices of being a scientist.

In the 'world of politics ... so deeply veined with both the traditional, the circumstantial and the transitory'[96] it is particularly important not to forget that theory abstracts from and presupposes that which political actors actually do. Oakeshott terms the former 'technical' or 'book' knowledge and the latter 'practical' knowledge and

[93] Graham Gee and Grégoire Webber, 'Rationalism in Public Law', 76(4) *Modern Law Review* (2013) 708–34, 713.

[94] Oakeshott associates the emergence of the rationalist character closely with the writings of Francis Bacon: see Michael Oakeshott, 'Rationalism in Politics', in n. 29, 19. An interesting perspective on the proper scope of scientific reasoning can be found in Isaiah Berlin, 'The Philosophical Ideas of Giambattista Vico', in *Three Critics of the Enlightenment: Vico, Hamann, Herder* (London: Pimlico, 2000).

[95] Michael Oakeshott, 'Rational Conduct', in n. 29, 123; see also Oakeshott, n. 94, 13; Oakeshott, n. 64, 56.

[96] Oakeshott, n. 94, 7.

the G20) has released a fifteen-point action plan designed to counter BEPS.[192] The OECD approach has attracted much criticism. Many contend that in seeking to work within the existing flawed regime and with problematic concepts such as the arms-length standard, that the proposals stand little chance of effecting major change.[193] This might very well be the case, but it is clear from the strong opposition of US MNEs and lawmakers to the proposed measures that there is at least a *belief* that the measures will have some impact.[194]

In any event, all agree that any effective solution will require international cooperation even though the proposals put forward might differ.[195] Perhaps the most hope of change might be solutions that require less than full cooperation.[196]

B. Is the VAT Faring Any Better?

No one denies the seriousness of harmful tax practices. However, it should be noted that the income tax is not alone in facing these existential threats. Although taxation of consumption is frequently advocated as a superior alternative to the income tax,[197] the VAT—the dominant form of consumption taxation around the globe—has proved

put before the Commonwealth parliament: see Exposure Draft—Tax Laws Amendment (Tax Integrity Multinational Anti-Avoidance Law) Bill 2015 (Cth); Explanatory Memorandum to the Exposure Draft Tax Laws Amendment (Tax Integrity Multinational Anti-Avoidance Law) Bill 2015 (Cth).

[192] The BEPS Action Plan is guided by three principles: (1) coherence, ensuring that national laws that tax deductible payments by one taxpayer result in the inclusion of income of another; (2) the adoption of rules that better match economic substance; and (3) greater transparency including openness and better data on the issue: see OECD, n. 161, 13–14, http://dx.doi.org/10.1787/9789264202719-en.

[193] Devereux and Vella, n. 157, 461–9. Some allege that the BEPS action plan is just a political measure which fails to highlight the real issues and rejects potential solutions, such as formulary apportionment, as unfeasible: Yariv Brauner, 'BEPS: An Interim Evaluation', 6(1) *World Tax Journal* (2014) 10, 12, 17; Devereux and Vella, n. 157, 463; OECD, n. 161, 14.

[194] See e.g. Thomson Reuters, 'US Senate Finance Committee Chairman Outlines US Concerns with BEPS Project', 32 *Weekly Tax Bulletin* (24 July 2015), [1210]; Thomson Reuters, 'BEPS Transfer Pricing Proposals Could Create Tax and Trade Chaos: MNE Group', 31 *Weekly Tax Bulletin* (17 July 2015), [1167].

[195] See, e.g., Brauner, n. 193, 12.

[196] Avi-Yonah and Benshalom propose maintaining the existing ALS approach for easy-to-price transactions but supplementing this with a formulary solution for the residual component of MNE income attributable to sources that are hard to allocate and/or value, such as income derived from hard-to-value intangible and financial assets. In general terms, formulary apportionment allocates income by approximation based on a number of factors, rather than attempting to do so precisely through alternative measures such as the use of market values. The relevant formula in this instance would attempt to allocate this residual income component through measuring easier to observe and harder to manipulate factors that contribute to that income, such as retail sales (by country of purchaser); overall sales in a given jurisdiction (including sales by agents); payroll expenses (of employees and contractors working for more than thirty hours per week on MNE premises); and moveable assets and fixed assets (real estate, including the value of leasehold): see Avi-Yonah and Benshalom, n. 164, 380. Whereas unitary formulary apportionment applies to the whole of the income of a corporate group (as happens at the state level in the United States), Avi-Yonah and Benshalom propose to only do so for this residual hard-to-value sources of income. The authors state that the approach will work with less than full cooperation, but that a 'critical majority of countries that includes some of the major developed and emerging economies' would be required: Avi-Yonah and Benshalom, n. 164, 381, 383–5, 391, 393–5.

[197] For instance, the IMF contends that, because '[t]axing consumption is equivalent to taxing accumulated assets and labor income' consumption taxation 'falls partly on a completely inelastic base—previously existing assets—and partly on a base less internationally mobile than capital income.' IMF, n. 90, 80.

susceptible to taxpayers exploiting disparate taxing laws that also result in nontaxation when certain goods and services cross borders. This is despite the same principle ostensibly informing the VAT at an international level, namely, that a transaction giving rise to consumption should be taxed once (but not twice).[198]

The VAT offers some advantages over the income tax at an international level. For example, the VAT universally applies on a destination basis (goods and services are taxed at the place of consumption rather than production) and this therefore mostly avoids transfer-pricing issues, because the design of the VAT shifts all liability to the end consumer.[199] This also avoids tax arbitrage opportunities around the debt/equity distinction under the income tax and other methods to shelter income because, in theory, a consumption tax is a wash for companies (other than a compliance cost). The VAT similarly avoids the susceptibility of the income tax in relation to tax competition regarding, for example, the setting of rates (because business in theory does not pay VAT; consumers do and they are generally less mobile) or even the base (pressure to reduce this is more at the domestic political level).

Nevertheless, the VAT has its own compliance issues at an international level. Although levying the VAT on a destination basis avoids transfer-pricing issues, in practice to achieve this exports must be tax-free and imports subject to tax. To achieve this end, the VAT has traditionally been administratively dependent on borders and more specifically on the effective administration of those borders to allow for VAT refunds on exports and to impose VAT on imports.[200] Weak borders therefore make taxing the end consumption of goods and services harder to achieve. Specific practical challenges are posed by: the removal of border controls (as for intracommunity trade in the EU and subnational VATs);[201] weak border controls (as is often the case in developing countries); and technological advances which have facilitated a massive shift towards trade in intangible goods and cross-border services that do not respect traditional borders (such as global telecommunications and international transport). Just as the income tax has difficulties in tracing and valuing highly mobile intangible assets (as a source of income), the VAT has similar difficulties in locating and tracing intangible assets and consumable services for the purposes of establishing the place of taxation. Although in theory consumption is a relatively immobile base, legal rules are needed to predict where consumption might occur and therefore where tax is payable, such as rules specifying the place of taxation, and indeed what constitutes the underlying supply. In the absence of a globally coordinated or harmonized approach, different place of taxation rules between jurisdictions can sometimes result in either double taxation (where more than one jurisdiction's place of taxation rules tax the same supply) or nontaxation (where the place of taxation rules of more than one

[198] *OECD*, 'International VAT/GST Guidelines' (Paris: OECD, 2015), Preface [5], http://www.oecd.org/ctp/consumption/international-vat-gst-guidelines.htm.

[199] In theory, source and residence issues should be avoided, but they are replaced by issues surrounding the need to define the place of taxation which in practice has relied on income tax concepts such as establishment and residence to do so: Shaviro, n. 92, 107–9; Ibid., n. 24; Guideline 3.6.

[200] Peggy Musgrave, 'Consumption Tax Proposals in an International Setting', 12(2) *International VAT Monitor* (2001) 56, 61.

[201] For an overview of the issues, see Rita de la Feria, *The EU VAT System and the Internal Market* (Amsterdam: IBFD, 2009).

jurisdiction fail to tax the supply at all).[202] The VAT has proved markedly vulnerable to fraud and evasion, which, at an international level, exploit these cross-border issues in relation to globally traded goods and services, especially intangible goods and services. Moreover, the VAT possesses its own key vulnerability: the refund mechanism. In theory, everyone pays VAT on purchases but business is entitled to a refund on VAT paid upon producing an invoice. Although the refund mechanism distinguishes the VAT from other sales tax alternatives, it is also regarded as its 'Achilles heel' because a VAT invoice can be a cheque written on the government.[203] A number of schemes have developed to wrongfully claim VAT refunds, from the simple falsification of invoices, to missing trader fraud (setting up an entity that claims VAT refunds, but then disappears before remitting VAT liabilities), to the large-scale carousel fraud prevalent in the EU which exploits the lack of border controls.[204] The revenue lost through VAT-fraud and non-compliance is likewise staggering. A recent estimate for the EU put it in the order of 17 per cent of theoretical VAT revenues or €193 billion, or 1.5 per cent of GDP.[205] The scale of VAT fraud and evasion has led some to conclude that the 'VAT's reliance on credits and refunds makes the tax more susceptible than an income tax ... to the compliance risks of fraudulent refund claims'.[206]

Our point is not to suggest the VAT is necessarily worse on this measure than the income tax but that, like the income tax, it has its own points of vulnerability and weakness. Both the income tax and the VAT have struggled to adapt to globalization and technological change and are informed by international tax rules that were in some cases drafted over a century ago (in the case of the income tax) and at least half a century ago in the case of the VAT. Although the content of the solutions for both the VAT and the income tax might differ, the prescription is the same, namely, global cooperation and coordination.[207]

[202] *OECD*, 'International VAT/GST Guidelines' (Paris: OECD, 2015), http://www.oecd.org/ctp/consumption/international-vat-gst-guidelines.htm, 1.12.

[203] Richard Bird and Pierre-Pascal Gendron, *The VAT in Developing and Transitional Countries* (New York: Cambridge University Press, 2007), 20, 133.

[204] Carousel fraud involves missing trader fraud with a twist. Goods, for example, might be imported from a Member State (no VAT is payable at the time of importation but rather is payable with the next periodic return), then sold to the missing trader who absconds before remitting the VAT due on its sale of the goods. The goods might then pass through a number of intermediaries before being exported again (with a refund being claimed by the exporter that matches the VAT that was invoiced but never paid by the missing trader). The carousel is complete when the goods end up back with the original exporter. See Ian Crawford, Michael Keen, and Stephen Smith, 'Value Added Tax and Excises', in *Dimensions of Tax Design*, n. 155, 312, Figure 4.3.

[205] Center for Social and Economic Research, Warsaw and Central Planning Bureau, Netherlands Bureau for Economic Policy Analysis, *Study to Quantify and Analyse the VAT Gap in the EU-27 Member States—Final Report*, TAXUD/2012/DE/316; FWC No. TAXUD/2010/CC/104 (Warsaw: European Commission, 2013), 10, 28.

[206] US Government Accountability Office, *Value-Added Taxes: Lessons Learned from Other Countries on Compliance Risks, Administrative Costs, Compliance Burden, and Transition*, GAO-08-566 (Washington, DC: Government Accountability Office, 2008), 14.

[207] The OECD realeased consolidated guidelines to encourage the harmonization of VAT regimes in relation to cross-border supplies of services and intangibles: *OECD*, 'International VAT/GST Guidelines' (Paris: OECD, 2015), http://www.oecd.org/ctp/consumption/international-vat-gst-guidelines.htm. The Guidelines are heavily dependent on administrative cooperation between jurisdictions to be effective and rely on existing legal frameworks—including those established for the income tax—to achieve this: see Chapter 4.

C. Conclusion

While international cooperation in relation to taxation is notoriously difficult to achieve, there exist some precedents. The mere existence of the European Union including its framework around taxation, such as the 1967 decision to adopt the VAT as the common form of sales tax in the European Economic Community (EEC), shows that cooperation towards a common end is possible. This is not to suggest that the path is easy or necessarily successful.[208] The EU offers many instances of failure, including the failure to achieve a similar level of cooperation in relation to the corporate income tax base: the long-proposed common consolidated corporate income tax base (which, as the name suggests, seeks to a adopt a unified corporate tax base across member states to, among other things, address BEPS in the EU) is yet to be introduced.[209] Nevertheless, even limited successes show that collective action is possible, given a framework that creates the right incentives to encourage states to cooperate.

[208] The EEC Treaty instructed the European Commission to 'consider how the legislation of the various Member States concerning turnover taxes, excise duties and other forms of indirect taxation ... can be harmonized in the interest of the common market': *European Treaty (Treaty of Rome, as amended)* Art 99 (ex Art 93). Following the Single European Act, Art. 17, the Treaty on the Functioning of the European Union now directs the Council to 'adopt provisions for the harmonization of legislation concerning turnover taxes, excise duties and other forms of indirect taxation to the extent that such harmonization is necessary to ensure the establishment and the functioning of the internal market and to avoid distortion of competition': Art 113 TFEU (ex Art 93 EC). The First Council Directive outlined the definition and aims of the proposed VAT: *First Council Directive 67/227/EEC of 11 April 1967 on the Harmonisation of Legislation of Member States Concerning Turnover Taxes* [1967] OJ L 1/14; [1967] OJ Spec Ed 14. The Second Council Directive of 11 April 1967 provided the details for the new system (by, for example, outlining concepts such as taxable transaction and place of supply) but gave Member States considerable scope to determine the content of their domestic VATs with freedom to determine their own VAT rate structure and exemptions: *Second Council Directive 67/228/EEC of 11 April 1967 on the Harmonisation of Legislation of Member States Concerning Turnover Taxes—Structure and Procedures for Application of the Common System of Value Added Tax* [1967] OJ L 1/14; [1967] OJ Spec Ed 16. The passage of the Sixth Directive in May 1977 provided greater guidance on the operation of the common VAT: *Sixth Council Directive 77/388/EEC of 17 May 1977 on the Harmonisation of the Laws of the Member States Relating to Turnover Taxes—Common System of Value Added Tax: Uniform Basis of Assessment* [1977] OJ L 145/1. The current Directive is a recast of the Sixth Directive: *Council Directive 2006/112/EC of 28 November 2006 on the Common System of Value Added Tax* [2006] OJ L 347/1. See generally: Ben Terra and Julie Kajus, *A Guide to the European VAT Directives—2014* (Amsterdam: IBFD, 2014); Rita de la Feria, *The EU VAT System and the Internal Market* (Amsterdam: IBFD, 2009); Walter van der Corput and Fabiola Annacondia (eds), *EU VAT Compass* (Amsterdam: IBFD, 2007). The imposition of the VAT through Directives, which bind member states to a shared result but allows each state the flexibility to choose the means to this end, have resulted in the enactment of a variety of VAT laws across the European Union. The passage of later Directives, including the Recast VAT Directive, have attempted to narrow the flexibility of earlier Directives through defining key terms and limiting exemptions, but moves towards a truly harmonized European VAT have met intractable domestic resistance. The end result is far from harmonious, with twenty-eight different regimes with more than ten different standard rates, twenty-eight different registration thresholds, twenty-eight unique sets of exemptions and twenty-eight different administrative regimes: see e.g. *European Commission*, 'VAT Rates Applied in Member States of the European Union—Situation as at 1st September 2016', Taxud.c.1 (Brussels: European Commission, 2013), https://ec.europa.eu/taxation_customs/sites/taxation/files/docs/body/vat_rates_en.pdf.

[209] The European Commission has relaunched this project in response to the recent publicity surrounding BEPS: European Commission, 'Common Consolidated Corporate Tax Base (CCCTB)' (2015), http://ec.europa.eu/taxation_customs/taxation/company_tax/common_tax_base/index_en.htm. The proposal is a type of unified formulary apportionment, and the repeated failure to adopt it suggests the merits of considering an approach which requires something less than full cooperation: Avi-Yonah and Benshalom, n. 164, 383.

While we have highlighted the threats to the income tax at a global level, we have not set out to identify the precise technical solutions required. What we have shown is that fundamental principles of justice pertaining to political and civic equality demand that such solutions be implemented. While no single solution is likely to generate total consensus at the international level, that does not mean that the income tax cannot be strengthened. The fact that reform proposals have attracted fierce opposition from some US MNE and lawmakers suggests that they may achieve something, and some options might be effective even in the absence of total cooperation.[210]

Irrespective of the specific technical means adopted, the key is to generate a sufficient commitment to the principles that underlie the income tax to make change possible. The fact that the issue of multinational tax avoidance has generated increasing media coverage and political interest is at least a start in the right direction. By showing that the income tax is grounded in fundamental considerations of justice, this chapter has shown how important it is to continue along this path.

[210] See above n. 196.

7

Tax Policy and the Virtuous Sovereign

Dworkinian Equality and Redistributive Taxation

David G. Duff

I. Introduction

Among the purposes of a tax system, it is generally accepted that one role is to implement a society's conception of distributive justice.[1] Indeed, if justice is, as John Rawls famously declared, 'the first virtue of social institutions',[2] the specification of tax policies to implement this conception of distributive justice is properly regarded as the first or sovereign virtue of a society's tax system—to which a virtuous sovereign should properly attend.

In practice, however, there are various conceptions of distributive justice, with different implications for the design of a society's tax system. Classical utilitarianism, for example, conceptualizes justice as the maximization of aggregate welfare, and supports tax and spending policies that weigh the utility gains from redistributive transfers against the utility losses attributable to the imposition of different taxes.[3] Based on these precepts, contemporary welfarist approaches to tax policy have generally favoured proportionate or declining-rate income taxes combined with redistributive transfer payments,[4] or the taxation of personal consumption at progressive rates.[5]

In contrast to classical utilitarianism, which he rejects,[6] Rawls advances a liberal-egalitarian conception of justice, according to which each person is accorded 'an equal right to the most extensive basic liberty compatible with a similar liberty for others' (the first principle of justice),[7] and social and economic inequalities are permitted only to the extent that they work to everyone's advantage (the difference principle)[8] and are attached to positions and offices that are reasonably accessible to all (the principle of fair equality of opportunity).[9] On this basis, he recommends progressive gift and

[1] See e.g. Liam Murphy and Thomas Nagel, *The Myth of Ownership; Taxes and Justice* (Oxford: Oxford University Press, 2002), 3.

[2] John Rawls, *A Theory of Justice* (Cambridge, MA: Harvard University Press, 1971), 3.

[3] See e.g. James A. Mirrlees, 'An Exploration in the Theory of Optimum Income Taxation', 38(2) *Review of Economic Studies* (1971) 175–208.

[4] See e.g. Joseph Bankman and Thomas Griffith, 'Social Welfare and the Rate Structure: A New Look at Progressive Taxation', 75(6) *California Law Review* (1987) 1905–67.

[5] See e.g. Daniel Shaviro, 'Replacing the Income Tax with a Progressive Consumption Tax', 103 *Tax Notes* (2004) 91–113; Joseph Bankman and David A. Weisbach, 'The Superiority of an Ideal Consumption Tax Over an Ideal Income Tax', 58 *Stanford Law Review* (2006) 1413–56.

[6] Rawls, n. 2, 26–7. [7] Ibid., 60. [8] Ibid., 61. [9] Ibid., 73.

Philosophical Foundations of Tax Law. First Edition. Edited by Monica Bhandari.

inheritance taxes 'to gradually and continually … correct the distribution of wealth and to prevent concentrations of power detrimental to the fair value of political liberty and fair equality of opportunity',[10] and a proportional expenditure tax (a flat-rate tax on personal consumption) to raise revenues so that 'the government … can provide for … public goods and make the transfer payments necessary to satisfy the difference principle'.[11]

Classical libertarian theories of justice, on the other hand, criticize utilitarian and Rawlsian conceptions of distributive justice on the grounds that these 'patterned' or 'end-result' approaches violate people's rights to the ownership of property that is justly acquired and justly transferred.[12] From this perspective, Robert Nozick maintains, all redistributive taxes and transfers are objectionable,[13] except to the extent that they correct for past injustices in the acquisition or transfer of property.[14] As a result, most libertarians would limit taxation to the collection of revenues necessary to support a minimal state dedicated to the protection of persons and property,[15] and allocate tax burdens according to the benefits that taxpayers receive.[16] In practice, these libertarian theories appear to be compatible with all major tax bases, including income, consumption, and wealth,[17] though most libertarian approaches to tax policy conclude that whatever tax is adopted should be levied at a flat or proportional rate.[18]

Like Nozick, Ronald Dworkin also rejects patterned or end state conceptions of distributive justice—which he criticizes as 'ethically insensitive' in that they 'deploy standards of just distribution that … do not reflect the distinctions and assignments of responsibility we make in leading our lives'.[19] In opposition to classical libertarianism, however, Dworkin regards a conception of equality as central to a theory of distributive justice, insisting that '[n]o government is legitimate that does not show equal concern for the fate of all those citizens over whom it claims dominion and from whom it claims allegiance.'[20] Drawing on each of these principles, Dworkin proposes a theory of distributive justice as 'equality of resources' that aims to provide 'a unified account of equality and individual responsibility that respects both'.[21]

This chapter reviews Dworkin's theory of equality of resources and its implications for redistributive taxation, arguing that it provides a persuasive argument for progressive income and wealth transfer taxes as essential elements of a just tax system. Section II examines the theory itself in contrast to other prominent theories of distributive justice, concluding that Dworkin's approach provides a more compelling conception of distributive justice than welfare-based theories that do not take rights and

[10] Ibid., 277. [11] Ibid., 278.

[12] Robert Nozick, *Anarchy, State, and Utopia* (New York: Basic Books, 1974), 149–231.

[13] Ibid., 168. [14] Ibid., 230–1. [15] Ibid., ix.

[16] See e.g. Eric Mack, 'Self-Ownership, Taxation, and Democracy: A Philosophical-Constitutional Perspective', in Donald P. Racheter and Richard E. Wagner (eds), *Politics, Taxation and the Rule of Law: The Power to Tax in Constitutional Perspective* (Boston: Kluwer Academic, 2002), 9, 29, note 11.

[17] See David G. Duff, 'Private Property and Tax Policy in a Libertarian World: A Critical Review', 18(1) *Canadian Journal of Law and Jurisprudence* (2005) 23–45, 32–4.

[18] Ibid., 34–6.

[19] Ronald Dworkin, *Sovereign Virtue: The Theory and Practice of Equality* (Cambridge, MA: Harvard University Press, 2000), 323–4.

[20] Ibid., 1. [21] Ibid., 7.

responsibilities seriously; Rawlsian theory, which is insufficiently attentive to individual rights and responsibilities; and classical libertarianism which fails to take equality seriously. Section III considers the implications of Dworkin's theory for redistributive taxation, addressing both the kinds of taxes that a virtuous sovereign should collect for this purpose and key features in the design of these taxes. Section IV concludes.

II. Theory

In order to understand Dworkin's idea of equality of resources, it is perhaps best to contrast this theory of distributive justice with other prominent theories that he explicitly rejects. The theory's emphasis on 'resources' as a standard for measuring equality, for example, represents a marked departure from theories based on utility or welfare, which Dworkin subjects to detailed criticism. At the same time, the theory's reliance on a concept of 'ethical individualism' that evaluates the justice of distributive outcomes based on the distinction between people's choices and their circumstances differs significantly from the approach taken by John Rawls. Finally, the analytical devices and institutional arrangements on which Dworkin's theory relies in order to achieve 'equality' in the distribution of resources are fundamentally opposed to those that underlie libertarian conceptions of private property.

The following sections outline Dworkin's concept of equality of resources: (1) reviewing Dworkin's critique of welfare as a measure of distributive equality; (2) explaining Dworkin's concept of resources and the idea of ethical individualism that distinguishes Dworkin's theory from that of John Rawls; and (3) contrasting the procedural and institutional devices on which Dworkin's theory relies in order to ensure equality in the distribution of resources from the procedural and institutional arrangements contemplated in classical libertarianism. In each case, I conclude, Dworkin's theory offers a more compelling account of distributive justice than the alternative theories that he rejects.

A. What's Wrong with Welfare?

Beginning with welfare, it is useful to begin by recalling Rawls' objections to classical utilitarianism—that it does not automatically exclude offensive or illegitimate preferences;[22] does not necessarily guarantee the protection of rights and liberties which are contingent on their utility at a particular time and place;[23] does not concern itself, except indirectly, with how welfare is distributed;[24] and 'does not take seriously the distinction between persons'.[25] Extending this critique of aggregate welfare as a criterion of distributive justice, Dworkin rejects welfare as a standard for measuring distributional equality, arguing that the concept of 'resources' constitutes a better measure for this purpose.

In order to make this argument, Dworkin begins by acknowledging the initial appeal of welfare as a criterion for distributive justice—noting that the concept of

[22] Rawls, n. 2, 30–1. [23] Ibid., 26. [24] Ibid. [25] Ibid., 27.

welfare was devised 'precisely to describe what is fundamental in life rather than what is merely instrumental' whereas 'resources are valuable so far as they produce welfare'.[26] As a result, he observes:

> The basic, immediate appeal of equality of welfare ... lies in the idea that welfare is what really matters to people, as distinct from money and goods, which matter to them only instrumentally, so far as these are useful in producing welfare. Equality of welfare proposes, that is, to make people equal in what is fundamentally important to them.[27]

Notwithstanding this initial appeal, however, Dworkin makes three arguments against welfare as a suitable metric for equality.

First, to the extent that the concept of welfare does not exclude political and impersonal preferences, a concept of distributive justice premised on equality of welfare implies that individuals should be compensated for all such preferences that are not realized—even if these preferences are offensive or unreasonable, such as those attributable to racial prejudice or unrealistic aspirations about some desired state of the world.[28] In contrast, Dworkin argues, in a society that is committed to distributional equality, the conception of equality that is adopted would presumably exclude the satisfaction of offensive and unreasonable political and impersonal preferences—thereby precluding any compensation for unrealized preferences of this sort.[29] More importantly, he adds, since an unrestricted conception of welfare cannot account for this result, it is necessary to rely on some independent theory of distributive justice for this purpose.[30]

Second, even if the concept of welfare is limited to purely personal preferences, equality of welfare would require a society to allocate relatively more resources to individuals with expensive tastes that are costly to satisfy and expansive goals that are difficult to realize, rather than to other individuals with more modest tastes and limited ambitions—even if these expensive tastes and expansive goals are deliberately cultivated.[31] These 'troubling counterexamples', Dworkin argues, 'are embarrassing for the theory that equality means equality of welfare precisely because we believe that equality ... condemns rather than recommends compensating for deliberately cultivated expensive tastes'.[32]

Finally, and more generally, Dworkin argues that the concept of 'welfare' is itself so abstract and ambiguous that it is impossible to assess its merits for a theory of distributive justice until 'a particular understanding or conception of welfare is specified'—at which point the ideal invariably loses 'whatever appeal it might have had'.[33]

If 'welfare' is understood in classical utilitarian fashion as an excess of pleasure over pain or more broadly as 'enjoyment' over 'dissatisfaction',[34] for example, an obvious objection to the concept is that people differ in the extent to which they regard

[26] Dworkin, n. 19, 14. [27] Ibid., 31. [28] Ibid., 21–8. [29] Ibid., 23.
[30] Ibid., 25, 27. [31] Ibid., 14–15. [32] Ibid., 48, 55.
[33] Ibid., 285; Ronald Dworkin, 'Ronald Dworkin Replies', in Justine Burley (ed.), *Dworkin and His Critics* (Malden: Blackwell, 2004), 339–95, 340.
[34] Dworkin, n. 19, 18.

pleasure or enjoyment as essential to a good or successful life.[35] On the contrary, Dworkin maintains:

> [M]ost of us ... are dedicated to something whose value to us is not exhausted or captured in the enjoyment its realization will bring, and some are dedicated to more things in that way, or more strongly dedicated, than others. Even when we do enjoy what we have or have done, we often enjoy it because we think it valuable, not vice versa. And we sometimes choose ... a life that we believe will bring less enjoyment because it is in other ways a better life to lead.[36]

For this reason, what Dworkin calls 'conscious-state' theories of welfare do not correspond to the standards by which most people govern their own lives, making it a questionable metric for a conception of equality and a theory of distributive justice.[37]

Alternatively, if 'welfare' is understood more plausibly as a matter of a person's 'success in fulfilling his [or her] preferences, goals, and ambitions',[38] it is vulnerable to another objection—regardless of whether the concept of 'success' is understood by reference to the preferences, goals, and ambitions that people set for themselves ('relative success') or by reference to more general judgements that people make regarding the value of their lives ('overall success').[39] Since reasonable people necessarily define their preferences, goals, and ambitions and assess the value of their lives 'against a background of assumptions about the rough type and quantity of resources they will have available with which to lead different sorts of lives',[40] a theory of distributive justice must first determine the resources to which people are entitled before it can properly assess either their relative success in achieving their preferences, goals, or ambitions or their overall success in leading a valuable life.[41] For this reason, Dworkin concludes, success theories of welfare are no better than conscious-state theories of welfare as a standard for measuring distributional equality and 'cannot be used to justify or constitute a theory of fair distribution'.[42]

Although some of Dworkin's critics have sought to reassert welfare as a metric for distributive justice,[43] these objections fail to articulate a specific meaning of welfare,[44] and remain vulnerable to Dworkin's objections that they do not correspond to the pluralistic standards by which people lead their lives, do not provide an adequate account of equality as a limitation on the recognition of individual preferences, and do not adequately recognize the role of individual responsibility as a criterion for assessing the justice of distributive outcomes. As the following section explains, principles of equality and individual responsibility are at the core of Dworkin's conception of distributive justice, distinguishing his theory not only from welfare-based approaches but also from Rawls.

[35] Ibid., 42–3. [36] Ibid., 43. [37] Ibid., 44. [38] Ibid., 17. [39] Ibid., 28–42.
[40] Ibid., 28. [41] Ibid., 29, 39. [42] Ibid., 39.
[43] See, especially, Richard Arneson, 'Welfare Should Be the Currency of Justice', 30(4) *Canadian Journal of Philosophy* (2000) 497–524.
[44] See e.g. Ibid., 501, admitting that 'a particular welfare-based theory of justice ... is beyond the scope of this essay'.

B. Resources, Ethical Individualism, and Distributive Justice

Having criticized welfare as a standard for measuring distributional equality, Dworkin introduces the concept of resources as an alternative criterion for this purpose. Unlike welfare, he explains, which reduces all values and preferences to a single conception of well-being that may not be universally shared, resources constitute the means through which people are able to pursue their own ends—making it a more suitable metric for distributional equality in a liberal society which generally assumes not only that 'people differ, sometimes radically, in their opinions about what makes their lives go overall better or worse', but also that 'people should govern their lives according to their own convictions on that matter'.[45]

By resources, Dworkin generally means impersonal marketable resources that individuals may privately own and exchange[46]—though this is not always clear in Dworkin's work, since he also refers to various 'personal qualities' such as 'strength, talent, character, and ambition' as other 'categories of resource'.[47] Although these personal qualities enter into his theory of distributive justice, however, they do so, as he emphasizes, 'in different ways'[48]—not as resources that are themselves the objects of distribution in accordance with equality of resources, but as factors that may (or may not) affect the meaning of an equal distribution.[49] As a result, Dworkin explains, the problem for his theory of distributive justice is 'one of determining how far the ownership of independent material resources should be affected' by differences in personal qualities.[50]

For this purpose, Dworkin relies on two principles of what he calls 'ethical individualism': (1) a principle of 'equal importance' that requires any political community that exercises dominion over and demands allegiance from its citizens to treat them with equal concern; and (2) a principle of 'special responsibility' that regards individuals as having a particular responsibility for the choices that shape their lives.[51] While the first principle 'requires government to adopt laws and policies that insure that its citizen's fates are, so far as government can achieve this, insensitive to who they otherwise are—their economic backgrounds, gender, race, or particular sets of skills and handicaps', the second principle 'demands that government work, again so far as it can achieve this, to make their fates sensitive to the choices that they have made'.[52] Together, these principles define a conception of distributive justice that distinguishes between a person's circumstances and their choices, making the justice of distributive outcomes as insensitive as possible to people's circumstances and as sensitive as possible to their choices.[53]

While the distinction between a person's circumstances and their choices is not always easy, Dworkin's approach relies on ordinary ethical judgements that normally distinguish between chance and choice in making assignments of consequential responsibility,[54] and typically regard individuals as responsible for their own

[45] Dworkin, n. 33, 340–1. [46] Dworkin, n. 19, 65. [47] Ibid., 286. [48] Ibid.

[49] Ibid., 80. In this respect, Dworkin's theory differs from that of John Rawls, who regards natural talents as 'a common asset' the benefits of which are shared with the least well off by virtue of his difference principle; see Rawls, n. 2, 101.

[50] Dworkin, n. 19, 80. [51] Ibid., 5–6. [52] Ibid., 6. [53] Ibid., 287. [54] Ibid.

personalities in the sense that individuals usually identify with the various convictions, preferences, tastes, and ambitions that comprise their personalities and regard the decisions that they make as their own choices rather than matters of good or bad luck.[55] On this basis, Dworkin generally understands a person's circumstances to include factors that are completely beyond a person's control (such as genetic endowments as well as other fortuitous circumstances that Dworkin labels 'brute luck'[56]), and a person's choices to include attributes and actions to which it is reasonable to assign individual responsibility (which generally include the various elements that comprise a person's personality,[57] as well as deliberate decisions to assume known risks, which Dworkin calls 'option luck'[58]). As a result, although acknowledging that people's choices are not 'causally independent of their culture, history, and circumstance',[59] nor of unchosen 'convictions, ambitions, and tastes that influence their choices',[60] Dworkin concludes that concepts of individual choice and responsibility are crucial to 'a political morality that makes sense in terms of—and of—each citizen's internal practices of moral and ethical criticism, including self-criticism'.[61]

In this respect, equality of resources differs not only from welfarist conceptions of distributive justice, but also from the political liberalism of John Rawls—whose principles of justice are derived from a hypothetical social contract entered into in an 'original position of equality' behind a 'veil of ignorance' that shields the contracting parties not only from knowledge of their 'place in society', but also of their 'natural assets and abilities' and their 'conceptions of the good' and their 'special psychological propensities'.[62] From this perspective, Rawls argues, the attributes and actions that define a person's choices are regarded as morally arbitrary,[63] so that agreed upon principles of justice define only 'the basic structure of society'[64] rather than individual entitlements to distributive shares—which Rawls conceptualizes not as rights in any foundational sense but instead as 'legitimate expectations' for 'those who, with the prospect of improving their condition, have done what the system announces that it will reward'.[65]

In contrast to this approach, Dworkin emphasizes that his theory of distributive justice does not attempt 'to insulate political morality from ethical assumptions and controversies about the character of a good life', but seeks its support in 'the more general ethical values to which it appeals'[66] including the distinction between a person's circumstances and their choices. On this basis, he explains, equality of resources 'defines a relation among citizens that is individualized for each'—determining 'what they are, as individuals, entitled to have' as 'a matter of individual right rather than one of group position'.[67]

While one might question the extent to which it is reasonable to attribute any particular distributive outcome to good or bad fortune versus individual responsibility,

[55] Ibid., 290. To the extent that this is not the case, these attributes of one's personality are, as Dworkin explains, best regarded as addictions or obsessions 'that we wish we did not have, and struggle to conquer or dispel'. Ibid., 293.
[56] Ibid., 73. [57] Ibid., 82. [58] Ibid., 73.
[59] Ronald Dworkin, 'Sovereign Virtue Revisited', 113(1) *Ethics* (2002) 106, 107. [60] Ibid.
[61] Ibid., 107. [62] Rawls, n. 2, 12. [63] Ibid., 312. [64] Ibid., 7.
[65] Ibid., 103. See also Ibid., 310–15. [66] Dworkin, n. 19, 5. [67] Ibid., 114–15.

the Rawlsian view that individual choices and actions have no normative significance for distributive justice is highly problematic given the ethical distinction that persons ordinarily draw between chance and choice in making assignments of consequential responsibility. For this reason, Dworkin's theory of distributive justice represents a useful improvement on Rawls's difference principle, which is insufficiently attentive to individual rights and responsibilities. Although classical libertarians have criticized the difference principle on similar grounds,[68] the following section explains how Dworkin's emphasis on equality as an essential criterion for distributive justice differentiates his approach from classical libertarianism.

C. Equality of Resources: Original Acquisition and Subsequent Redistribution

While Dworkin's theory of distributive justice includes a principle of individual responsibility for the consequences of one's choices, it also affirms a conception of equality in the distribution of resources. In order to reconcile these two values, which are often seen as mutually inconsistent, Dworkin relies on the idea of 'an economic market of some form' as both 'an analytical device' and 'an actual political institution'.[69] Although Dworkin notes that the market is often regarded as 'the enemy of equality' and 'a necessary condition of individual liberty',[70] equality of resources is designed to make the market serve both objectives by requiring that people enter the market 'on equal terms'.[71] In this respect, Dworkin's approach differs sharply from classical libertarianism.

For classical libertarianism, the justice of any distribution in the ownership of property depends not on a 'patterned' or 'end result' principle such as utility or the difference principle, but instead on the justice of its initial acquisition and the justice of its subsequent transfer.[72] According to John Locke, for example, even if all resources were originally held 'in common', individuals could legitimately appropriate these resources without any express agreement based on a right to self-preservation and entitlement to the fruits of one's labour—subject to a prohibition against the appropriation of resources that spoil before they are used which is overcome through the development of money, and a requirement that 'enough, and as good' is 'left in common for others' which is effectively satisfied by the productivity of private property.[73] Similarly, Robert Nozick concludes that individuals may acquire ownership of originally 'unheld things' so long as private appropriation satisfies a 'Lockean proviso' that others are not made worse off— which is fulfilled by the increased social output and varied employment opportunities that private property creates.[74] In each case, these theories presume that the property rights so acquired include the right to transfer property through exchange or bequest.[75]

[68] Nozick, n. 12. [69] Dworkin, n. 19, 66. [70] Ibid. [71] Ibid., 70.

[72] Nozick, n. 12, 149–231.

[73] John Locke, *Second Treatise of Government* (1690), C.B. Macpherson (ed.) (Cambridge: Hackett, 1980), 18–24 (ch. V, paras 25–47). For an overview of Locke's argument, see Duff, n. 17, 24–8.

[74] Nozick, n. 12, 175–81. [75] See, e.g., Locke, n. 73, 39 (ch VI, para. 72); Nozick, n. 12, 178.

In contrast to classical libertarianism, Dworkin's concept of original acquisition imagines a division of a society's resources through an auction or other market procedure among members of the society who are assumed to enter into this procedure on equal terms.[76] Through this arrangement, each individual would acquire a bundle of resources based on his or her willingness to pay for these resources relative to the willingness to pay of other individuals—making this opportunity cost the measure of the resources that each individual could justly acquire.[77] Although individuals wanting to acquire relatively expensive resources might regret that these are not less costly, they could not reasonably complain that they have been treated unfairly because the cost of the resources that they choose to acquire would reflect their opportunity cost to society as a whole.[78] In the end, Dworkin concludes, no one would prefer anyone else's bundle of resources to their own, and an equal division of the society's resources—'equality of resources'—would prevail.[79]

Once a society's resources have been divided in this manner, of course, people would continue to transfer and exchange resources and would also produce more resources—making different decisions about work and leisure, consumption and savings, gifts and bequests, the development of skills and talents, and the riskiness of investments; obtaining different rates of return from different market activities; and accumulating different resources over time from those originally acquired.[80] Although a 'starting-gate theory' of equality would permit subsequent inequalities without any adjustment on the basis that it would be unjust to interfere with the property rights acquired through original acquisition, Dworkin rejects this conclusion on the grounds that equality is no less relevant to the justification of subsequent holdings than it is for the justification of initial holdings,[81] so that any system of property rights established through an equal division of a society's resources should be subject to subsequent adjustment in the name of equality.[82] Having outlined a basic conception of equality of resources for the purpose of original acquisition, therefore, Dworkin must extend the idea to contemplate a 'dynamic economy' with production, savings, and investment.[83]

In order to do so, Dworkin begins by returning to the concept of ethical individualism on which his theory of distributive justice ultimately rests—arguing that a dynamic conception of equality of resources must allow distributive outcomes to vary with people's deliberate choices, while simultaneously protecting them as much as possible against adverse distributional consequences attributable to brute luck.[84] As

[76] Dworkin, n. 19, 66–71, employing the analogy of shipwrecked survivors who are washed up on an island with no indigenous population and abundant natural resources, which they seek to divide equally by allocating an equal number of clamshells to all survivors who can exchange these clamshells for the available resources. Although Dworkin's example assumes that all of the society's resources are subject to private appropriation, his theory does not exclude the possibility that some resources might also be held in common. As a result, the theory addresses the only the distribution of privately-owned resources, not the division of resources between public and private ownership.

[77] Ibid., 70. [78] Ibid., 69.

[79] Ibid., 67, equating the idea of an equal division of resources with an 'envy test' requiring that no one would prefer someone else's bundle of resources to their own.

[80] Ibid., 73. [81] Ibid., 87–8. [82] Ibid., 88. [83] Ibid., 71.

[84] Ibid., 89, arguing that 'we must, on pain of violating equality, allow the distribution of resources at any particular moment to be ... ambition-sensitive' (reflecting 'the cost or benefit to others of the choices people make'), but not 'endowment-sensitive' (reflecting 'differences in ability of the sort that produce income differences in a laissez-faire economy among people with the same ambitions').

a result, he explains, equality of resources is not violated if a person obtains more or less resources than others by choosing to work more or less or in occupations that pay more or less,[85] by deliberately taking or not taking risks,[86] by winning or losing intentional gambles,[87] or by saving rather than spending.[88] Where people's chances to obtain resources are not equally distributed, however, because natural talents differ,[89] inheritances vary,[90] and opportunities to take risks diverge,[91] equality of resources demands that any resulting inequalities be neutralized.[92] Since it is impossible to eliminate all inequalities attributable to brute luck, however, Dworkin must devise another method to ensure that equality of resources continues to apply over time.

For this purpose, Dworkin draws on the basic conception of equality of resources for an equal division of a society's resources—imagining a market mechanism that all members of society would have been willing to enter into on equal terms in order to offset the effects of brute luck on distributive outcomes. In this respect, Dworkin explains, equality of resources aims to achieve a condition of equality *ex ante* rather than *ex post*[93]—making people 'equal, so far as this is possible, in the resources with which they face uncertainty'[94] as opposed to the resources they possess 'after the uncertainties of risk' have transpired.[95]

According to Dworkin, this market mechanism is best represented by a hypothetical insurance arrangement in which individuals who are presumed not to know the economic returns that their skills and talents will command (and are therefore equally situated in this respect) would purchase insurance against the risk of low returns,[96] and individuals who are presumed not to know what if any inheritance they might receive would purchase insurance against the risk of 'bad inheritance luck'.[97] Although recognizing that the type and level of insurance that individuals would acquire in this hypothetical arrangement is somewhat 'speculative',[98] Dworkin identifies four features that are broadly consistent with those of actual insurance markets.

First, since the administration of any insurance arrangement is not costless and the costs of insurance benefits and insurance administration must be funded from premiums that reduce the resources available to those paying these premiums, it is reasonable to assume that coverage would extend only to relatively substantial and low probability risks for which the expected welfare losses exceed the welfare losses attributable to the payment of relatively small but certain premiums.[99] For this reason,

[85] Ibid., 85. [86] Ibid., 74. [87] Ibid., 74–5. [88] Ibid., 479, note 8. [89] Ibid., 91.
[90] Ibid., 347. [91] Ibid., 76. [92] Ibid., 91. [93] Dworkin, n. 59, 120–2.
[94] Ibid., 107.
[95] Ibid., 121. Although Dworkin's approach is designed to provide *ex post* compensation based on a presumed state of *ex ante* equality, equality of resources might also enhance actual equality *ex ante*, for example through educational programs designed to minimize the effects of natural talents and class backgrounds on economic opportunities. Dworkin appears to contemplate this *ex ante* approach to equality of resources, suggesting that 'an egalitarian society ought, just in the name of equality, to devote special resources to training those whose talents, as things fall out, place them lower on the income scale', but does not address this issue in any detail on the basis that this 'is part of the larger question of an egalitarian theory of education, which I have not even attempted to take up here'. Ibid., 108.
[96] Ibid., 73–109. [97] Ibid., 347. [98] Ibid., 79.
[99] Ibid., 97–8. Although Dworkin's analysis on this point draws on the notion of welfare and the principle of diminishing marginal utility, it does so in a very different way than welfare-based conceptions of distributive justice—as an account of the kinds of insurance that equally situated individuals would acquire rather than an independent measure of the justice of distributive outcomes.

Dworkin explains, 'the lower the income level chosen as the covered risk, the better the argument becomes that most people given the chance to buy insurance on equal terms would in fact buy at that level'.[100] Although Dworkin does not specify precisely what this income level might be, he suggests that '[t]he argument becomes compelling ... well above the level of income presently used to trigger transfer payments for unemployment or minimum wage levels in either Britain or the United States'.[101]

Second, since individuals are much less likely to insure against losses for which they are personally responsible than losses for which they are not responsible (and insurers are reluctant to insure losses for which individuals are personally responsible given the problem of 'moral hazard' whereby the availability of insurance encourages more and larger claims), the kinds of risks that this hypothetical insurance arrangement would be expected to cover are those that are attributable primarily to the brute luck that determines a person's circumstances rather than the attributes and actions that define their choices (including the deliberate assumption of known risks). For this reason, Dworkin suggests, a dynamic conception of equality of resources would provide health and income insurance for individuals who experience an illness or disability for which they are not responsible and against which they could not insure, but not for illnesses and disabilities that are primarily attributable to their own actions or against which they could have insured if insurance were available on equal terms.[102] For the same reason, equality of resources would generally provide insurance for individuals with skills and talents that command low economic returns,[103] though presumably not where these low returns are clearly attributable to an individual's deliberate decision to pursue less remunerative activities.[104] In addition, Dworkin maintains, equality of resources would not provide insurance against losses resulting from risks and gambles that people voluntarily assume,[105] though he also suggests that 'paternalistic reasons' might justify 'limiting how much any individual may risk'.[106] In

[100] Ibid., 97.

[101] Ibid. For a more detailed examination, see Daniel Markovits, 'How Much Redistribution Should There Be?', 112 *Yale Law Journal* (2003) 2291, 2305–13, concluding that 'people would insure only up to talent levels that fall significantly—more than 25%—below the mean'.

[102] Dworkin, n. 59, 73–4, distinguishing between someone who 'develops cancer in the course of a normal life' where 'there is no particular decision to which we can point as a gamble risking the disease' and someone who 'smoked cigarettes heavily'; and at 77, arguing that 'the bare idea of equality of resources, apart from any paternalistic additions, would not argue for redistribution from the person who had insured to the person who had not if, horribly, they were both blinded in the same accident'. Although Dworkin is not clear on the relationship between paternalistic concerns and equality of resources, this passage suggests that paternalistic considerations can be integrated with his idea of equality of resources—for example, by imagining what additional insurance an individual might have acquired in a hypothetical position of equality if cognizant of the distribution of persons who do and do not purchase accident insurance.

[103] Ibid., 92–9.

[104] Ibid., 91, distinguishing between 'the effects of differential talents' against which hypothetical persons would insure and 'the consequences of choosing an occupation' in response to a sense of what one wants to do with one's life, against which hypothetical persons would not insure.

[105] Dworkin, n. 19, 74–5.

[106] Ibid., 75. Although Dworkin does not appear to contemplate the possibility, one way to limit the amount that any individual may risk is to provide some kind of compensation in the event of losses—presumably on the basis of the same paternalistic considerations that might justify limits on how much any individual might risk. As explained earlier, these paternalistic considerations might reasonably be integrated with what Dworkin calls 'the bare idea of equality of resources' by imagining what additional

contrast, he argues, equality of resources would provide insurance against the risk of receiving little or no inheritance, the prospect of which depends more on the luck of one's birth than one's own actions.[107]

Third, because it is often difficult to distinguish between economic outcomes for which an individual is primarily responsible and economic outcomes that are primarily attributable to brute luck, the coverage that a hypothetical insurance arrangement would provide might be expected to include common features of standard insurance contracts that are designed to reduce moral hazard—such as co-insurance that limits the amount of benefits paid to a percentage of a claimant's losses,[108] and a requirement that claimants prove their losses.[109] Coverage levels might also differ based on the extent to which it is possible to differentiate categories of claims for which the risk of moral hazard varies—with higher coverage for losses for which individuals are less likely to bear any responsibility and lower coverage for losses for which individuals are more likely to bear some responsibility.

Finally, and most significantly for the purpose of this chapter, Dworkin argues that the premiums under the hypothetical insurance arrangements that he contemplates would likely be measured as 'an increasing percentage of the income the policy owner turns out to earn' in the case of insurance against the risk of a low income,[110] and 'a steeply progressive rate' in the case of inheritances.[111] Since insurers would be able to offer a higher level of coverage by charging higher premiums, and individuals would have reason to purchase this insurance if it increased their expected welfare, the principle of diminishing marginal utility suggests that equally situated individuals who are presumed not to know what they would earn or inherit would prefer to buy insurance with premiums that are an increasing function of their income or inheritances.[112] In each case, therefore, the concept of a hypothetical insurance market constitutes the basis for redistributive taxes, conceptualized as 'premiums' that equally-situated individuals would agree to pay.

Although one might question the emphasis that equality of resources places on *ex ante* equality over *ex post* outcomes, the extent to which brute luck can be distinguished from option luck, and the types of insurance that equally-situated individuals might reasonably be expected to purchase in a hypothetical insurance market,[113] Dworkin's ideas of original acquisition and subsequent redistribution represent compelling alternatives to classical libertarianism, affirming a conception of equality as essential to a theory of justice not only for the original acquisition of resources but also

insurance individuals might have acquired in a hypothetical insurance market if cognizant of the risks of various losses. See n. 102.

[107] Ibid., 346–9. [108] Ibid., 101. [109] Ibid., 101–2. [110] Ibid., 100.

[111] Ibid., 348. [112] Ibid., 100–1, referring specifically to insurance against a low income.

[113] See e.g. Michael Otsuka, 'Luck, Insurance and Equality', 113(1) *Ethics* (2002) 40–54, 50, arguing that Dworkin's *ex ante* approach fails to reconcile equality of resources with inequalities that arise *ex post*; and Elizabeth Anderson, 'How Should Egalitarians Cope with Market Risks?', 9 *Theoretical Inquiries in Law* (2008) 239–70, arguing that an egalitarian conception of distributive justice requires constraints on distributive shares that markets may generate. To the extent that Dworkin's concept of a hypothetical insurance market can incorporate paternalistic considerations and provide insurance against the risk of inhabiting a society characterized by extreme inequalities, it may be possible to incorporate these concerns within an expanded conception of equality of resources.

for their subsequent distribution. The remainder of this chapter considers the implications of Dworkin's theory for redistributive taxation.

III. Practice

As a legal and political philosopher, not a tax scholar, it is not surprising that Dworkin's comments on redistributive taxation are limited and basic—emphasizing primarily the conceptual rule of these taxes in a society committed to equality of resources as 'premiums' that equally situated individuals would have been willing to pay to insure against the risks of illness, disability, or low market returns, and the risk that they might receive little or no inheritance.

The following sections build on Dworkin's account of redistributive taxation, considering the implications of his theory for the kinds of taxes that a society should levy in order to promote equality of resources, as well as the design of these taxes. The first section considers the form of a personal tax to insure against illness, disability, and low market returns, and the second examines the design of a tax to insure against little or no inheritance.

A. Personal Taxation

With respect to personal taxation, tax policy analysts generally contemplate three different kinds of taxes, which apply to different tax bases: (1) income taxation, which applies to revenue less expenses over a period of time, typically a year, and in principle includes all income from labour and capital;[114] (2) consumption or expenditure taxation, which also applies to revenue less expenses over a period of time, but excludes all income that is saved during this period rather than spent;[115] and (3) wealth taxation, which generally applies to the aggregate value of a person's assets less liabilities at a particular time such as the end of a taxation year.[116] To this traditional trio of personal

[114] This description emphasizes the source of the income, which generally corresponds to the concept of income in source-based income tax regimes like those in Canada and the United Kingdom. In contrast to this source concept of income, much US tax policy analysis refers to the comprehensive concept of income proposed by Henry Simons, which defines income in terms of its uses for consumption or saving. Henry C. Simons, *Personal Income Taxation: The Definition of Income as a Problem of Fiscal Policy* (Chicago: University of Chicago Press, 1938), 50.

[115] This description applies to a cash-flow personal consumption tax in which tax is paid when income is spent on consumption rather than saved. See, e.g., William D. Andrews, 'A Consumption Type or Cash Flow Personal Income Tax', 87(6) *Harvard Law Review* (1974), 1113; Nicholas Kaldor, *An Expenditure Tax* (London: Routledge, 1955). Alternatively, a yield-exemption consumption tax would exempt all capital income from tax, making this form of consumption tax equivalent to a so-called wage tax that would apply exclusively to labour income. See e.g. David Bradford, *Untangling the Income Tax* (Cambridge, MA: Harvard University Press, 1986), 89–94. Although the yield-exemption approach is often considered to be equivalent to the cash-flow approach, this equivalence holds only if several assumptions apply, including that investment returns are certain, taxpayers can borrow and lend unlimited amounts at a risk-free rate, and that tax rates are not progressive and remain constant over time—assumptions that are unlikely to be satisfied in practice. See e.g. Michael J. Graetz, 'Implementing a Progressive Consumption Tax', 92(8) *Harvard Law Review* (1979) 1575, 1602.

[116] See e.g. C.T. Sandford, J.R.M. Willis, and D.J. Ironside, *An Annual Wealth Tax* (London: Heinemann Educational Books, 1975); David Shakow and Reed Shuldiner, 'A Comprehensive Wealth Tax', 53 *Tax Law Review* (2000) 499.

tax bases, tax theorists have also added ability or endowment taxation, which would in principle apply to a person's income-earning ability, irrespective of the amount of income that the person actually earns.[117]

Beginning with income taxation, proponents generally extol the fairness of this tax base, which in principle applies comprehensively to all categories of income, and is often said to provide the most equitable measure of each person's 'ability to pay' tax.[118] Although many arguments for the taxation of personal income are explicitly welfarist, viewing the concepts of income and ability to pay as substitutes or surrogates for individual welfare or utility,[119] some rely on nonwelfarist conceptions of distributive justice which regard personal income taxation as the legitimate assertion of a social claim to a share of all output based on 'the role of fortuity in income distribution and the dependence of producers on consumers and other producers to create value in our society'.[120]

For those favouring personal consumption or expenditure taxation, on the other hand, tax fairness is best measured by reference to the resources that one consumes during a taxable period, rather than the income that one earns during any period (which may be spent on current consumption or saved in order to finance future consumption)—on the grounds either that individual welfare ultimately depends on personal consumption rather than income,[121] or that judgements about legitimate distributive shares properly concern the resources that one withdraws from society through personal consumption rather than the resources to which one is entitled by virtue of one's labour and investment.[122] Consumption tax advocates also challenge the fairness of the income tax, arguing that it discriminates against persons who choose to save rather than spend[123]—differentiating between individuals who are equally situated *ex ante* based solely on their preference for future consumption over current consumption,[124] and imposing a 'double tax' on saving by taxing the returns that compensate savers for deferred consumption.[125] On these grounds, proponents argue, a personal consumption or expenditure tax is both fairer and more efficient than a personal income tax.[126] As with the taxation of personal income, therefore,

[117] See e.g. Lawrence Zelenak, 'Taxing Endowment', 55 *Duke Law Journal* (2006) 1145. Although it is widely recognized that a tax on earning ability would be impossible to administer, ability or endowment might nonetheless be regarded as an ideal to which an actual tax system should aspire in various ways.

[118] See, e.g., Alan Gunn, 'The Case for an Income Tax', 46 *University of Chicago Law Review* (1979) 370.

[119] See e.g. Richard Goode, 'The Economic Definition of Income', in Joseph A. Pechman (ed.), *Comprehensive Income Taxation* (Washington, DC: The Brookings Institution, 1977), 1, 9.

[120] Alvin Warren, 'Would a Consumption Tax Be Fairer Than an Income Tax?', 89(6) *Yale Law Journal* (1980) 1081, 1091.

[121] See e.g. Irving Fisher, *The Nature of Capital and Income* (London: Macmillan, 1906).

[122] See e.g. Edward J. McCaffery, 'The Uneasy Case for Capital Taxation', in Ellen Frankel Paul, Fred D. Miller, Jr, and Jeffrey Paul (eds), *Taxation, Economic Prosperity, and Distributive Justice* (Cambridge, UK: Cambridge University Press, 2006), 166, 167, 168, arguing that 'the moment of spending ... is the right time to make social judgments over the appropriate level of taxation' and that 'our ordinary and reflective moral intuitions ought to consistently run out to the *uses* of material resources, and not to their *sources*'. For an early version of this argument, see Thomas Hobbes, *Leviathan*, C.B. Macpherson (ed.) (Harmondsworth, UK: Penguin, [1651] 1985), 386–7.

[123] See e.g. Edward J. McCaffery, *Fair Not Flat: How to Make the Tax System Better and Simpler* (Chicago: University of Chicago Press, 2002), 35.

[124] See e.g. Bradford, n. 115, 315. [125] See e.g. Andrews, n. 115, 1167.

[126] See e.g. Bankman and Weisbach, n. 5.

arguments for personal consumption or expenditure taxation invoke both welfarist and non-welfarist conceptions of distributive justice.

This is also the case with arguments for personal wealth taxation and ability or endowment taxation. The former, for example, is defended both on the welfarist grounds that wealth confers a form of ability to pay that is not recognized in most measures of income or consumption,[127] and on the non-welfarist basis that wealth taxation can curb extreme concentrations of wealth which can threaten democratic institutions, social stability, and economic growth and prosperity.[128] The latter is similarly supported on the welfarist basis that earning ability corresponds more closely to individual welfare than income, consumption, or wealth,[129] and the nonwelfarist basis that earning ability is a better measure of unjustified economic inequality than proxies such as income, consumption, or wealth—which reflect the combined effect of one's ability or endowment and one's choices regarding work or leisure and savings or consumption.[130]

With its emphasis on *ex ante* equality and its reliance on a principle of ethical individualism that distinguishes a person's choices from their circumstances, one might have expected that equality of resources would regard a consumption or expenditure tax or an ability or endowment tax as the ideal tax base for personal taxation. Indeed, Dworkin's conclusion that equality of resources is not violated if a person obtains more or less resources than others by deliberately taking or not taking risks, by winning or losing intentional gambles, or by saving rather than spending,[131] would appear to support consumption or expenditure taxation as an ideal tax base, while his insistence that equality of resources allows the distribution of resources to be 'ambition-sensitive' but not 'endowment-sensitive'[132] seems to support ability or endowment taxation as an ideal tax base. Not surprisingly, therefore, advocates of each of these tax bases have referred to Dworkin for support.[133]

In fact, however, Dworkin rejects endowment, consumption, and wealth as ideal tax bases for redistributive taxation and explicitly endorses the income tax for this purpose.[134] Regarding endowment, Dworkin objects that talents and ambitions are 'too closely intertwined' to differentiate for tax purposes,[135] and that requiring people to pay for their talents would require those with high earning abilities to 'purchase leisure time or the right to a less productive occupation at the cost of other

[127] See e.g. Richard M. Bird, 'The Case for Taxing Personal Wealth', in *Report of the Proceedings of the Twenty-Third Tax Conference* (Toronto: Canadian Tax Foundation, 1972), 6, 8, arguing that personal wealth affords advantages of 'opportunity, flexibility and security' beyond the income that it may generate; and Shakow and Shuldiner, n. 125, arguing that 'substantial income from wealth effectively goes untaxed under the current income tax system' which generally does not apply to gains until they are realized and does not apply to the imputed income from assets that are not used to generate a market return.

[128] See, e.g., James R. Repetti, 'Democracy, Taxes, and Wealth', 76(3) *New York University Law Review* (2001) 825; Thomas Picketty, *Capital in the Twenty-First Century* (Cambridge, MA: Harvard University Press, 2014), 515–34.

[129] See, e.g., Dan Shaviro, 'Endowment and Inequality', in Joseph J. Thorndike and Dennis J. Ventry, Jr (eds), *Tax Justice: The Ongoing Debate* (Washington, DC: The Urban Institute Press, 2002), 123, 128–9.

[130] Ibid., 140. [131] Dworkin, n. 19, 74–5, 479, note 8. [132] Ibid., 89.

[133] See, e.g., Edward J. McCaffery, 'Tax's Empire', 85 *Georgetown Law Journal* (1996) 71, 141–4; Shaviro, n. 129, 140–2.

[134] Dworkin, n. 19, 90–1, 478–9, note 8. [135] Ibid., 91.

resources'—violating equality of resources by causing those whose skills and talents command the highest economic returns to envy those whose earnings abilities are less.[136] Consumption and wealth, on the other hand, are rejected on the grounds that the former would exclude investment returns which are presumed to reflect more than 'preferences for later consumption',[137] while the latter would impose an additional burden on income that a person chooses to save rather than spend.[138]

Although welfarists are generally sympathetic to the idea of ability or endowment taxation on the grounds that it would eliminate tax disincentives to work,[139] most liberal-egalitarians share Dworkin's aversion to this tax base on the grounds that a tax on earning abilities would force those whose skills and talents command the highest economic returns to engage in these pursuits for a period of time in order to pay the tax—interfering with their freedom to conduct their lives as they choose within a framework of equal justice.[140] As others have observed, however, if liberal egalitarians consider it acceptable for a tax system to require people to work longer hours or in particular occupations in order to obtain sufficient after-tax income in order to satisfy their consumption preferences, it is not clear why it is unacceptable for a tax system to require people to work at least some hours in some occupations in order to satisfy the requirements of a redistributive tax.[141] While an answer may lie in a distinction between market returns that are realized through social interaction and potential returns that are not realized through market exchanges, this argument requires further elaboration.[142]

Even if ability or endowment taxation is considered normatively indefensible (and administratively infeasible), however, it might be possible to imagine specific features of a tax and transfer system that might aim to track Dworkin's distinction between a person's ambitions and their endowments in ways that are both administratively feasible and normatively acceptable.[143] Public health insurance, for example, arguably redistributes along one dimension of endowment by transferring resources from the healthy to the sick,[144] as do disability support programs which transfer resources from the 'able' to the 'disabled'. The same may also be said of public pension plans, which redistribute resources from 'the short-lived to the long-lived'.[145] Others have proposed endowment-related taxes that would vary according to average parental income during childhood,[146] or Scholastic Aptitude Test (SAT) scores achieved in high

[136] Ibid., 90. [137] Ibid., 479, note 8. [138] Ibid. [139] See e.g. Mirrlees, n. 3.

[140] See, e.g., John Rawls, *Justice as Fairness* (Cambridge, MA: Harvard University Press, 2001), 158; Eric Rakowski, 'Can Wealth Taxes Be Justified?', 53 *Tax Law Review* (2000) 263, 267, note 10.

[141] See e.g. Kirk J. Stark, 'Enslaving the Beachcomber: Some Thoughts on the Liberty Objections to Endowment Taxation', 18 *Canadian Journal of Law & Jurisprudence* (2005) 47, 49. As Stark notes, however, this conclusion may not apply if labour markets are 'lumpy' so that a particular level of income can be obtained only by working full time. Ibid., 59, note 64.

[142] For an argument along these lines, see David M. Hasen, 'Liberalism and Ability Taxation', 85 *Texas Law Review* (2007) 1057, 1113.

[143] See, e.g., Zelenak, n. 117, 1172–81.

[144] See, e.g., Kyle Logue and Ronen Avraham, 'Redistributing Optimally: Of Tax Rules, Legal Rules, and Insurance', 56 *Tax Law Review* (2003)157, 226–7.

[145] Ibid., 227, note 211.

[146] Bruce Ackerman and Anne Alstott, *The Stakeholder Society* (New Haven: Yale University Press, 1999), 155–77.

school[147]—though these approaches might well raise the same concerns about 'talent slavery' that motivate liberal egalitarian concerns about ability or endowment as an ideal tax base. More appealing, perhaps, are tax rules that would provide graduated cost recovery for investments in education and training, thereby reducing the tax on returns from these investments, on the basis that the income derived from the skills and talents acquired through these investments is more closely related to ambitions and efforts than endowments and circumstances.[148]

Dworkin's opposition to consumption or expenditure as an ideal tax base is more puzzling given the emphasis that equality of resources places on *ex ante* equality, and his conclusion that taxation should not alter the distributive consequences of individual decisions to take risks or gambles or to save rather than spend—arguments that are often used to support the taxation of personal consumption or expenditure. With respect to risks and gambles, however, Dworkin acknowledges that 'paternalistic' considerations might affect this conclusion, so that a hypothetical insurance market might compensate persons who suffer the consequences of bad option luck as well as bad brute luck.[149] Indeed, to the extent that the gambles involved in most investments entail both known risks and unknown risks, these gambles are apt to combine elements of option luck and brute luck, justifying at least some *ex post* redistribution from winners to losers. For both reasons, equality of resources might reasonably reject a yield-exemption consumption tax as incompatible with distributive justice.[150]

Since a cash-flow consumption tax would apply on an *ex post* basis to all investment returns that are used for personal consumption, it is not vulnerable to this objection to the yield-exemption approach.[151] By excluding saved income from tax, however, the effect of a cash-flow consumption tax is to exempt the risk-free return on invested capital, which is included in the base of an income tax.[152] Although consumption-tax

[147] Zelenak, n. 117, 1180.

[148] See, e.g., David S. Davenport, 'Education and Human Capital: Pursuing an Ideal Income Tax and a Sensible Tax Policy', 42(3) *Case Western Law Review* (1992) 793.

[149] Dworkin, n. 19, 75, 77. See also nn 102 and 106 and accompanying text, suggesting that these paternalistic considerations might be integrated with Dworkin's idea of equality of resources by imagining what additional insurance individuals in a hypothetical position of equality might have purchased if cognizant of the risks of not insuring against bad option luck.

[150] For a similar argument against a yield-exemption consumption tax, see Graetz, n. 115, 1600–1, arguing that 'lucky gamblers are not the same as unlucky gamblers' and that 'the tax base must distinguish those who are lucky from those who are unlucky, even though they might have been in the same position with respect to their expectations before the gamble'. This conclusion assumes that a tax system can, in fact, apply to returns to risk—which economic analysis demonstrates is not the case in a flat-rate income tax with full loss offsets in which investors can borrow at the risk-free rate of return in order to increase the size of investments that are subject to taxation in the event of success and loss offset in the case of failure. See, e.g., Joseph Bankman and Thomas Griffith, 'Is the Debate Between and Income Tax and a Consumption Tax a Debate About Risk? Does it Matter?', 47 *Tax Law Review* (1992) 377; David A. Weisbach, 'The (Non)Taxation of Risk', 58 *Tax Law Review* (2004) 1. Since the assumptions on which this conclusion rest are unlikely to apply in practice, it seems reasonable to conclude that 'reports of the death of principles taxation of risk premium … have been greatly exaggerated'. Lawrence Zelenak, 'The Sometimes-Taxation of the Returns to Risk-Bearing Under a Progressive Income Tax', 59 *Southern Methodist University Law Review* (2006) 879, 915.

[151] Edward J. McCaffery, 'A New Understanding of Tax', 103 *Michigan Law Review* (2005) 807, 812 arguing that a 'postpaid' or cash-flow personal consumption taxes are fairer than a 'prepaid' or yield-exemption personal consumption taxes because the former 'can and do burden the yield to capital'.

[152] For a numerical demonstration, see Warren, n. 120, 1102–7.

advocates often argue that this risk-free return should be exempt from tax on the basis that it merely compensates savers for deferring their consumption to a later period,[153] others have challenged this theory of the risk-free rate of return on the grounds that individuals wanting to smooth their consumption over different taxation periods might reasonably save income for this purpose without requiring any return[154]—suggesting that positive returns on invested capital are due entirely to the productivity of capital rather than compensation for deferral.[155] As well, if the risk-free return on savings should be exempt because it compensates for deferred consumption, one might argue that labour income should also be exempt on the basis that it compensates workers for giving up leisure time.[156]

Although Dworkin's rejection of a personal consumption tax does not consider these tax policy arguments for or against personal consumption as an ideal tax base, his assumption that investment returns reflect more than 'preferences for later consumption' is consistent with the tax policy argument that these returns are attributable to the productivity of capital and are therefore properly included in the base of a redistributive tax. More generally, his support for income as a tax base and his view that the purpose of this tax is to insure against the risk of low market returns reflect a clear rejection of the argument by some consumption tax advocates that redistributive taxation should address the resources that one withdraws from society through personal consumption, rather than the resources that one receives through labour and investment. On the contrary, as one critic of personal consumption taxation has argued:

> There is ... a sense in which consumption taxation is less consistent with individual freedom than is income taxation. The distributive premise of the consumption tax is that quantitative consumption decisions are for collective, not individual, judgment. It certainly does not seem obvious that this premise shows more respect for individual liberty than does the income tax view that distribution of product is for collective decision. A person's collective responsibilities are concluded at the time of production under the income tax; by contrast, under the consumption tax those responsibilities are not discharged until a person consumes his [or her] last resource.[157]

For this reason as well, a redistributive tax based on personal income seems more consistent with equality of resources than a redistributive tax aimed at personal consumption or expenditure.

In contrast to personal income, on the other hand, liberal egalitarians generally oppose wealth as an ideal tax base on the grounds that a personal wealth tax would impose a tax on income that individuals choose to save rather than spend.[158] Unlike

[153] See especially Irving Fisher, *The Theory of Interest as Determined by Impatience to Spend and Opportunity to Invest It* (New York: Macmillan, 1930). For a useful review of this 'supply-side' account of the origin of interest, see Mark Kelman, 'Time Preference and Tax Equity', 35(4) *Stanford Law Review* (1983) 649, 658–70.

[154] See e.g. Warren, n. 120, 1100, suggesting that a rational consumer might reasonably treat consumption in each period equally: 'Marooned on a desert island with a lifetime store of goods, a consumer might well allocate an equivalent amount of goods to each of the remaining years of his life.'

[155] Ibid., 1100–1; Kelman, n. 153, 670–5, reviewing 'demand side' accounts of the origin of interest based on the productivity of capital.

[156] Warren, n. 120, 1107.

[157] Warren, n. 120, 1120–1.

[158] See, e.g., Rakowski, n. 140.

a personal income tax, which applies to the return from saved income, a personal wealth tax would apply to saved income itself—imposing a second tax on saved income that would not apply to income that is devoted to consumption in the same taxation period. For this reason, Dworkin rejects personal wealth as an ideal base for redistributive taxation, concluding that '[s]omeone's decision to spend rather than save ... is precisely the kind of decision whose impact should be determined by the market uncorrected for tax under this analysis'.[159]

Crucially, however, this conclusion depends on the assumption that income is subject to redistributive taxation before it is saved or spent, and that inheritances are also subject to a system of just redistribution, so that personal wealth is justly held.[160] To the extent that neither assumption holds, which might be true of an income tax that generally does not apply to unrealized gains, equality of resources might contemplate a role for personal wealth taxation as a supplement to an income tax or a tax on the transfer of wealth. Equality of resources might also contemplate a role for personal wealth taxation to reduce extreme concentrations of wealth, on the basis that equally situated individuals participating in a hypothetical insurance market might reasonably have insured against a society of extreme inequalities in which they might suffer the 'distinct harm of occupying a low tier in the class system'.[161] In principle, however, Dworkin and other liberal-egalitarians appear to regard well-designed income and inheritance taxes as sufficient for this purpose.

Finally, it is useful to reiterate two important aspects of Dworkin's proposal for a redistributive income tax: that it should be levied at progressive rates, and that revenues should be devoted exclusively to benefits paid to those whose skills and talents command low market returns. Although Dworkin's rationale for progressive rates relies on a principle of diminishing marginal utility of income, which equally-situated individuals are assumed to take into account in a hypothetical insurance market,[162] equality of resources might also favour progressivity on the basis that higher market returns are more likely to reflect an element of brute luck than ordinary returns—a presumption that is consistent with the phenomenon of 'winner-take-all' markets in which certain positions offer returns that greatly exceed those available to marginally less successful competitors.[163] It might also contemplate higher rates on speculative gains that are also apt to reflect a significant element of brute luck (combined with option luck).

[159] Dworkin, n. 19, 479, note 8.

[160] These assumptions are implicit in Dworkin's view that equality of resources requires that individuals be situated equally *ex ante*.

[161] Dworkin, n. 19, 348, explaining the rationale for taxes on estates or inheritances. A personal wealth tax along these lines might be consistent with the view that an egalitarian society should place constraints on the extent to which markets are allowed to produce extreme inequalities. See, e.g., Anderson, n. 113.

[162] Dworkin, n. 19, 100–1. Although Dworkin's reliance on this principle might seem to suggest that his justification for progressivity is based on welfare or utility, Dworkin emphasizes that the 'the point of the strategy is fairness to individuals' who are presumed to consider the impact of different income levels on their welfare. Ibid., 349–50.

[163] See, e.g., Robert H. Frank and Philip J. Cook, *The Winner-Take-All Society* (New York: Penguin Books, 1995); Martin J. McMahon, Jr and Alice G. Abreu, 'Winner-Take-All Markets: Easing the Case for Progressive Taxation', 4 *Florida Tax Review* (1998) 1.

As for the idea that income tax revenues should be devoted exclusively to redistributive transfers, this approach would contradict both traditional public finance theory which rejects the idea of dedicated taxes, and prevailing practice in most developed countries which adds revenues from income taxes to general tax revenues. It might also suggest a more limited role for progressive income taxation as part of a tax system in which governments rely more extensively on other taxes including sales taxes and benefit-related taxes in order to finance public goods and services.[164] At the same time, however, dedicating income tax revenues to redistributive transfer programs might provide a more compelling rationale for progressive income taxation than welfarist rationales based on ability to pay which do not adequately account for individual entitlements.

B. Inheritance Taxation

In addition to a progressive income tax, Dworkin argues that equality of resources would also favour 'an inheritance tax, at a steeply progressive rate'.[165] Although fiercely opposed by some commentators on the welfarist grounds that taxes on the transfer of wealth allegedly discourage capital accumulation and impede economic growth,[166] and the non-welfarist basis that these taxes constitute a 'double tax' on hard-working and thrifty donors who managed to accumulate wealth during their lifetimes,[167] these taxes are widely supported by liberal egalitarians on the grounds that substantial transfers of wealth from one generation to another are essentially unearned by their recipients; undermine ideals of fair equality of opportunity; and perpetuate dynastic concentrations of wealth that undermine social, economic, and political equality.[168]

[164] See, e.g., Michael J. Graetz, *100 Million Unnecessary Returns: A Simple, Fair and Competitive Plan for the United States* (New Haven: Yale University Press, 2008), recommending a reduced role for the income tax as an explicitly redistributive tax alongside a broad-based sales or value-added tax; and David G. Duff, 'Benefit Taxes and User Fees in Theory and Practice', 54(4) *University of Toronto Law Journal* (2004) 391, supporting benefit taxes and user fees as an element of a tax system that includes redistributive taxes.

[165] Dworkin, n. 19, 348.

[166] See, e.g., Edward J. McCaffery, 'The Uneasy Case for Wealth Transfer Taxation', 104(2) *Yale Law Journal* (1994) 283. Notwithstanding these claims, empirical evidence suggests that wealth transfer taxes have relatively little impact on capital accumulation—a finding that is consistent with theoretical analysis suggesting that the motives for transferring wealth are mixed, including accidental bequests on which taxes have no impact and altruistic gifts and bequests for which wealth transfer taxes can actually encourage increased accumulation in order to maintain a targeted gift or bequest after tax. See e.g. Wojciech Kopczuk and Joel Slemrod, 'The Impact of the Estate Tax on Wealth Accumulation and Avoidance Behavior', in William G. Gale, James R. Hines, and Joel Slemrod (eds), *Rethinking Estate and Gift Taxation* (Washington, DC: Brookings Institution, 2001), 299; David Joulfaian, 'The Behavioral Response of Wealth Accumulation to Estate Taxation: Time Series Evidence', 59 *National Tax Journal* (2006) 253. For an excellent summary of the literature, see Lily L. Batchelder, 'What Should Society Expect from Heirs? The Case for a Comprehensive Inheritance Tax', 63(1) *Tax Law Review* (2009) 1, 36–8.

[167] See e.g. Edward McCaffery, 'Grave Robbers: The Moral Case Against the Death Tax', 85 *Tax Notes* (1999) 1429, 1436–40.

[168] See e.g. David G. Duff, 'Taxing Inherited Wealth: A Philosophical Argument', 6 *Canadian Journal of Law & Jurisprudence* (1993) 3; Eric Rakowski, 'Transferring Wealth Liberally', 51 *Tax Law Review* (1996) 419; Anne L. Alstott, 'Equal Opportunity and Inheritance Taxation', 121(2) *Harvard Law Review* (2007) 469; Miranda Perry Fleischer, 'Divide and Conquer: Using an Accessions Tax to Combat Dynastic Wealth Transfers', 57 *Boston College Law Review* (2016) 913.

According to Rawls, for example, progressive gift and inheritance taxes are necessary 'not to raise revenue ... but gradually and continually to correct the distribution of wealth and to prevent concentrations of power detrimental to the fair value of political liberty and fair equality of opportunity'.[169] Dworkin's argument for a progressive inheritance tax is broadly consistent with these concerns, though his emphasis on ethical individualism as a principle of distributive justice dictates that his account turns on considerations of individual right rather than collective good.

For Dworkin, the argument for inheritance taxation requires a reconciliation between two 'competing demands' of equality of resources: (1) that individuals are generally free 'to spend what is rightfully theirs' after tax as they choose—'on expensive cars or art or travel, for example'—without restriction through 'further taxes';[170] and (2) that 'it is unjust when some people lead their lives with less wealth available to them, or in otherwise less favorable circumstances, than others, not through some choice or gamble of their own but through brute bad luck'.[171] Taking both principles into account, Dworkin rejects the idea that gifts and bequests should be prohibited altogether,[172] but concludes that 'people may be taxed on what they give or leave to others because this ... form of expenditure ... produces injustice in the next generation.'[173]

In order to fully justify and specify the form of this tax, Dworkin resorts to the same device that he employs to justify a progressive income tax, imagining 'another hypothetical insurance market in which hypothetical people may all buy insurance on equal terms'.[174] According to Dworkin:

> Inheritance insurance would make sense ... to guarantee ... against the ... harm of occupying a low tier in a class system—against, that is, a life in a community where others have much more money, and consequently more status and power, than they do and their children will.[175]

On this basis, he maintains, equally situated individuals would insure against 'bad inheritance luck'—accepting a structure of premiums that would 'rise ... steeply from zero in the case of modest gifts or a modest estate to a very high marginal proportion of very great wealth'.[176] In addition, he suggests, since 'it falls to income taxes' to finance medical benefits and redistributive transfers to individuals whose skills and talents command low market returns, inheritance tax revenues should be used 'for improved public education, education and training loans for would-be professionals,

[169] Rawls, *A Theory of Justice*, n. 2, 277.

[170] Dworkin, n. 59, 125; Dworkin, n. 19, 347. Although Dworkin is not clear on this point, the general prohibition against 'further taxes' that he contemplates presumably would not exclude broad-based sales or value-added taxes or more targeted benefit taxes or user fees that finance public goods and services, nor regulatory taxes such as environmental taxes that are deliberately designed to discourage behaviour that imposed negative externalities on others. In contrast, equality of resources would appear to exclude luxury taxes that might be designed to discourage 'conspicuous consumption'.

[171] Dworkin, n. 19, 347. [172] Dworkin, n. 59, 125. [173] Dworkin, n. 19, 347.

[174] Ibid. For a critical assessment of Dworkin's reliance on a hypothetical insurance market for inheritance, see Daniel Halliday, 'Inheritance and Hypothetical Insurance', in S. Sciaraffa and W. Waluchow (eds), *The Legacy of Ronald Dworkin* (Oxford: Oxford University Press, 2016), 99–114.

[175] Dworkin, n. 19, 348. [176] Ibid., 347, 348.

and other programs that ease the impact of whatever economic stratification remains after the tax has been levied'.[177]

While Dworkin contemplates that these premiums would be paid by donors, in the form of a gift and estate tax that is 'measured by the assets given or bequeathed',[178] liberal egalitarians generally favour donee-based taxes that are measured by the assets that individuals receive by way of gift or inheritance.[179] Since a donee-based tax would apply tax-exempt thresholds and progressive rates to the value of assets received by beneficiaries rather than the value of assets accumulated by donors, it is more finely attuned to concerns about unequal inheritance than a donor-based tax—imposing the largest tax obligations on the most fortunate beneficiaries who receive the largest gifts and inheritances, encouraging donors to distribute their wealth more widely, and thereby reducing the impact of gifts and inheritances on unequal opportunities and the dynastic concentration of wealth.[180] For these reasons, a donee-based gift and inheritance tax should also be easier to justify as a tax on the fortunate beneficiaries of substantial gifts and inheritances, rather than a tax on hard-working and thrifty donors, and less vulnerable to the criticism that it constitutes double taxation of accumulated wealth on which tax has already been paid.[181]

Although Dworkin does not consider these arguments for a donee-based tax on the intergenerational transfer of wealth, his justification for a progressive inheritance tax is arguably more compatible with gift and inheritance tax levied on donees than it is with a gift and estate tax levied on donors—since it seems most reasonable to assume that hypothetical individuals would pay for insurance against the risk of 'bad inheritance luck' with premiums corresponding to the manifestation of 'good inheritance luck'. Indeed, in a subsequent comment on his inheritance tax proposal, Dworkin appears to accept that this tax should 'fall not on the donor, ... but on the recipient of the gift or bequest'.[182]

Finally, Dworkin's argument that inheritance tax revenues should be devoted to public education and other programs designed to reduce economic stratification seems reasonable given that a central purpose of these taxes to reduce unequal

[177] Ibid., 349. [178] Ibid., 348.

[179] See e.g. Rawls, n. 2, 277. In principle, such a tax would apply to all gifts and inheritances received by individuals over the course of their lifetimes, in the form of a lifetime accessions tax. See, e.g., Duff, n. 168.

[180] See e.g. David G. Duff, 'Alternatives to the Gift and Estate Tax', 57(3) *Boston College Law Review* (2016) 893, 911–12.

[181] Michael J. Graetz and Ian Shapiro, *Death by a Thousand Cuts: The Fight over Taxing Inherited Wealth* (Princeton: Princeton University Press, 2006), 255.

[182] Dworkin, n. 33, 353. In a footnote to this comment, Dworkin appears to suggest that this approach would include gifts and inheritances as 'income' to the donee. Ibid., note 41. See also the brief discussion in Ronald Dworkin, *Is Democracy Possible Here?* (Princeton: Princeton University Press, 2006), 117–18, remarking that 'it does seem unprincipled to tax an estate at the same rate without regard to the number or wealth of its beneficiaries' and suggesting that 'it would be much fairer ... to treat substantial gifts of any form, including bequests, as income subject to ordinary taxes'. Although the income-inclusion approach is one way to tax donees on the value of gifts and inheritances, the aggregation of gifts and inheritances with ordinary income and the taxation of these aggregate amounts at income tax rates are arguably inappropriate for the taxation of inherited wealth and are incompatible with Dworkin's argument for a distinct tax on inherited wealth. For a critical assessment of the income-inclusion approach to taxing gifts and inheritances, see Duff, n. 180, 910–11.

opportunities—though one might also imagine other uses such as the payment of a 'social inheritance' to individuals reaching the age of maturity,[183] and is important to recognize that additional resources should also be devoted to public education and other programs to support advanced education and training on the grounds that these programs constitute public services that confer societal benefits in addition to those enjoyed by individual recipients. As with Dworkin's argument for the dedication of income tax revenues to redistributive transfers, this approach to the use of inheritance tax revenues would contradict traditional public finance theory and prevailing practice in most developed countries that levy taxes on transfers of wealth,[184] but could help to enhance public understanding and support for inheritance taxation as an essential element of a just tax system.

IV. Conclusion

While this chapter does not endorse all aspects of Dworkin's theory, it argues that equality of resources provides a more compelling account of distributive justice than welfare-based theories, Rawlsian theory, and classical libertarianism—combining a conception of economic equality with principles of individual freedom and responsibility in a way that affords better recognition to both sets of values than these other approaches. On this basis, it examines Dworkin's arguments for redistributive taxation, building on his brief remarks to defend progressive income and inheritance taxes for this purpose.

To the extent that justice is the first virtue of social institutions, it follows that a just society should attend to the distributive justice of its tax system as its first or sovereign virtue. Relying on Dworkin's conception of equality of resources as a guide, a just tax system would include progressive income and inheritances taxes.

[183] See e.g. Ackerman and Alstott, n. 146, 21–64.

[184] Over the past few decades, several countries have scaled back or repealed taxes on the transfer of wealth, which Dworkin suggests 'may well be unjust'. Dworkin, n. 19, 349. For an account of the repeal of these taxes in several countries, see David G. Duff, 'The Abolition of Wealth Transfer Taxes: Lessons from Canada, Australia and New Zealand', 3 *Pittsburgh Tax Law Review* (2005) 72.

PART III

DESIGN AND MECHANICS OF THE TAX SYSTEM

WEALTH AND PROPERTY

8

A Forced Labour Theory of Property and Taxation

*Theodore P. Seto**

I. Introduction

Two memes dominate principled academic opposition to taxation. The first—that taxation is equivalent to forced labour—was famously articulated by Robert Nozick in *Anarchy, State, and Utopia*: 'Seizing the results of someone's labour is equivalent to seizing hours from him and directing him to carry on various activities.'[1] This, he implied, was wrong. His intellectual progeny rephrase his claim more pungently: taxation is theft.[2]

The second is the assumption that underlies much of optimal tax theory: that in the absence of taxation taxpayers would work and save in welfare-maximizing amounts and that taxation distorts these choices, thereby reducing aggregate social welfare. Arnold Harberger's conclusion that taxes produce deadweight loss[3] and James Mirrlees's conclusion that progressive marginal rates reduce welfare[4] both rest on this assumption. So do optimal tax theory's 'double distortion premise' (that distributive consequences should never be taken into account in structuring non-tax rules), its support for lump sum taxation, and its opposition to taxing income from capital.

This chapter offers an account of the history of property and tax law that challenges both these memes. It begins with the observation that we were not evolved to work hard and save. We were evolved to expend just as much effort on such activities as would maximize our likelihood of surviving and reproducing.[5] In the era of evolutionary adaptation (from the beginning of humankind until about 10,000 years

* This chapter was inspired in significant part by a presentation by Prof Neil Buchanan entitled 'Forced Labor, and Taxation as Theft: Debunking Some Confused Philosophical Attacks on the Income Tax' at the National Tax Association Annual Meeting, Santa Fe, New Mexico, 15 November 2014.

[1] Robert Nozick, *Anarchy, State, and Utopia* (New York: Basic Books, 1974).

[2] See e.g. Edward Feser, 'Taxation, Forced Labor, and Theft', 5 *Independent Review* (2000) 219–35; Murray N. Rothbard, *The Ethics of Liberty* (New York: NYU Press, 1998).

[3] Arnold C. Harberger, 'The Measurement of Waste', 54(3) *American Economic Review* (1964) 58–76.

[4] James Mirrlees, 'An Exploration in the Theory of Optimum Income Taxation', 38(2) *Review of Economic Studies* (1971) 175–208.

[5] Anthropological studies of modern hunter-gathers elaborate this premise. See e.g. Brian Coddington et al., 'Provisioning Offspring and Others: Risk–Energy Trade-Offs and Gender Differences in Hunter–Gatherer Foraging Strategies', 278 *Proceedings of the Royal Society B* (2011) 2502–9; Rebecca Bird et al., 'What Explains Differences in Men's and Women's Production', 20(2) *Human Nature* (2009) 105–129; Michael Gurven and Kim Hill, 'Why Do Men Hunt? A Reevaluation of "Man the Hunter" and the Sexual Division of Labor', 50(1) *Current Anthropology* (2009) 51–74; Rebecca Bird et al., 'The Hunting Handicap: Costly Signaling in Human Foraging Strategies', 50(1) *Behavioral Ecology and Sociobiology* (2001) 9–19; Rebecca Bird, 'Cooperation and Conflict: The Behavioral Ecology of the Sexual Division

Philosophical Foundations of Tax Law. First Edition. Edited by Monica Bhandari.

ago), opportunities for productive investment were low and the risk of death high. The rational individual discount rate—an actor's preference for present over future benefits—was therefore extremely high; modern economists would call it 'hyperbolic'. Ancient hunter-gatherer labour-leisure substitution curves depended on the environment within which they lived. In a harsh or overpopulated land, they struggled to survive. In a thinly-populated, resource-rich land, they likely worked to the extent necessary to produce a successful next generation, but no more. Our work-hard-and-save ethos is a modern invention, a culturally-maintained complex of carrots, sticks, and socialization; it would have been maladaptive in hunter-gatherer society and is not innate in newborns today.[6]

The development of agriculture and the large-scale social structures it made possible changed everything. The importance of arable land made investments in land adaptive: conquering it,[7] asserting property rights to it, sometimes even improving it. Those able to enforce property rights in land could extract surplus from those who worked it, forcing the latter to work harder than they otherwise would. History records that the former often lived lives of ease; the latter, lives of bleak and unremitting drudgery. The dominant class generally consumed the resulting surplus immediately, reflecting humans' previously adaptive preference for present over future benefits. Nevertheless, the institution of property concentrated resources in a set of decision makers that had more than they needed for individual survival and reproduction, making investment a realistic possibility.

In some societies, the result was to lower the apparent discount rate. For the first time, those in power could dream of becoming effectively immortal—Alexander through conquest, Cheops by building monuments. Concentration of surplus also allowed the creation of capital: immediately productive assets like irrigation systems, mills, and boats, but also, and at least as importantly, public goods such as systems for the orderly distribution of the products of labour, mechanisms for the peaceful resolution of disputes, defence against outsiders, grain stored against droughts, and other forms of social insurance, roads, communication networks, productivity-enhancing know-how, and community cohesion. Even if the discount rates of ordinary members remained hyperbolic, some societies began to behave as if their discount rates were lower: some began to invest. I will call the rate that describes a society's aggregate investment behaviour its 'social discount rate'. In my model, social discount rates are

of Labor', 8(2) *Evolutionary Anthropology* (1999) 65–75; Kristen Hawkes et al., 'Why Hunter-Gatherers Work: An Ancient Version of the Problem of Public Goods', 34(4) *Current Anthropology* (1993) 341–61.

[6] This does not mean that our hunter-gatherer ancestors only ate, slept, fought, and procreated. Play can be adaptive; so can social bonding, conflict diffusion, art, curiosity, and invention—the list encompasses much of what makes life worth living. Any motivation requiring an expenditure of energy, however, is costly; at the very least, it requires calories and may involve opportunity costs. Unless its survival or reproductive benefits equal or exceed such costs, any such motivation will reduce its carriers' ability to survive and reproduce vis-à-vis their more adaptively motivated competitors. The mathematics of probability tell us that overly industrious individuals and individuals who place too high a value on the future, like other maladaptively motivated phenotypes, will diminish over time as a percentage of the population as a whole, not because they should, but because that is simply how the mathematics of probability work.

[7] William of Normandy, for example, reaped enormous returns from his investment in the conquest of England.

functions of societies' institutional, legal, and normative structures; they are not mere aggregations of the discount rates of their constituent members.[8]

In the long run, societies with lower social discount rates tend to prevail over those with higher. Stated another way, societies that invest will, on average, outperform societies that do not. This is not because their members are smarter, stronger, or more virtuous. It is simply because, over time, investment results in increased capacity and with it, competitive advantage. Please note that this is a purely descriptive claim. We may fervently believe in liberty or the maximization of some social welfare function. If either such belief results in significantly less investment, however, a society that implements it will eventually recede into the annals of history, not because it is wrong or deserves to, but simply because of the power of compound interest. Thus do lower social discount rates and the institutional, legal, and normative structures that support them evolve.

For most of history, property and taxation were simply alternative techniques for appropriating labour value from a society's working members and transmitting that value upstream to a ruler or dominant class. A ruler might assert the right to control property, typically through force, and then grant rights to use that property to others in exchange for what we would today call rent. Norman England and pre-Roman Egypt both used this model. Or the ruler might instead leave existing property relationships in place and extract 'taxes'. If the latter were proportional to property values, rents and taxes were effectively indistinguishable.

I will call any mechanism through which labour value is appropriated from those who produce it 'taxes'. I will call taxes 'explicit' if they are labelled 'taxes' and 'implicit' if they are labelled anything else—for example, land rents or, more generally, returns to capital. I do so for several reasons. First, if one is genuinely concerned about the ethics of such appropriation, all such mechanisms raise the same concerns. Similarly, if one objects to the distortion of pre-tax welfare-maximizing decisions, all such mechanisms distort such decisions. In subsistence societies, both force workers to work harder than they otherwise would; in non-subsistence societies, they both create substitution and income effects. And both operate to increase savings and investment over the minimal levels that would have been rational for our hunter-gatherer ancestors. Finally, in much of premodern history, implicit and explicit taxes were indistinguishable; as will be seen, in the Anglo-American tradition their modern separation was, to a significant extent, an accident of history.

A unified account of property and taxation allows, in turn, a simple, coherent model of civilization. Taxes, implicit and explicit, force ordinary members to work harder than they otherwise might. They also make investment of the resulting surplus

[8] For reasons beyond the scope of this chapter, my model assumes that cultures and institutions may have evolutionary interests independent of those of their human stakeholders. Cultural evolutionary theory treats cultures and institutions as interdependent sets of learned behaviours. The latter, in turn, may survive and reproduce for reasons independent of their adaptivity to their human carriers—what biologists sometimes refer to as the 'levels of selection' phenomenon. See e.g. Theodore Seto, 'Is Bookburning Bad?', in John T. Parry and Welat Zeydanlıoğlu (eds), *Rights, Citizenship and Torture: Perspectives on Evil, Law and the State* (Freeland, UK: Interdisciplinary Press, 2009), http://papers.ssrn.com/sol3/papers.cfm?abstract_id=1140302, 8.

more likely. Investment produces capital; capital makes work more productive and the creation of additional capital easier. Capital, in other words, ultimately inures to the benefit of a society's ordinary members. Eventually, it makes life more pleasant, allowing ordinary members to move beyond mere subsistence. By recognizing the private ownership of property, property law deprives humans of their natural liberty. Taxation and the resulting investment in capital then permit civilization to make payment for this deprivation and justify the resulting forced labour. This is civilization's grand bargain.

As Figure 8.1 suggests, this bargain may play out differently in different societies, depending on the extent to which the dominant class diverts the resulting surplus to its personal use. In late medieval England, for reasons I will explore in Section II, it produced large accumulations of capital, an innovative and evolving polity and economy, and eventually a large and comfortable middle class. In ancient Egypt, much of the resulting surplus was devoted instead to monument building, funerary preparation, and consumption by the dominant class. As a result, Egypt, one of the most naturally well-endowed societies of the ancient world, remained culturally, politically, and economically stagnant for three millennia, from 3150 BCE to the Greek and Roman conquests, with relatively little additional return to its ordinary citizens for 3,000 years of hard work.

To the extent I am right, my account has significant implications for tax theory. First, it challenges Nozick's claim that explicit taxation in excess of that required to maintain a minimal state is an illegitimate taking of property. Consistency requires that Nozick object as well to implicit taxation, and with it, to property rights vested in other than those who work the land or other capital. Ultimately, he may be even forced to argue that the grand bargain upon which civilization is based is itself illegitimate. His progeny assert that taxation is theft. I assert, to the contrary, that the uneven distribution of property rights without the creation of social capital is theft, and that taxation, explicit or implicit, facilitates the creation of such capital.

Second, my account calls into question optimal tax theory's claim that taxation distorts otherwise welfare-maximizing choices between labour and leisure, on the one hand, and consumption and saving, on the other. If civilization forces members to spend time generating surplus that they are then not allowed to keep, we cannot assume that 'pre-tax' labour-leisure decisions are welfare-maximizing; indeed, the

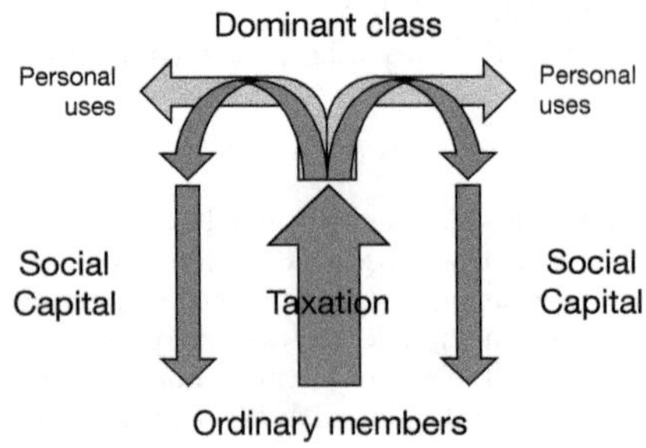

Figure 8.1 Dominant class

very purpose of property and tax law is to force levels of labour and savings in excess of those to which ordinary members would otherwise be inclined. If so, many of optimal tax theory's canonical conclusions are called into question.

Section II explores the implications of my account for theories of property law. In the process, it recounts the history of the separation of property and tax law in the Anglo-American tradition, beginning with Magna Carta. Section III then explores its implications for the morality of property and taxation. Magna Carta required consent for explicit taxation, but not for implicit. Implicit taxation remains highly regressive, and the rates at which it is imposed vary markedly from country to country. Section IV, finally, explores implications of my account for the economics of taxation—that is, for optimal tax theory.

II. Theories of Property Law

Property law poses two fundamental questions: (1) Should its rules be instrumental or based in moral right? and (2) if instrumental, what goals should they seek to further? My account suggests that property law rules are and should be primarily instrumental—that purely rights-based theories lack sufficient moral force to justify their often unpalatable consequences and fail to predict the structure of existing law. It suggests further that if property, tax, and other rules are structured so as to maximize the production of social capital while minimizing regressive implicit taxation, societies are more likely to flourish in the long run.

Two theories currently dominate property law.[9] The first is John Locke's rights-based theory of acquisition, as elaborated by Nozick. Locke asserts that labourers are entitled to the products of their labour and, in consequence, acquire property rights in items in the common pool by mingling their labour with those items.[10] Thus, for example, a farmer might acquire rights to unoccupied land by farming it. The problem with this account is that in reality very few workers end up owning either the products of their labour or the capital with which they mix that labour. Locke's origin story describes a world that does not exist. Nozick solves this problem with an aphorism: 'Whatever arises from a just situation by just steps is itself just.'[11] In the beginning, he implies, humans were all homesteaders, acquiring worker-owned parcels through the sweat of their brows. Our current radically unequal distribution of property resulted from

[9] Many structural theories also exist. For a review of the current state of play and a suggested integration, see Adam Mossoff, 'What is Property? Putting the Pieces Back Together', 45 *Arizona Law Review* (2003) 371.

[10] John Locke, *The Second Treatise of Government*, ¶ 27, reprinted in John Locke, *Two Treatises of Government*, Peter Laslett (ed.) (Cambridge, UK: Cambridge University Press, 1988), 287, '[E]very Man has a *Property* in his own *Person*.... The *Labour* of his Body, and the *Work* of his Hands, we may say, are properly his. Whatsoever then he removes out of the state that Nature hath provided, and left it in, he hath mixed his *Labour* with, and joined to it something that is his own, and thereby makes it his *Property*.... For this *Labour* being the unquestionable Property of the Labourer, no Man but he can have a right to what that is once joined to, at least where there is enough, and as good left in common for others' (emphasis in original). Following convention, I will refer to sections in the Treatises by Treatise and section, e.g., Locke II §27.

[11] Nozick, n. 1, 151.

sales, inheritances, and other transfers deemed voluntary and therefore just. It follows that the Koch brothers have a moral right to their property unless it can be shown that their rights did not arise from a just situation by just steps. If they have a moral right to their property, government cannot rightfully take it by taxation or any other means.[12] The result is a prima facie moral right to immunity from taxation. Both Locke and Nozick use this to justify what Locke calls 'night-watchman' and Nozick 'minimal' government—government that provides personal and property security, contract enforcement, and little else.

The second theory is the welfarist approach of law and economics, which begins with the premise that we should structure property rights so as to maximize efficiency and thereby the size of the economic pie. The tragedy of the commons is used to justify division of rivalrous commons into individual parcels, and the need to provide creation incentives to justify recognition of intellectual property rights in created nonrivalrous capital.[13] This first premise is then modified by a second—that because of the declining marginal utility of property (the fact that the more one has, the less utility one derives from each additional unit), we may be able to increase aggregate social welfare by redistributing property from those who have more to those who have less.[14] This second premise is limited by yet another, the double distortion premise, i.e. that all redistribution should be undertaken through a society's system of explicit taxation, not through modifications of property or other non-tax rules.[15] Welfarism is currently the most popular academic implementation of the utilitarianism of Jeremy Bentham, who asserted that property was purely a creature of law, devoid of inherent ethical

[12] If the Kochs have a moral right to their property, there is a stronger argument that they should be morally free to use it for any purpose, including influencing elections. Under an instrumental view of property rights, by contrast, we might assign them the right to determine the most efficient use of capital, but limit their use of the resulting power to influence the rules under which they operate.

[13] See e.g. Marc K. Temin, 'The Irrelevance of Creativity: Feist's Wrong Turn and the Scope of Copyright Protection for Factual Works', 111 *Pennsylvania State Law Review* (2006) 263; Kenneth J. Arrow, 'Economic Welfare and the Allocation of Resources for Invention', in *The Rate and Direction of Inventive Activity: Economic and Social Factors* (Princeton: Princeton University Press, 1962); William M. Landes and Richard A. Posner, 'An Economic Analysis of Copyright Law', 18 *Journal of Legal Studies* (1989) 325, 326; William D. Nordhaus, *Invention, Growth, and Welfare: A Theoretical Treatment of Technological Change* (Cambridge, MA: MIT Press, 1969), 70; Jeremy Bentham, 3 *The Works of Jeremy Bentham/published under the superintendence of his executor, John Bowring* (Edinburgh: W. Tait, 1843), 71, http://galenet.galegroup.com/servlet/MOML?af=RN&ae=F100668833&srchtp=a&ste=14 (accessed 4 October 2016) ('He who has no hope that he shall reap, will not take the trouble to sow. But that which one man has invented, all the world can imitate.').

[14] See e.g. Sarah B. Lawsky, 'On the Edge: Declining Marginal Utility and Tax Policy', 95(3) *Minnesota Law Review* (2011) 904.

[15] See e.g. Louis Kaplow and Steven Shavell, 'Should Legal Rules Favor the Poor? Clarifying the Role of Legal Rules and the Income Tax in Redistributing Income', 29 *Journal of Legal Studies* (2000) 821; Louis Kaplow, 'The Optimal Supply of Public Goods and the Distortionary Cost of Taxation', 49(4) *National Tax Journal* (1996) 513; Louis Kaplow and Steven Shavell, 'Property Rules versus Liability Rules: An Economic Analysis', 109 *Harvard Law Review* (1996) 713; Louis Kaplow and Steven Shavell, 'Why the Legal System Is Less Efficient Than the Income Tax in Redistributing Income', 23 *Journal of Legal Studies* (1994) 667; Steven Shavell, 'A Note on Efficiency vs. Distributional Equity in Legal Rulemaking: Should Distributional Equity Matter Given Optimal Income Taxation?', 71 *American Economic Review* (1981) 414; Aanund Hylland and Richard Zeckhauser, 'Distributional Objectives Should Affect Taxes But Not Program Choice or Design', 81 *Scandinavian Journal of Economics* (1979) 264.

content.[16] The law and economics literature is replete with works on how the foregoing premises require that property and tax law be structured.

A. Property as Taxation

As may be apparent, I agree with Nozick that taxation involves a significant element of forced labour (hence the title of this chapter). Where we part company is in our accounts of how property rights originated. In most societies, over most of history, I assert, property was first acquired by force. Even on the American frontier—the best exemplar of Nozick's theory—white homesteaders acquired their land only after its forceful expropriation from indigenous peoples. Nozick's theory might be read to suggest that the right to use and perhaps the right to alienate are the most important aspects of property. In historical reality, however, the single most important aspect of property was the power to force others to pay for access to the means to earn a living, what we would today call the right to exclude.

Although my claims are not limited to the Anglo-American tradition, their defence in all cultures and times is beyond the scope of this chapter. I note, however, that the creation of monuments requires vast amounts of social surplus, which in turn require an extended and systematic appropriation of labour. We can infer that any civilization that has created monuments—the Great Pyramid of Giza, Versailles, Schönbrunn Palace, Ankor Wat, the Rapa Nui statues, Qin Shi Huang's terracotta army, the Taj Mahal, and Chichen Itza come immediately to mind—has employed some dynamic of the sort I describe.

Here I will use the Anglo-American tradition from the Norman Conquest as my exemplar; each of my claims is illustrated by that tradition. Early inhabitants of Britain, like early inhabitants elsewhere, were hunter-gatherers, free to hunt and gather where they would; the products of their labour were theirs to use or give away as they saw fit. In his history of English and Welsh game laws, Locke notes that 'ancient Britons enjoyed the chase in common, it being their principal means of subsistence, and at that time the land, as well as the game, was equally the property of all, as the arts of husbandry had not yet been introduced.'[17]

Things had changed dramatically by the time of the Conquest. The core of the feudal system imposed by William and his immediate successors was a set of rules for the appropriation of the products of labour and their transmission upstream. Land was worked by commoners, generally holding in lesser tenures—tenancy at will, tenancy for term of years, or copyhold—in exchange for payments in kind or services to those of whom they held. Freeholders, in turn, held of their superiors in return for services or payments in lieu of services ('scutage'), plus financially valuable auxiliary obligations known as 'incidents'—wardship, forfeiture, relief, and aids, among others.

[16] See Jeremy Bentham, 'A Critical Examination of the Declaration of Rights', in Bhikhu Parekh (ed.), *Bentham's Political Thought* (London: Croon Helm, 1973), 257, 269 ('Natural rights is simple nonsense: natural and imprescriptible rights, rhetorical nonsense, nonsense upon stilts.').

[17] John Locke, *A Treatise on the Game Laws of England and Wales* (Gilmore Evans; London: H Sweet, 1866) 11. This is not the John Locke of philosophy fame, whose work is referenced elsewhere in this chapter.

Their superiors held of their superiors, who held in turn of theirs, and so on. Tenants-in-chief held ultimately of the king.[18] Transmission of value upstream was required at each stage.

The hunter-gatherer way of life was effectively criminalized.[19] 'At the Norman Conquest, … the right of pursuing and taking all beasts of chase or venery, and such other animals as were accounted game, was claimed by the crown, and with it, that of restraining all other others from that privilege, except those authorized under the crown.'[20] Robin of Locksley and his band were outlaws to some and heroes to others in part for asserting their ancient hunter-gatherer liberties and attempting to live outside the system. For the most part, however, Norman property and forest laws forced ordinary members of English society into a land-for-rent-or-services system highly profitable to the dominant class, with the king at its apex.

Modern descriptions of the resulting payments upstream sometimes call them 'taxes'. At the time, however, no firm distinction was drawn between taxes and feudal property obligations. Indeed, the word 'task', a cognate of 'tax', originally meant 'a fixed payment to a king, lord, or feudal superior'[21] required as a matter of property law. Today, we might characterize the resulting upstream payments as rent and those paying them as tenants. In early Norman England, however, the property and tax systems were, for the most part, one and the same. To assert property rights but object on moral principle to 'tasks' or 'taxes', as Nozick does, would have made no sense.

Magna Carta, sealed by King John in 1215, began the process of disentangling tax from property law. Today, we commonly celebrate a single clause in the second half of the document, clause 32: 'No free man shall be arrested or imprisoned … except by the lawful judgment of his peers or by the law of the land.' When forced on the English crown, however, Magna Carta was first and foremost a rent control agreement, fixing the amount of services and incidents owed by freeholders to those of whom they held, quintessentially the King.[22] The rules of knight's service,[23] relief,[24] wardship,[25] and aid[26] were regularized and the amount collectible limited. What were to become today's 'taxes' were given special treatment: Clause 12 provided that no additional scutage or aid could be levied without the kingdom's general consent, except in limited circumstances,[27] and Clause 14 established the rudiments of a collective body through which the required consent could be given.[28]

The history of Anglo-American law thereafter reflects a continued gradual disentangling of property and tax; the fiscal history of England, an extended contest over the scope of Clause 12. The statute *quia emptores terrarum*,[29] enacted in 1290, limited implicit tax avoidance techniques—especially the use of subinfeudation to reduce the

[18] The term 'real' in 'real property' is a variant of 'rial' or 'royal', meaning royal, regal, or kingly. See *The Compact Oxford English Dictionary*, 2nd edn (Oxford: Clarendon, [1519] 2002). Real property was property held, directly or indirectly, of the king.

[19] Locke, n. 17, 11–12. [20] Ibid., 12. [21] *Oxford*, n. 18.

[22] 1215 Magna Carta, reprinted in English translation in Daniel Barstow Magraw et al., *Magna Carta and the Rule of Law* (Chicago: American Bar Association, 2014), 389–98.

[23] Ibid., Clause 16. [24] Ibid., Clauses 2, 3. [25] Ibid., Clauses 4, 5.

[26] Ibid., Clause 15. [27] Ibid., 391. [28] Ibid.

[29] *Statutum domini Regis de terris vendendis & emendis* (sometimes known as the 'Statute of Westminster the Third'), 18 Edw. 1, ch. 1.

value of wardship to a deceased freeholder's lord—by eliminating subinfeudation in fee simple absolute and requiring that all such transfers be made instead by assignment. What was intended as an anti-tax-avoidance statute had two unintended but profound side effects. First, it made English real property freely assignable—the core of the modern law of real property. Second, over time, elimination of subinfeudation in fee simple absolute resulted in more land being held directly of the King. Instead of a feudal pyramid defined by loyalty and personal obligation, England transitioned to a system of alienable real property in which most freeholders were of roughly equal legal status (holding directly of the king), payments upstream within the property system were of limited and decreasing value, and explicit taxes could only be imposed with the consent of Parliament.

English land law was thoroughly reformed in 1925.[30] In the United States, however, the process of eliminating the now irrelevant implicit tax functions of property law remains incomplete even today. The rule of destructibility of contingent remainders, which prevented gaps in the payment of knight's service or scutage, is still the law in Florida and perhaps six other states.[31] The Rule in Shelley's Case, which precluded use of a grant for life followed by a remainder to grantee's heirs to avoid payment of relief on grantee's death, has been abolished in most but not all states.[32] The *inter vivos* branch of the doctrine of worthier title, which precluded use of a remainder to grantor's heirs to avoid payment of relief on grantor's death, appears to survive in a majority of states, although sometimes only as a rule of construction.[33] The fee simple conditional, abolished in 1285 by the statute *de donis conditionalibus*[34] in a tussle between the barons and the crown over the incident of forfeiture,[35] remains the law in South Carolina.[36] The rules against springing and shifting interests, designed to prevent gaps in the payment of knight's service or scutage and ensure that conditions could be enforced only by the holder's feudal lord, were only partially nullified by the Statute of Uses in 1536, itself a compromise in yet another tussle with the King.[37] One

[30] Law of Property Act 1925, 15 & 16 Geo. 5, ch. 20.

[31] See *Blocker v Blocker*, 103 Fla. 285, 137 So. 249 (1931); *In re Rentz' Estate*, 152 So.2d 480 (Fla. Dist. Ct. App. 1963). See also 2A. R. Powell, *Powell on Real Property*, P. Rohan (ed.) (New York: M. Bender, 1993), ¶ 314; Jesse Dukeminier, 'Contingent Remainders and Executory Interests: A Requiem for the Distinction', 43 *Minnesota Law Review* (1958) 13; Samuel M. Fetters, 'Destructibility of Contingent Remainders', 21 *Arkansas Law Review* (1967) 145; Jack D. Jones and William R. Heck, 'Destructibility of Contingent Remainders in Tennessee', 42 *Tennessee Law Review* (1975) 761.

[32] See Powell, n. 31, ¶ 380.

[33] See Sheldon F. Kurtz et al., *Cases and Materials on American Property Law*, 6th edn (St. Paul: Thomson West, 2012), 335.

[34] Statute of Westminster II, 1285, 13 Edw. 1, ch. 1 (repealed 1879).

[35] The King's judges had held that a tenant in fee simple conditional could convey in fee simple absolute once he had issue born alive. This allowed the King to take a rebellious baron's estate by forfeiture in fee simple absolute. *De donis conditionalibus* eliminated this right. As a result, once the King beheaded the rebellious baron, his estate passed instead to the baron's eldest son. The statute therefore reduced the crown's control over the barons, contributing eventually to the state of internal turmoil known as the War of the Roses. A year after Edward IV defeated the Lancastrians at the Battle of Tewkesbury in 1471, his judges decided Taltarum's Case, which recognized a procedure known as the 'common recovery' through which the King could disentail rebellious barons, once again allowing him to take their estates by forfeiture.

[36] See *Scarborough v Scarborough*, 249 S.C. 331 (1967).

[37] See Sir John Baker, *The Oxford History of the Laws of England*, vol. 6 (Oxford: Oxford University Press, 2003), 672–3.

unrepealed remnant of those rules—that possibilities of reverter and rights of reentry are neither alienable nor devisable—remains the law in at least some US states.[38] And *Purefoy v Rogers*,[39] decided in 1671 but cited more than fifty times by American courts since the Revolution, reaffirmed the need to prevent gaps in the payment of knight's service or scutage and reinforced the rule of destructibility.

Magna Carta, however, did little to protect the nonfreeholders who actually did most of the work, except to require their assent to explicit taxes.[40] Nor did it limit in any regard the new forms of implicit taxation made possible by the industrial revolution. Industrial employers could impose terms on employees without any limits other than those defined by supply and demand. Residential landlords could do the same to tenants. The resulting terms were sometimes extremely onerous; sometimes far more so than those tenants had faced in the countrysides from which they had been forced. As a result, a substantial portion of the value created by labour continued to flow upstream through implicit taxation, just as it had in Norman England—indeed, just as it had in ancient Egypt.

B. What Is Property?

How we define property should turn on why we assign and protect property rights. My theory suggests that civilization does so for two main reasons: to (1) make the products of labour more easily transferable and therefore appropriable and (2) facilitate the allocation of decision-making powers with respect to capital.

1. *'Labour'*—I call an activity 'labour' or 'work' if it produces transferable value—value subject to possible appropriation. Whether we undertake the activity for pleasure, because we have been socialized to do so, because we are paid, or because we will be punished if we refuse is irrelevant. For example, activities in the production of food, whether through hunting, home gardening, or agribusiness, are all 'work' because the resulting product (food) is transferable and therefore potentially appropriable. Enjoying the beauty of the sunset is not; the value we thus produce for ourselves, although perhaps very real, is not transferable.

The raising of one's own children, by this definition, is not 'work'. Although one might characterize children as separate from their parents and the services provided in raising them as value transferred to others, from an evolutionary perspective reproduction is something we do for ourselves. Raising the children of another may be 'work'. Raising children that we treat as our own is not. Please note that I am not claiming that child-rearing is in any sense less important or less difficult than work for which we receive monetary compensation. What I am claiming is that when we care for our own children, we do so primarily for our own benefit; we are not generally creating appropriable value.

[38] See, e.g., *Mahrenholz v County Board of School Trustees of Lawrence County*, 93 Ill.App.3d 366 (Ill. App. Ct. 1981).

[39] 2 Wm. Saund. 380, 85 Eng. Rep. 1181 (1671).

[40] The United Kingdom's forty-shilling freeholder sufferage requirement was not formally abandoned until the early twentieth century. In the meantime, freeholding had become much more widespread, including many workers.

My definition of 'labour' is, for the most part, consistent with the definitions used by the memes I am challenging. Nozick, of course, is worried about appropriation. My definition, limited to activities that produce appropriable value, is consistent with his usage. It is also similar but not identical to that generally invoked in welfare economics. Economists also treat the raising of one's own children as something other than labour; they call it 'leisure' (most of them are male). Where our definitions diverge is in the treatment of imputed income. In economics, imputed income is value we create for ourselves: washing our own dishes, growing food in our own garden, raising our own children, making pottery, watching a beautiful sunset. Welfare economics treats activities that produce imputed income (generally not taxed) as 'leisure'. Because market income is taxed and imputed income is not, economists argue, taxation distorts our choices—leading us, for example, to spend more time with our children than we otherwise would. This, economists claim, is welfare-reducing.

Because my theory is not limited to monetary economies with explicit taxation, however, I draw the relevant line somewhat differently: between activities that produce transferable value and activities that do not. The former constitute 'labour' or 'work' within my definition; the latter do not. Thus, for example, home gardening and pottery-making produce transferable and therefore potentially appropriable value; they therefore constitute 'work' for purposes of my theory even if we do not take the resulting products to market. Activities that economists classify as 'labour', of course, are already monetized and therefore necessarily involve the production of transferable value.

2. *'Capital'*—I define 'capital' as anything that makes activity, including but not limited to labour, more productive or otherwise valuable. Land suitable for agriculture, when combined with farming know-how, can dramatically increase the value of activities directed to the production of food. Both the land and the know-how are capital. A television set makes sitting on a couch more valuable. The resulting value is not transferable; sitting on the couch is therefore not work. But the television is capital nonetheless.

Social technologies can constitute capital as well. Mechanisms for the orderly distribution of the products of labour reduce losses through conflict. So do mechanisms for the peaceful resolution of disputes. So do common defences against marauders. So do just mechanisms for the funding of collective action. Grain stored by the community and other forms of social insurance reduce the necessity of individual precautions against famine and other risks, take advantages of economies of scale, and reduce the costs of dealing with such risks. The value-enhancing properties of roads and communication networks are obvious. Economists should find none of these aspects of my definition objectionable.

My definition does differ from that of some financial disciplines, however, in three regards. First, for my purposes, although the institution of money makes many activities more valuable, money itself is not capital; it is merely an accounting mechanism. We do not, by printing more money, increase our society's productive capacity. Second, economists often limit use of the term 'capital' to assets with extended useful lives. I do not. Annual stores of seed stock, for example, are not normally treated as capital. Nevertheless, seed stock makes farming activities more valuable; a society without seed stock is far less likely to be able to put its farmers to productive use.

Third, in my model, society assigns ownership rights temporarily and for instrumental reasons; all capital is ultimately part of a society's commonwealth—the repository of capital to which it has not assigned property rights. I therefore use the terms 'capital' and 'social capital' interchangeably.

3. *'Property'*—If my account has merit, the concept of property should be limited to items of transferable value. And it is. Physical fitness and peace of mind, no matter how valuable and no matter how much labour one has invested in them, are not transferable and are generally not given the status of property. Nontransferability need not be inherent; it may result as well from considerations of public policy. Thus, modern societies generally decline to recognize property rights in human beings; recognizing such rights might imply rights of transfer and therefore the right to sell oneself into slavery.[41]

4. *Lockean theory compared*—Lockean theory is less successful in its definitions. It offers no principled basis upon which to distinguish a chair from peace of mind; each may be the product of its creator's labour. Nor can it tell the difference between a chair and a human being. Locke unconvincingly avoids the slavery problem by claiming that since no one has the right to take his or her own life, no one has the right to go voluntarily into slavery;[42] he then defends black slavery on the ground that captives taken in just wars have thereby forfeited their lives and that all black slaves can be so categorized.[43] Nozick, to his credit, simply concedes that 'a free system will allow [an individual] to sell himself into slavery.'[44]

5. *Welfarist theory compared*—Like my account, welfarist theory views property law as instrumental. Its goals, however, are different: as a moral system, welfarism generally maintains that whatever maximizes aggregate social welfare is right. Voluntary decisions are generally assumed to have been made for welfare-maximizing reasons. It follows that if someone decides to become a slave, slavery must be welfare-maximizing. If so, then slavery is right. Thus, it is said, 'property rights develop in a society when the benefits of having them exceed the costs of getting them.'[45] As will be seen in the remainder of this Part I, my account and welfarist theory often end up in the same place. Welfarism, however, focuses on individuals, with the greatest weight given to the welfare of those alive today. My account focuses instead on societies and their success or failure in the long run.

C. Property in Natural Capital

Property can be divided into several functional classes. The first consists of things not created by human activity: land, the Pacific Ocean, a deer in the forest, consistent rainfall, a beautiful view. I will call such things 'natural'. To the extent they make activity more valuable, they constitute 'capital'. Like a television set, a beautiful view

[41] See e.g. Philippe Ducor, 'The Legal Status of Human Materials', 44 *Drake Law Review* (1996) 195; Margaret Jane Radin, 'Property and Personhood', 34(5) *Stanford Law Review* (1982) 957.

[42] Locke II §23. [43] Locke II §24. [44] Nozick, n. 1, 331.

[45] James E. Krier, 'Evolutionary Theory and the Origin of Property Rights', 95 *Cornell Law Review* (2009) 139, 139–40. Krier might object to being cited in this context, but the logic of his statement fits slavery as well as it does other forms of property. See also Harold Demsetz, 'Toward a Theory of Property Rights', 57(2) *American Economic Review* (1967) 347, 350 ('the emergence of new property rights takes place in response to … new benefit-cost possibilities').

may make looking in a particular direction more valuable; it is therefore 'natural capital'. The state of Utah, for example, has extraordinary stores of such capital, from which it derives large amounts of revenue.

Natural capital comes in two varieties: rivalrous and nonrivalrous. Something is 'rivalrous' if use by one precludes or limits its use by another. Use of the Pacific Ocean for shipping is currently nonrivalrous; there is no effective limit on the number of ships the Pacific can bear. Use of the Great Plains to travel to Oregon was effectively nonrivalrous; use of the same land for farming, however, precluded its use by others and therefore became rivalrous. Use of land for hunting and gathering is nonrivalrous at low population densities; as population increases, however, use by one reduces its value to others.

Like welfarism, my theory suggests that there is no reason to assign property rights to natural capital until tragedy of the commons problems arise and cannot otherwise be regulated. Unlike welfarism, however, my theory predicts that as societies implement forced labour systems, they will limit the use of hunter-gatherer commons even in the absence of such problems, just as English law did. Welfarism justifies property rights in rivalrous natural capital on the grounds that assigning persistent decision-making and revenue rights to the same private party will maximize productive use of such capital.[46] Note, however, the unintended cost of the use of property law for this purpose: property owners may end up using the value of appropriated labour for personal purposes, instead of creating social capital. My account leaves open the possibility that we may someday develop social technologies that will allow us to motivate efficient decision-making with regard to capital at lower social cost.

In the context of rivalrous natural capital, however, Locke's and Nozick's arguments fall apart. Locke applies his theory of the acquisition of property rights to rivalrous natural capital only if supply always exceeds demand: 'Nor was this appropriation of any parcel of Land, by improving it, any prejudice to any other Man, since there was still enough, and as good left; and more than the yet unprovided for could use. So that in effect, there was never the less left for others because of his inclosure for himself.'[47] He gives two reasons to believe supply will always exceed demand: (1) that God is good,[48] and (2) that his theory justifies acquisition of property rights only in what one can use personally: '*As much Land* as a Man Tills, Plants, Improves, Cultivates, and can use the Product of, so much is his *Property*.'[49] 'Whatever is beyond this, is more than his share, and belongs to others.'[50]

Nozick accepts the same basic limitation of Locke's theory of acquisition, which he calls Locke's 'proviso': 'A process normally giving rise to a permanent bequeathable property right in a previously unowned thing will not do so if the position of others no longer at liberty to use the thing is thereby worsened.'[51] He does not accept—indeed, does not even address—Locke's conclusion that one can only acquire property rights in what one can use personally, and certainly does not appeal to God's generosity. This leaves a hole in his argument, which he attempts to minimize by arguing that property rights acquired in natural capital hurt others only if the owner obtains a monopoly.[52]

[46] See e.g. Abraham Bell and Gideon Parchomovsky, 'A Theory of Property', 90 *Cornell Law Review* (2005) 531.

[47] Locke II §33.

[48] Ibid., §31 ('God gives us all things richly, 1 Tim. 6: 17').

[49] Ibid., §32.

[50] Ibid., §31.

[51] Nozick, n. 1, 178.

[52] Ibid., 179–81.

Apparently aware of the problematic nature of this assertion, he lamely concludes: 'Here I make an empirical historical claim; as does someone who disagrees with this.'[53] He does not, however, offer any evidence in support of his 'empirical historical claim.'

Unfortunately, in the process of trying to fill the resulting hole, he makes an unnecessary concession: 'Someone whose appropriation otherwise would violate the proviso still may appropriate provided he compensates the others so that their situation is not thereby worsened.'[54] Compensated takings, it would seem, are legitimate. It follows that no compensation is required if the taking results in a net benefit to the one whose rights have been abridged.[55] This corollary appears in footnote in response to an argument by François Marie Charles Fourier, a French socialist: 'that since the process of civilization had deprived the members of society of certain liberties (to gather, pasture, engage in the chase), a socially guaranteed minimum provision for persons was justified as compensation for the loss'.[56] Since civilization makes all of its members better off, Nozick seems to claim, no such compensation is required.

One might read the Fourier footnote and accompanying text to mean that Nozick would accept my descriptive account and concede further, as a normative matter, that the benefits civilization funds with taxation justify the taking that taxation represents. I think this unlikely. I think it more likely that Nozick wrote what he did without fully exploring its implications, simply to be rid of difficulties he found irksome. The implications of the Fourier footnote and accompanying text are fundamentally at odds with the rest of his text. If government can legitimately take so long as it gives fair value in return, any level of taxation can be justified, and government of any size.

In any event, the argument does not help him much. Upon defeating Harold, William I claimed a monopoly on real property in England—just the sort of situation in which Nozick conceded that his theory of acquisition would not work. All who held of William were required to pay 'tasks'—undeniably a harm. But Nozick must nevertheless contend that the Conquest and William's monopoly claims were just. Otherwise, applying his own aphorism—'Whatever arises from a just situation by just steps is itself just'—Nozick must conclude that no land title in England is legitimate. And since much American wealth was originally derived from English wealth, the problem is not limited to England. American history further compounds the problem. As I have already noted, to establish that land titles in the Americas are just, Nozick must contend that the dispossession of Native Americans by English and Spanish invaders[57] was just. This becomes disturbingly reminiscent of Locke's defence of black slavery.

D. Property in Created Capital

Created capital is capital created by human activity. Although it can be categorized across two dimensions—rivalrous versus nonrivalrous and tangible versus intangible—most created tangible property is rivalrous and most created intangible

[53] Ibid., 182. [54] Ibid., 178. [55] Ibid., 178–9 fn. [56] Ibid.

[57] See e.g. Ronald Wright, *Stolen Continents: The Americas Through Indian Eyes Since 1492* (New York: Houghton Mifflin, 1992).

property is nonrivalrous, specifically information as to which use by one does not preclude or limit its use by another.[58] Thus created capital falls into two principal categories: (1) tangible artefacts like ploughs and houses and (2) know-how.

Created capital necessarily involves the defiance of entropy to produce unnatural order—forms and quantities not found in nature. If it did not, creation would be unnecessary. Tangible created capital generally resuccumbs to entropy quickly; as a result, items of tangible created capital typically have short useful lives. By contrast, techniques exist for the inexpensive preservation and transmission of information, the bulk of all intangible created capital; its useful life is therefore effectively indefinite.

Because tangible created capital expires and intangible created capital does not, the largest part of any society's accumulated created capital is intangible—specifically, information, most of which is held as part of society's commonwealth. We do not need to reinvent farming or bookkeeping or steel-making. Notwithstanding the destruction of much of Germany's and Japan's physical capital in World War II, their economies recovered quickly. Steel mills could be rebuilt without reinvention, farms restarted, books of account reestablished. Another significant portion of a society's accumulated created capital consists of public goods: night-watchman institutions, public rights-of-way, schools, and the like. Ownership of the remainder, productive physical capital, is commonly vested in private hands. The speed of Germany's and Japan's recoveries after the war suggests that the Allies' thoroughgoing destruction of this last segment was not a significant limiting factor.

Welfarist theory assigns property rights to rivalrous created capital—tangible artefacts—at least in part for the same reason it assigns property rights to rivalrous natural capital: its belief that assigning persistent decision-making and revenue rights to the same private party will maximize productive use of such capital. In the case of nonrivalrous created capital, however, this rationale does not justify property rights. Since use by one cannot, by hypothesis, preclude or limit use by another, there is no such reason for government to regulate such use. Instead, welfarism justifies the assignment of property rights to nonrivalrous created capital—primarily information—on a different ground: to provide incentives for the creation of such capital. Although much nonrivalrous created capital effectively lasts forever, only rights of limited duration are believed necessary to provide such incentives. As a result, property rights in created intangibles are generally limited in term. Once they expire, the resulting capital falls back into society's commonwealth, open to all.

The same incentive rationale applies to tangible artefacts. Because tangible artefacts generally have relatively short useful lives, however, there is no need to limit the duration of ownership rights. Indeed, an owner with rights of unlimited duration will have greater incentive to resist entropy, keep such artefacts in repair, and extend their useful lives.

Locke's and Nozick's argument that the user has a moral right to the fruits of his labour might appear to have stronger intuitive appeal in the context of created capital. The problem is that modern created capital is always an admixture of the labourer's

[58] Although rivalrous, trademarks constitute a small part of society's total store of intangible property.

efforts and society's vast stores of accumulated social capital. Yes, the potter throws the pot. But the potter's understanding of how to throw pots is the result of millennia of trial and error by others long dead. If we were to allocate the fruits of the potter's labour based on the relative contributions of the potter, on the one hand, and society's commonwealth, on the other, we would probably be able to justify tax rates far in excess of any now generally imposed.

The one context in which the Lockean argument is sometimes claimed to make a difference is in the *duration* of intellectual property rights. If the labourer has a perpetual right to the fruits of his labour, intellectual property rights should be perpetual.[59] But if my theory is correct, they should also only be partial; society deserves to be compensated for its contribution to the work as well. A full right for a finite duration is almost always worth more than a partial right of infinite duration, depending, of course, on percentages and discount rates. Even if we are Lockeans, therefore, we might prefer the former to the latter.

E. Theories of Property Law Compared

In sum, Nozick's rights-based approach to property law fails to fit or justify existing law. Welfarism, a purely instrumental approach, does a much better job of predicting the structure of existing law, although it too sometimes misses the mark. Although my goal is somewhat different—to maximize the production of social capital and with it long-term flourishing, rather than aggregate social welfare discounted to present value[60]—welfarist rules are often consistent with both goals. At some point, we may discover techniques for maximizing the productive use of capital that rely less on the possibility that members of the dominant class may divert the resulting surplus to personal use. At that point, implementation of welfarist ideals and those implicit in my account may diverge.

III. The Morality of Property and Taxation

In Nozick's account, the morality of taxation is inherently related to the morality of property. The same is true in mine. Nozick, however, claims that because property is moral, embodying as it does the labour to which the worker has an inherent right, taxation of income from labour is inherently immoral. I, by contrast, claim that property is still, to some extent, a mechanism for the appropriation of labour and is still, to that same extent, a form of implicit taxation. In my account, therefore, to assess the morality of implicit and explicit taxation, it is first necessary to understand how each operates in the real world.

In democracies since Magna Carta, explicit taxation has only been imposed with the consent of some portion of those taxed. This has tended to ensure that its proceeds would be expended for their benefit, not solely for the personal use of the dominant

[59] See e.g. Linda J. Lacey, 'Of Bread and Roses and Copyrights', 38(6) *Duke Law Journal* (1989) 1532.

[60] I elaborate this goal more fully in ethical, rather than economic, terms in my article 'Intergenerational Decision Making: An Evolutionary Perspective', 35 *Loyola Los Angeles Law Review* (2001) 235.

class. This, in turn, has made it more likely that explicit taxation would result in the production of social capital. To the extent this is so, 'no taxation without representation' lies at the core of Anglo-American economic success.

Implicit taxation, by contrast, has never been subject to a Magna Carta equivalent. Since *quia emptores terrarum*, the institution of alienable private property has generated great wealth, albeit unevenly distributed, in societies that have adopted it. For this reason, because implicit taxation is less salient than explicit, and because the separation of political from economic power is far from complete, even in nominally democratic countries, implicit taxation has generally been subject to fewer constraints than explicit.

To elaborate this last point, it may be useful to state more clearly what I mean by 'dominant class'. I mean to refer to the set or sets of persons persistently empowered to make individual or small group decisions that affect others—not merely to participate in community-wide decisions like voting. Such powers tend to be of three kinds: (1) the power to make the rules, (2) the power to determine the productive use of capital, and (3) the power to divert value for personal purposes. In pre-modern civilizations, these powers were often vested in the same members. Modern systems generally attempt to separate them. Soviet Communism combined (1) and (2) in an attempt to minimize (3). Liberal capitalism combines (2) and (3) in an attempt to maximize efficiency; its attempts to separate (1) are often only modestly effective: those with power to make the rules still often use that power to divert value for personal purposes, and those with power over resources still often make the rules. This may, at least in part, explain why implicit taxes have only gradually faced limits on rate and structure.

What else can we say about implicit taxes? In particular, who do they hit and how large are they? They are almost certainly sharply regressive. This is inherent in their nature: they necessarily involve appropriation of labour value from society's ordinary members by property-owning members of the dominant class. Unfortunately, we do not know precisely either how regressive or how large they are. Their average magnitude can, however, be estimated. Property results in implicit taxation when capital is owned by persons other than those who work. We can therefore derive a rough estimate of a society's average implicit tax rate by subtracting its labour share (the share of national income that flows to labour) from 100 per cent and multiplying the result by its Gini index (a measure of the society's wealth or income inequality, zero representing perfect equality and one perfect inequality). Rough estimates of average implicit tax rates for a number of contemporary economies follow:[61]

Iceland	3.77%	
Switzerland	4.11%	
Denmark	4.94%	*
Sweden	6.56%	
United Kingdom	6.84%	*
Austria	7.01%	

[61] Labour shares are taken from Marta Guerriero, 'The Labour Share of Income Around the World: Evidence from a Panel Dataset', Paper prepared for the 4th Economic Development International Conference of GREThA/GRES 'Inequalities and Development: New Challenges, New Measurements?'

Finland	7.59%	
Germany	7.83%	
Belgium	8.00%	
Norway	8.29%	
Netherlands	8.40%	
France	8.94%	
Ireland	9.43%	
United States	9.44%	*
Poland	9.72%	
Spain	10.41%	
Italy	10.55%	
Estonia	10.94%	
Brazil	12.16%	
Greece	12.47%	
Russian Federation	16.64%	
Philippines	16.79%	
Chile	17.15%	
Iran	20.17%	
Colombia	20.33%	
Turkey	20.49%	
Mexico	20.67%	
South Africa	24.72%	

Note that these are average rates, not the rates applicable to any given group of workers. Because implicit taxation is regressive, the rates applicable to a society's ordinary members are likely to be higher, perhaps significantly so. The foregoing averages are also probably low; the income Ginis used in their computation are generally lower than the more theoretically correct but less widely available wealth Ginis.

Nevertheless, several observations are worth making. First, implicit tax rates appear to vary widely from country to country; this suggests that they are not inevitable but are rather the products of political choice.[62] Implicit tax rates are limited

University of Bordeaux, France, 13–15 June 2012 available at http://piketty.pse.ens.fr/files/Guerriero2012.pdf (accessed 6 October 2016). Guerriero's LS6 estimates are used, except where no such estimates are provided, in which case LS5 estimates are used (indicated by *). The United Nations' International Labour Organization reports lower labour shares, implying higher implicit tax rates: 'Labour shares typically vary between forty and sixty per cent of GDP, and are generally higher in industrialized than in developing countries. They average just over 50 per cent of GDP in the OECD countries and Asia, around forty per cent in Latin America, the Middle East and North Africa, and around thirty per cent in sub-Saharan Africa.' See also Malte Lübker, *Labour Shares*, Int'l Labour Org. Tech. Brief No. 01 (2007), www.rrojasdatabank.info/laborshare.pdf (accessed 6 October 2016). I have used the World Bank's income Gini estimates as proxies for wealth Ginis, which are difficult to come by. See http://www.indexmundi.com/facts/indicators/SI.POV.GINI/rankings (accessed 6 October 2016).

[62] Ian Morris has argued that 'each age has gotten the inequality it needs, different economic systems functioning best with different levels of inequality.' Ian Morris, 'To Each Age Its Inequality', *New York*

most saliently by labour laws; a recent IMF study of advanced economies, for example, concluded that '[o]n average, the decline in unionization explains about half of the 5-percentage-point rise in the top 10 per cent income share. Similarly, about half of the increase in the Gini of net income is driven by deunionization.'[63] They may also be affected by other non-tax rules. Second, average implicit tax rates appear to be lowest in the social democracies of western Europe, highest in the developing world, including the BRICs.[64] The United States has one of the highest average implicit tax rates in the developed world. Finally, implicit tax rates appear to be significant, particularly if one takes into account the fact that effective rates at the bottom are probably higher than the computed averages.

Here, then, is the question: which is more morally problematic, progressive explicit taxation subject to the consent of those taxed, the proceeds of which are more likely to benefit society as a whole, or regressive implicit taxation not subject to any general consent requirement, proceeds of which are freely appropriable to personal use by the dominant class? Political conservatives tend to seek as many limits as possible on explicit taxation and as few as possible on implicit taxation. The consequence is to maximize appropriation by the dominant class while minimizing benefits provided pursuant to the will of the governed and presumably for their benefit. In theory, it remains possible that maximizing appropriation by the dominant class will, in the long run, reduce the social discount rate and maximize investment. But this is true only if the dominant class invests. To the extent the dominant class consumes, the conservative approach merely benefits the dominant class at the expense of those who actually do the work.

My theory also suggests that moral objections to the taxation of income from capital are weaker, as Nozick himself admits.[65] In the modern world, privately owned capital is an admixture of pre-existing social capital, already in the common pool, and some private contribution by the person to whom we award ownership rights. The former almost always vastly outweighs the latter. We award private ownership rights in capital primarily for instrumental reasons.[66] To the extent income from capital can

Times (9 July 2015), http://www.nytimes.com/2015/07/10/opinion/to-each-age-its-inequality.html. To accept this assertion requires that we ignore public choice theory—to assume that those with the power to make the rules exercise that power so as to maximize the welfare of all, not just their own.

[63] Florence Jaumotte and Carolina Osorio Buitron, 'Power from the People', 52(1) *Finance & Development* (March 2015), available at *IMF* http://www.imf.org/external/pubs/ft/fandd/2015/03/jaumotte.htm.

[64] The World Bank does not supply recent Ginis for China or India, nor does Guerriero compute labour share estimates for those countries.

[65] 'In a fuller discussion we would have (and want) to extend our argument to include interest, entrepreneurial profits, and so on. Those who doubt this extension can be carried through, and those who draw the line here at taxation of income from labor, will have to state rather complicated patterned historical principles of distributive justice, since end-state principles would not distinguish sources of income in any way. It is enough for now to get away from end-state principles and to make clear how various patterned principles are dependent upon particular views about the sources or the illegitimacy or the lesser legitimacy of profits, interest, and so on; which views may well be mistaken.' Nozick, n. 1, 170–1.

[66] 'Why isn't mixing what I own with what I don't own a way of losing what I own rather than a way of gaining what I don't.... Why should one's entitlement extend to the whole object rather than just to the added value one's labor has produced? ... No workable or coherent value-added property scheme has yet been developed', Ibid., 174–5.

be taxed without jeopardizing the desired incentive effects, it is harder to assert moral objections to doing so.

In any event, my theory implies that, to the extent taxation of any form is justified, it must be by reference to the social capital thereby created. With this caveat, taxation—appropriation of the fruits of labour for reallocation by a dominant class—lies at the core of civilization; indeed, it may be civilization's *sine qua non*.[67]

IV. The Economics of Taxation: Optimal Tax Theory

I turn, finally, to the implications of my account for optimal tax theory, a topic that merits much more extensive treatment than the few pages remaining here permit. My claim, however, is simple: to the extent my account has merit, much of optimal tax theory requires reconsideration and possible restatement.

A. Assumption that Pre-Tax Labour-Leisure Substitution Decisions Are Welfare-Maximizing

As I noted at the outset, much of optimal tax theory is based on the assumption that, in the absence of explicit taxation, taxpayers' labour-leisure decisions would be welfare-maximizing and that explicit taxation that distorts those decisions must therefore be welfare-reducing. This logic underlies some of optimal tax theory's most canonical results.[68]

But if civilization forces ordinary members to spend time generating surplus that they are not allowed to keep, there is no reason to believe that the amount of time they would 'choose' to devote to generating that surplus in the absence of explicit taxation would be welfare-maximizing. The critical underlying premise—that, in the absence of externalities, rational actors behave so as to maximize their own welfare—no longer applies. Appropriated surplus, in economic terms, is an externality; its size depends on nontax law and varies from economy to economy.

Indeed, implicit taxation should distort taxpayers' hypothetical welfare-maximizing pre-tax labour-leisure decisions as well. If there were just one natural implicit tax rate for each economy, we might treat it as part of the set of exogenous constraints subject

[67] The saying 'Taxes are what we pay for a civilized society' is carved above the door of the Internal Revenue Service in Washington, DC. It has been attributed, in various versions, to Oliver Wendell Holmes, Jr., but was also invoked by Franklin Delano Roosevelt. See *Quote Investigator*, http://quoteinvestigator.com/2012/04/13/taxes-civilize/ (accessed 15 March 2015).

[68] See e.g. James Mirrlees, 'An Exploration in the Theory of Optimum Income Taxation', 38(2) *Review of Economic Studies* (1971) 175. Several influential articles have built on Mirrlees's work, e.g. Joseph Bankman and Thomas Griffith, 'Social Welfare and the Rate Structure: A New Look at Progressive Taxation', 75(6) *California Law Review* (1987) 1905; Joseph Bankman and David A. Weisbach, 'The Superiority of an Ideal Consumption Tax over an Ideal Income Tax', 58 *Stanford Law Review* (2006) 1413, 1414; Edward J. McCaffery and James R. Hines, Jr., 'The Last Best Hope for Progressivity in Tax', 83(5) *Southern California Law Review* (2010) 1031.

to which taxpayers maximize utility. But implicit tax rates appear to represent political choices. If so, treating them as exogenous is arbitrary.

Indeed, if my theory is correct, one of the essential functions of civilization—now that we have survived its most bleak and dreary days—is to make ordinary members better off. It does so through taxation, implicit and explicit, extracting surplus from labour to invest in social capital, which in turn makes life more pleasant and more productive in the long run. As I have noted, the long run is not optimal tax theory's focus. It focuses instead on efficiency and redistribution. My model focuses on investment.

B. Lump Sum Taxation

Optimal tax theory's reification of lump sum taxes—including taxes on endowment[69]—is part of the same quest to protect hypothetical welfare-maximizing pre-tax labour-leisure decisions from distortion. The theory, recall, is that, in the absence of taxation, taxpayers choose the mix of labour and leisure that maximizes their welfare. Lump sum taxes, optimal tax theory asserts, avoid substitution effects and are therefore minimally distortive.

There are at least two problems with this argument. First, it does not work on its own terms, even if we ignore the forced labour aspects of civilization suggested by my account. Taxation actually produces two effects: (1) substitution effects, which purportedly cause taxpayers to spend more time on leisure, which is not taxed, and less on labour, which is, and (2) income effects, which cause taxpayers to work more to try to end up with the same income after tax.[70] Both distort labour-leisure decisions, the first by inducing taxpayers to work less, the second by forcing them to work more. If labour-leisure choices in the absence of taxation are welfare-maximizing, either should be welfare-reducing. And lump sum taxes commonly create income effects.

American history vividly illustrates this problem. Shortly after the Civil War, former slave states used lump sum taxes payable only in specie—head or 'poll'[71] taxes—to force newly freed slaves to return to work on the plantations from which they had just been freed.[72] Those who failed to pay were seized and their services rented to plantation owners in lieu of taxes. The income effects of head taxes, in other words, were used to force former slaves back to work. It is hard to characterize these as either non-distortive or welfare-maximizing.

[69] See e.g. Kirk J. Stark, 'Enslaving the Beachcomber: Some Thoughts on the Liberty Objections to Endowment Taxation', 18 *Canadian Journal of Law & Jurisprudence* (2005) 47, 48–9; Lawrence Zelenak, 'Taxing Endowment', 55 *Duke Law Journal* (2006) 1145.

[70] There are two types of income effects, often confused. The first are consumption effects. Consider, for example, a taxpayer with \$50,000 of pre-tax income. If we exact \$10,000 in taxes, taxpayer will have \$40,000 of income left to spend. Assuming no change in taxpayer's work patterns, taxpayer will spend like someone with \$40,000 in income, not like someone with \$50,000 in income. Income effects of this type are not treated as distortive, and are therefore not welfare-reducing. But taxpayer may also, in response to that same tax, work harder so as to earn \$48,000 of income after-tax. If taxpayer's prior labour-leisure choice was welfare-maximizing, this behavioural change must be welfare-reducing.

[71] 'Poll' originally meant 'head'.

[72] See Brian Sawers, *The Poll Tax before Jim Crow* (unpublished manuscript on file with the author). At the same time, former slave states began to criminalize trespass and restrict hunting. More slowly, they

Second and more fundamentally, the purportedly ideal nature of lump sum taxes depends entirely on the assumption of an undistorted, welfare-maximizing baseline. If my account is correct, there is no such baseline.

C. The Double Distortion Premise

Kaplow and Shavell assert that 'redistribution through legal rules offers no advantage over redistribution through the income tax system and typically is less efficient. The reason is that using legal rules to redistribute income distorts work incentives fully as much as the income tax system—because the distortion is caused by the redistribution itself—and also creates inefficiencies in the activities regulated by the legal rules.'[73]

Their proof can be summarized as follows: assume a non-tax rule that redistributes exactly as the income tax system redistributes, but does so only upon an incident of behaviour or event with respect to which an efficient rule would produce an optimal quantity. The example they use is a negligence rule pursuant to which tortfeasor pays damages computed by reference to his taxable income. Such a rule will distort the tortfeasor's labour-leisure decision much as the income tax would (the first distortion), but will also distort the amount of care the tortfeasor takes in the activity in question (the second distortion). High-income actors will take too much care; low-income actors too little. Therefore, they conclude, nontax rules should be structured so as to maximize efficiency, and redistribution should be left to the tax system: the 'double distortion premise'.

The premise implicitly assumes an ideal income tax—a tax based solely on income and not dependent on other behaviours or events. In the real US income tax system, however, liability turns on countless behaviours and events other than income. A redistributive nontax rule based solely on income or wealth would avoid all such distortions, introducing only one new distortion: a distortion with respect to the behaviour or event that triggers it. There is no reason to believe, a priori, that any such rule would be more distortive than current US tax law.

The double distortion premise also assumes redistribution of the kind optimal tax theory cares about: redistribution based on the smooth curves consistent with an assumed declining marginal utility of money. Not all nontax redistribution, however, takes this form. Minimum wage laws focus exclusively at the very low end of the income scale and apply regardless of the income of the employer. Unionization changes market power relationships, again regardless of the income of the employer. The implied warranty of habitability protects all consumers, regardless of income.

closed the open range, first in counties with large black populations. The motive, as evidenced by contemporary newspapers, farm journals, and travelogues, was to deprive landless blacks of any economic alternative to returning to work on the plantations, through sharecropping or other arrangements. See Brian Sawers, 'Property as Labor Control in the Postbellum South', 33 *Law & Historical Review* (2015) 351. These rules performed the same function as Norman England's forest laws.

[73] Louis Kaplow and Steven Shavell, 'Why the Legal System Is Less Efficient than the Income Tax in Redistributing Income', 23(2) *Journal of Legal Studies* (1994) 667, 667–8.

Each may introduce distortions to the markets to which it applies, but the redistributive benefits may exceed the distortionary costs if targeted redistribution creates greater normative benefits than simple declining-marginal-utility-of-money utility curves would imply.

The most fundamental problem with the double distortion premise, however, is that implicit tax rates are almost certainly sharply regressive and are the products of political choice. Ultimately, Kaplow and Shavell must prove that reducing such sharply regressive rates is inherently more distortive than effecting redistribution through an explicit tax and transfer system. This they have not done.

D. Taxation of Income from Capital

Optimal tax theory's opposition to taxing income from capital derives from a similar assumption—that in the absence of taxation, taxpayers would save some welfare-maximizing amount and that taxing income generated by that saving therefore distorts savings behaviour and reduces welfare.

My account suggests many problems with this claim. First, it is not at all clear that taxpayers' innate discount rates are welfare-maximizing; indeed one of the principal functions of both implicit and explicit taxation in my model is to lower the social discount rate and increase rates of investment over those to which taxpayers might otherwise be inclined.

Assume *arguendo*, however, that current rates of saving and investment are too low. Optimal tax theory's solution is to reward the dominant class for investing rather than consuming the implicit taxes we allow them to collect by allowing them to keep all of what they have collected. Doing so, however, begs an important question: why should we allow them to collect implicit taxes in the first place if all they are going to do is consume the proceeds? Recall how we treat those who actually do the work that produces the surplus in question: we force them to work and then appropriate part of the fruits of their labour. Why should members of the dominant class only face carrots when ordinary members face sticks?

There is, of course, a simple way to assure adequate investment: have the state tax and invest. Objection might be made that we do not want government making decisions about whether to build buggy whips or smartphones. Fair enough. But government can at least make adequate investment in public goods: education, transportation infrastructure, a sustainable environment, technology. It is also possible, however, to use explicit taxation to generate surplus that can then be made available to private enterprise: have the state tax and lend. If the state lends to intermediaries—for example, banks—which face profit-maximizing incentives to pick winners, the state can do so while remaining completely neutral as among industries and entrepreneurs.

E. Changing the Goal

Edward Kleinbard has recently argued that fiscal policy academics might usefully spend more time examining how most effectively to spend the money raised through taxation and less on how to distribute the explicit tax burden across taxpayers.[74] I agree in part, but would go further. My theory suggests that the question should ultimately be how to maximize the production of social capital and with it long-term flourishing. This is in part a spending question. But to accomplish this in a stable manner over the long run requires that society view the relevant mechanisms as fair. To rely more than necessary on regressive implicit taxation is likely to be counterproductive. In the meantime, we should be searching for techniques for maximizing the productive use of capital that rely less on the possibility that members of the dominant class may divert the resulting surplus to personal use.

Currently, pre-tax income disparities—a predicted but undesirable side effect of civilization—are increasing, not decreasing.[75] A better understanding of how implicit and explicit tax systems contribute to those disparities might help us ensure that civilization works for us, not we for civilization.

V. Conclusion

One of the great accomplishments of civilization is to force its ordinary members to spend time generating surplus that they are not then allowed to keep. It does this, first and foremost, through property law rules, which restrict access to the means of production of the necessities of life unless the member pays for access to those means. In exchange, civilization facilitates the accumulation of social capital which makes that work more productive and life more pleasant. Taxation permits the creation, preservation, and expansion of civilization's stock of social capital.

Civilization is therefore an exchange: you work; society takes a portion of the fruits of your labour; and in return, society makes your work more productive and your life more pleasant. The foregoing, like all memorable memes, is simpleminded and to some extent inaccurate. Nevertheless, it captures a significant portion of anthropological and historical reality. To this extent, it allows a principled response to both Nozick's critique of taxation and the foundational assumptions of optimal tax theory.

[74] Edward D. Kleinbard, *We Are Better Than This: How Government Should Spend Our Money* (Oxford: Oxford University Press, 2015).

[75] See e.g. Thomas Piketty, *Capital in the Twenty-First Century*, Arthur Goldhammer (trans.) (Cambridge, MA: Harvard University Press, 2014).

9

The Philosophical Foundations of Wealth Transfer Taxation

Jennifer Bird-Pollan

I. Introduction

Taxation performs a variety of roles in contemporary society. Primarily, levying taxes raises the funds necessary to pay the costs of government.[1] However, an ideal tax system could also be understood as the expression of a society's beliefs about distributive justice.[2] Almost all taxation involves some degree of redistribution.[3] Redistribution accomplished through the tax code should not be haphazard or accidental. If a society believes redistribution is socially desirable, then it can use taxation (usually in accordance with other tools[4]) to achieve that redistribution. If society believes redistribution is undesirable, then the tax system must be carefully structured to avoid or at least minimize such redistribution. However, the creation and implementation of tax laws have historically responded primarily to the input of economic analyses, while paying

[1] Of course, this elides a significant debate regarding the size of government. Do governments raise taxes in order to pay for the necessary costs of governing, or are the costs determined by the amount of taxes raised? For a useful discussion of this debate, *see* Susannah Tahk, 'Everything is Tax', 50 *Harvard Journal of Legislation* (2013) 67. In addition, taxation can itself be a form of spending. For instance, the establishment of a tax base includes some forms of income, and excludes others. When items are excluded from the tax base the government releases its taxing power over that amount. This is no different from the government collecting the tax, and then paying out that same amount as part of a spending programme. For a discussion of this issue, see Stanley S. Surrey, 'The Tax Expenditure Concept and the Budget Reform Act of 1974', 17 *Boston College Law Review* (1976) 679. This is also a central theme in the work of Ed Kleinbard. 'All of our technical knowledge on the economic side effects of taxation cannot resolve the fundamental fiscal issue that dominates contemporary political discourse, which is how much tax revenue our technical expertise should be harnessed to collect in the first place.' Edward D. Kleinbard, *We Are Better Than This: How Government Should Spend Our Money* (Oxford: Oxford University Press, 2014), XXI.

[2] 'In a capitalist economy, taxes are not just a method of paying for government and public services: they are also the most important instrument by which the political system puts into practice a conception of economic or distributive justice.' Liam Murphy and Thomas Nagel, *The Myth of Ownership* (Oxford: Oxford University Press, 2002), 3.

[3] 'Redistribution' here means moving money, or the benefits that money can buy, from one member of society to another. This could be upward redistribution (as in scenarios where tax is collected from all members of society, including the poor, to pay for roads or defence, where the benefit is enjoyed by all members of society, including the rich; or in scenarios where tax is collected from all members of society to pay for benefits enjoyed primarily by the rich, such as securities regulation) or it could be downward redistribution (when taxes are levied more heavily on wealthier members of society to pay for welfare programmes targeted at less well-off members of society).

[4] Louis Kaplow and Steven Shavell, 'Why the Legal System Is Less Efficient than the Income Tax in Redistributing Income', 23(2) *Journal of Legal Studies* (1994) 667.

Philosophical Foundations of Tax Law. First Edition. Edited by Monica Bhandari.

little to no attention to the philosophical justifications for one model or another. While this attitude towards philosophical input into tax policy analysis has started to change[5], the taxation of wealth transfers remains relatively undertheorized.[6] In the United States, the taxation of wealth transfers has become a political hot potato. While many economists and theorists write in support of the continued existence of the tax, many oppose it, often claiming to demonstrate the economic inefficiency of taxing wealth transfers.[7] However, as I will show in this chapter, the taxation of wealth transfers, as examined from the most commonly accepted political philosophical systems, achieves desirable ends and should be included in any robust system of taxation.[8]

Contemporary tax systems rely very little to not at all on the taxation of wealth transfers. As of 2016, forty-four countries in the world impose some sort of tax on wealth transfers, but this number is shrinking.[9] Indeed, thirteen countries have

[5] '[I]t turns out that all fiscal policy recommendations rest on a foundation of moral philosophy: the only question is whether we are conscious of that fact.' Edward D. Kleinbard, n. 1, XXII.

[6] There are numerous exceptions to this generalization. See e.g. Ed McCaffrey, 'The Uneasy Case for Wealth Transfer Taxation', 104(2) *Yale Law Journal* (1994) 283; Anne Alstott, 'The Uneasy Case Liberal Case Against Income and Wealth Transfer Taxation: A Response to Professor McCaffrey', 51 *Tax Law Review* (1995) 363, 364; Paul L. Caron and James R. Repetti, 'Occupy the Tax Code: Using the Estate Tax to Reduce Inequality', 40 *Pepperdine Law Review* (2013) 1255; Linda Sugin, 'Theories of Distributive Justice and Limitations on Taxation: What Rawls Demands from Tax Systems', 72 *Fordham Law Review* (2004) 1991. In addition, my own recent work has explored the relationship between philosophy and the taxation of wealth transfers. See Jennifer Bird-Pollan, 'Death, Taxes, and Property (Rights): Nozick, Libertariansim, and the Estate Tax', 66 *Maine Law Review* (2013) 1 [*hereinafter* 'Death, Taxes, and Property (Rights)']; Jennifer Bird-Pollan, 'Unseating Privilege: Rawls, Equality of Opportunity, and Wealth Transfer Taxation', 59 *Wayne Law Review* (2014) 713 [*hereinafter* 'Unseating Privilege']; Jennifer Bird-Pollan, 'Why Tax Wealth Transfers? A Philosophical Analysis', 57 *Boston College Law Review* (2016) 859 [*hereinafter* 'Why Tax Wealth Transfers?']; and Jennifer Bird-Pollan, 'Utilitarianism and Wealth Transfer Taxation', 69 *Arkansas Law Review* (*forthcoming*) [*hereinafter* 'Utilitarianism and Wealth Transfer Taxation'].

[7] '[F]ollowing significant estate tax rate increases, estate tax revenue as a share of GDP has been shown to decrease, and alternatively increase as a share of GDP when the estate tax rate is significantly lowered. The resultant loss of capital from the estate tax could be serving economically productive uses; but as it is, the loss translates into less wealth and reduced economic activity, thus leading to a smaller tax base for income tax.' *Joint Economic Committee Republicans*, 'Staff Study: Cost and Consequences of the Federal Estate Tax' (25 July 2012) at 16, http://www.jec.senate.gov/public/_cache/files/bc9424c1-8897-4dbd-b14c-a17c9c5380a3/costs-and-consequences-of-the-federal-estate-tax-july-25-2012.pdf (last accessed 27 October 2016).

[8] The direct taxation of wealth would, in many instances achieve many of the same goals as the taxation of wealth transfers (an indirect tax). However, direct taxation of wealth is often less politically palatable than wealth transfer taxation. In addition, in the United States, direct federal taxation of wealth is unconstitutional and would therefore require a constitutional amendment. See e.g. Beverly Moran, 'Wealth Redistribution and the Income Tax', 35 *Howard Law Journal* (2010) 319.

[9] Forty-four OECD countries impose wealth transfer taxation. Many countries that do not tax wealth transfers did so in the recent past, and many that do currently tax wealth transfers may not do so for long, given current political discussions. Therefore, finding the correct number for this list is difficult. The Tax Foundation is, however, a reliable source for such statistics. The current list of countries that impose some form of wealth transfer taxation is: Japan, South Korea, France, United Kingdom, United States, Ecuador, Spain, Ireland, Belgium, Germany, Chile, Venezuela, Bermuda, Greece, Netherlands, Philippines, South Africa, Finland, Angola, Denmark, Lebanon, Malawi, Cameroon, Equatorial Guinea, Iceland, Puerto Rico, Taiwan, Turkey, Brazil, Poland, Switzerland, Aruba, Curacao, Guatemala, Sint Maarten, Botswana, Croatia, Zimbabwe, Italy, Guinea, Senegal, Mozambique, Jamaica, and Bulgaria. See *Tax Foundation*, 'Estate and Inheritance Taxes Around the World', http://taxfoundation.org/article/estate-and-inheritance-taxes-around-world#_ftn2 (last accessed 27 October 2016).

repealed their wealth transfer tax laws since the year 2000.[10] By contrast, almost every country in the world taxes the receipt of income. Why is the taxation of income so much more common than the taxation of wealth and wealth transfers? Is this form of taxation merely more familiar and more accepted, and therefore more politically palatable? Or does income taxation accord more directly with the distributive justice views held by the citizens (and voters) of countries with these tax systems? In this chapter, I argue that, in fact, when we consider the most common views of distributive justice, we should see more taxation of wealth and wealth transfers, as those forms of taxation more closely track philosophical views held today.[11] This chapter proceeds as follows: Section I introduces the basic concepts, Section II describes the three basic forms of wealth transfer taxation, Section III identifies four central political philosophical theories and applies those theories to an analysis of wealth transfer taxation, and Section IV sums up the chapter and concludes.

II. Forms of Wealth Transfer Taxation

There are two major forms of wealth transfer taxation that are most common in the world today and which embody two distinct approaches to the taxation of wealth transfers. The first focuses on the amount held by the transferor, what I will call 'estate taxation', and the second focuses on the amounts received by the transferee, what I will call 'inheritance taxation'.[12] Both taxes would likely, for the sake of coherent enforcement, incorporate the taxation of gifts in addition to the taxation of transfers at death. I contemplate each of these forms of taxation in turn.

A. Estate Taxation

An estate tax taxes the estate of a decedent, before transfers are made. Upon the death of an individual, the estate becomes a legal entity, made up entirely of assets held by the individual during her lifetime. The US federal government currently assesses this form of wealth transfer taxation.[13] The US estate tax determines the value of the estate either on the date of death, or on an 'alternate valuation date' six months after the

[10] Wealth transfer tax systems have been repealed in Macau (2001), Portugal (2004), Slovakia (2004), Sweden (2005), Russia (2005), Hong Kong (2006), Hungary (2006), Singapore (2008), Austria (2008), Liechtenstein (2011), Brunei (2013), Czech Republic (2014), and Norway (2014). *Tax Foundation*, n. 9.

[11] Wealth transfer taxation can be used to more quickly respond to changing philosophical goals than income taxation can. The income tax is used in most countries for the majority of revenue raising (in the United States the income tax raises about $1.1 trillion annually, while the estate tax raises only about $20 billion), and therefore policy goals must often be subsumed under revenue raising goals. At the same time, income taxation is often used to achieve particular incentive measures (encouraging charitable contributions, home ownership, or energy efficiency, for instance) and those particular incentive goals may be inconsistent with larger theoretical goals about redistribution or other philosophical beliefs. For these reasons, wealth transfer taxation is a theoretically 'purer' place than income taxation to talk about the philosophical justifications for tax policies.

[12] I note that the system of wealth transfer taxation in place in the United Kingdom is referred to as an 'inheritance tax', although it more closely resembles what I refer to as an estate tax in this chapter.

[13] The estate tax is imposed under 26 United States Code section 2001. Hereinafter all references to the 'Code' will be references to title 26 of the United States Code.

individual's death.[14] The US estate tax then allows a deduction for all amounts transferred to charity, transferred to the spouse of the deceased, and for certain other small amounts.[15] Tax is then assessed on the value of the estate over a specific exemption amount.[16] In 2016 the US estate tax is nominally imposed at a flat rate of 40 per cent on all assets over $5.45 million[17], although that generality glosses over important nuances in the law.[18]

The most important characteristics of an estate tax are the focus of the tax on the assets of the decedent after her death, and the uniform assessment of the tax without regard to the identity of the heir-recipients of the transfers.[19] So, for example, an estate with a taxable value of $10 million that is transferred entirely to one heir is subject to the same amount of tax as a $10 million estate that is divided among ten or even 100 heirs. In this way, estate taxation focuses on taxing large estates, regardless of whether they are divvied up post-death, or transferred in their entirety to one heir.

B. Inheritance Taxation

An inheritance tax focuses on the recipient of a wealth transfer, rather than on the transferor of the wealth. The United States does not have a federal inheritance tax, but some states in the United States have state-level inheritance taxes.[20] By contrast with an estate tax, an inheritance tax is assessed on the recipient of the wealth transfer. This can be done either by including the amount of the wealth transfer in the income of the recipient[21], or by assessing a separate inheritance tax on the amounts received via wealth transfers.[22] An inheritance tax often includes a per-heir

[14] The default date of valuation of the estate is the date of death. §2013. However, by election, a representative of the estate may use an alternate valuation date. §2032.

[15] Transfers to a surviving spouse are fully deductible without limit under §2056. Transfers from the estate to charity, as long as they satisfy the statutory requirements, are deductible under §2055. Finally, deductions are available for funeral and administrative expenses, indebtedness of the decedent, and for claims against the estate. §2053.

[16] The mechanical application of the rule actually works by permitting a credit against tax equal to an exemption of a certain amount. In 2016 the credit available against estate tax liability is equivalent to an exemption of $5.45 million per individual, $10.9 million per married couple. §2010.

[17] Ibid. The exemption equivalent credit is adjusted annually for cost of living and inflation.

[18] The existence of a large number of estate tax exemptions and deductions reduces the base of the tax, thereby lowering the effective tax rate. See, e.g., n. 13, §2032A (offering an alternate valuation for farm property), §2056 (deducting all amounts transferred to a surviving spouse), and §2055 (exempting amounts transferred to charity, including to a private foundation entirely controlled by the decedent's family).

[19] The exceptions to this are that, as mentioned above, transfers to surviving spouses and charities are deductible to the estate. §§2056, 2055, n. 16.

[20] Inheritance taxes are assessed at the state level by Iowa, Kentucky, Nebraska, and Pennsylvania. In addition, Maryland and New Jersey have wealth transfer tax laws with inheritance tax-like characteristics. Connecticut, Delaware, the District of Columbia, Illinois, Maine, Massachusetts, Minnesota, New York, Oregon, Rhode Island, Tennessee, Vermont, and Washington all impose state-level estate taxes, http://www.taxfoundation.org/sites/taxfoundation.org/files/docs/Estate%20and%20Inheritance%20taxes_0.png (last accessed 27 October 2016).

[21] This is specifically excluded in the United States by §102.

[22] For instance, in the Commonwealth of Kentucky in the United States, the rate of tax assessed on the value of the inheritance is determined by reference to the relationship between the heir and the decedent. Kentucky Revised Statutes 140.070. In addition, the exemption amount also varies based on the relationship between the two parties. Spouses, direct ancestors, and direct decedents, as well as siblings, receive

exemption amount. So, for instance, if an inheritance tax has a $1 million per heir exemption, then a $10 million estate that is distributed to ten different heirs would not be subject to any tax. However, a $10 million estate distributed to one heir would be subject to tax on the $9 million excess over the exemption amount. In this way, an inheritance tax encourages the breaking up of concentrations of wealth more than an estate tax does. An inheritance tax can be designed with either a per transfer or a per lifetime exemption amount. If the tax has a per transfer exemption, then an individual can receive several transfers during her lifetime, and as long as each transfer is below the exemption amount, then she will owe no tax. However, a per lifetime exemption amount will allow only a total of that exemption amount to be transferred during the individual's lifetime before tax is due. Each of these tax design elements focuses on a different policy goal. A per lifetime exemption amount focuses on the total amount of wealth that can be accumulated by means of inheritance before taxes are assessed. A per transfer exemption amount focuses on breaking up estates by encouraging donors to transfer their wealth to several heirs, in order to minimize the tax due. This strategy emphasizes breaking up dynastic wealth, and pays little attention to the wealth status of the recipient of the transfer. Each tax system achieves a different goal, and the political or philosophical end to be achieved helps to determine which system best meets the needs of the society in question.

C. Gift Tax

Both an inheritance tax and estate tax would likely be complemented by a gift tax. Without a gift tax, post-death wealth transfer taxation could be avoided altogether by making transfers during the transferor's lifetime. The current gift tax in the United States was enacted for just this reason.[23] It serves as a backstop to the estate tax, ensuring that death bed transfers do not gut the estate tax by avoiding transfer taxation altogether. As a tax-exclusive, rather than tax-inclusive, tax, the gift tax allows *inter vivos* transfers to occur less expensively than post death transfers,[24] but without the gift tax,

a 100 per cent exemption from the inheritance tax under Kentucky law. See Kentucky Revised Statutes 140.080, http://www.lrc.ky.gov/statutes/statute.aspx?id=28984 (last accessed 27 October 2016).

[23] 'The stated purpose of the proposed introduction of the gift tax in the House Committee report was "To assist in the collection of the income and estate taxes and prevent their avoidance through the splitting of estates during the lifetime of a taxpayer." See House of Representatives (1932, 8).' David Joulfaian, *The Federal Gift Tax: History, Law, and Economics*. OTA Paper 100, US Department of the Treasury, 2007, http://www.irs.gov/pub/irs-soi/11pwcompenaddgift.pdf (last accessed 27 October 2016).

[24] Imagine a donor wants to transfer $100,000 post tax to a donee. Assuming a 50 per cent flat tax rate, assuming that the exemption equivalent credit has been fully used, and that the entire transfer is subject to tax, an analysis of the transfer before *death* and after death makes clear why *inter vivos* transfers are less expensive than post death transfers. If the transfer happens during the donor's lifetime, then the base of the tax is the transferred amount of $100,000. Applying the 50 per cent rate to that transfer results in a tax liability of $50,000. By contrast, if the donor wants the donee to receive $100,000 after the donor's death, there must be $200,000 available to achieve that result. If the estate holds $200,000, then the application of the 50 per cent tax rate leaves $100,000 to be transferred to the donee. Therefore, the same result ($100,000 in the hands of the recipient) costs $150,000 if the transfer occurs during the transferor's lifetime, but $200,000 if it occurs after death.

the estate tax would be all too easy to avoid. An inheritance tax may have less need of a separate gift tax, as long as the rule was drafted to tax the receipt of all gratuitous transfers, not only those effected after the death of the transferor.

III. Political Philosophical Theories

Philosophy does not have a unified response to taxation generally or to wealth transfer taxation specifically. Philosophical inquiry into tax policy adds to the discussion by helping to determine which tax law best reflects the needs and beliefs of the society to which it applies. As a discipline with more than 2,000 years of recorded history, there are obviously more philosophical perspectives than can fit into this chapter. However, contemporary political philosophy arguably represents, at least generally, the philosophical beliefs and needs of most western societies. Therefore, in this chapter I will focus on four of the most prevalent theories in contemporary political philosophy: socialism, liberalism, libertarianism, and utilitarianism.[25] As I will demonstrate, examining wealth transfer taxation from the perspective of each of these theories results in the same central conclusion—the taxation of wealth transfers is justified and is an essential element of any robust contemporary tax system.[26]

A. Socialism

Contemporary socialist theory stems originally from the nineteenth-century writings of Karl Marx.[27] Marx's communism had as its ultimate goal not only social equality of opportunity, but also true equality of outcome. As Marx famously wrote, 'from each according to his ability, to each according to his needs.'[28] Read literally, Marx seems

[25] Each of these theories is, in fact, composed of many different threads, representing a variety of interpretations of the central claims. In each case I focus primarily on one foundational articulation of the view: Marxist socialism, Rawlsian liberalism, Nozickian libertarianism, and Millian utilitarianism.

[26] Throughout the course of the analysis I demonstrate the differences in the form of wealth transfer taxation most strongly endorsed by the particular philosophical theory in question. While we clearly cannot conclude that one particular form of wealth transfer taxation is unanimously endorsed by all philosophical views, I do claim that most major philosophical political theories endorse wealth transfer taxation as such. In my view this advances the conversation. If we debate what form the tax should take, rather than whether or not we should have such a tax at all, we have already made progress.

[27] The current socialist structure of many European countries is, of course, not a model of Marx's ultimate goal. However, Marx theorized that the ultimate achievement of communism would occur only over time, and that there were necessary stages of social development before achieving that final goal. 'Marx [makes] the stages of the development of communism parallel the stages of development of communist ideas. The less sophisticated stage of communism seems also to correspond to a less sophisticated and more primitive socialist theory.' Shlomo Avineri, *The Social and Political Thought of Karl Marx* (Cambridge: Cambridge University Press, 1968), 222.

[28] The famous phrase was first issued, not by Marx, but by Louis Blanc, although it was popularized by Marx. Marx saw this as the motto of the future communist society: 'after labour has become not only a means of life but life's prime want; after the productive forces have also increased with the all-round development of the individuals, and all the springs of cooperative wealth flow more abundantly—only then can the narrow horizon of bourgeois right be crossed in its entirety and society inscribe on its banner: "From each according to his ability, to each according to his needs!" Karl Marx, 'Critique of the Gotha Program', in Robert Tucker (ed.), *The Marx-Engels Reader* (New York: W.W. Norton & Co. 1978), 531.

to be endorsing an endowment tax, which raises many interesting questions, but goes beyond the scope of this chapter.[29] However, the emphasis on distribution according to need illustrates Marx's concern that well-being in society should not hinge on one's performance.

History has generally demonstrated that communism is unsuccessful as a strategy for political systems,[30] but most major European countries include elements of socialism, including publicly held wealth, high taxes, and a robust social safety net.[31] This form of contemporary European socialism is a direct decedent of the communism endorsed by Marx. Even in the United States, not traditionally a socialist stronghold, 2016 Presidential candidate Bernie Sanders embraced the term 'socialist', explicitly endorsing the shared social responsibility implied by the term.[32] While these governments and political candidacies are not purely Marxist, such political structures are influenced by Marx and his philosophical heirs, who valued the regulation of economic transactions to ensure the greatest possible public benefit.

Socialism tends towards relatively heavy taxation, so that members of society share responsibility for the provision of public benefits. Socialist theory endorses the taxation of wealth transfers, since the concentration of wealth, or the transfer of wealth based merely on familial relationships violates the fundamental premises of socialism.[33] Both forms of wealth transfer taxation (estate taxation and inheritance taxation) seem consistent with the goals of socialism. Indeed, applying socialism to tax policy may result in a system that taxes such transfers both at the point of the transferor and the transferee. In this way, wealth transfer taxation could both work towards the breaking up of concentrated wealth (taxing large estates at the moment of death), and also ensure that new concentrations of wealth are not created by wealth transfers (by taxing the newly transferred wealth in the hands of the recipient).

[29] Many interesting things have been written about endowment taxation, both explaining its advantages and highlighting its problems. In this book, Henk Vording's chapter addresses the issue. See also, Kirk J. Stark, 'Enslaving the Beachcomber: Some Thoughts on the Liberty Objection to Endowment Taxation', 18 *Canadian Journal of Law and Jurisprudence* (2005) 1.

[30] Neither is it necessarily an accident that communism in practice regularly led to authoritarian dictatorships. 'The vulgarization of Marx's theory thus becomes a necessary component in the make-up of those historical movements brought to life by Marx's own philosophical speculation and historical analysis.' Shlomo Avineri, *The Social and Political Thought of Karl Marx* (Cambridge, UK: Cambridge University Press, 1971), 251.

[31] Countries with more spending as a percentage of GDP tend to be those with socialist characteristics. For a list of countries with the highest spending, on these measures, see *OECD*, 'General Government Spending', https://data.oecd.org/gga/general-government-spending.htm (last accessed 27 October 2016).

[32] Sanders first publicly identified as a socialist in 1990, when he was elected to the House of Representatives. 'I am a socialist and everyone knows that. They also understand that my kind of democratic socialism has nothing to do with authoritarian communism.' See Philip Bump, 'Bernie Sanders Is an Avowed Socialist. 52 Percent of Democrats Are Okay With That', *Washington Post*, http://www.washingtonpost.com/news/the-fix/wp/2015/04/29/bernie-sanders-is-an-avowed-socialist-and-democrats-are-actually-pretty-ok-with-that/ (last accessed 27 October 2016).

[33] Because socialist theory endorses wealth transfer taxation, it is unsettling to see that many European countries traditionally identified with socialist policies have eliminated their wealth transfer taxation in recent years. See n. 9.

B. Liberalism

Political liberalism is perhaps the most prevalent theory in contemporary political philosophy. As articulated in its most well-known form by twentieth-century philosopher John Rawls, liberalism generally endorses political systems that guarantee equality of opportunity, while not seeking the equality of outcome preferred by Marxist socialism. Rawls famously proposes a so-called 'veil of ignorance' in order to determine the most just political structures.[34] Possible political systems are evaluated from behind the veil, ensuring that the self-interest of those currently in power is not the determining element of political system design. Rawls' argument is that, if one must choose a political system before knowing where in that system one will end up, then one will prefer a system that tends towards equality. When applied to questions of tax design, the veil of ignorance seems to lean towards relatively more redistributive taxation. When thinking about wealth transfer taxation from behind the veil of ignorance, it seems likely that most rational actors would endorse a system of wealth transfer taxation that breaks up concentrations of wealth, if it were demonstrated that such concentrations of wealth were generally bad for society at large, or if the concentrations of wealth were held primarily by an extremely small percentage of the population, often at the expense of the remaining members of society.

Most commentators writing about Rawls and tax law generally agree that Rawlsian liberalism is consistent with heavy redistribution.[35] But most of those who have thought about Rawls and tax, specifically in the context of redistribution, have written about the income tax.[36] The income tax alone is unlikely to satisfy the goals of Rawlsian equality of opportunity.[37] Achieving true equality of opportunity requires finding some way to combat the early in life advantages experienced by those who inherit significant wealth. The estate tax is the appropriate tool to use in order to achieve true equality of opportunity.[38]

Importantly, Rawls's theory of liberalism endorses equality of opportunity rather than strict equality. That is, Rawls focuses on the equality of members of society at

[34] Rawls believed that political structures should be analysed from the 'original position', which was only available to those who placed themselves behind the veil of ignorance. From such a position, wrote Rawls, 'no one knows his place in society, his class position or social status; nor does he know his fortune in the distribution of natural assets and abilities, his intelligence and strength, and the like.' John Rawls, *A Theory of Justice*, rev. edn (Cambridge, MA: Belknap, 1999), 118.

[35] Most, if not all, tax law articles that make reference to Rawls do so in support of the proposition that Rawls endorsed a redistributive liberal position. See, e.g., Anne Alstott, 'Equal Opportunity and Inheritance Taxation', 121 *Harvard Law Review* (2007) 469; Eric Rakowski, 'Transferring Wealth Liberally', 51 *Tax Law Review* (1996) 419; Kerry Ryan, 'Human Capital and Transfer Taxation', 62 *Oklahoma Law Review* (2010) 223.

[36] See e.g. Barbara H. Fried, 'The Puzzling Case for Proportionate Taxation', 2 *Chapman Law Review* (1999) 157; Linda Sugin, 'Theories of Distributive Justice and Limitations on Taxation: What Rawls Demands from Tax Systems', 72(5) *Fordham Law Review* (2004) 1991; Charles R.T. O'Kelley, 'Rawls, Justice, and the Income Tax', 16 *Georgia Law Review* (1981) 1. Notable exceptions include Alstott, n. 35, and Ryan, n. 35.

[37] Sugin argued that '[Rawls'] analysis of philosophical principles does not require commitment to any particular tax system at all. Numerous tax systems could conceivably satisfy Rawls's principles of justice.' Sugin, n. 36, 1998.

[38] 'Equal opportunity ... is widely understood to be the bedrock principle for wealth transfer taxation'. Alstott, n. 35, 542.

the outset of their lives, rather than on whether or not there is an equal distribution of assets within society at any given moment.[39] This is an important distinction. A pure egalitarian might require a regular and ongoing redistribution of wealth in an attempt to achieve an equal distribution of goods among all, but such redistribution would not necessarily be required by applying Rawls's equality of opportunity theory. Redistribution over time would not be required, as long as a sufficiently fair distribution of goods is available to allow all members of society an equal opportunity for success. Once equality of opportunity is assured, any later uneven distribution within society would arguably be attributable to differences in effort.[40] That later arising inequality of outcome would not, on an equality of opportunity theory, require reallocation, because the individual members of society all had the same opportunity for success. Of course, it is not entirely clear what it means for goods to be equally distributed to provide equality of opportunity. Specifically, an unequal distribution of natural abilities seems impossible to account for *ex ante*.[41] Even the ability and desire to work hard could be considered an asset creating an inequality of opportunity. However such thorny issues are resolved, the central concern of those seeking equality of opportunity is that distributions of material goods and economic assets must be evaluated with regard to whether or not they tend towards fairness.

Wealth transfer taxes are not the only tool a government can use to try to ensure equality of opportunity. Indeed, in most societies, wealth transfer taxes have been a relatively small part of the tax system. Government revenues are primarily generated through taxation, but imposing taxes alone cannot achieve the kind of equality of opportunity that Rawlsian liberalism requires.[42] An analysis of the justice of any particular society must involve an examination of both the tax system and the transfer systems or expenditure programmes that are funded by the revenues raised through that tax system.[43] A society that demonstrates the equality of opportunity required by Rawls must have robust expenditure programmes in place in order to ensure that education, health care, housing, and more are made available to all members of that society. The revenues needed to provide these programmes must be raised by taxation, and the revenue required to fund such programmes is unlikely to be able to be raised only through wealth transfer taxation.[44] Achieving Rawlsian equality of opportunity

[39] As Linda Sugin wrote, 'the benefits from individual effort appropriately produce inequalities in income and wealth, and should not require adjustment under the difference principle.' Sugin, n. 36, 2004.

[40] Ibid. [41] See e.g. Alstott, n. 35.

[42] For example, in 2012, the revenue collected by the US federal government was $2,450,164,000,000. See *Historical Tables*, Office of the Management and Budget, http://www.whitehouse.gov/omb/budget/historicals (last accessed 27 October 2016). The tax system was responsible for collecting over 95 per cent of that amount.

[43] Louis Kaplow, *The Theory of Taxation and Public Economics* (Princeton: Princeton University Press, 2008).

[44] This has primarily been true because the base of the wealth transfer tax has always been small (and has been shrinking dramatically in recent years). If the base were increased by shrinking the exemption equivalent credit, and if the rate were increased beyond the current 40 per cent level, then the wealth transfer tax system would generate more revenue. Indeed, the estate and gift tax systems in the United States raised significantly more revenue in years past. See *Internal Revenue Service*, Statistics of Income, Historical Data Tables, https://www.irs.gov/uac/soi-tax-stats-historical-table-17 (last accessed 27 October 2016).

may require a robust income tax in addition to a wealth transfer tax.[45] But an income tax alone cannot address the concerns of equality of opportunity proponents, because the income tax, at least in its current form in the United States, does not address the particular advantages made available to the heirs of the wealthy.[46]

The twentieth and twenty-first centuries have seen growing inequality in the western world, in particular in the United States.[47] This growing inequality does not in itself violate Rawls's theory, because Rawls is focused on equality of opportunity rather than equality of position or egalitarianism. If present inequalities arose only through differences in effort, then Rawlsian equality of opportunity might accept the current distribution of wealth as just. Those who endorse equality of opportunity theories do not necessarily believe that equality of condition results from such equality of opportunity. Inequality of condition can be consistent with a just society. Even with equal original opportunities, different members of a society can end up in different positions. Equality of opportunity does not necessarily view as unjust the uneven distribution of talents or ability to exert effort.[48] However, if an uneven distribution of talents and effort resulted in advantages to the *heirs* of the talented, that might violate the principles of Rawlsian equality of opportunity. If wealth is permitted to transfer unobstructed from one generation to another, it is easy to see how a society that began with an equality of opportunity could quickly morph into a society with very different opportunities available to the heirs of the first generation.

[45] Anne Alstott explained the concerns associated with using an income tax to fund the expenditure programmes necessary to achieve equality of opportunity. Because an income tax can violate the principles of equality of opportunity, tending instead towards egalitarianism, Alstott saw risks in funding her proposed public inheritance (one form of an expenditure programme meant to equalize opportunity) with income tax revenues. She wrote, 'Whether this solution [a 100% inheritance tax] is the right one depends on the justice and injustice of the alternative revenue sources. Lowering inheritance tax rates below 100% means tolerating private inheritance, which is unjust. But raising other taxes—say, income taxes—may also work an injustice. For example, the income tax tends to penalize market work relative to leisure and nonmarket work (as does a consumption tax). An income tax also penalizes savers relative to spenders (which a consumption tax arguably does not). Thus, raising income taxes may require weighing an affront to equal opportunity (unequal inheritance) against an affront to neutrality (penalizing certain ways of life).' Alstott, n. 35, 495.

[46] The current US federal income tax does not include gifts and inheritances in income. See §102. Because of that, even a robust income tax would not tax amounts received in gratuitous transfers. One possible solution to this part of the problem would be to include gratuitously transferred amounts in income. Indeed, several commentators have proposed this. See e.g. Joseph M. Dodge, 'Comparing a Reformed Estate Tax with an Accessions Tax and an Income-Inclusion System, and Abandoning the Generation-Skipping Tax', 56 *SMU Law Review* (2003) 551. However, even including these amounts in income would be insufficient to achieve equality of opportunity because those who are born into positions of privilege would receive wealth merely as a result of their position, even if the amount of that transfer is reduced via the income tax. Treating earned and inherited amounts in the same way (rather than preferencing inherited amounts, as our current tax system does) will not resolve the problem Rawls saw.

[47] For an analysis of the current state of inequality in the world, see Thomas Piketty, *Capital in the Twenty-First Century*, Arthur Goldhammer (trans.) (Cambridge, MA: Belknap, 2014).

[48] However, proponents of equality of opportunity might actually view the uneven distribution of talents as unfair.

C. Libertarianism

A third widely held view of political philosophy is libertarianism. Libertarianism generally embraces freedom and liberty above other political goals, and evaluates political systems by their tendency towards the protection or infringement of individual freedoms. Twentieth-century proponents of libertarianism include Milton Friedman and Robert Nozick, both of whom argued for limited taxation. In general, libertarian analyses of taxation endorse only taxation as payment for services—a version of the benefit principle of taxation.[49] The central tenet of libertarianism is that the government cannot coerce action by its citizens. Only free consent to the law can result in just governance.

Another critical feature of libertarian thinking is a strong view of property rights. Libertarians generally believe property rights are naturally held, rather than created as a result of governmental grace. Because property rights pre-date social membership, the government cannot curtail or eliminate property rights, with the exception of instances of consent by the property holder. As a result, on the libertarian view, most taxation is seen as an unjust violation of property rights by the government. Wealth transfer taxation is generally subject to the same libertarian criticisms as all other forms of taxation, namely that the tax is immoral unless it is explicitly consented to by the property holder. However, the estate tax provides a unique opportunity for just taxation under the libertarian model.[50] Because the entity subject to taxation (the estate) is not a person with natural rights, the normal libertarian arguments regarding unassailable property rights and the requirements of consent do not apply.

Some forms of tax have historically been accepted even by libertarians who view property rights as inviolable. Libertarians have regularly disputed the level of consent required in order to legitimately tax property owners. Nozick's writings seem to indicate that explicit consent must be received from every individual who will be subject to the tax. More pragmatic authors have argued that remaining within the society or accepting government-provided benefits are sufficient forms of implicit consent to legitimate the tax.[51] Despite potentially significant differences regarding the necessary level of consent, libertarians have generally agreed that taxpayers' payment for services received from the government justifies a minimal amount of tax.[52] Such a tax,

[49] Milton Friedman, *Capitalism and Freedom* (Chicago: University of Chicago Press, 1967).

[50] See, Bird-Pollan, 'Death, Taxes, and Property (Rights)', n. 6.

[51] Nozick makes clear his views of implicit consent when he writes that 'everyone realizes that tacit consent isn't worth the paper it's not written on'; see Robert Nozick, *Anarchy, State, and Utopia* (New York: Basic Books, 1974), 287. Earlier in the book he claims to have demonstrated that the reason a minimal state is not redistributive, when the amounts paid by some are used to pay for the protection of others, stems from the fact that those who are receiving protection without paying are getting that protection for free in compensation for the rights they may have given up. (Ibid., 114.) However, Fried demonstrates that Nozick's lack of a coherent theory of property rights and consent leads to the result that, in certain circumstances (such as the move from a minimal state to a slightly more than minimal state), consent to limit the rights of citizens does not have to be explicitly attained. Fried claims that ' in place of actual or implied consent, Nozick does away with consent entirely' (Fried, n. 36, 235).

[52] In Nozick's explanation of the shift from anarchy to a minimal state he demonstrates the situation in which an individual could be compelled to pay for protection, since she is benefitting from the provision of that protection. See *Anarchy, State, and Utopia*, n. 51, 110–18.

explained by the so-called benefit principle of taxation, views the government as a provider of services, collecting payment for those services (in the form of taxes) as part of a freely engaged in transaction.[53] Taxpayers could legitimately argue that the government should limit the kinds of services it provides to those that *only* a government could provide, or to services where efficiency is increased or cost is reduced when the service is provided by a collective body. Such services might include the maintenance of roads and sewers or the provision of security (both local and national).[54] On a benefit theory of taxation, the government would be justified in collecting taxes for the payment of the provision of these services. In a more expansive state, services might include public education, the regulation of markets, or the provision of public health care. These more 'intrusive' services might be unpalatable to a classical libertarian, but the essential feature of the legitimacy of any such payment for and provision of services will be the consent of the taxed.[55]

Thinking of tax as merely a payment for services benefit-principle model seems to fit most neatly with an income tax, rather than an estate tax or other wealth transfer tax. The services provided (such as maintenance of roads, national security, and garbage collection, for example) would be provided regularly, such that an annual accounting of the cost of the services, and the amount of that cost due from any particular taxpayer, would be administratively easier to account for than a lifetime calculation done via the estate tax and 'settled up' upon the death of the taxpayer. In addition to the ease of calculation, an income tax fits the payment for services model better than the estate tax, since it charges the taxpayer for the services in the general time period in which the services were received, rather than waiting until the end of the taxpayer's life to calculate the amount due.[56] But this administrative ease does not mean that a society could not choose to administer a 'payment for services' tax in the form of an estate tax. Such a tax would calculate the benefits enjoyed over a lifetime, and would assess tax to compensate the government for the benefits it had provided to the deceased. Of course, this might be a less than ideal strategy, especially if the decedent, having enjoyed a lifetime of government provided benefits, died a pauper.[57]

[53] The benefit principle of taxation, authorizing taxation only to the extent that it compensates the government for services it provides to its taxpaying citizens, is not a view held only by libertarians. For a discussion of the benefit principle of taxation, and an explanation of its ongoing role in tax policy debates, see Jon Bakija and Joel Slemrod, *Taxing Ourselves* (Cambridge, MA: MIT Press, 2008), 86.

[54] Milton Friedman even acknowledged that a government should provide certain services, and could collect tax from its citizens in order to receive payment for those services. Friedman, n. 49, 65.

[55] There is a tradition known as Left Libertarianism, in which a more expansive state, such as one that might provide the second set of services listed above, is more likely to be endorsed. What Left Libertarianism shares with the tradition of Right Libertarianism is the insistence on the importance of consent in providing moral legitimacy to the government and its curtailing of property rights. For examples of Left Libertarianism, see, e.g., Michael Otsuka, *Libertarianism Without Inequality* (Oxford: Oxford University Press, 2003); Peter Vallentyne and Hillel Steiner, *The Origins of Left-Libertarianism: An Anthology of Historical Writings* (Basingstoke: Macmillan, 2000).

[56] In most payment-for-services scenarios payment is made in the general time frame in which the services are provided. Providing a lifetime of services and waiting for payment until the end of that lifetime seems to leave significant room for error.

[57] Under the current system, individuals receive the benefits of government services, and then must pay an annual income tax. If an individual does not have sufficient funds available to pay the income tax that the government assesses against her, then the government has a variety of methods available to help it decide whether to forgive some amount of the assessed taxes, or collect from the individual in future

Most libertarians approve of the use of a tax to collect payment for the provision of government provided benefits, although there is some debate about what constitutes 'consent' to receive or pay for such benefits. Unsurprisingly, however, most libertarians, and certainly Nozick himself, would find a wealth transfer tax primarily organized to redistribute wealth across society, morally unpalatable.[58] Because it would likely violate the principle of taking from the taxpayer only with her (implicit or explicit) consent, government-facilitated redistribution through the tax code is immoral, on the libertarian view.[59] Importantly, there is no fundamental libertarian objection to the estate tax as such. It may be easiest to administer the kind of benefit principle taxation of which libertarians approve through an income tax, but that is not a moral claim. An estate tax would be permitted on libertarian grounds, as long as it were used only for the collection of payment for services consented to by the taxpayers and provided by the government. The Nozickian view of absolute property rights objects to taxation intended to redistribute when that redistribution has not been explicitly consented to. The form of the taxation (whether the tax is assessed as an income tax or as an estate tax) does not affect the analysis.

D. Utilitarianism

Stemming from the nineteenth-century writings of John Stuart Mill, utilitarianism evaluates the morality of actions on the basis of the utility produced by those actions. The ethically correct action is that which maximizes utility the most overall, including in the utility calculus both the production of utility and the offsetting production of disutility. Utilitarianism has generally evolved into contemporary theories of welfare economics. In this model, the utilitarian calculus is done by determining the utility of particular outcomes based on the social preferences of the relevant society. Within utilitarianism, actions are not a priori moral or immoral. On the contrary, the rightness or wrongness of an action can only be determined by examining its consequences. In this sense, utilitarianism is deeply contextual, and utilitarian analyses would likely result in different moral outcomes in different social scenarios. In evaluating tax policies from a utilitarian theoretical perspective, one must determine what outcomes each policy will likely have. Here empirical economic research plays an important role, making predictions about the likely economic consequences of various

years. For a discussion of the way the government makes these decisions, see Shu-Yi Oei, 'Who Wins When Uncle Sam Loses? Social Insurance and the Forgiveness of Tax Debts', 46 *UC Davis Law Review* (2012) 421. However, if a government held its collection of taxes until the end of an individual's life, it seems significantly more likely that there would be no money left to pay the bills accumulated over that lifetime.

[58] G.A. Cohen, *Self-Ownership, Freedom and Equality* (Cambridge, UK: Cambridge University Press, 1995), 68.

[59] Of course, redistribution could be consistent with a libertarian model, as long as the redistribution was explicitly consented to by the taxpayers involved. Here one might imagine Warren Buffett, Bill Gates, and others insisting that they should be taxed more heavily in order for the government to have more funds available to support social welfare programmes. "Patriotic Millionaires" Lobby Congress for Higher Taxes on Rich', *PBS Newshour* (16 November 2011), http://www.pbs.org/newshour/bb/politics-july-dec11-millionaires_11-16/ (last accessed 27 October 2016).

tax policy actions. However, classical utilitarianism as articulated by Mill included objective utility values.

Mill's theory of utilitarianism cannot be reduced to a mere ethics of self-interest, because the theory requires that one refrain from privileging one's own happiness over that of any other person.[60] When determining how much happiness any particular action will produce, all potentially affected individuals must be counted equally.[61] Even actions that have the possibility of imposing pain on individuals might still be held to be ethical as long as the utilitarian calculus, objectively applied, determined that the result created more pleasure than pain. Because of this universal calculus, taxation is ethically permitted under utilitarianism, as long as the 'pleasure' created by the actions of the government funded through taxation exceeds the 'pain' created by the action of taxation.[62]

Mill's view that the general category of 'pleasure' can be broken down into 'higher' and 'lower' pleasures, and his argument that the higher pleasures have more ethical value than the lower ones, motivates the claim that there is more to utilitarianism than mere self-interest. In Mill's utilitarianism 'justice' is a higher pleasure that must be included with its higher value in the utilitarian calculus. Mill argues that justice has meaning only inside of the utilitarian calculus. The fact that society values 'justice', even in some instances giving it absolute dominance over all other values, only demonstrates that what we call justice must be given great worth in the utilitarian calculus. A world that is just, by utilitarian measures, will tend towards as equality, as those with means will experience happiness by sharing what they have with those who have less.[63]

Mill ultimately holds that there are meaningful differences between the higher and lower pleasures, and that the higher pleasures are those that tend towards equality and justice. And since motives are irrelevant, from an ethical perspective, laws can and should create ethical behaviour by mandating happiness-producing actions. Wealth transfer taxes, by creating more justice and equality in society, will be judged worthy projects by a Millian utilitarian calculus.

[60] '[Impartiality] is involved in the very meaning of Utility, or the Greatest-Happiness Principle. That principle is a mere form of words without rational signification, unless one person's happiness, supposed equal in degree (with the proper allowance made for kind), is counted for exactly as much as another's.' John Stuart Mill, *Utilitarianism*, Roger Crisp (ed.) (Oxford: Oxford University Press, 1998), 105.

[61] '[T]he happiness which forms the utilitarian standard of what is right in conduct, is not the agent's own happiness, but that of all concerned. As between his own happiness and that of others, utilitarianism requires him to be as strictly impartial as a disinterested and benevolent spectator.' Mill, n. 60, 64.

[62] Mill discusses taxation towards the end of *Utilitarianism*, primarily by criticizing non-consequentialist analyses of the justice of taxation. Mill claims that the only way out of the debate about the appropriate way to tax is with the application of utilitarian principles. Having pointed out that some theories of justice will demand equal taxation from all, and others will require graduated tax, Mill states 'from these confusions there is no other mode of extrication than the utilitarian.' Mill, n. 60, 102.

[63] 'In a properly constituted world, the individual's happiness will be found in doing what is morally right.' Mill, n. 60, Editor's Introduction, 5.

IV. Conclusion

Good tax policy depends not only on empirical work and economic theories. While those inputs are important, and help us to determine how best to achieve the ends we set for ourselves, economics and empirics cannot tell us what those ends should be. Established and generally endorsed philosophical theories provide an ideal starting place for doing that tax policy work. When philosophy is applied to tax policy decisions, the result can be a more consistent, coherent, and justifiable set of rules. Despite becoming increasingly unpopular politically, I have demonstrated in this chapter that wealth transfer taxation is endorsed by four very different leading political philosophical theories. While we are still left with important tax policy questions regarding the design of the particular form of wealth transfer taxation to apply in any particular scenario, this consistent endorsement should finally resolve the question 'should we tax wealth transfers'. The answer is a resounding yes.

10

Talents, Types, and Tags

What Is the Relevance of the Endowment Tax Debate?

Henk Vording

I. Introduction

Elizabeth was born in to a well-to-do family, went to expensive schools, graduated in law, and now works on a part-time basis as an advisor to millionaires, most of them recruited from the social network of her own family. Her average working time is twenty hours a week, and her annual income is €100,000.

Ahmed was born in Iraq, in a peasant family. He came to Europe as a refugee. He started working as a taxi driver and, by living frugally, was able to open his own mini-market. His average working time is eighty hours a week, and his annual income is €100,000.

Under the personal income tax, Elizabeth and Ahmed are taxed equally. This makes sense, as they have equal incomes. But it also raises uncomfortable questions. Shouldn't we say that Ahmed made much more effort to get his current position in life than Elizabeth did? And should that matter when we compare their economic positions for income tax purposes? And in addition, shouldn't we say that, even ignoring starting positions, Ahmed has to work much harder than Elizabeth does? If Ahmed worked twenty hours a week, he would only earn €20,000, and under a progressive income tax, he would perhaps pay no more than 10 per cent of what Elizabeth pays with the same working hours. Or reversely, if Elizabeth worked eighty hours a week, she would earn €400,000.

These types of questions explain why many scholars in the field of taxation are inclined to believe that an endowment tax is morally preferable over an income tax. Others, however, object that an endowment tax, being based on what people could earn rather than what they choose to earn, is an unwarranted interference with personal autonomy. And then there is the concern that the concept of endowment is problematic, both in its measurability and in its normative underpinning. Over the last two or three decades, the literature on endowment taxation has developed a kind of consensus on what the relevant arguments are, if not on the relative weight of each of these arguments. As the idea of taxing individuals' endowments is generally considered purely academic in the sense of impracticable, the corpus of literature on the topic is still manageable. The central theme of the debate is: would taxing 'endowment' have surplus value over taxing 'income'? That would be the case if individuals' incomes would under- or overestimate their ability to contribute to society; or, under

Philosophical Foundations of Tax Law. First Edition. Edited by Monica Bhandari.

an economic approach, when taxing endowment would be more efficient (cause fewer distortions) than the income tax.

This chapter is aimed at discussing some of the 'open' issues in the debate. First, and probably because an endowment tax is generally accepted to be unfeasible, there is a tendency to discuss a form of endowment tax that is fully impossible. Perhaps, one day, we will be able to make reliable predictions of an individual's expected income, based on the average of individuals with comparable background characteristics. But we will not be able to predict statistical outliers—those who perform much better than their peer group by earning, e.g., more than $250,000 a year.

Secondly, the popular 'slavery of the talented' objection to endowment taxation does not deserve the prominence that it has received. And this is not just because we are unable to predict extraordinary talent (or at least, its fruits in terms of income). A brief discussion of both Rawls and Dworkin shows that both of them paid undue reverence to the freedom of only the highly talented. Rawls ignored that systems of redistribution (including one that would be based on his maximin rule) tend to interfere heavily with the freedom of people with limited talent to choose their own life plans. And Dworkin's 'slavery of the talented' argument only holds for a limited case.

The decisive argument against an endowment tax is not 'talent slavery', but the difficulty in making a workable distinction between endowment and personal choice. On a conceptual level, the interaction between people's talents and their choices cannot be ignored. On the empirical level, no good 'predictor' of an individual's future economic performance is within reach, nor is there a nonarbitrary way to attribute unpredicted individual economic performance to either choice or luck.

While an endowment tax is impossible to achieve—but for other reasons than usually advanced—it definitely focuses our attention on a simple question: are there measurable signs of (dis)advantage that, in addition to a person's income, could be relevant when discussing tax burden distribution? The arguments here are more pragmatic—e.g. we do know that the labour market discriminates against, roughly speaking, non-'white male' persons. And again, it is obvious that 'being born in a privileged family' brings advantages during later life, in terms of education, skills, etc. Both conditions are ignored by income taxation. In addition, the income tax discriminates against those with a low preference for leisure, and against those with a high preference for money-intensive leisure. The point is not that these are all, by definition, shortcomings of income taxation which need to be resolved urgently. And if solutions are needed, it is not a priori clear whether new tax rules would be the best approach. The point is that discussing endowment taxation helps us to get a clearer view of aspects of equality not captured by the income tax.

II. A Flawed Idea of the 'Model' Endowment Tax

A. The Concept of Endowment

In the endowment tax literature,[1] definitions of endowment abound, usually more of them within the same contribution: 'well-being', 'ability to earn income',

[1] Daniel Shaviro, 'Endowment and Inequality', in Joseph J. Thorndike and Dennis J. Ventry, Jr. (eds), *Tax Justice: The Ongoing Debate* (Washington DC: Urban Institute Press, 2002) 123–48; Kirk

'characteristics such as IQ, parental wealth, income, and education', 'the initial set of wealth and talent resources', and 'a social construct used to measure the relative well-being of a certain individual within a certain social setting';[2] 'an individual's innate lifetime earning capacity', the 'innate capacity to command and enjoy economic resources', the 'innate capacity to produce income or well-being'.[3] Or, to take a deliberately open definition: 'Intellect may be a part of ability, along with sound judgment, self-discipline, and the other aspects of what some call "emotional intelligence". The same, however, may hold for good looks, the exercise of parental influence, possessing a white skin if customers are racists, having widely shared bad taste as an artist or performer, and a willingness to stoop to fraud or violence when they pay off.'[4]

It can be argued that in a traditional, nondynamic society, individuals' endowments can reasonably be measured by their descent and social class. Some pre-modern taxes, such as the French *Capitation* and the Prussian *Klassensteuer*,[5] did indeed connect tax consequences to social class differentials. Family background still seems to be a significant determinant of an individual's future position in life. But a modern society—with considerable changes in technology and economy over an average individual's lifetime—generates much higher levels of social mobility.

Even allowing for a shift from 'background' to 'prospects', the question remains what are we looking for, what the True Tax Base is that we try to approach. Are we looking for what individuals could earn if they strove for maximum economic result? Or is it rather their ability to grasp opportunities and cope with the drawbacks of life, their ability to achieve a happy life? Perhaps the best we can make of all these attempts at definition is that the True Base of an endowment tax would be:

(1) an individual's prospect of a good life, with the focus on the economic side;
(2) as measured by relevant criteria such as the individual's gender and ethnicity, family background, IQ and other cognitive and non-cognitive skills, personality traits, etc.;
(3) at a fixed moment in life, presumably in early adulthood.

Stark, 'Enslaving the Beachcomber: Some Thoughts on the Liberty Objection to Endowment Taxation', 18(1) *Canadian Journal of Law and Jurisprudence* (2005) 47–68; David Hasen, 'Liberalism and Ability Taxation', 85(5) *Texas Law Review* (2007) 1057–113; Kristi A. Olson, 'The Endowment Tax Puzzle', 38(3) *Philosophy & Public Affairs* (2010) 240–71; Linda Sugin, 'A Philosophical Objection to the Optimal Tax Model', 64 *Tax Law Review* (2011) 229–81. Good and recent reviews of the literature are Ilan Benshalom and Kendra Stead, 'Values and (Market) Valuations: A Critique of the Endowment Tax Consensus', 104(4) *Northwestern University Law Review* (2010) 1511–58, Lawrence Zelenak, 'Taxing Endowment', 55 *Duke Law Journal* (2006) 1145–81. Other relevant contributions: Liam Murphy and Thomas Nagel, *The Myth of Ownership* (Oxford: Oxford University Press, 2002); Kyle D. Logue and Joel Slemrod, 'Genes as Tags: The Tax Implications of Widely Available Genetic Information', 61 *National Tax Journal* (2008) 843–63.

[2] Benshalom and Stead, n. 1, 1515, 1517, 1524, footnote 15.

[3] Logue and Slemrod, n. 1, 2–4.

[4] Shaviro, 'Endowment and Inequality', n. 1, 131.

[5] For the latter tax: Stephen Utz, 'Ability to Pay', 23(3) *Whittier Law Review* (2001) 867–950, 898–9.

B. The Measurement of Endowment

It is widely acknowledged that no simple 'endowment test' is available. But let us assume, for a moment, that we would indeed have a reasonably reliable predictor of an individual's future earnings at age 20. Such a test would probably use heterogeneous information on individuals' measurable characteristics and on their social context. We may expect the test to generate estimated average earnings capacity of, e.g. the group of all white middle-class men having an 125+ IQ, the group of all black women raised in poor single-parent families, etc. We would not be surprised to find widely divergent results for these groups, the former having (had) much better average economic opportunities in life than the latter. The white males may well expect average incomes of $200,000; the black females perhaps no more than an average of $20,000. But that is what the test will do, at the best. It will not be able to predict who the future Bill Gates or Oprah Winfrey will be.

It is, therefore, surprising that much of the literature is based on the assumption that an endowment tax could achieve much more than taxing expected averages. The classical problem in the debate is the 'beachcomber'.[6] Imagine a lawyer able to earn $5 million a year, who rather prefers a leisurely life along the beaches. An endowment tax would effectively make it impossible for him to lead the life he prefers; it would result in 'slavery of the talented'. But the point is: an endowment test would never be able to estimate any 20-year-old's potential income at $5 million a year, or, for that sake, even at $0.5 million.

Figure 10.1 provides a stylized presentation of the yearly earnings of all US lawyers (2013). We find a bell-shaped distribution with a long tail to the right, around an average of $130,000.[7]

An even remotely workable endowment tax would take the cohort's average expected yearly earnings as a point of reference; using the earnings of 2013 as our guide, that would be about $130,000. To stay on the reasonable side, the tax might well take, e.g., the 25th percentile wage level as the base of assessment. The tax would then impute $75,000 in potential earnings to everyone with an academic grade in law. It would make no sense to expect the full cohort to be able to achieve a $5 million wage, if only one in fifty or a hundred will ever achieve that salary. Of course, to track the potential big earners, it could help to use extra information (such as the status of the law school,[8] or additional information on skills and backgrounds of the students[9]).

[6] Stark, n. 1, 50; Zelenak, 'Taxing Endowment', n. 1, 1156. The strongest critic of the beachcomber 'frame' is Sugin, 'Philosophical Objection', n. 1, 243–4.

[7] For all lawyers (2013), the US Bureau of Labor Statistics reports a mean wage of $131,990, with the 25th percentile on $75,540, the 75th on $169,880. Bureau of Labor Statistics, Occupational Employment Statistics, www.bls.gov/oes/current/oes231011.htm.

[8] See *NYU Law*, Employment Data for Recent Graduates, www.law.nyu.edu/careerservices/employmentstatistics: nine months after graduation, NYU's 2013 law alumni earned $120,983 on average. The 25th percentile was a meagre $64,390. The 75th percentile was equal to the median ($160,000) which suggests that the large law firms all make the same wage offers to starters. Anyway, these salaries are high compared to the average for all US lawyers.

[9] Peter Kuhn and Catherine Weinberger, 'Leadership Skills and Wages', 23(3) *Journal of Labor Economics* (2005) 395–436 show that having performed leading functions at high school increases lifetime earnings, especially in managerial functions.

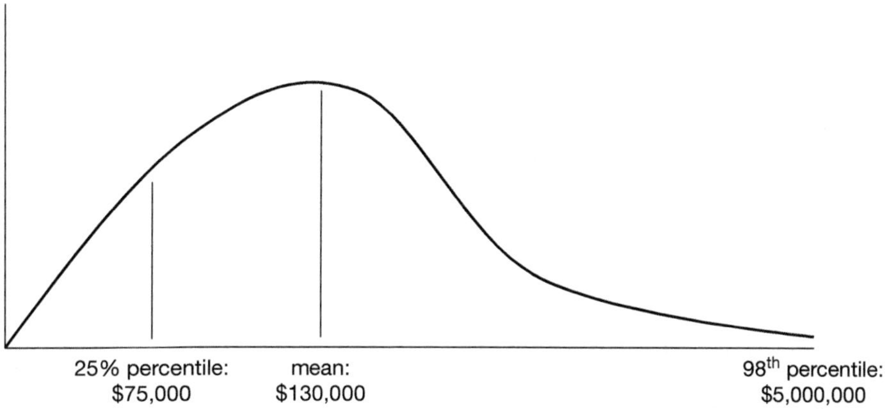

Figure 10.1 earnings distribution of US lawyers (2013)

That might, however, imply that we tax personal choices in addition to endowments, adding potentially considerable distortions to the process of measurement. And even then, it would be very difficult to find a sound statistical basis for imputing more than $250,000 in yearly expected earnings to that more successful subgroup of lawyers.[10]

The type of endowment tax that we should be debating would be based on a classification of individuals in broad categories of social background, gender, ethnicity, perhaps early educational performance and other indicators of skills, etc. It would not be able to track in advance those individuals who will strongly outperform the statistical average of their broad groups.

The 'beachcomber case' pollutes the endowment tax debate in several respects. To start with, it is simply wrong to deal with questions of tax design by referring to extreme statistical outliers.[11] When we accept the beachcomber problem as hypothetical, the underlying test is: 'we can qualify a tax regime as unjust if we are able to construe one case, however unlikely to occur, in which it would work out unjust'. I would suggest that many if not all tax regimes could shipwreck on that test.

Secondly, while a more realistic (or at least less unrealistic) idea on the possible results of an endowment test cannot fully do away with 'talent slavery' concerns, it certainly reduces those concerns.

And thirdly, the (probably unintended) implication of the beachcomber example is that one obvious objection to endowment taxation is usually ignored. It could be an enormous tax cut for the rich. To be sure, proponents of an endowment tax will generally accept that the results of higher-than-average individual effort will go untaxed. But they may not have realized that all incomes exceeding, say, $250,000 will be

[10] Given the figures on NYU law alumni, the mean earnings in the 4th quartile (so excluding the 75 per cent lower-earning lawyers) cannot much exceed $200,000. Murphy and Nagel, n. 1, 123 and, in response, Stark, 'Enslaving the Beachcomber', n. 1, 49 using figures of $500,000, may therefore still be within the realm of hard-to-predict outliers.

[11] Sugin, n. 1, 244, argues that 'beachcombers who have truly opted out of civilized society are too scarce to care about. And even if they were more common, why should they be relevant to the question of society's ordering, given that they are not part of it?'

unpredictable and consequently remain tax-free. Some critics of endowment taxation have, however, noticed that high incomes, when caused by pure luck, will indeed escape taxation. And the question (to be discussed in Section IV) then becomes whether we can distinguish between the results of effort and choice and of pure luck.[12] Probably, the CEO earning $5 million will see effort as the cause of his payment. But others may believe that much of it is luck, and there may be no empirical way to decide the matter. If we want to tax CEOs' earnings capacity, the best instrument is the income tax, not an endowment tax.

III. The Asymmetry of the 'Talent Slavery' Objection

A. Rawls's Argument

The idea of endowment taxation looks attractive from a liberal perspective. It separates individuals' starting positions in economic life from their choices and efforts—they have no moral claim to the fruits of the former, but the more so to the latter. Advantageous positions are taxed, efforts go untaxed. But what to think of those individuals with high estimated earning capacity, who choose not to exploit that capacity, because they prefer a leisurely life, or perhaps because they feel more socially useful in a lower-paying occupation? This concern for the highly talented is known as the 'talent slavery' objection to endowment taxation. It should be noted, as Cohen does, that in this context the word 'talent' just means: high earning capacity, whatever the reason for it.[13]

The objection has been worded by Rawls, by Dworkin, and by many others. I will argue that both Rawls and Dworkin give too much weight to the problem of talent slavery, in part because they both seem to have in mind an endowment tax that is able to track statistical outliers (the $5 million CEOs), but also because they tend to give precedence to the rights of the talented to choose their own levels of effort.

Rawls argues that an endowment tax may take away the freedom of talented people to choose the life plans that they prefer.[14] This argument cannot be rejected by arguing that many lawyers would pay less tax under an endowment tax than under an income tax.[15] The point is that lawyers who 'opt out' of economic life are accommodated under an income tax (with no income, they pay no tax), while under an endowment tax they would be taxed as if they still worked as lawyers. Therefore, an endowment tax forces leisure-loving people to work more than they want, and perhaps in professions that they don't want.

The interesting debate whether there is a qualitative difference between steeply progressive taxation of earnings and an obligation to use one's talents on the labour

[12] Olson, n. 1, stresses the role of luck; see also Sugin, n. 1, 254.

[13] Gerald A. Cohen, 'Where the Action Is: On the Site of Distributive Justice', 26(1) *Philosophy & Public Affairs* (1997) 3–30, 6–7.

[14] John Rawls, *Justice as Fairness: A Restatement*, Erin Kelly (ed.) (Cambridge, MA: Harvard University Press, 2001), 158.

[15] Olson, n. 1, makes the valid point that (my choice of words) hard-working people would pay less under an endowment tax than under an income tax. This is because an endowment tax shifts the tax burden to those who work less than average.

market is, for that same reason, also irrelevant in this context. To Nozick, these were comparable constraints on liberty in the strong sense of self-ownership.[16] Many liberals, including Rawls, hold that paying high taxes on individual earnings does not reduce one's freedom in the same way that an obligation to work (full-time and/or in a high-salary job) would do. And indeed, under an income tax, paying tax is not equivalent to forced labour. People can reduce or avoid the tax by working less, or not at all. The relevant comparison, in Rawls's argument, is not between paying 40 per cent income tax and doing forced labour for 40 per cent of your time; it is between paying no tax at all because you have no income and paying $20,000 because you could have earned income. Therefore, Rawls's argument cannot be rejected summarily.[17]

The main objection to Rawls' argument is that the loss of freedom of the talented is not a matter of principle, but just of degree.[18] With a tax rate of, e.g., 20 per cent, all lawyers would pay $20,000 a year. The choice not to work is, therefore, not available to them. But they could earn $20,000 by working part-time, or by working one year in every five.[19] The result is that individuals with a strong preference for money-intensive leisure are disadvantaged by an endowment tax. That is the exact opposite of an income tax, which discriminates against individuals with money-intensive leisure preference.[20] And the question would then be, not whether we are allowed to distort talented individuals' preferences, but whether some preferences deserve special protection.[21]

The point is underlined by the consideration that all taxes (except prohibitive ones) have income effects, and therefore induce individuals to work more, or seek better-paying jobs, than they would prefer.[22] Taxes differ in their substitution effects: the effects that, by changing relative prices, cause dead weight losses. Substitution effects depend on the type of tax. A tax on earned income reduces the relative price (opportunity cost) of leisure; a tax on expensive cars increases the relative price of those cars. The income effects of taxes do not depend on the type of tax. An individual who faces a $10,000 income tax burden, and another $10,000 car tax, faces a total income effect of $20,000. When his income tax burden is doubled and the car tax abolished, his income effect would still be $20,000. When comparing the economic effects on an income tax of $20,000 with the effects of an endowment tax of $20,000, the only thing that matters is substitution effects, as the income effects of both alternatives are equal.[23]

[16] 'Taxation of earnings from labor is on a par with forced labor', Robert Nozick, *Anarchy, State, and Utopia* (New York: Basic Books, 1974), 169.

[17] Apart from the observation that reiterations of the argument which speak of people being 'forced' into specific jobs are too rhetorical, see Barbara Fried, 'Left-Libertarianism: A Review Essay', 32(1) *Philosophy & Public Affairs* (2004) 66–92, 80.

[18] Murphy and Nagel, n. 1, 123.

[19] For the problem of 'lumpiness' of the labour market (meaning that employees cannot freely choose their own amount of hours worked): Shaviro, n. 1, 138, and Zelenak, n. 1, 1150.

[20] Think of Stark's example ('Enslaving the Beachcomber', 64) of the individual whose hobby is (expensive) Himalaya climbing, and has to work harder during four years to save the money needed for a year off. See also Olson, n. 1, for hypothetical cases where an income tax interferes more strongly with personal choices than an endowment tax would do.

[21] Fried, n. 17, 82. [22] Ibid., 81–2.

[23] Therefore I think that Sugin's reasoning in 'Philosophical Objection' (n. 1, 231–7) on the distorting impact of income effects is mistaken. The distortion that she points at may exist in extreme cases, but (as

However, that the tax has no substitution effect is a consequence of it taking no account of any economic choices that individuals make, nor of any economic results that they achieve, or fail to achieve. An endowment tax is literally unavoidable. And that makes, indeed, a qualitative difference between an endowment tax and most other taxes. The result can be seen in cases where individuals (e.g. because of bad luck, or because they prefer leisure) fail to live up to their endowments, and in cases where they (e.g. because of good luck, or because they work extremely hard) exceed it. An endowment tax does not respond. All taxes on income and consumption do respond sooner or later. The only clear analogy to a tax on endowments is a tax on property. Just for once accepting the beachcomber frame: if the CEO has a seaside resort that he wants to live in as a beachcomber, he will be 'forced' to some form of paid labour to pay his property tax assessment.

Returning to Rawls's argument: indeed, the lawyer who opts out of economic life will not pay income tax (and *ceteris paribus*, his fellow citizens will face a higher tax rate), while he does pay under an endowment tax. But whenever he wants to buy something in the market place, he will have to work, and the more so for the taxes imposed on the consumption goods that he wants. Again, the issue is one of degree rather than principle. Modest taxation has modest income effects; heavy taxation will induce people to make strong adaptations to their preferred way of living. But an endowment tax is qualitatively different in that it is a permanent curse/blessing for those with bad/good luck and for those with a high/low preference for leisure. The question is: what exactly is wrong with that?

The insensitivity of an endowment tax to the incidence of good and bad luck can to some (perhaps considerable) extent be repaired by insurance (to be discussed subsequently). The remaining normative question would be: may we expect high-talented individuals to (more or less) live up to their endowments in terms of their labour efforts?

One reason to consider an affirmative answer is symmetry: we do impose work obligations, and other obligations as well, on low-talented people. The interesting thing is that Rawls has almost ignored the issue. His maximin rule holds that society should maximize the position of the least advantaged of its members. He remained vague about who these least advantaged people were. But, in the discussions following his *Theory of Justice*, he conceded that a Malibu surfer would not qualify; he would not be entitled to public funds for his lack of income.[24] We may assume that this surfer is also good at beachcombing.

But how to distinguish between low-advantaged individuals and Malibu surfers? To exclude people with a high preference for leisure, recipients of social security benefits are typically required to be available for jobs. Their right to refuse job offers is limited, both in terms of type and hours of work. In addition, for many social security benefits, it matters whether one is single or part of a household. Availability of property may

she acknowledges) it is due to the fact that tax must be paid in money, instead of working hours or goods. That is a contingency of modern tax systems, but not a matter of principle. See also Shaviro, n. 1, 134.

[24] John Rawls, 'The Priority of Right and Ideas of the Good', 17(4) *Philosophy & Public Affairs* (1988) 251–76, 257, footnote 7.

also matter. In the end, social security systems typically use anti-abuse rules which are highly intrusive, and may definitely interfere with people's life plans.[25]

For Rawls, the maximin rule was not a matter of providing social security; in fact, he argued against the welfare state[26] for its demoralizing impact on the underclass. He stressed that the least advantaged are those with the poorest life perspectives (or endowments?[27]). Maximizing their positions would mean: improving their market power, their perspectives on realizing their life plans. But that does not reduce the problem: we would still need intrusive rules to keep out the Malibu surfers. And in addition: neither does it rule out that middle-class ideas of the good life are imposed on the least advantaged.

Most libertarians would have no problem with intrusive rules for recipients of social benefits: after all, they are spending taxpayers' money. For Rawls, such a position was not possible.[28] He defended that people have no moral right to the benefits of an unequal distribution of endowments. The logical inference is that they cannot be blamed for it, either. His solution for the problem of the Malibu surfer was the one proposed by Musgrave: take account of leisure in the redistribution process.[29] As a result, the Malibu surfer would get lower support because he enjoys so much leisure. This looks like a poor solution indeed. Either all involuntarily unemployed will share the fate of the surfer, or we would still need intrusive rules.

Summing up, Rawls largely ignored that his maximin rule would require intrusive rules to be applied on the low-talented—a consequence that has been dubbed 'illiberal',[30] mirroring the more familiar qualification of talent slavery.[31] And indeed, this intrusiveness seems in conflict with Rawls's contention that one of the primary goods is respect, 'understood as those aspects of basic institutions normally essential if citizens are to have a lively sense of their worth as persons and to be able to advance their ends with self-confidence'.[32]

One possible explanation of Rawls' position is that 'realization' has a normative meaning. It has been argued that an endowment tax could not, except in limited cases, be generated by a Rawlsian social contract, as individuals will only agree to a contract that makes them better off. And when we accept the view that, absent a social contract, people will not be able to develop and employ their talents, then their gain by agreeing with the contract is precisely measured by realization—that is by their actual income, consumption, and wealth.[33] 'Offering your talents on the market' is

[25] Jonathan Wolff, 'Fairness, Respect, and the Egalitarian Ethos', 27(2) *Philosophy & Public Affairs* (1998) 97–122, extensively discussing the need for 'shameful revelation' of one's circumstances at 113–15.

[26] Rawls, n. 14, 137–40.

[27] It has been argued that the maximin rule, by focusing on the individuals with lowest lifetime expected advantages, comes much closer to the idea of endowment taxation than Rawls realized. Philippe van Parijs, 'Basic Income and Social Justice—Why Philosophers Disagree', Joseph Rowntree Foundation lecture, 13 March 2009, www.uclouvain.be/cps/ucl/doc/etes/documents/2009.Rowntree.pdf.

[28] Simon Birnbaum, 'Radical Liberalism, Rawls and the Welfare State: Justifying the Politics of Basic Income', 13(4) *Critical Review of International Social and Political Philosophy* (2010) 495–516.

[29] In Rawls's terms: include leisure in the index of primary goods. Richard A. Musgrave, 'Maximin, Uncertainty, and the Leisure Trade-Off', 88(4) *The Quarterly Journal of Economics* (1974) 625–32; John Rawls, 'Reply to Alexander and Musgrave', 88(4) *The Quarterly Journal of Economics* (1974) 633–55, 654.

[30] Birnbaum, n. 28, 509.

[31] Zelenak, n. 1, 1169, referring to an unpublished article by Hasen.

[32] Rawls, n. 14, 59.

[33] Hasen, n. 1, esp. 1087, 1099, 1106.

what should trigger an individual's tax liability.[34] In the private sphere, people arrange their relations in the ways that they choose. Only when they enter the public sphere do they become subject to tax rules.[35]

There are two objections to this type of defence. One is that it involves a post-contractarian judgement. In Rawls's contract setting, there is no room for individuals to evaluate their positions and 'opt out' of the contract as soon as the veil of ignorance is lifted. Ex-post individual net gains cannot be the measure of success of the social contract. And if we would accept the view that people may expect to receive net gains from social cooperation (or else opt out), the question would still be how to measure those net gains. Is it what they actually earned, or rather, what social cooperation allowed them to earn, e.g., if their preference for leisure (or unpaid work) had not been so strong in comparison to their fellow citizens?[36] The second objection to giving normative status to realization is that it assumes a specific setting, in which the negotiators, agreeing with Rawlsian redistribution, are not concerned about shirking behaviour of the talented-to-be. It could well be argued that the social contract must contain some provisions requiring the talented to make a contribution to society.[37]

The conclusion need not be that the liberty objection to endowment taxation is invalid, nor that high-talented individuals should be obliged to realize their endowments. But the conclusion that should indeed be drawn is that Rawls's liberty objection is remarkably one-sided in its concern for the high-talented only. And, if we accept that the care for low-endowment individuals requires intrusive interference with their life plans, it is not clear why high-endowment individuals should not be asked to make some reasonable contribution to the functioning of the maximin rule.[38]

B. Dworkin's Argument

Now turning to Dworkin: he also objected to the 'slavery of the talented' caused by an endowment tax. In Dworkin's concept of equality of resources,[39] the benchmark for

[34] Kelman has explained the resistance to taxing household production as income as 'basic human resistance to commoditization', Mark G. Kelman, 'Personal Deductions Revisited: Why They Fit Poorly in an "Ideal" Income Tax and Why They Fit Worse in a Far from Ideal World', 31 *Stanford Law Review* (1979) 831–83; see his discussion at 841–4, and Shaviro's comments, n. 1, 133–4.

[35] The public/private distinction is not identical to the labour/leisure distinction, as argued convincingly by Sugin, n. 1; much useful work is being done in the private sphere.

[36] It may be added that the treatment of nonmarket production in traditional income tax doctrine is fairly pragmatic. The relevance of pure leisure ('doing nothing') is clear: it does not add to taxable income in any way. The status of non-paid work is more ambiguous. Non-paid efforts can be reciprocal (barter), or non-reciprocal (gifts), and in both cases, there are obvious market analogies which do attract income tax. Under the concept of comprehensive income, non-paid labour is not excluded in principle; if it remains outside the definition of taxable income, the only reason is pragmatic. See discussion by Hasen, n. 1, 1071–2; Shaviro, n. 1, 135. In the European tradition—e.g. the German *Quellentheorie* which requires the presence of a 'source of income' (Utz, n. 5, 903–10) —there is more of a normative objection to taxing non-paid work.

[37] Or alternatively, as Cohen, n. 13, 8–10, has argued, the social contract confers on the talented an obligation to contribute to redistribution.

[38] Stark in 'Enslaving the Beachcomber' makes a comparable point in arguing that an income tax implies a privileged status of non-market over market activities at 63–5.

[39] Ronald Dworkin, 'What is Equality? Part 2: Equality of Resources', 10(4) *Philosophy & Public Affairs* (1981) 283–345.

equality is that individuals have equal bundles of resources available. He introduces a group of people emigrating to an uninhabited island. They organize an auction to establish a fair distribution of the resources available on that island. The decisive criterion is the envy test: when no individuals want to trade their bundles of resources with someone else's, everyone has equal resources. What they do with those resources depends on their own preferences. An endowment tax, one would assume, fits in perfectly.

But Dworkin argues that equality of resources is to be 'devoted to whole lives'.[40] This means that an initially fair distribution of resources may need constant reconsideration as those resources are valued on markets. An additional and separate problem is the interaction between individuals' initial endowments and their choices and ambitions. From a lifetime perspective, the problem is that one's resources have no specific value apart from the world in which they will be used. That world includes the overall distribution of resources (which decides how special one's talents really are), and the preferences and choices of other people (which decides the demand for one's talents). As a result, individuals with equal initial resources and equal ambitions would face different economic opportunities and end up with different levels of resources. Dworkin rejects that result, and considers two solutions. One is to include endowments (i.e. the capacity to put one's resources to economic use at given market conditions) in the initial auction, the other is an insurance against the risk of having low-value endowments.

The auction approach entails 'to include, as resources to be auctioned, the labor of the immigrants'.[41] Dworkin rejects that option out of hand, as resulting in 'indeed the slavery of the talented'.[42] The reasoning is that an individual with higher potential earnings would have to pay more to become the owner of his own labour; and if he prefers to spend his time writing poetry, he 'will have spent a large part of his initial endowment on a right that will bring him little financial benefit'.[43]

That may sound as a welfarist objection, but Dworkin argues that this outcome would not pass the envy test. Adrian and Claude start with equal external resources (e.g. parcels of land) so they do not envy each other's bundles. But as Adrian, being a better farmer, has a higher earning capacity than Claude, Adrian has more opportunity to either acquire more resources, or spend time writing poetry. If we want to make Adrian pay for his higher earning capacity, we effectively give him a smaller parcel of land in the initial auction. But then, Dworkin argues, if he wants to write poetry, he will be envious of Claude's position that would allow him more time to write poetry.

It is quite unclear why this should be so; at the very least, additional assumptions seem to be required. It may be true that, to achieve some minimum subsistence level, Adrian would have to work more hours than Claude, now that his parcel of land is smaller. It has been argued that this, in itself, does not warrant the conclusion that Adrian will envy Claude under all circumstances. Adrian may still feel that the type of work that Claude is able to do on his land is too boring; or he may understand that if he were Claude, he would never feel like writing poetry.[44] But when we drop the

[40] Dworkin, n. 39, 310. [41] Dworkin, n. 39, 311. [42] Ibid., 312. [43] Ibid., 312.

[44] Miriam Cohen Christofidis, 'Talent, Slavery and Envy in Dworkin's Equality of Resources', 16(3) *Utilitas* (2004) 267–87.

specific restriction that both Adrian and Claude just aim at achieving the subsistence level, Adrian's opportunities prove much better than Claude's. Any extra effort that Adrian makes generates more income than Claude's similar hours of effort. If Adrian would get a smaller parcel of land than Claude, he might be envious of Claude when considering the minimum work effort required, but Claude might equally be envious of Adrian when considering higher levels of effort. On balance, we simply need extra assumptions about preferences and restrictions to be able to decide who envies whom, and when—and under which conditions talent slavery occurs.

Dworkin prefers to address differences in individual endowments through insurance. Having resources or talents that prove to be valuable or worthless is a matter of good or bad luck. The role of luck was pointed at previously: as an endowment test leaves unpredicted high incomes untaxed, it effectively favours lucky persons along with the hard-working ones. However, Dworkin argues that insurance can do much to convert 'brute (bad) luck' into 'option luck'. He needs that assumption to make the outcomes of the initial auction sensitive to the incidence of (good and bad) luck in later life. In that way he, so to speak, dynamizes the measurement of initial endowments. Whether individuals want to take out an insurance against their risks of disability, unemployment, etc., is a matter of their personal choice. Those who choose to carry their own risks apparently feel better off that way; to those people, the net present value of expected benefits is lower than the net present value of the prospective insurance contributions. If the residue of noninsurable luck is too large, that would be fatal not just to the idea of endowment taxation, but also to Dworkin's concept of equality of resources.

Dworkin discusses a hypothetical insurance market based on the assumption that individuals know the distribution of talents but are uncertain on their own position in that distribution (e.g. because they have no knowledge on the market value of their own specific talents). They will then want to insure their risk of not being able to achieve some level of earnings, at the cost of paying a premium when they exceed that level. Dworkin discusses different target levels of relative earnings without being fully aware that it is logically impossible to insure more-than-average levels of earnings. His thought experiment is nevertheless intriguing. As he assumes compulsory insurance and a standardized contribution scheme to achieve a workable market, his result comes close to an actual income tax. People who fall short of average earnings will get a benefit, paid by those who earn more (and progressively so). The bad luck of having commercially uninteresting talents is (partially) compensated by those who have the good luck of having valuable talents. In the extreme case of a full insurance against the risk of having below-average endowments, all income in excess of the average is needed to fund the benefits, and the result of the insurance scheme is that everyone enjoys equal incomes.[45]

[45] Even an insurance against the risk of having just below-average talent would require draconic contribution levels. See Daniel Markovits, 'How Much Redistribution Should There Be?', 112 *Yale Law Journal* (2003) 2291–329. Dworkin, however, has addressed that point in R. Dworkin, 'Sovereign Virtue Revisited', 113(1) *Ethics* (2002) 106–43, esp. 125–9. There is a comparable debate on Dworkin's idea of how auctions work; see Joseph Heath, 'Dworkin's Auction', 3(3) *Politics, Philosophy & Economics* (2004) 313–35.

We can easily apply this reasoning to the situation that people would be taxed according to their endowments. The only difference is the risk to be covered: not the risk of having talents with below-average value, but the risk of not being able to live up to your own endowment. Arguably, when individuals were to pay a yearly tax based on their estimated earning capacity, they would want to insure the risk of not being able to realize that capacity (or not being able to pay the tax, which is basically the same thing). Again, compulsory insurance and a standardized progressive contribution scheme would result in something much like an income tax. There will be two differences. The insurance would not cover the (expensive) taste for leisure, while it would compensate for measurable labour market discrimination. Anyway, a careful analysis based on the economics of insurance would be required to clarify the relevant issues; for the moment it may be assumed that such an insurance scheme is no more feasible than the endowment tax that it would accompany. But the point is that an endowment tax looks much more like a conventional income tax as soon as we consider the impact of insurance against not being able to pay the tax.

IV. The Fundamental Problem: Endowment Versus Choice

We will return once more to the talented lawyer who prefers to be a beachcomber. We noted that his preference is highly atypical. If we assume that most people have more or less identical life plans (and preferences with respect to leisure, risk, timing of consumption) there is not too much 'choice' left. Any discrepancies between individuals' endowments and their incomes would likely be due to (good or bad) luck. In that case, an income tax, which takes account of luck, would probably be preferable to an endowment tax, which needs additional insurance to achieve that result.

Another question raised by the beachcomber story is, whether his behaviour is a matter of choice, preference, or personal traits. The man can also be regarded as simply a beachcomber who is, for whatever reason, not (or no longer) able to do anything useful with his legal skills. That is to say, when effort and ambition are not personal choices but results of nature or nurture or bad luck, the best available expression of what people could earn is what they actually earn. Anyway, James Mirrlees showed few hesitations: 'One might obtain information about a man's income-earning potential from his apparent IQ, the number of his degrees, his address, age or colour: but the natural, and one would suppose the most reliable, indicator of his income-earning potential is his income.'[46]

The concept of endowment is problematic for other reasons as well. Individual endowments and choices may well interact over a lifetime; it may be very difficult to draw a plausible and workable line at any moment in that life. Concepts like 'preferences' and 'personal traits' demonstrate the problem: should these be considered parts of one's endowment, as a constraint on choice, or as the underlying explanation of

[46] J.A. Mirrlees, 'An Exploration in the Theory of Optimum Income Taxation', 38(2) *The Review of Economic Studies* (1971) 175–208, 175. One of the simplifying assumptions made in this seminal article is that people have identical preferences; and as luck is not modelled, the relation between income and endowment indeed becomes straightforward.

choice, as the life plan that we realize? Note that Dworkin draws the line in a way that allocates to the field of 'choice' ambitions, tastes, preferences, and personality traits, while considering as 'circumstances' health and ability, including the 'innate capacity to produce goods or services that others will pay to have'. This requires that one's 'innate capacity' is assessed without taking notice of one's ambitions, tastes, traits, etc.[47] It is hardly surprising that Dworkin's criteria for distinguishing endowments from choices have remained contested.[48]

To be sure, social cooperation requires an idea of personal responsibility; our legal systems need it; and courts, both civil and criminal, decide cases applying notions of free will and responsibility. But that is quite a few steps removed from a set of generally applicable rules for taxation. It should be noted that both Rawls and Dworkin have noted this fundamental demarcation problem, even while both relied primarily on (their own versions of) the slavery objection to explain why they rejected endowment taxation.

Rawls argued: 'there may be no measure of native endowments (as opposed to realised endowments) sufficiently accurate for us to have confidence that we can justify such a coercive tax ... native endowments such as intelligence and various natural abilities ... are, as such, merely potential, and their actual realization depends on social conditions, among which are the social attitudes directly concerned with their training, encouragement, and recognition. A usable measure of native endowments seems out of the question, even in theory'.[49] And Dworkin: 'we will be thwarted by the reciprocal influence that talents and ambitions exercise on each other. Talents are nurtured and developed, not discovered full-blown, and people choose which talents to develop in response to their beliefs about what sort of person it is best to be'.[50] As Sugin sums up: 'Either endowment is a moving target that makes taxing it subject to the same criticisms directed at income and consumption taxes, or it is limited in a way that fails to reflect important differences among individuals and across lifetimes.'[51]

An endowment tax would need to meet—or at least not evidently fail to meet—two criteria to be feasible:

1. It is possible to predict individuals' 'capabilities'—innate and/or acquired, at a specific moment in life—for economic achievement.
2. It is possible to explain individuals' actual achievements (as distinct from their predicted achievements) in terms of personal choice and (bad) luck, with choice being the dominant factor. Both assumptions have an empirical aspect, that I will briefly comment on.

[47] Ronald Dworkin, n. 41, 322. In a broad review of economic psychology, Almlund and others discuss personality traits as constraints (limiting our choices) but also as preferences (leading our choices); see M. Almlund, A.L. Duckworth, J.J. Heckman, and T.D. Kautz, 'Personality Psychology and Economics', National Bureau of Economic Research Working Paper 16822, 2011, 108–13.

[48] A prominent example: Gerald A. Cohen, 'On the Currency of Egalitarian Justice', 99(4) *Ethics* (1989) 906–44. His criterion that responsibility, not choice should guide what we hold people accountable for, is conceptually interesting but also shows how difficult it will be to find a legal definition of endowment.

[49] Rawls, n. 14, 157–8.

[50] Dworkin, n. 39, 313.

[51] Sugin, n. 1, 254.

A. Predicting Differences in Individuals' Economic Performance

Over the last decades, the determinants of differences in earnings have been studied from several angles, such as labour market discrimination based on gender,[52] ethnicity, etc.; the relevance of cognitive versus noncognitive skills;[53] intergenerational mobility in earnings;[54] and the return to education.[55] There is now a considerable corpus of literature on each of these topics. To some extent, these strands of research integrate, e.g., when the wage gap between whites and blacks is explained by test scores for skills, and when intergenerational mobility and the return to education are related to ethnicity and gender. Most of this literature is aimed at explaining observed wages; it typically concludes that a 1 per cent higher IQ leads to a $500 higher wage, that women earn 20 per cent less than men at the same level of education, that height and beauty add considerably to one's wages,[56] etc.

Unfortunately, potential causalities abound. Education matters to prospective earnings, as do personal traits, IQ, ethnicity, and family background. But these factors are not evidently independent. For example, family background may correlate with education level, IQ, and personality traits. Another example: some of the most important preferences concern individual attitudes towards risk and time. Both of these seem to be related to IQ. People with lower IQ are more risk-averse, and their discount rate is higher, than people with higher IQ.[57] Vital economic 'choices' can apparently be explained by 'endowments'. These and other interdependencies make the impressive body of empirical findings difficult to interpret in coherence. It is quite unclear which share of total inequality in earnings can now be explained by endowment-like

[52] D. Weichselbaumer and R. Winter-Ebmer, 'A Meta-Analysis of the International Gender Wage Gap', 19(3) *Journal of Economic Surveys* (2005) 479–511.

[53] Jay L. Zagorsky, 'Do You Have to Be Smart to Be Rich? The Impact of IQ on Wealth, Income and Financial Distress', 35(5) *Intelligence* (2007) 489–501. A recent review is Matthew Hall and George Farkas, 'Adolescent Cognitive Skills, Attitudinal/Behavioral Traits and Career Wages', 89(4) *Social Forces* (2011) 1261–85. Reviewing the literature, they sum up: 'while a consensus has not been reached, the empirical research to date has tended to find either equal-sized wage effects of cognitive skills and attitudinal/behavioral traits ... or somewhat larger effects of attitudinal/behavioral traits than of cognitive skills', at 1263.

[54] S. Bowles and H. Gintis, 'The Inheritance of Inequality', 16(3) *The Journal of Economic Perspectives* (2002) 3–30, noting at page 22 that while the larger part of intergenerational correlation in earnings remains unexplained, wealth, race, and education are important to the inheritance of economic status while IQ is not. A recent literature review puts the intergenerational elasticity of earnings in a range between 0.25 and 0.5, implying that when a father earns 10 per cent more than average, his children may be expected to earn 2.5 to 5 per cent more than average. This may well be a low estimate: elasticities tend to be higher as better data (over longer lifespans) are used. See Florencia Torche, 'Analyses of Intergenerational Mobility, An Interdisciplinary Review', 657(1) *The Annals of the American Academy of Political and Social Science* (2015) 37–62.

[55] Anthony P. Carnevale, Stephen J. Rose, and Ban Cheah, *The College Payoff: Education, Occupations, Lifetime Earnings* (Washington, DC: Georgetown University Center on Education and the Workforce, 2011).

[56] N. Gregory Mankiw and Matthew Weinzierl, 'The Optimal Taxation of Height: A Case Study of Utilitarian Income Distribution', NBER Working Paper 14976, 2009; Roy Wada and Erdal Tekin, 'Body Composition and Wages', 8(2) *Economics and Human Biology* (2010) 242–54; Timothy A. Judge and Daniel M. Cable, 'When It Comes to Pay, Do the Thin Win? The Effect of Weight on Pay for Men and Women', 96(1) *Journal of Applied Psychology* (2011) 95–112.

[57] See the literature review in Almlund et al., n. 47, 108–9.

factors.[58] And using these factors to predict someone's economic prospects in early adulthood has never been undertaken.

An additional difficulty is that there are no signs that a large share of an individual's earning capacity is 'innate'; much of it depends on socialization. There may well be a 'folk believe' in innate personal characteristics[59] which, it is argued, is reinforced by simplistic presentations of human genetics.[60] But the results of empirical research suggest that education, socialization, training, and experience are at least as important. It may be true that not everyone can become a top violinist or long-distance runner. But even those with some natural advantage in those fields will get nowhere without dedicating their lives to it.[61] This has two implications. One is that 'developing your innate skills' may be described as choosing a life path, while that choice may, on the other hand, well depend on educational environment and family background. In that case, the distinction between endowment and choice becomes weak. The other implication is that 'developing your innate skills' may be a lifetime process, in which case it could be arbitrary to measure endowment at a specific age.

B. Understanding Differences in Individuals' Economic Performance

Turning to the empirical basis for distinguishing between choice and luck, there is scant evidence. Let us assume that the basic issue is simply to attribute all non-predicted economic achievements of individuals to luck, unless we have reason to attribute these achievements to the choices these individuals made. The question then is: how to measure the impact of choices on people's economic results?

The economists' rational choice theory might look promising, as it makes the assumption of rational choice behaviour testable. But *homo economicus* can function without agency; plausibly the behaviour of animals can also be interpreted in terms of

[58] Bowles, Gintis, and Osborne have argued that, overall, individuals' educational achievements, years of work experience, and family background have 'surprisingly little' to say about their earnings, and that a better understanding of relevant cognitive and especially noncognitive skills is required to improve on that. See Samuel Bowles, Herbert Gintis, and Melissa Osborne, 'The Determinants of Earnings: A Behavioral Approach', 39(4) *Journal of Economic Literature* (2001), 1137–76. A recent example of such research on the impact of noncognitive traits on lifetime earnings is A. Duckworth and D. Weir, 'Personality, Lifetime Earnings, and Retirement Wealth', Michigan Retirement Research Centre Research Paper Working Paper WP 2010-235, 2010, 235. Using the well-known Big Five personality traits (openness, conscientiousness, extraversion, agreeableness, and neuroticism) they find a significant and sizeable positive effect of conscientiousness, and a negative effect of neuroticism, on lifetime earnings. Overall, these noncognitive traits explain nearly as much of the variation in lifetime earnings as do cognitive measures (such as numeracy, memory, and vocabulary).

[59] Mameli and Bateson speak of 'folk wisdom', and show the many ambiguities of the concept. Matteo Mameli and Patrick Bateson, 'Innateness and the Sciences', 21(2) *Biology and Philosophy* (2006), 155–88.

[60] Dar-Nimrod and Heine show how popular (press) presentations of the findings of genetic research convert weak into strong explanations, arguing that the general public is led into deterministic beliefs. I. Dar-Nimrod and S.J. Heine, 'Genetic Essentialism: On the Deceptive Determinism of DNA', 137(5) *Psychological Bulletin* (2011) 800–18.

[61] Howe et al., while perhaps extremely 'nurturist', nevertheless argue refreshingly against the idea of innate talents. M.J. Howe, J.W. Davidson, and J.A. Sloboda, 'Innate Talents: Reality or Myth?', 21(3) *Behavioral and Brain Sciences* (1998) 399–407.

rationality. Irrational economic behaviour may be measurable, but is hard to interpret in terms of choice.[62]

What we do know is that people tend to believe in choice (labelled a 'folk belief' as well[63]), and probably that they take 'free will' to mean 'making choices'. However, the belief in individuals as 'choosing' agents is significantly determined by social context. In the Western world, especially in the United States, personal identity tends to be defined as striving for realization of individual preferences and having impact; in many non-Western societies, identity is defined as being responsive to the social context and expectations of others.[64]

The only thing that can positively be concluded from the evidence is that the belief in both innate characteristics and free will has a heuristic meaning for people to understand their lives. But there will always be the fallacy of what psychologists call 'cognitive dissonance': a lack of correspondence between the things we believe to be true. We tend to ascribe our successes to our deliberate choices, while attributing our failures to adverse circumstances. In the end, we all face the millionaire's illusion: having started once as a newsboy, he believes that every newsboy can become a millionaire if he makes the right choices.

The question as to the causal relationship between processes in our brains and the actions we perform can be left to neuroscience.[65] The philosophical point is of course that even if no equivalent for free will or choice could be found in the functioning of our brains, it would still be possible for us to believe in free will. Both Rawls and Dworkin can be understood as arguing conditionally: we have to assume that people are moral beings, being able to evaluate alternative courses of action, and bearing responsibility for their courses of action taken. Without the assumption, social contract theory might be impossible in the first place.[66] It is the assumption that makes a political society possible, even when we are not sure how our brains work.

Summing up, the 'true tax base' of an endowment tax might well be a very arbitrary one. The reason is not just empirical (as our knowledge has definitely been increasing), but to a large extent conceptual. The base of an endowment tax that uses indicators like family background, educational achievement, personality traits, etc. could

[62] For example, it can be argued that rationality is making the 'good choice' (in terms of self-interest) which simply leaves irrationality as making the 'wrong choice'.

[63] Emad H. Atiq, 'How Folk Beliefs About Free Will Influence Sentencing: A New Target for the Neuro-Determinist Critics of Criminal Law', 16(3) *New Criminal Law Review* (2013) 449–93.

[64] K. Savani, H.R. Markus, N.V.R. Naidu, S. Kumar, and N. Berlia, 'What Counts as a Choice? US Americans Are More Likely Than Indians to Construe Actions as Choices', 21(3) *Psychological Science* (2010) 391–8. Henrich et al., discussing the use of American college students as respondents in empirical social science, show that these students tend to be extreme outliers on many aspects of preferences, choices, and behaviour, in comparison to the world population. J. Henrich, S.J. Heine, and A. Norenzayan, 'The Weirdest People in the World?', 33(2–3) *Behavioral and Brain Sciences* (2010) 61–135.

[65] O'Connor and Joffe argue that modern neuroscience, by stressing the role of the brain in behaviour, may actually strengthen the idea of individual agency. Cliodhna O'Connor and Helene Joffe, 'How Has Neuroscience Affected Lay Understandings of Personhood? A Review of the Evidence', 22(3) *Public Understanding of Science* (2013) 254–68, 259.

[66] Therefore I think that Ramsay is mistaken to claim that Rawls and Dworkin should have assumed that determinism is true, even when she does address fundamental difficulties in both authors. Maureen Ramsay, 'Problems with Responsibility: Why Luck Egalitarians Should Have Abandoned the Attempt to Reconcile Equality with Responsibility', 4(4) *Contemporary Political Theory* (2005) 431–50.

in fact have a hard-to-define relation with people's experience of personal choice and responsibility.

The history of taxation provides ample evidence of taxpayers' desire to limit the state's taxing power to definable tax bases. That may explain why the idea of 'ability to pay' taxation has never achieved much legal recognition; instead, it has been specified into 'taxation of income'. Of course, discussions on the meaning of 'income' tend to be lengthy and inconclusive; but 'ability to pay' is evidently much more imprecise.

Taxing poorly observable 'endowment' may therefore sound as an apology for unlimited taxation. The archetypal form of unlimited taxation (and the perfect general anti-avoidance rule) is 'Morton's fork': when you look rich, you can evidently pay tax; when you look poor, you hoarded your money so you can evidently pay tax.[67]

V. What's Left? The Challenges of an Endowment Tax

In the previous sections, it was argued that an endowment tax must be conceived as being based on statistical information concerning identifiable social groups. As a consequence, such a tax will never be very good at predicting outliers: remarkable achievements and windfall gains. This insight has not received the prominent place in the debate that it deserves; instead, an implausible version of endowment taxation keeps hanging around. And as the slavery objection to endowment taxation is typically one of degree rather than principle, it matters a lot what image of a tax we are actually using. It was further argued that a distinction between endowment, choice and luck as needed for a workable endowment tax is likely to be arbitrary. Not only is our empirical knowledge still developing; the conceptual problems are important, perhaps insurmountable.

More generally, the search for 'true tax bases' is fruitless and potentially damaging. The search for the 'true meaning' behind our ideas of the good society, and in this case, the good tax system, may lead to a focus on remote ideals rather than practical opportunities for improvement.[68] The question should not be what endowment 'really' is. It should rather be: are there measurable signs of (dis)advantage that, in addition to a person's income, could be relevant when discussing tax burden distribution?[69] This implies that we may not require a new tax; a system of tax credits within existing income taxes could perhaps do the job.

[67] Cardinal John Morton, Archbishop of Canterbury, was chancellor to Henry VII. His 'fork' is first mentioned by Francis Bacon, *The History of the Reign of King Henry the Seventh* (1622), reprint by The Folio Society London 1971, 120. Desmond Seward, *The Wars of the Roses* (London: Constable, 1995) believes this attribution to be incorrect. He argues that Edward IV first used it when talking London merchants into providing huge loans.

[68] This is Amartya Sen's criticism on 'transcendent' theories such as Rawls's. See Amartya Sen, *The Idea of Justice* (Cambridge, MA: Belknap, 2009).

[69] And even with such a fairly practical question, the risk of myopia is always there. The debate on endowment tax assumes that something like 'equal taxpayer treatment' or 'ability to pay taxation' is indeed a decisive criterion in the design of tax systems. It can be argued, instead, that tax system design cannot be separated from general government policy design, in which case separate norms for tax burden distribution make no sense. See Murphy and Nagel, n. 1.

An interesting starting point is John Roemer's practical approach to what he calls equality of opportunity. The idea can be illustrated by an example.[70] Assume that we want to redistribute income to compensate for unequal starting positions in life, as measured by the educational level achieved by people's parents. We proceed by dividing all individuals into four types, conditional only on the schooling of their parents (from 1: basic up to 4: university). For each of these four types, we determine the distribution of incomes and the mean income. We will find that the mean income per type increases with parents' educational achievements, while the distribution of incomes within each type will be comparably bell-shaped with a long tail to the right. Differences in mean income between types can now be considered a measure of unequal opportunity. The type with low-educated parents may have done worse at school, or prefer low hours of work—whatever the explanation for their low average income, we impute it to their background. On the other hand, the variance within each type is regarded as the consequence of differences in effort. That is to say: even if on average, the members of the type 'low-educated parents' work only thirty hours a week, a member who works twenty shows less effort than explained by his background.

The consequence of this approach (which can be repeated for other types, based on IQ, gender, ethnicity, etc.) is that we have a measure to redistribute between types: the difference in average earnings per type. We can also take account of effort: those who are seen to underperform may receive a reduced benefit (lower type) or be required to make a higher contribution (higher type). Note that in this approach, it is assumed that non-(group) average results can fully be attributed to effort (or 'choice') rather than luck.

Using recent information on lifetime earnings, educational achievement, gender and race in the United States, the idea can be illustrated in some more detail.[71] Basically, the data are there to follow Roemer's approach for differences in educational achievement. Of course, we would first have to decide whether we can indeed consider educational achievement as a relevant 'circumstance', not as a 'choice'.

Educational attainment is an important determinant of differences in lifetime earnings: those holding a professional degree earn nearly four times more than those who did not finish high school. Furthermore, women earn 25 per cent less than men at similar levels of education, even excluding women who work part time. Blacks earn 20 per cent less than whites, also with little variation over levels of education. This kind of data can be used to compensate between types. The result would be a redistribution from the highly educated (and especially the white males among them) to the poorly educated (and especially the nonwhite females among them). As Roemer argues: 'the difficult philosophical and neurophysiological problem of delineating exactly the cut between circumstances and effort need not, for most or all practical purposes, be solved. Social science has much to say about resource distributions that equalize

[70] With some adaptation based on John E. Roemer, 'Equality of Opportunity: a Progress Report', 19(2) *Social Choice and Welfare* (2002) 455–71, 464. The exposition of his approach by Richard Arneson 'Equality of Opportunity', in *Stanford Encyclopaedia of Philosophy* (8 October 2002), http://seop.illc.uva.nl/entries/equal-opportunity is more accessible.

[71] Carnevale et al., n. 55.

opportunities even before philosophers and students of the mind further refine our conception of personal responsibility'.[72]

As to *within*-type compensation from poor performers to high performers, such a transfer requires considerably more of a 'belief' in the idea of endowment taxation, and especially in the separability of effort (choice) and luck. For those who do not believe that such a distinction can be made in a workable way, the *between* type compensation is still possible as a measure of unequal opportunity in life.

The thing is then simply to use tags that reveal earning capacity. Dating back to Akerlof's *The Economics of Tagging*,[73] economists have accepted the view that the welfare costs of redistribution can be reduced by tagging.[74] Plausible tags are, e.g., age,[75] gender, ethnicity, parents' social position, and IQ. Individual genetic traits have been mentioned as (future) candidates for tagging.[76] Such tags could be the basis for tax credits within an income tax system. A normative question to be answered could be the choice between correlation and causality. For example, body height correlates with earnings, but the causality is not as clear as, e.g., race or gender. We could, therefore, want to limit the choice to those tags that show not just a significant correlation to income, but which make sense as causal explanations for income.[77]

VI. Conclusion

The dominant model of endowment taxation has led many commentators to overstate the talent slavery problem, and to ignore the more relevant point: a full-fledged endowment tax, if feasible, would offer a sizeable tax cut to all high-income earners. In the US context, one would have expected a more positive interest in endowment taxation from the libertarian right (as their favoured consumption tax is perhaps too obvious a tax cut for the rich).

The main problem of an endowment tax is, I argued, conceptual. When the aim is to tax the 'true tax base'—individual earning power not created by choice—we easily end up in sophisticated distinctions regarding tastes, traits, luck, and risk. It is probably fair to say that the distinction between individuals' 'endowments' and their 'choices' finds very limited support in the social sciences.

That does not mean that the debate on endowment taxation has generated nothing useful. It does point at identifiable sources of economic inequality that might

[72] Roemer, n. 70, 471.

[73] G.A. Akerlof, 'The Economics of Tagging', 68(1) *American Economic Review* 1978, 8–19.

[74] Logue and Slemrod, n. 1, offer a concise explanation of the economic analysis of (endowment) taxation.

[75] For the idea to (partially) replace progressivity in income taxation by age-related taxation: James Mirrlees et al., 'Conclusions and Recommendations for Reform', in *Tax by Design* (Oxford: Oxford University Press, 2011); James Banks and Peter Diamond, 'The Base for Direct Taxation', in *Dimensions of Tax Design* (Oxford: Oxford University Press, 2010), 548–647. Also: Matthew Weinzierl, 'The Surprising Power of Age-Dependent Taxes', 78 *Review of Economic Studies* (2011) 1490–518.

[76] Logue and Slemrod, n. 1; Jan-Emmanuel De Neve, Nicholas A. Christakis, James H. Fowler, and Bruno S. Frey, 'Genes, Economics, and Happiness', 5(4) *Journal of Neuroscience, Psychology, and Economics* (2012) 193–211.

[77] Chris William Sanchirico, 'Good Tags, Bad Tags', University of Pennsylvania, Institute for Law & Economics Research Paper 13-24 (2013).

be relevant to the distribution of the tax burden.[78] The salient examples are gender and ethnicity, but differences in family background, and differences in effort (hours worked), also matter. We should keep in mind of course that causalities may be complex or ambivalent. For example, the finding that, on average, women earn less than men can be interpreted in alternative ways: a higher preference for leisure, labour market discrimination, or higher effort in unpaid work.

When we would agree that one or more of these sources of inequality should be addressed by government policy (or should be addressed more firmly), the choice of instrument is a matter of expediency. The use of types and tags could be considered to develop tax credit systems within existing income taxes.

[78] The point that our idea of income taxation ignores important information about individuals' socio-economic position is argued cogently by Anthony C. Infanti, 'Tax Equity', 55(4) *Buffalo Law Review* (2008) 1191–2060.

11

How Is the Opera Like a Soup Kitchen?

*Miranda Perry Fleischer**

Over 150 years ago, Alexis de Tocqueville was struck by the importance of charitable associations in American life. As he noted in *Democracy in America*, 'Americans of all ages, of all conditions, of all minds, constantly unite.... Americans associate to celebrate holidays, establish seminaries ... erect churches, distribute books, send missionaries to the Antipodes; in this way they create hospitals, prisons, schools. If, finally, it is a matter of bringing a truth to light or of developing a sentiment with the support of a good example, they associate.'[1]

Even de Tocqueville, however, likely couldn't have imagined the size and scope of today's nonprofit sector: over 1.4 million nonprofit organizations were registered with the Internal Revenue Service in 2013. Of these, almost 1 million are 'charitable organizations', meaning they benefit the public at large instead of their own members (in contrast to labour unions or professional associations). In 2013, these charitable organizations had assets of $3.22 trillion and revenues of $1.72 trillion. Over a quarter of Americans volunteered for charities in 2014; the 8.7 billion hours volunteered equates to an estimated 5.1 million full-time employees whose time was worth $179.2 billion.[2] Lastly, Americans voluntarily donated over $373 billion to such organizations in 2015, either individually during life or at death, or through foundations and corporations.[3]

Given this special role, it is not surprising that American charities enjoy a variety of tax benefits. Charitable organizations are exempt from corporate income taxes and enjoy the ability to issue tax-exempt bonds. And at the individual level, donors may deduct their contributions when determining their federal income, gift, and estate tax liabilities. These benefits are not free, however. The income tax charitable deduction alone, for example, costs Treasury an estimated $38 billion a year.[4]

* Many thanks to Monica Bhandari and the participants of the 2015 University of College London Symposium on the Philosophical Foundations of Tax Law.

[1] Alexis De Tocqueville, *Democracy in America*, 2 vols, Eduardo Nolla and James T. Schleifer (eds) (Indianapolis: Liberty Fund, Inc., 2012), 896.

[2] Brice McKeever, 'The Non-Profit Sector in Brief 2015: Public Charities, Giving, and Volunteering', *The Urban Institute* (2015), http://www.urban.org/research/publication/nonprofit-sector-brief-2015-public-charities-giving-and-volunteering (last accessed 29 October 2016).

[3] Lilly Family School of Philanthropy, Indiana University Indianapolis, *Giving USA 2016 Highlights* 1 (2016).

[4] Jon Bakija, 'Tax Policy and Philanthropy: A Primer on the Empirical Evidence for the United States and its Implications', 80(2) *Social Research* (2013) 557, 558.

Philosophical Foundations of Tax Law. First Edition. Edited by Monica Bhandari.

Despite the prominent role of the sector and its special tax treatment, legal scholarship on the sector's tax treatment is undertheorized. Scholars have proffered a variety of theories to explain these tax provisions, the most accepted of which focus on efficiency and pluralism. While these theories provide valuable insights into the benefits of the charitable tax provisions, they ignore the fact that at heart, these provisions are redistributive: some individuals (the recipients of charitable goods and services, such as students, museumgoers, and soup kitchen patrons) receive benefits. Other individuals pay for these benefits, both voluntarily (through donations) and involuntarily (in the form of higher taxes or reduced benefits).

When viewed in this light, it seems logical to analyse the resulting redistribution in distributive justice terms. At first glance, it appears that the subsidies' structure violates commonly held notions of distributive justice, for it treats charities that serve the wealthy, like the opera, the same as it treats charities such as the soup kitchen that aid the poor. How can spending public funds on the wealthy in this manner be considered just? As this chapter shows, so doing is just under expansive interpretations of resource egalitarianism and left-libertarianism that account for expensive tastes and talent pooling. These understandings argue that individuals with expensive tastes deserve compensation to put them on equal footing with individuals with ordinary tastes when pursuing their visions of the good life, just as individuals who lack financial resources deserve compensation to put them on equal footing with the financially advantaged when pursuing their life plans. Subsidizing not only the soup kitchen but also the opera thus helps a variety of individuals who are disadvantaged in their ability to pursue their vision of a good life to achieve that life.

This chapter proceeds as follows. Section I describes the American charitable tax subsidies and their existing theoretical justifications, which emphasize efficiency and pluralism; Section II then explains why considerations of distributive justice are also relevant. Section III explores whether the subsidies are consistent with utilitarianism as most commonly used in tax policy. Sections IV and V, respectively, analyse the subsidies in terms of libertarian and equality of opportunity theories. Section VI concludes.

I. The Charitable Tax Subsidies: Existing Theoretical Justifications

A. A Brief Overview of the Charitable Tax Subsidies

Charities have received special tax treatment since America's earliest days. Even before the advent of the federal income tax, most American colonies exempted religious, educational, and poverty-relief organizations from taxation. This treatment continued with the advent of the federal income tax, which has exempted charities from the corporate income tax since 1894. On the personal side, individuals have been allowed to deduct donations when computing their individual federal income tax liability since 1917. Most states also provide a charitable deduction, and exempt charities not only from state corporate income taxes but also property and sales taxes.[5]

[5] John D. Colombo and Mark A. Hall, *The Charitable Tax Exemption* (Boulder: Westview, 1995), 3–5, 20.

To qualify for these benefits, organizations must comply with both positive and negative rules. First, to obtain the respective benefits of deductibility and tax exemption, an organization must be formed for one of the purposes listed in Sections 170(c) and 501(c)(3). These include several enumerated purposes (for example, religious, scientific, literary, or educational purposes) and the catch-all 'charitable' purpose. Organizations that qualify for exemption under Section 501(c)(3) almost always also qualify for tax-deductible contributions under Section 170(c), and vice versa. Groups qualifying for both sections are generally referred to as 'charitable' organizations, even if they further a specifically enumerated purpose instead of the general charitable purpose.

These purposes have been quite broadly construed. Groups ranging from mainstream churches to witches' covens to the Church of Body Modification serve religious purposes; organizations as diverse as Harvard University, the Vent Haven Ventriloquist Museum, and the Paper Industry Hall of Fame serve educational purposes. The catch-all charitable purpose has been interpreted especially broadly; it covers organizations ranging from disaster relief to arts organizations, environmental preservation, and cause-oriented public interest litigation.

Quite generally, groups qualifying under this prong must provide a 'community benefit', but little guidance exists as to what counts as a community benefit. What seems to count is fulfilling a need unmet by the private market or operating in a manner that a for-profit would not. In some cases, an organization must benefit the poor in order to provide a community benefit, but in other cases, no benefit for the poor is required. For example, art organizations are not required to provide special benefits for the poor, but recreation centres like YMCAs are not considered to provide a community benefit simply by offering facilities to the middle class.[6] To further confuse the issue, the Supreme Court has held that groups serving a specifically enumerated purpose (such as educational or religious organizations) must also be 'charitable' in the common law sense.[7] Even so, such groups are not required to help the poor to qualify for Sections 170 and 501.[8] Tax-exempt schools and universities, for example, are not required to offer any scholarship assistance at all.

In addition to serving one of the broadly interpreted statutory purposes, organizations must also comply with several negative prohibitions. For example, the commerciality doctrine precludes charitable organizations from engaging in 'too much' unrelated business activity or conducting their businesses in a manner similar to for-profits. The private inurement and private benefit doctrines prohibit insiders and other identifiable individuals from improperly benefiting from charitable assets.[9] A rule against deducting any quid pro quo received from a charity in exchange for a donation ensures that donors only deduct that part of their contribution that benefits others instead of themselves.[10] These requirements work backwards: they reason that

[6] John D. Colombo, 'The Role of Access in Charitable Tax Exemption', 82(2) *Washington University Law Quarterly* (2004) 343, 345, 384.

[7] *Bob Jones University v United States*, 461 U.S. 574 (1983).

[8] Colombo, n. 6, 343–6.

[9] For an explanation of these and other requirements for obtaining exemption, see Joint Committee on Taxation, JCX-29-05, Historical Development and Present Law of the Federal Tax Exemption for Charities and Other Tax-Exempt Organizations 48–61 (2005).

[10] Treasury Regulation §1.170A-1(h).

if an organization is neither acting 'too much' like a for-profit nor benefiting specific individuals, it must be doing something that benefits the community at large.

B. Current Theoretical Justifications

What justifies the treatment provided to such organizations by Sections 170(c) and 501(c)(3)? Although some argue that these provisions are necessary to accurately measure income,[11] most scholars agree that they act as tax subsidies for charitable activity. One set of rationales argues that charities should be subsidized because of the 'good things' charities do for society: relieve the government of burdens it would otherwise bear, provide creative solutions to societal problems, offer diverse and alternate viewpoints in the arts, serve as a counterweight to governmental power, and enhance experimentation.[12]

The more accepted set of rationales is grounded in economics. These theories argue that subsidizing charities helps them produce goods or services that would otherwise be underproduced due to market and government failure. These rationales start from the assumption that the market will underprovide public goods due to free-rider problems and other market failures. The government's taxing power can overcome free-rider problems, but a democratic process dependent upon majority preferences will only provide those public goods supported by the median voter. This means public goods that the median voter supports (perhaps national defence) will be provided but not others (maybe art museums). In response, individuals who support projects that do not have majority support join forces in a 'you scratch my back, I'll scratch yours' manner by agreeing to provide a partial subsidy for each other's projects.[13]

Next, these justifications argue that providing these subsidies via the tax system generates efficiency and pluralism benefits that direct governmental grants would not. With respect to efficiency, scholars have argued that using a tax deduction (or credit) to subsidize charitable activity allows the cost of subsidizing an activity to be allocated among individuals in proportion to how much each individual values the project. High demanders, the reasoning goes, will pay more than low demanders by making a donation to a project, but low demanders still pay something (albeit indirectly) through the tax system. In contrast, direct grants would trigger across the board tax increases, which would almost certainly not reflect how much a given taxpayer favours the subsidized project.[14]

Theorists have also emphasized that allowing individual taxpayers to determine which projects merit subsidies (by making a donation or creating a charity) serves pluralism goals. For example, Saul Levmore has portrayed the charitable deduction

[11] See, e.g., William D. Andrews, 'Personal Deductions in an Ideal Income Tax', 86(2) *Harvard Law Review* (1972) 309, 314–15; Boris I. Bittker and George K. Rahdert, 'The Exemption of Non-profit Organizations from Federal Income Taxation', 85(3) *Yale Law Journal* (1976) 299, 307–14.

[12] See Miranda Perry Fleischer, 'Theorizing the Charitable Tax Subsidies: The Role of Distributive Justice', 87(3) *Washington University Law Review* (2010) 505, 518.

[13] Colombo and Hall, n. 5, 107–8.

[14] See Mark P. Gergen, 'The Case for a Charitable Contributions Deduction', 74(8) *Virginia Law Review* (1988) 1393, 1399–1406 (summarizing work by Harold Hochman, James Rodgers, and Burton Weisbrod).

as a mechanism that allows individual taxpayers to 'vote' on which projects receive subsidies. He argues that this better matches the size of the government subsidy to the voters' enthusiasm for a given project, since the subsidy is only triggered when a donor makes a contribution. Levmore further posits that giving taxpayers a direct say in which projects to fund will lead them to be more active volunteers, develop deeper commitments to such projects, be more vigorous monitors, and tolerate greater amounts of redistribution and funding for public goods.[15] David Schizer has similarly contended that letting taxpayers have wide latitude in choosing which projects to subsidize boosts donor generosity and amplifies monitoring.[16] Lastly, John Colombo and Mark Hall have argued that the existence of donations from a threshold number of donors signals that a given organization both needs and deserves a subsidy.[17]

II. Distributive Justice and the Charitable Tax Subsidies: General Considerations

The justifications described above that are grounded in economics have enormous appeal to tax theorists. Namely, they seem to avoid value-laden judgments about which projects deserve a subsidy by focusing on objective tests: is the project a pure or impure public good? Does it suffer from market and government failure? Does the project have support from some threshold number of individuals? This appeal, coupled with the fact that only some organizations are required to help the poor, has led most scholars to ignore distributive considerations. If so few organizations help the poor, these scholars reason, then redistribution must not be a goal of the charitable tax subsidies. If so, and if the goal of the subsidies is to further efficiency and pluralism, they conclude, why assess them in terms of distribution?[18]

While it may be true that redistribution is not the primary goal of the sector, the fact remains that the charitable tax subsidies are inherently redistributive on two levels. First, they encourage voluntary redistribution from donors to the beneficiaries of charitable activities. And on a second, mandatory level, they take from some individuals (nondonating taxpayers) and give to others (charitable beneficiaries). As economist Charles T. Clotfelter has noted, '[a]lthough few would argue that redistribution is the most important justification for maintaining nonprofit institutions, distributional impact remains one significant consideration, as it is in most areas of public policy.'[19] Moreover, the assessment that the tax subsidies are not redistributive because so few organizations help the poor ignores the diverse forms of redistribution found in detailed examinations of common theories of distributive justice.

[15] Saul Levmore, 'Taxes as Ballots', 65(2) *University of Chicago Law Review* (1998) 387, 404–12.

[16] David M. Schizer, 'Subsidizing Charitable Contributions: Incentives, Information, and the Private Pursuit of Public Goods', 62 *Tax Law Review* (2009) 221, 229–42, 257–67.

[17] Colombo and Hall, n. 5, 104–7, 163–4.

[18] See e.g. Rob Reich, 'Philanthropy and Caring for the Needs of Strangers', 80(2) *Social Research* (2013) 517.

[19] Charles T. Clotfelter (ed.), *Who Benefits from the Non-profit Sector* (Chicago: University of Chicago Press, 1992), 3.

To that end, I have argued elsewhere that a full account of the charitable tax subsidies requires a closer look at distributive justice.[20] As highlighted below, several such theories countenance redistribution to individuals other than the financially poor. Of these theories, the current structure most closely reflects expansive readings of resource egalitarianism and left-libertarianism that incorporate expensive tastes and talent pooling. Under these views, subsidizing both the opera and the soup kitchen can be justified on distributive justice grounds. In contrast, the current structure does not closely reflect most utilitarian or right-libertarian theories of justice. This might seem surprising, given the heavy reliance that tax scholarship places on utilitarianism and the seeming impression that a broad set of charitable tax subsidies is consistent with right libertarianism because they divert resources away from the government. The remainder of this chapter fleshes out these observations.

III. Utilitarianism: Only a Partial Fit

Given the strong influence that utilitarianism exerts over current tax scholarship, it seems logical to start by exploring whether the current charitable tax subsidies reflect utilitarian theories of distributive justice. Under utilitarianism, the proper function of political institutions is to maximize the total amount of utility in society.[21] As most commonly used in tax scholarship, utilitarianism uses income or wealth as a proxy for utility. (I call this 'traditional utilitarianism'.) It further assumes that individuals experience declining marginal utility, and that utility curves are identical across individuals. Based on these assumptions, utilitarianism suggests that downward redistribution maximizes the total amount of utility in society. If a lower-income person who receives a dollar values it more than the higher-income person from whom that dollar is taken, then that transfer increases overall utility. This reasoning is often used to justify the increasing marginal rate structure and our estate and gift tax system.

Under this line of thought, any charitable giving that redistributes from a donor to someone poorer than herself is consistent with utilitarianism. It is easy to identify this redistribution in the case of donative organizations providing basic services to the poor. The transferor (the contributor to the soup kitchen) and the beneficiary (the person eating the soup) are each identifiable, and the donor is almost certainly higher income than the beneficiary. It is also relevant, however, even if the recipient is not financially disadvantaged, so long as the beneficiary is less well off than the donor. For example, although most donors to the opera and other arts organizations are wealthy, many attendees are middle- or upper-middle class. These examples reflect the conventional wisdom that the charitable deduction (setting aside tax exemption for now) is consistent with utilitarian principles even though most subsidized groups are not required to help the poor.

A closer look at this strand of utilitarianism, however, shows that the current structure only partly exemplifies this ideal for a number of reasons. First, many types of

[20] Fleischer, n. 12.

[21] For a fuller analysis of utilitarianism and the charitable tax subsidies, see Miranda Perry Fleischer, 'Charitable Giving and Utilitarianism: Problems and Priorities', 89(4) *Indiana Law Journal* (2014) 1485.

subsidized organizations do little in terms of downward redistribution but instead shuffle resources around among similarly situated individuals. Most American churches, for example, are heavily segregated by income.[22] Likewise, most contributions of Yale and Harvard alumni benefit children from similarly well-off families.[23] The same likely holds true of recreational organizations like little leagues, where the geographic emphasis often leads to segregation by income. A related problem is determining the extent of downward redistribution in organizations where both donors and recipients come from a wide range of income levels. This diversity makes it hard to argue that such a group redistributes downward.

Second, as applied in tax policy, utilitarianism turns on the idea that giving up a dollar decreases donor utility less than receiving a dollar increases beneficiary utility. In the case of many charitable organizations, however, identifying the transferor and beneficiary is difficult. Imagine a day care where some families pay full price but others receive a discount, and that the profit margin from the full-price-families makes up the difference. The families receiving a discount are identifiable as the recipients of redistribution, but who should be considered the source of the redistribution? The families who pay full price? Or are they merely receiving what they pay for? Or should the day care operators be considered the transferors, since they forego some profits in order to provide a discount to the less fortunate families?

Although identifying transferors may be difficult, in settings where for-profits also operate, it will generally be easy to identify beneficiaries. This is so because a market rate can be identified; anyone receiving a discount should be considered a beneficiary. But in many other cases where a nonprofit is selling something, there is no real market rate and therefore no way to know who is being subsidized. Consider the opera. Rich Schmalbeck and Larry Zelenak illustrate the difficulty of identifying who benefits from the opera by imagining that it costs the Houston Opera \$500 to perform *Porgy and Bess* in Durham. One opera lover who values the chance to see *Porgy and Bess* at \$200 buys a \$50 ticket and also makes a \$250 donation to the opera company. Assuming a 40 per cent tax rate, the charitable deduction lowers the after-tax cost of the donation to \$150. This opera lover has now paid \$200 for an experience she values at \$200. Four other opera buffs each buy a \$50 ticket without donating anything. According to Schmalbeck and Zelenak, since all five are buying attendance at the opera at the exact price at which they value it, nobody is getting subsidized.[24]

Their argument, however, overlooks the fact that someone who values an item at less than its purchase price is still being subsidized if that individual pays part of the price and someone else pays the difference. I might only be willing to pay \$500 for a \$5,000 fur coat, but I am still getting subsidized if my mother pitches in the remaining

[22] Jeff E. Biddle, 'Religious Organizations', in Clotfelder (ed.), n. 19, 92, 109. Some churches, of course, provide social services to the less fortunate. Subsidizing these activities is therefore consistent with traditional utilitarianism.

[23] While such schools do offer some scholarships, these schools struggle to enrol truly poor students. See Robert Reich, 'Why Government Spends More per Pupil at Elite Universities than Public Universities', *Huffington Post* (13 October 2014).

[24] Richard Schmalbeck and Lawrence Zelenak, *Federal Income Taxation*, 2nd edn (New York: Aspen, 2007), 417–18.

$4,500. The problem with applying this reasoning to the opera is that there is a working market for fur coats and a market price can be determined. In contrast, without the ability to price discriminate, the opera's cost structure would preclude it from performing.[25] That means there is no comparative baseline we can use to determine who is receiving a subsidized discount and therefore no way of identifying who is benefiting from the opera in terms of redistribution.

A related concern is valuation. Although the value of what the donor gives up can generally be valued in dollars, the same is not true of the value received by many charitable beneficiaries. Imagine a nonprofit that puts on a free production of *A West Side Story*. How should the value received by the audience be measured for purposes of determining whether donors lose less utility than beneficiaries receive? If a tourist in Times Square purchases a ticket to see *A West Side Story* for $100, she is assumed to value the experience at $100 because she chose to spend that money on that musical instead of on other items she could have purchased for $100. But the audience of a free performance at the park hasn't made the same choice, and this lack of a market transaction renders valuation difficult.

Lastly, the foregoing discussion has considered the utility only of individuals with some direct tie to the charity in question, such as a patron, donor, or employee. But the utility of the public at large also matters, since the costs of the subsidies are also borne by others in the form of higher taxes or reduced services.[26] How do we compare the reduced utility of other individuals for purposes of comparing it against the utility gained by the charitable beneficiaries? And to what extent should the public at large be considered beneficiaries of charitable activity? Imagine an after-school sports programme in a tough neighbourhood. The participating children and their families clearly benefit from the programme. But should other residents of the neighbourhood also be considered beneficiaries, on the grounds that they benefit when fewer children get in trouble after school? Perhaps one response to this dilemma is to dismiss it by arguing that although each member of the public at large gives up some utility via higher taxes or reduced benefits, she also gains utility because each of us likely benefits from some charity or another. Under this view, however, the subsidies are not redistributive in the sense contemplated by traditional utilitarianism.

IV. Most Libertarian Theories Justify a Much Narrower Structure

Although not frequently discussed by tax academics, libertarianism is frequently invoked by the public in discussing taxes and redistribution. Although the type of libertarianism popular with the public is not well reflected in the subsidies' current structure, the subsidies are consistent with less well known left-libertarian theories of justice.

[25] Henry B. Hansmann, 'The Role of Non-profit Enterprise', 89(5) *Yale Law Journal* (1980) 835, 854–9.

[26] See Eric M. Zolt, 'Tax Deductions for Charitable Contributions: Domestic Activities, Foreign Activities, or None of the Above', 63(2) *Hastings Law Journal* (2012) 361, 374.

Stated broadly, libertarianism is a family of theories that share the view that governmental power should be strictly limited and that celebrate strong private property rights, the right of individuals to be free from coercion, the importance of the free market, and the idea that its resulting distributions should generally not be disturbed. There is a wide range of thought within the libertarian camp, however, ranging from minimal state libertarianism (which calls for the strongest protection of private property rights and generally supports only the most minimal state); to classical liberals (who support more state activity than minimal state libertarians but still oppose much of what our current state does); to 'left-libertarians' (who allow for a great deal of redistribution).[27]

At first glance, one might assume that libertarianism provides a sound explanation for the charitable tax subsidies. After all, if Anna donates $100 to charity and is in the 40 per cent bracket, her taxes are reduced by $40. The government takes $40 less from her than otherwise, and has $40 less to redistribute to others against Anna's will. Moreover, the more vibrant the charitable sector is, the more it can act as a counterweight to government power and offer decentralized and diverse solutions to societal problems.

This reasoning, however, overlooks the fact that the charitable tax subsidies are inherently redistributive. Their costs are borne by other taxpayers and they are best viewed as indirect mechanisms for governmental redistribution. When Anna makes a charitable contribution and takes the charitable deduction, she is essentially acting as the government's agent. Anna decides which charity will receive $40 from other taxpayers in addition to $60 from her (using the numbers from the previous example). Although her gift to the charity is not coerced, the $40 transfer from other taxpayers is, and this coercion means that the relationship between libertarianism and the charitable tax subsidies is more complicated than it initially appears.

As this section will show, a closer look suggests that the most common conceptions of libertarianism do not support the current structure. Only the much less common left-libertarian theories could support something akin to our current structure. This analysis stems from the idea that if the state could not legitimately tax citizens to engage in an activity itself, it cannot validly tax citizens to subsidize third parties to provide that activity. If, however, a state could provide a given public good or service itself, it may justifiably subsidize third parties to provide that good or service. In fact, in that case, subsidization is likely preferable than direct governmental provision. The disparate actors who determine which charities receive subsidies have access to dispersed information that the government likely lacks, and the market for contributions in some respects mirrors the for-profit market. Moreover, subsidizing charities to provide a given service in lieu of the government enhances pluralism and experimentation and minimizes governmental power.[28]

[27] For useful summaries of libertarianism and classical liberalism, see Harry Brighouse, *Justice* (New York: Polity, 2004), 86–94; Will Kymlicka, *Contemporary Political Philosophy: An Introduction*, 2nd edn (Oxford: Oxford University Press, 2002), 102–65; Eric Mack and Gerald F. Gaus, 'Classical Liberalism and Libertarianism: The Liberty Tradition', in Gerald F. Gaus and Chandran Kukathas (eds), *Handbook of Political Theory* (Thousand Oaks: SAGE, 2004), 115–30; Matt Zwolinski, 'Classical Liberalism and the Basic Income', 6(2) *Basic Income Studies* (2011) 1–13.

[28] For a fuller account of the interaction between libertarianism and the charitable tax subsidies, see Miranda Perry Fleischer, 'Libertarianism and the Charitable Tax Subsidies', 56(4) *Boston College Law Review* (2015) 1345.

A. Minimal State Libertarianism

Most tax academics associate libertarian thought with Robert Nozick's entitlement theory, which contains three core principles: justice in acquisition, justice in transfer, and the rectification of past injustice in holdings. Under these principles, if Bonnie justly acquires a holding, she can do with it whatever she wants. If she freely transfers it to Chris, then Chris's ownership of that holding is just and cannot be interfered with. On the other hand, if Bonnie's acquisition of the holding was unjust, or the transfer to Chris was somehow unjust, then some type of compensation is due whoever was harmed.[29]

Nozick's theory, along with John Locke's natural theory of property rights, forms the basis of what is commonly referred to as 'minimal state libertarianism'. As summed up by Nozick, only 'a minimal state, limited to the narrow functions of protection against force, theft, fraud, enforcement of contracts, and so on is justified.'[30] Because 'taxation is on par with forced labor,'[31] redistributive taxation is unjust. Minimal state libertarianism thus seems to suggest that the charitable tax subsidies are unjust. If the state cannot validly provide anything beyond basic protective and enforcement services, then it cannot justifiably subsidize the provision of any other services by third parties. Moreover, the charitable tax subsidies violate the antidistributive norm embodied by minimal state libertarianism, for they involuntarily take from non-donors (in the form of higher taxes or reduced services) to give to charitable recipients.

1. *Non-absolutism and a safety net*

A nuanced look at minimal state libertarianism, however, shows a more complicated picture. For example, prominent libertarian philosopher Eric Mack 'confess[es] to a fondness for the dictum that all taxation is theft', while arguing that rights-based libertarianism could support taxation that would 'fund something like a minimal safety net for individuals who would faultlessly find themselves in dire straits without that net'.[32] Simplifying somewhat, Mack argues that property owners have a self-serving incentive to provide a minimal safety net so that those in dire straits do not need to steal food or shelter. Mack reasons that by removing justifications for incursions upon property rights, a minimal safety net would actually strengthen those rights.

This reasoning, however, would support only extremely limited redistribution via the charitable tax subsidies and not the current, broad structure. It suggests limiting the charitable tax subsidies to groups providing basic aid at a subsistence level to those truly unable to support themselves through no fault of their own. This would support aid to the disabled, children, and the elderly, but not to the able-bodied unless the latter was structured as some type of 'workfare'.[33] And while such aid would likely

[29] Robert Nozick, *Anarchy, State, and Utopia* (New York: Basic Books, 1974), 169.

[30] Ibid., ix. [31] Ibid., 169.

[32] Eric Mack, 'Non-Absolute Rights and Libertarian Taxation', 23(2) *Social Philosophy & Policy* (2006) 109.

[33] Mack would impose some type of workfare requirement, on the grounds that those who ignore property rights due to extreme need should compensate affected property owners wherever possible. See

include soup kitchens, homeless shelters, emergency medical care, and basic provisions such as clothes and toiletries, it would likely not include other goods and services to the truly destitute, such as recreation programmes, access to the arts, and the like.

2. *Rectification*

Nozick's notion of rectification could also support limited redistributive efforts, but again, nothing like our current structure. Recall that, for Nozick, if existing conditions result from unjust acquisitions or transfers, then redistribution on the grounds of rectifying past injustice is justified. This process involves three steps: identifying past injustices, determining what the distribution would be if those past injustices had not occurred, and then restoring victims to a position as good as the one they would have had without the injustices.[34]

To that end, tax subsidies for improving the situation of individuals who are victims of past injustices would be justifiable. Some instances of past injustice are clear, such as slavery, the treatment of Native Americans, and the internment of Japanese Americans during World War II. Rectification could therefore support subsidizing charitable organizations that helped improve the situation of these groups (and any similar groups). If poverty in these groups was traceable to past injustices, then providing basic necessities such as food, clothing, and shelter to members of these groups would be justified. If members of these groups have lesser educational and employment opportunities due to past injustices, then the state could legitimately subsidize efforts to improve their educational and employment opportunities. This might include private schools in neighbourhoods populated by these groups, tutoring programmes, job skills training, and so on. Rectification might go even further, and subsidize activities in any situation where the opportunities of the victim group fall short of the opportunities for nonvictims (such as white Americans or men). Consider recreation. Many African Americans and Native Americans lack recreational opportunities such as access to summer camps and swimming pools that others take for granted. If that lack of access is due to past injustice, then subsidizing such programmes would be justified.

Obviously, identifying past victims and determining what distributions would have resulted without past injustices is exceedingly difficult. Even if this were possible, it would not support subsidizing the broad array of groups that we currently do. Interestingly, Nozick himself floated the idea that something like Rawls's difference principle could offer a way around these implementation problems. Perhaps, he reasoned, the least advantaged in society are the most likely to be victims of past

text surrounding nn 50–1, however, for a discussion of whether making such distinctions involves too much governmental interference.

[34] Nozick, n. 29, 152–3; Lawrence Davis, 'Nozick's Entitlement Theory', in Jeffrey Paul (ed.), *Reading Nozick: Essays on Anarchy, State and Utopia* (Totowa: Rowman & Littlefield, 1981), 344, 350–1; Adam James Tebble, 'The Tables Turned: Wilt Chamberlain versus Robert Nozick on Rectification', 17(1) *Economics and Philosophy* (2001) 89, 91–3. Rectification does not involve returning the precise holding that was the subject of an unjust transfer to its proper owner, nor does it turn on inheritance rights of victims' descendants. Davis, n. 34, 348–51.

injustice.[35] Even this reasoning, however, would not support the current structure but would only justify subsidizing groups that assisted the financially disadvantaged.

B. Classical Liberalism

In contrast to the 'minimal state libertarianism' of Nozick and the self-ownership tradition, classical liberal theories justify a slightly more active state that could legitimately provide additional public goods and infrastructure, reduce negative externalities, and prohibit monopolies. These theories, however, reject the current scope of government as unjustified, and oppose most government regulations and the implementation of large-scale redistributive programmes. While classical liberal principles likely justify a broader set of subsidies than minimal state libertarianism, they do not support the breadth of the current structure. As explored below, they would subsidize public goods that truly suffer from market failure, and potentially a limited safety net for the extremely destitute.

1. Public goods

Classical liberal theorists recognize that even a functioning market might underprovide public goods due to free-rider and similar market failures. Why might market failure occur in the case of public goods? One characteristic of such goods is that they are nonexcludable. Consider clean air: once clean air is provided for one person, it is impossible to preclude others from also enjoying it. This nonexcludability is thought to lead to free-riding, which in turn causes private actors to underproduce such goods. If so, the government may justifiably act to remedy market failure so that the optimal level of public goods is produced.[36]

While this reasoning may appear to validate the current, broad structure of the charitable tax subsidies, a closer look shows that it does not. Instead, classical liberalism justifies a much narrower set of subsidies. In some cases, a given good may lack the nonexcludability that characterizes true public goods. In other instances, free-riding may be less prevalent than commonly thought or private actors may be able to overcome an initial market failure on their own without government intervention.

a. Excludability

Consider excludability. If individuals who do not pay for a given good or service can be excluded, then the private market should generally be able to provide it at optimal levels. And a number of activities currently subsidized are, in fact, excludable. Schools could educate only paying students, hospitals could treat only paying patients, and

[35] Nozick, n. 29, 231.

[36] See e.g. Milton Friedman, *Capitalism and Freedom*, 40th anniv. edn (Chicago: University of Chicago Press, [1962] (2002), 27–32; Lionel Robbins, *The Theory of Economic Policy in English Classical Political Economy* (London: Macmillan, 1953), 188–9; Gerald F. Gaus, *Social Philosophy* (Armonk: M.E. Sharpe, 1999), 170, 188–91.

museums could admit only paying patrons. And given technology such as cable and satellite, public television could be offered only to those willing to pay.[37]

Subsidizing such activities therefore cannot be justified on the grounds of nonexcludability. There are, however, two other potential rationales for subsidizing such activities. The first relates to contract failure. As Henry Hansmann first noted, many subsidized activities are complex personal services such as health care, education, and day care. He theorized that because purchasers cannot easily judge the quality of these services, firms will organize as nonprofits to reassure purchasers that payments will be used to increase quality instead of to benefit personally the firms' managers. The drawback of organizing as a nonprofit, however, is that the nondistribution constraint hampers a firm's ability to raise capital. According to Hansmann, tax subsidies compensate for that disability.

To the extent such services do suffer from contract failure, classical liberalism would support subsidization. In contrast, subsidization would not be warranted if private actors could solve the information asymmetry problem. Given the myriad ways one may now obtain information about a potential service provider—internet review sites, consumer message boards, third-party certifications, and so on—it is quite plausible that contract failure is less prevalent than in the past. Moreover, Anup Malani and Eric Posner have identified several contractual mechanisms that could reassure potential customers that resources are being used as promised instead of being diverted. In both instances, if consumers have some means of determining on their own which providers are trustworthy, then both the nondistribution constraint and subsidization are extraneous.[38]

A second potential rationale for subsidizing excludable activities, the concept of merit goods, likely holds little sway with classical liberals. According to Richard Musgrave, merit goods are goods such as education or cultural activities for which individual preferences as expressed in the market do not reflect societal preferences concerning the proper amount of such goods. Such a mismatch might occur for two reasons. First, perhaps the activity generates positive externalities if its benefits are widened to those unwilling to purchase it in an unsubsidized market, and those positive externalities exhibit nonexcludability. Secondly, maybe individuals underestimate their preferences for merit goods because their benefits are far in the future or are indirect. To 'correct' individual preferences, subsidization is justified to lower the price and thereby increase demand.[39]

A classical liberal, however, would likely be sceptical of the foregoing for the following reasons. How does society know which preferences should be corrected in this manner? Why the ballet but not cult zombie movies? How does society identify which

[37] See Harold Demsetz, 'The Private Production of Public Goods', 13(2) *Journal of Law and Economics* (1970) 293 (using the example of pay television throughout the article); Gergen, n. 14, 1443–4. Anyone doubting that willingness to pay for public television exists need look no further than the public's willingness to pay to rent or buy shows such as *Downton Abbey*.

[38] Anup Malani and Eric A. Posner, 'The Case for For-Profit Charity', 93(8) *Virginia Law Review* (2007) 2017, 2035–9.

[39] Richard A. Musgrave, *The Theory of Public Finance* (New York: McGraw Hill, 1959), 13–14.

goods generate positive externalities? Provocative modern art is a positive externality to some and a negative externality to others. As others have noted, most examples of merit goods—education and cultural amenities—reflect the tastes of the middle class cultural elite. Why allow the tastes of a few to override the expressed preferences of others?

b. Free-riding

Classical liberal tenets would go further, however, than simply insisting on stricter adherence to the criteria of nonrivalry and nonexcludability. Such principles would also require (1) that free-riding actually be a problem and (2) that government intervention be necessary to overcome that problem. Some evidence exists that free-riding may be less common than many believe. In one experiment, for example, individuals were told that they would not be excluded from viewing goods like theatre performances and television programming even if they did not pay. Nonetheless, most individuals still revealed their true demand for the product, instead of strategically understating demand so as to free-ride off of others.[40]

Moreover, a variety of social and contractual mechanisms can overcome potential free-rider problems. Such problems are minimized in churches, for example, by their club-like nature.[41] Social pressure and moral suasion have the same effect. At my daughter's school, for example, the first class in each grade whose parents reach 100 per cent participation in the annual fund wins a special pizza party. The desire to benefit one's child by giving them the party and the stigma of being the holdout who ruins the party minimize free-riding. Many organizations harness the power of social recognition to encourage giving; consider the prominent lists of donors in theatre programmes and university alumni magazines. Robert Cooter's proposed donation registry, which would publish how much of one's income one donates to charity, has a similar effect.[42]

In other contexts, contractual mechanisms such as tie-ins can overcome free-riding. When using a tie-in, providers charge not for the public good itself but for a private good whose purchase closely correlates with use of the public good. Consider the lighthouse, often used as the quintessential example of a public good. Until the mid-1800s, private operators actually operated numerous lighthouses in England. To avoid the free-rider problem, operators charged ships that docked at nearby ports. Ships could avoid the fee only by avoiding the port, which meant docking somewhere more dangerous or spending a much longer time at sea.[43] In the nonprofit context, pew rents are a form of tie-in, as are preferred seats for concerts and shows. Offering donors extra benefits, like the ability to meet performers after a show, has a similar effect.

[40] See Peter Bohm, 'Estimating Demand for Public Goods: An Experiment,' cited in Earl R. Brubaker, 'Free Ride, Free Revelation, Or Golden Rule', 18(1) *Journal of Law and Economics* (1975) 147, 158–61.

[41] See Gergen, n. 14, 1438.

[42] Robert D. Cooter, 'The Donation Registry', 72(5) *Fordham Law Review* (2004) 1981.

[43] See R.H. Coase, 'The Lighthouse in Economics', 17(2) *Journal of Law and Economics* (1974) 357, 357–8.

c. Final thoughts on classical liberals and public goods

As described above, a strict reading of classical liberal tenets would support subsidizing truly public goods via the charitable tax subsidies. This would almost certainly encompass activities such as environmental protection, animal welfare, medical and scientific research, and poverty relief (excluding poor individuals who can't pay for poor relief defeats the purpose). It would also likely include activities such as education and health care; it is fairly easy to imagine positive externalities in addition to the benefits enjoyed by the direct recipient (such as an educated and healthy workforce). But a number of cultural amenities (theatres, museums, public radio) and other groups that bring together those of common interests (a group devoted to fostering an appreciation of knitting) would likely not be subsidized, on the grounds that such groups do not generate identifiable positive externalities.

This reading, of course, conceptualizes the sector as providing a variety of discrete public goods (and legitimately providing those goods only if the government itself could have provided them). Some classical liberals, however, might argue that the charitable sector itself should be considered a public good.[44] A strong charitable sector, for example, can act as a counterweight to governmental power by minimizing the extent of activity undertaken by the government, keeping governmental growth in check, and ensuring that nongovernmental voices are heard on important issues. The sector (and the subsidies) also encourages voluntary giving and a communitarian ethos that minimizes the need for coercive taxation.

Under this view, the sector should be thought of in the same manner as national defence or a working market. All citizens—rich and poor alike—benefit from these institutions with broad public benefits. The fact that wealthy individuals benefit from the charitable tax subsidies (just as they benefit from national defence) simply reflects this fact. Just as it would be silly to worry about the distributional consequences of national defence, this reasoning continues, it is silly to worry about the distributional consequences of the charitable tax subsidies.

Despite the appeal of the notion that the sector acts as a counterweight to governmental power, the above arguments do not convince me that the distributional consequences of the subsidies should be ignored. Namely, the charitable tax subsidies—unlike, say, national defence—are often touted by opponents of large government for their redistributive capabilities. Some contend that governmental welfare efforts, for example, should be replaced by increased private giving. And whenever reforms to the sector are discussed, proponents of the status quo argue that any changes would harm the poor. For these reasons, the distributional consequences of the various activities conducted by the sector are relevant.

[44] See Fleischer, n. 28, 1402–3.

2. Classical liberalism and a safety net

In addition to funding truly public goods, a number of classical liberal scholars support providing a minimal safety net to the very poor. Four major justifications predominate, though scholars tend to be vague about their arguments or mix and match them. Like Eric Mack, some argue that a safety net provides self-protection or insurance to the non-needy.[45] Another set of arguments emphasizes free-rider problems, conceptualizing poor relief as a public good of the type discussed above.[46] Other scholars focus on a moral duty to the poor and/or the need to justify a liberal scheme to all its members.[47]

Due to classical liberalism's other principles, however, none of these arguments lead to broad redistributive measures or redistribution for equality's sake. Instead, these concerns are sufficientarian. Hayek, for example, supports the provision of a minimum income that would provide 'security against severe physical privation' but he opposes the idea of assuring 'a given standard of life ... determined by comparing the standard enjoyed by a person or a group with that of others'.[48] He reasons that aiming for a 'more even or more just distribution of goods'[49] intolerably interferes with freedom.

Along those lines, classical liberal concerns justify subsidizing activities like homeless shelters, soup kitchens, emergency medical care, and basic provisions such as clothes and toiletries but not endeavours such as recreation programmes and access to the arts. Even if the latter set of activities benefit the destitute, they go beyond the basic necessities envisioned by these theorists. What remains unclear is the treatment of programmes like job training or day care that go beyond basic subsistence but make it more likely that the diligent can provide for themselves in the future.

Libertarians continue to debate, however, whether or not this safety net should be restricted to the 'deserving poor', meaning people who cannot support themselves through no fault of their own such as children, the elderly, and the disabled. On one hand, many scholars who support a basic safety net—including Hayek, Locke, and Eric Mack—distinguish the deserving poor from the undeserving.[50] On the other hand, limiting assistance in this way may require a level of government intrusion repugnant to libertarian principles, for it would require that the government be involved in determining who was 'deserving' for purposes of knowing which charities merited a subsidy.[51] Regardless of how this debate is resolved, it is clear that providing a

[45] Friedrich A. Hayek, *Law, Legislation and Liberty*, vol. 2: *The Mirage of Social Justice* (Chicago: University of Chicago Press, 1978), 87 [*hereinafter* Hayek, *Mirage*]; Friedrich A. Hayek, *The Constitution of Liberty* (Chicago: University of Chicago Press, 1960), 285–6 [*hereinafter* Hayek, *Constitution*].

[46] Friedman, n. 36, 191; Mack and Gaus, n. 27, 124.

[47] Friederick A. Hayek, *Law, Legislation and Liberty*, vol. 1: *Rules and Order* (Chicago: University of Chicago Press, 1973) 152 [*hereinafter* Hayek, *Rules*]; Hayek, *Constitution*, n. 45, 285; Hayek, *Mirage*, n. 45, 87; John Locke, 'First Treatise on Government', cited in Jeremy Waldron, 'Nozick and Locke: Filling the Space of Rights', 22(1) *Social Philosophy and Policy* (2005) 81, 91; Loren Lomasky, *Persons, Rights, and the Moral Community* (New York: Oxford University Press, 1989), 125–9. For a summary of these arguments, see Zwolinski, n. 27, 7–8; Gaus, n. 36, 188–91.

[48] Hayek, *Constitution*, n. 45, 259. [49] Ibid.

[50] Friedrich A. Hayek, *The Political Order of a Free People* (Chicago: University of Chicago Press, 1979), 55, reprinted in Tebble, n. 34, 595–6; Waldron, n. 47, 96–7.

[51] See Zwolinski, n. 27, 8–9.

sufficientarian safety net would justify a much narrower set of charitable tax subsidies than under current law.

C. A Brief Word About Left-Libertarianism

Minimal state libertarianism and classical liberalism are the most common interpretations of libertarianism; most laypeople who self-identify as libertarian likely subscribe to one or the other. Both are versions of 'right libertarianism', whose reasoning turns on the assumption that natural resources are initially unowned. In contrast, less well-known 'left libertarian' theories argue that prior to appropriation, natural resources should be considered as commonly owned. Due to this common ownership, left-libertarians argue that an individual who appropriates more than her fair share of natural resources must compensate others.[52]

This leads to debates as to what counts as natural resources and what 'fair shares' in those resources are that largely mirror the debates among resource egalitarians discussed in more detail below. 'Equal share left-libertarianism'[53] is roughly equivalent to basic resource egalitarianism and does not take into account disabilities and other nonfinancial characteristics that affect one's opportunity for welfare. The more common left-libertarian interpretation, however, is that initial shares should give each individual an equal opportunity for welfare.[54] This conceptualization recognizes that innate differences in individuals, such as disabilities, affect their ability to generate welfare.[55] And as with resource egalitarianism, some theorists also argue that individuals with expensive tastes or below average talents also merit extra resources. To that end, what left-libertarianism suggests for the charitable tax subsidies overlaps in many respects with what resource egalitarianism suggests, discussed below. Notably, this version comes much closer to supporting the current structure than do the more popular right-libertarian theories.

V. Expansive Resource Egalitarianism: A Better Fit

The final set of distributive theories common to tax scholarship consists of those which rely on the principle of equality of opportunity. It is under these theories—when interpreted to account for expensive tastes and talent pooling—that the current structure can most easily be viewed as just.

Quite generally, equality of opportunity refers to the idea that one's choices should determine one's life path, instead of the chance characteristics of birth (such as race). Equality of opportunity thus tolerates divergent outcomes that are due to choice, in

[52] For useful discussions, see Peter Vallentyne, 'Left-Libertarianism and Liberty', in Thomas Christiano and John Christman (eds), *Contemporary Debates in Political Philosophy* (Malden, MA: 2009), 138–44; Michael Otsuka, *Libertarianism without Inequality* (Oxford: Clarendon, 2003), 11–22.

[53] See Vallentyne, n. 52, 148; Hillel Steiner, 'The Natural Right to the Means of Production', 27 *Philosophical Quarterly* (1977) 41, 49.

[54] See Vallentyne, n. 52, 149; Otsuka, n. 52, 25.

[55] See Otsuka, n. 52, 27, 29. Otsuka believes that a disabled person merits compensation even if her opportunity for welfare is as great as the nondisabled due to a sunny disposition or other traits.

contrast to traditional utilitarian theories that seek to minimize inequality regardless of the cause. Not surprisingly, a rich debate exists as to what it means to ensure that chance characteristics of birth do not predetermine life outcomes.[56] One interpretation, known as 'the merit principle' or 'careers open to talents', basically requires nothing more than precluding discrimination in the awarding of jobs and similar opportunities. It does not, however, countenance any redistribution to enable individuals to compete for those opportunities and therefore shall not be addressed further. (Many who hold this view also consider themselves classical liberals or libertarians, however, and may support on those grounds the limited redistributive efforts discussed in the prior part).

Although the concept of careers open to talents is popular with the general public, many scholars believe that it offers equal opportunities in name only. In their view, the resources available at birth heavily influence one's ability to develop one's talents in order to compete for positions such as jobs and college admissions. They further argue that the resources available at birth are just as arbitrary as one's skin colour or gender. To that end, these 'liberal egalitarian' theorists support programmes that seek to equalize *ex ante* resources, so that later differences in outcomes will be due to choice instead of the chance circumstances of birth. These theories, which include Rawls's democratic equality and resource egalitarianism, thus require redistribution in addition to nondiscrimination. Of these, an expansive reading of resource egalitarianism that allows for talent pooling and expensive tastes provides the closest justification for the charitable tax subsidies as currently structured.

A. Democratic Equality and Basic Resource Egalitarianism

Most readers are likely familiar with Rawls's conception of democratic equality, which reflects his view that both the financial resources and natural endowments one is born with are arbitrary. Democratic equality (very generally) consists of two principles. 'Fair equality of opportunity' requires limits on the differing ability that equally talented individuals from different social classes have to develop their skills and talents. The 'difference principle' then requires that society be arranged so that better endowed individuals gain financially from their talents only if the less advantaged also benefit. Democratic equality thus tolerates inequalities that result from differing choices and from unequal endowments, but individuals with differing endowments are not owed any compensation ipso facto.[57]

In many respects, this overlaps with the interpretation of resource egalitarianism most common to tax scholarship. This conception, which I shall call 'basic resource egalitarianism', also seeks to minimize the role that the financial resources available at one's birth play in determining life outcomes. In its most basic version, basic resource egalitarianism concerns itself only with financial resources and ignores differences in natural endowments. As with Rawls's democratic equality, outcomes that diverge

[56] For useful discussions of various equality of opportunity theories, see Kymlicka, n. 27, 53–97; Anne Alstott, 'Equal Opportunity and Inheritance Taxation', 121(2) *Harvard Law Review* (2007) 470, 476–85.

[57] John Rawls, *A Theory of Justice*, rev. edn (Cambridge, MA: Harvard University Press, 1999), 63–87.

because of chance are unjust and initial financial resources should therefore be equalized. Unequal natural endowments, however, do not trigger compensation.[58] Neither Rawls's democratic equality nor basic resource egalitarianism seeks to equalize *ex post* resources. Because of these parallels and their similar implications for the charitable tax subsidies, I shall discuss these theories together from here on and simply refer to this set of ideas as 'basic resource egalitarianism'.

As translated to public policy, basic resource egalitarianism generally expresses itself as programmes for children and parents. Recall its essential goal of equalizing *ex ante* resources so that later outcomes will reflect choices. In the real world, of course, *ex ante* equalization is impossible. The real world is an ongoing state, composed of a mix of people of all ages. Some are just starting out, some are in the middle of careers of varying levels of success, and some are near the end of their lives. At any given moment, the distribution of resources reflects a mix of choices and luck. Imagine a confiscatory tax coupled with the distribution of equal amounts of resources across society in Year 10. This would provide for *ex ante* equalization for the following years, but ignores the choices made before Year 10.

But the circumstances of any given child are not the product of their past choices; nobody chooses to be born into a given family. Assisting disadvantaged children (and their parents, to help the children indirectly) can further *ex ante* equality of resources at the individual level.[59] Consider programmes such as Head Start; scholarship programmes for poor students; Children's Health Insurance Program; and the Women, Infants, and Children Nutrition Program. All attempt to augment the resources of poor children so that they have the same opportunities to develop their talents and abilities as do wealthier children. Thus, the programmes most consistent with basic resource egalitarianism are those that aid children and their parents, as well as adults whose plight is clearly due to bad luck (those who have suffered an accident at work, perhaps).

These theories provide only a partial explanation for the current structure of the charitable tax subsidies and do not justify subsidizing the broad array of groups we currently assist. Because such theories emphasize equalizing the financial resources available to children at birth, they do not justify subsidizing programmes that do not assist poor children. In contrast, basic resource egalitarianism validates assisting only those organizations that somehow enable financially disadvantaged children to develop their talents. Obvious examples include pre- and post-natal care for poor mothers (such as the Nurse/Family Partnership); tutoring programmes, libraries, and schools in poor neighbourhoods; and projects like the Harlem Children's Enterprise Zone. (Perhaps) less obvious examples are groups that help poor children develop skills that at first might seem frivolous because they don't directly teach academic or job skills. This would include groups that teach things like music, dance, sports, and chess to poor children. Since such groups develop skills like patience, discipline, and teamwork, it seems likely that resource egalitarianism would suggest subsidizing them. Going a step further, basic resource egalitarianism would also suggest

[58] Alstott, n. 56, 476–85. [59] Ibid., 477.

subsidizing opportunities for poor children to enjoy cultural programmes like museums, theatres, and dance performances.

This is obviously a much smaller group of activities than those subsidized under current law. Activities like youth recreation programmes and 'elite' cultural activities like the opera and art museums would be subsidized only if they offered free or discounted admission to poor children (or other programmes that help them develop their abilities).[60] The same holds true of nonprofit hospitals. And many organizations that aid adults would not be subsidized, so as not to reward past bad choices on the part of their clients. Instead, aid to poor adults would be validated only if they were parents (as an indirect way of assisting the children) or if their plight was due to circumstances beyond their control. (Of course, in many instances it may be difficult to identify when adults are poor due to their own choices or not. Is someone who grew up in a poor area with terrible public schools, didn't go to college, and was just laid off from a factory the victim of choice, chance, or both?)

B. Resource Egalitarianism that Accounts for Disabilities

Basic resource egalitarianism focuses only on the extent to which different material resources at birth affect life outcomes. Some theorists, however, believe that society should also minimize the extent to which chance differences in physical and mental abilities at birth affect outcomes. In their view, physical and mental disabilities at birth deserve compensation, just as a lack of financial resources does. To take a common example: imagine two individuals, Dana and Emma, with equal financial resources at birth. If Dana is born with a disabled leg and cannot walk, then she does not have the same opportunities as Emma. Some resource egalitarians thus argue that Dana should be compensated for her disability, since she will have to spend resources on a wheelchair or crutches to gain mobility and have the same opportunities as Emma.[61]

In terms of the charitable tax subsidies, this supports a slightly broader set of subsidies than under the most basic resource egalitarianism but still nothing like our current structure. Accounting for disabilities, for example, would support subsidizing groups such as the Special Olympics and Paralympics that provide opportunities for the disabled to develop their skills and talents. It would also subsidize treatment and research on diseases and disabilities that strike solely by chance, such as Down's Syndrome. A trickier question would be organizations whose activities are things like lung cancer research and prevention. Although many people who get lung cancer are smokers and are in some sense responsible for their plight, a large portion of lung cancer victims are not smokers. Aiding them would not be rewarding past bad choices.

Notably, resource egalitarianism that accounts for disabilities also suggests subsidizing hospitals and health care services even if they provide no free or discounted services to children. Instead, simply providing health care services for a fee (even without

[60] This of course sets aside the question of 'how much' aid to poor children would be required of a youth recreation league or the opera.

[61] Amartya Sen, 'Equality of What?', in Sterling M. McMurrin (ed.), *The Tanner Lectures on Human Values* (Cambridge, UK: Cambridge University Press, 1980), 196, 218.

a discount, and even to adults) should be considered charitable. Recall Hansmann's justification for the charitable tax subsidies. Activities such as medical care that suffer from contract failure will organize as nonprofits to overcome informational asymmetries. At the same time, however, the nonprofit form hinders their ability to raise capital, which justifies a tax subsidy.[62] Thus subsidizing health care providers allows them to offer a good or service that is necessary to remedy a physical disadvantage and that would not be provided absent the subsidy—in Dana's case, perhaps an operation to fix her leg.[63]

Of course, once Dana pays for this operation, she has fewer financial resources left than Emma. In a world with equal initial financial resources, fully compensating Dana would also require providing some financial compensation to her so that she has the same financial resources as Emma after her disability is fixed. This suggests that health care providers that do offer free or reduced-cost services should be eligible for an extra subsidy: one for providing Dana with access to the operation she needs, and one for compensating her for the resulting difference in material resources. This is especially true if the normal price was out of Dana's reach. In that case, the hospital's existence would do nothing to remedy her disability; only free or reduced-price care would help Dana. (In theory, resource egalitarianism would require such free or reduced-price care. But it might be the case that such a requirement would put health care organizations out of business. If so, it makes more sense to forego such a requirement so that health care organizations can exist in the first place and remedy disabilities for at least some individuals.)

C. Expensive Tastes and Talent Pooling: The Best Explanation for the Current Structure

In addition to compensating for unchosen disabilities, some theorists would go even further and compensate for expensive tastes and lacks of talent. Recall the resource egalitarian notion that the chance circumstances of one's birth should not affect one's ability to live her conception of a good life. To some theorists, being born with expensive tastes is just as arbitrary as being born with one leg, and puts one at a disadvantage compared to those without expensive tastes when it comes to one's ability to live her view of the good life.[64] For example, because champagne is more expensive than beer, I require more resources than my beer-guzzling husband to further my welfare. Some theorists further argue that the distribution of skills such as a good voice or the ability to play basketball well is likewise arbitrary and should be viewed in the same light. In their view, a tone-deaf accountant with a poor voice who wants to be a pop singer

[62] Henry Hansmann, 'The Rationale for Exempting Nonprofit Organizations from Corporate Income Taxation', 91(1) *Yale Law Journal* (1981) 54, 69–71, 72–5.

[63] It should be noted here that resource egalitarians are much less sceptical of government activity than classical liberals, and likely would not insist on as rigid standards concerning market or contract failure as do classical liberals.

[64] Richard J. Arneson, 'Equality and Equality of Opportunity for Welfare', 56(1) *Philosophical Studies* (1989) 77, 79.

instead is also the victim of chance when it comes to his inability to live his version of the good life. Both the accountant and I merit compensation under this view.

Although this expansive interpretation of resource egalitarianism is controversial,[65] it best explains the broad array of groups currently subsidized. For example, it would support subsidizing groups like the opera and community theatre, even if they did not provide opportunities to poor children or discounts to the poor. The reasoning is similar to that of health care organizations. Take a group like the opera. The operagoer has the bad luck of having expensive tastes, and the opera singer has the bad luck of wanting to engage in an occupation she likely would not be able to without subsidized operas. The very existence of the opera, therefore, furthers resource egalitarianism by making it possible for these individuals to lead their conception of the good life. As with health care, however, operas, schools, museums, and the like that do offer free or reduced-cost services should be eligible for additional subsidies. This reasoning also applies to other nonprofit activities that we might not think of as expensive in the sense that the opera is. In a sense, anyone who has minority preferences that are not funded by the market or government suffers from bad luck. By providing such individuals with an opportunity to obtain welfare, the charitable tax subsidies are compensating them for that bad luck.

And while the current structure most closely reflects this interpretation of resource egalitarianism, it is not a perfect match. For example, even this expansive interpretation does not justify aid to adults who are not parents and who are poor due to their own choices. A structure that perfectly reflected resource egalitarianism, for example, would require soup kitchens or homeless shelters to inquire into the causal circumstances of adult clients who were not parents. Likewise, subsidized hospitals shouldn't treat someone who breaks her leg after voluntarily climbing a dangerous tree or who had the opportunity to insure but did not.

D. Levelling Down

The current structure also departs from resource egalitarian ideals in that it does not require levelling down. Both Rawls and the resource egalitarians would require levelling down, that is, limiting the financial resources one can transfer to one's children for two reasons. First, it lessens the arbitrary advantages that children born to wealthy families have when it comes to developing their talents and abilities. Second, it minimizes wealth concentrations, which Rawls believed could injure democracy and therefore impair the primary liberties of individuals with lesser financial resources.[66]

A set of subsidies more closely aligned with these ideals would therefore only subsidize transfers that actually level down. Although it may appear that all charitable contributions necessarily level down by removing assets from outright family use, a closer look shows that many donations do not level down as a practical matter and in some cases may even exacerbate inequality of opportunity. When Francie contributes to a private school her daughter attends or to a foundation supporting her son's public

[65] See Alstott, n. 56, 481–2 for a discussion of these criticisms.
[66] See, e.g., Rawls, n. 57, 245–7.

school, this increases the resources available for her children's education. Little or no levelling down occurs, and in fact, the differences between her children's educational opportunities and those of children who attend public schools in poor areas may be magnified.[67] Alternatively, Francie might contribute to her family's private foundation or to a public charity controlled by her family. Even if the recipient organization ultimately uses the funds to help others, Francie's family still retains a large amount of power over those assets. This control can constitute economic and political power over others, which is in contention with equality of opportunity ideals. To that end, charitable donations that benefit the donor or her family (even indirectly) would not be deductible. Nor would contributions to charities controlled by the donor's family be deductible.

E. Structural Issues

A final way in which the current scheme departs from liberal egalitarian ideals is the fact that the charitable deduction is structured as an itemized deduction. This arrangement creates two results that are troubling to a liberal egalitarian: it gives wealthier individuals more of a 'vote' over how government resources are spent than less wealthy individuals, and it only subsidizes the expensive tastes of a small subset of the population.

1. *The mechanics of itemized deductions*

The fact that the subsidy is structured as an itemized deduction (as opposed to an above-the-line deduction or a credit) means only donors who itemize have their choices subsidized. When computing one's taxes, each taxpayer may take either the standard deduction ($6,300 in 2016) or the sum of one's itemized deductions. Other common itemized deductions include home mortgage interest, unreimbursed business expenses, and state and local taxes.

Roughly two-thirds of American taxpayers do not itemize and instead take the standard deduction. These taxpayers receive no additional tax benefits from making a charitable contribution. If Georgia, a non-itemizer, donates $100 to the local soup kitchen, her taxes are not affected one whit. The after-tax cost to Georgia of the donation remains $100, and the government has subsidized no part of her gift. In contrast, the one-third of American taxpayers who itemize do receive a tax benefit from making a contribution. Imagine that Henry, an itemizer who is in the 40 per cent bracket, donates $100 to the local homeless shelter. The deduction reduces his taxable income by $100 and drops his tax bill by $40. The after-tax cost to Henry of his donation is $60, and the government has subsidized $40 of his gift.

The higher one's income, the more likely a taxpayer is to itemize. It is not hard to imagine why. The more income one has, the more likely she is to own her own home

[67] See Rob Reich, 'Philanthropy and its Uneasy Relation to Equality', in William Damon and Susan Verducci (eds), *Taking Philanthropy Seriously: Beyond Noble Intentions to Responsible Giving* (Bloomington: Indiana University Press, 2006), 27, 40–5.

and take the mortgage interest deduction, the higher her state and local taxes will be, and the more disposable income she will have available with which to make charitable contributions. Although over 90 per cent of taxpayers with incomes over $200,000 itemize, only 55 per cent of taxpayers with incomes between $50,000 and $100,000 do, and only 28 per cent of taxpayers with incomes below $50,000 itemize.

Moreover, deductions provide greater tax benefits to taxpayers in higher brackets than to taxpayers in lower brackets. Imagine that Iris (who is in the 35 per cent bracket) and Katherine (who is in the 15 per cent bracket) each make a $100 contribution. The deduction reduces *Iris*'s after-tax cost to $65. The government has subsidized the remaining $35 gift to her chosen charity, which means that she has essentially directed where $35 of the government's money goes. But the deduction only reduces *Katherine*'s after-tax cost to $85. The government subsidizes only $15 of her gift and she directs where only $15 of the government's money goes.

2. *The shortcomings of this structure*

This feature of the charitable tax subsidies seems at odds with liberal egalitarian ideals by giving what is essentially a vote over government resources to only a subset of the donor population.[68] Moreover, it gives wealthier taxpayers more of a vote than less wealthy taxpayers. Given that resource egalitarianism does not tolerate these types of inequalities with respect to basic rights elsewhere (richer Americans are not given more votes on Election Day, for example), it seems odd to tolerate them here.

Lastly, this structure does not account for the tastes of nondonors unless their tastes match up with those of donors and founders of nonprofits. Consider Lola, who does not have enough disposable income to make a charitable donation but would like to enjoy modern dance performances. Unless other individuals with enough money to create and fund a modern dance company near her do so, she is out of luck. If such individuals instead create and fund an opera, Lola is not compensated for the bad luck of being born with a taste for modern dance.

The first problem could be remedied by replacing the deduction with a credit. There may not, however, be a way around the second problem (of nondonor tastes). Having the government decide which charities receive subsidies returns us to the situation where only projects with the support of the median voter are funded. In theory, each person could be given a 'charitable' voucher, much like a school choice voucher, that could be used to fund whatever charity one wished. There would still be some activities, however, which didn't receive enough funding to operate, and individuals with a taste for that activity would still find themselves left out. Thus, it is hard to conceptualize a system that could provide for the expensive tastes of all citizens, and many scholars have noted the benefits of attaching the subsidies to the affirmative act of a donor making a donation.[69]

[68] See Levmore, n. 15, 411–12.

[69] Ibid., 405–12; Schizer, n. 16, 229–42, 257–67.

VI. Conclusion

This chapter has explored the theories of justice most common to tax scholarship in order to assess the distributional consequences of the charitable tax subsidies. Running throughout this analysis is the view that the subsidies should be considered redistributive because they take from one set of individuals (other taxpayers) and give to another set (those who enjoy charitable goods and services). Under this view, the type of utilitarianism traditionally used in tax policy analysis and the more popular right-libertarian theories of justice are not reflected in the breadth of the current structure's redistribution. In contrast, the subsidies' current structure is most likely to be considered just under expansive readings of resource egalitarianism and left-libertarianism that account for expensive tastes and talent pooling. This recognition provides one answer to critics who argue that the charitable tax subsidies are not just because they do not do enough to help the poor; these critics are essentially criticizing the use of expansive notions of resource egalitarianism and left-libertarianism. Theorists who argue that the deduction should be turned into a credit, however, do find support in these egalitarian and left-libertarian theories.

12

The Right to Autonomy as a Moral Foundation for the Realization Principle in Income Taxation

Charles Delmotte

The work of Thomas Piketty has engendered a twofold change in the economic viewpoint of many academics, policymakers, and laymen. Not only did his empirical analyses lead to a revitalization of the relevance of relative inequality, but his *Capital in the Twenty-First Century* also opened up a debate on tax justice. Given the accumulating nature of capital unravelled by Piketty, two tax measures are championed to decelerate the increasing wealth gap. In addition to wealth taxes—that is, levies imposed on the market value of one's fortune—Piketty delivers arguments for increasing the taxation of capital gains.

Given this greatly increased public interest in the taxation of capital, the present chapter supplements the debate on the *ideal capital gains tax* through its examination of a suitable technique for assessing income. On the one hand, one's assets can be taxed according to the annual increase in market value (the mark-to-market approach). On the other hand, the taxation of capital can be imposed on the income that one realizes from one's assets—the monetary benefits received in exchange for a transfer of property (the realization approach). Importantly, tax scholars quasi-unanimously decry the former practice in terms of equity and efficiency. Theoretically, the (diminishing) acceptance of the taxation of realized gains is merely founded on pragmatic concerns.

I will show that the taxation of realized gains is by no means an unfounded principle. Departing from a normative appreciation of each person having a specific end of his or her own, I will outline the problematic nature of the mark-to-market approach. In particular, I will exemplify that when we take general market prices as the basis for interpersonal comparisons—that is, to assess peoples' incomes—we violate people's autonomy. Specifically, the automatic attribution of market value underlying a mark-to-market approach measures people's incomes with standards and valorizations that are alien to their own views. The value of a realization-based tax lies exactly in the fact that such taxation replicates people's own valorizations, expressed in their confirmation of a particular price within an agreement (such as a sale).

By delivering a deontological defence of the realization principle, the current contribution intends to:

1. Establish a possible normative foundation for this theoretically denounced practice, and

Philosophical Foundations of Tax Law. First Edition. Edited by Monica Bhandari.

2. Supplement the debate on tax reform by suggesting the promotion of efficiency or redistribution in an autonomy-friendly fashion.

I. Thomas Piketty and the Manifestation of Relative Inequality

There are two basic normative assessments for an economic distribution. The first analyses peoples' absolute level of welfare. One approach states that what matters is not that people have the same level of income or wealth, but rather that they have enough, according to some standard of sufficiency.[1] The prioritarian tradition aims higher and states that we should target economic distributions that maximize the level of the least well-off.[2] When judging a particular economic situation, an underlying system is valued positively if it benefits those who are worst off more than an alternative system does, in terms of some particular standard.[3] A third application targets the maximization of welfare gains, without any particular regard for the distribution between persons.[4]

An alternative way of scrutinizing a specific distribution uses relative terms—that is, it does not matter how much people have; what matters is their economic relation. To judge a situation we do not look at what level of welfare people attain; what is important is whether others have more or less than they have.[5] A situation will be deemed to be positive if the differences between people's holdings are small, and deemed to be negative if there are huge differences between people's holdings.[6]

Applied to income—the accretion of wealth—the following comparison of alternative social situations can trigger our proper intuitions regarding the matter:

Society A	**Society B**
Richest 10% earn £30,000 per year	Richest 10% earn £100,000 per year
Poorest 10% earn £10,000 per year	Poorest 10% earn £20,000 per year

[1] A sufficientarian approach to social justice can be found in: Harry Frankfurt, 'Equality as a Moral Ideal', in Harry Frankfurt (ed.), *The Importance of What We Care About: Philosophical Essays* (Cambridge: Cambridge University Press, 1988), 134–58.

[2] The most famous variant of the 'prioritarian standard' was established by John Rawls's maximin principle, arguing that justice demands maximizing the primary goods for the worst off with in society. See John Rawls, *Theory of Justice* (Oxford: Oxford University Press, 1978), 152–6.

[3] A recent defence of social justice's primary aim to maximize welfare gains for the least well-off can be found in: John Tomasi, *Free Market Fairness* (Princeton: Princeton University Press, 2012).

[4] This is what is classically understood under (outcome) utilitarianism. See Amartya Sen, 'Utilitarianism and Welfarism', 76(9) *The Journal of Philosophy* (1979) 468.

[5] Such a position is defended by, for example, Larry Temkin in: 'Equality, Priority, and the Levelling Down Objection', in Matthew Clayton and Andrew Williams (eds), *The Ideal of Equality* (Houndmills: Macmillan, 2000), 126–61. Many other political philosophers defend such a comparative view on equality, albeit one that is limited in scope. Welfare inequality between persons is deemed principally wrong, but only to the extent that it is caused by inequality of endowment or opportunity for welfare. See Ronald Dworkin, 'What Is Equality? Part 2: Equality of Resources', 10(4) *Philosophy & Public Affairs* (1981) 283–345; John Roemer, 'A Pragmatic Theory of Responsibility for the Egalitarian Planner', 22(2) *Philosophy & Public Affairs* (1993) 146–66.

[6] Such a form of egalitarianism is discussed by Derek Parfitt in: 'Equality and Priority', 10(3) *Ratio* (1997) 202–21.

Some of us will intuitively opt for Society B as being the preferred situation, if we focus on *absolute* figures: a prioritarian approach would value Society B for yielding the most benefit for the least well-off, and a utilitarian approach would value it for generating the most overall welfare. Within this framework it does not matter that the richest 10 per cent own more than 80 per cent of the assets of Society B; what matters is how well off 'the poor' are, or how well off society as a whole is in terms of absolute numbers.

Others will opt for a *strict egalitarian standard*, and will choose Society A as the preferred situation. What people have is only relevant with respect to how much others have, and our final goal is to mitigate inequalities. Within this framework it does not matter that the poorest 10 per cent are above a certain standard of living and able to acquire a decent income; what matters is that the richest 10 per cent do not earn five times as much as them. Equality thus has value in itself.

Although for many years the International Monetary Fund (IMF), the World Bank, and almost all Western leaders promoted economic growth, and consequently focused on welfare gains in absolute numbers as a normative evaluation for an economic system, the ideal of maximizing standards and absolute numbers is currently fading. In the aftermath of the financial crisis in the first decade of this century, public attention shifted from a focus on growth and absolute welfare gains to an analysis of the distributive character of economic gains in relative terms. Many popular contributions have addressed this issue in terms of what part of 'the pie' goes to which percentile, confirming the relevancy of a notion of relative inequality.[7] It is significant that public authorities mirror this moral conversion and express political indignation at huge economic gaps. President Obama stated that 'the basic bargain at the heart of our economy has frayed' in response to the fact that the top 10 per cent of the population in the United States yields 50 per cent of the national income.[8] Furthermore, at the World Economic Forum (WEF) this year the subject of relative economic inequality was promoted as the core topic and the preferred economic prism, thus dethroning the notion of a maximizing analysis.[9] Prior to this, the IMF had already launched the idea of 'inclusive capitalism', aiming at a better distribution of profits between the members of society.[10]

[7] An illustration of the growing public importance of relative inequality can be found in: Danny Dorling, 'Growing Wealth Inequality in the UK is a Ticking Timebomb', *The Guardian* (15 October 2014), http://www.theguardian.com/commentisfree/2014/oct/15/wealth-inequality-uk-ticking-timebomb-credit-suisse-crash; Stewart Lansley, 'Why Economic Inequality Leads to Collapse', *The Guardian* (5 February 2012), http://www.theguardian.com/business/2012/feb/05/inequality-leads-to-economic-collapse; Christopher Ingraham, 'If You Thought Income Inequality Was Bad, Get a Load of Wealth Inequality', *The Washington Post* (21 May 2015), https://www.washingtonpost.com/news/wonk/wp/2015/05/21/the-top-10-of-americans-own-76-of-the-stuff-and-its-dragging-our-economy-down/; Michael Fletcher, 'White People Have 13 Dollars for Every Dollar Held by Black Americans', *The Washington Post* (12 December 2015), https://www.washingtonpost.com/news/wonk/wp/2015/05/21/the-top-10-of-americans-own-76-of-the-stuff-and-its-dragging-our-economy-down/.

[8] Remarks by the President on Economic Mobility, *Whitehouse.gov* (4 December 2013), http://www.whitehouse.gov/the-press-office/2013/12/04/remarks-president-economic-mobility.

[9] See World Economic Forum, Report 2015, 'Top 10 Trends 2015', http://reports.weforum.org/outlook-global-agenda-2015/top-10-trends-of-2015.

[10] See Christine Lagarde, 'Economic Inclusion and Financial Integrity—an Address to the Conference on Inclusive Capitalism' (27 May 2014), https://www.imf.org/external/np/speeches/2014/052714.htm.

Among many factors, the revival of an egalitarian normative outlook was certainly caused by a series of studies informing us of a tendency towards the accumulation of wealth and income in the hands of a few over the last few decades. The Organization for Economic Co-operation and Development (OECD) recently reported a concentration of wealth since the 1970s, and found that since around the year 2000 in many Western countries the bottom 50 per cent of the population has been holding a small fraction of the national wealth, while the top 10 per cent often holds about 50 per cent of it.[11] Credit Suisse confirms this observation and has identified a concentration of wealth over the last 40 years, when the relative share for the top 10 per cent started rising in the United States, in eight European countries, and in Australia.[12] Concerning the highly correlated issue of income inequality, the OECD found that the gap has never been so high: in its member countries today, the richest 10 per cent have an income 9.5 times the size of the poorest 10 per cent, whereas this ratio was only 7.1 in 1980.[13] Davies et al. confirm this concentration of wealth, and estimate on the basis of research in thirty-nine countries that the top 10 per cent of the population in 2000 held 71 per cent of all holdings.[14] Last but not least, Piketty's research in *Capital in the Twenty-First Century* certainly corroborates this current normative transition, revealing that for many Western countries, since the 1970s the top 10 per cent—and certainly the top 1 per cent—are holding an increasing proportion of national wealth.[15]

Piketty provides us not only with numbers but also with a causal analysis of the growing inequality of wealth, which together form an important empirical justification for certain theoretical (fiscal) measures that can oppose this trend.[16] The central thesis of his book is that over the last forty years the return on capital—by which Piketty means income from stocks, bonds, participations, shares, annuities, intangible assets, and real estate—has exceeded public economic growth.[17] This explains why wage earners have seen their wealth accrue to much smaller proportions than that of the capital owners; capital is highly unequally distributed and—given its cumulative nature—it is getting progressively more so. This corresponds with the findings of the Global Wealth Report, which emphasizes the correlation between the capital assets of a household and its wealth level.[18] Furthermore, the

[11] Kaja Bonesmo Fredriksen, 'Less Income Inequality and More Growth—Are they Compatible? Part 6. The Distribution of Wealth', *OECD Economics Department Working Papers*, No. 929, OECD Publishing 2012, 5–6.

[12] Credit Suisse, *Global Wealth Report 2014*, https://www.credit-suisse.com/uk/en/news-and-expertise/research/credit-suisse-research-institute/publications.html, 37.

[13] Federico Cingano, 'Trends in Income Inequality and Its Impact on Economic Growth', *OECD Social, Employment and Migration Working Papers*, No. 163, OECD Publishing 2014, http://dx.doi.org/10.1787/5jxrjncwxv6j-en, 9.

[14] James Davies, Susanna Sandström, Anthony Shorrocks, and Edward Wolf, 'The Level and Distribution of Global Household Wealth', 121(551) *The Economic Journal* (March 2011) 250.

[15] Piketty delivers evidence for a widening wealth gap in the countries for which sufficient information was available, such as Sweden, the United Kingdom, France, and the United States. See Thomas Piketty, *Capital in the Twenty-First Century*, Arthur Goldhammer (trans.) (Cambridge: Belknap, 2014), ch. 10; see Figures 10.1–10.5.

[16] See Section II for some redistributive measures in response to Piketty's observation.

[17] Piketty, n. 15, ch. 6. For Piketty's definition of capital (income), see Ibid., 18.

[18] *Global Wealth Report 2014*, n. 12, 34.

OECD points in the same direction, showing a noticeable effect of inclusion of capital gains on the share of the top 1 per cent of incomes in countries for which information was available.[19] This further coincides with the findings of Davies, which indicates that a disproportionate number of high incomes are derived from capital assets.[20]

We can thus observe the manifestation of economic inequality on two levels. First, empirically speaking, wealth is unequally distributed, and a tendency towards greater inequality can be observed in many Western countries. Capital plays a key role in this evolution, yielding relatively high revenues when compared with labour, leading to a concentration of wealth. Second, normatively speaking, by underwriting the problematic nature of this evolution, academics and public discourse are—often implicitly—adhering to an egalitarian standard, as they are confirming economic inequality to be intrinsically bad.

This development in economic philosophy cannot be perceived as an isolated matter—Piketty's analysis of relative inequality has already sparked a widespread debate on the political measures that should be taken, especially with regard to the key role that taxation should play.[21] Moreover, if taxation is supposed to be levied in accordance with the ability to pay, Piketty has raised awareness of tax codes' failure to reach capital owners.[22] In the light of current economic inequality, Piketty and others underline how current policies exacerbate this effect, and highlight the preferential treatment of capital income.[23]

[19] OECD, *Divided We Stand: Why Inequality Keeps Rising* (Paris: OECD Publishing, 2011), 349, 359.

[20] James B. Davies, 'Wealth and Economic Inequality', in Wiemer Salverda, Brian Nolan, and Timothy M. Smeeding (eds), *The Oxford Handbook of Economic Inequality* (Oxford: Oxford University Press, 2009), 137.

[21] In response to the regained interest in taxation from the prism of relative inequality, the New York University School of Law and the UCLA School of Law hosted a symposium on *Capital in the Twenty-First Century* on 4 October 2014, with the papers being published in the *Tax Law Review* in 2015. Another illustration of tax scholars' reaction is: Paul Caron and James Repetti, 'Occupy the Tax Code: Using the Estate Tax to Reduce Inequality and Spur Economic Growth', 40(5) *Pepperdine Law Review* (2013): 1255–90. See also Paul Caron, 'Thomas Piketty and Inequality: Legal Causes and Tax Solutions', 64 *Emory Law Journal Online* (2015) 2072–82; Shi-Ling Hsu, 'The Rise and Rise of the One Percent: Considering Legal Causes of Wealth Inequality', 64 *Emory Law Journal Online* (2015) 2043–72.

[22] Among other things, Piketty mentions low tax rates for capital income (and a decrease in progressive rates) as one of the factors causing growing wealth inequality. See Piketty, n. 15, ch. 14, 495–6.

[23] See, for example, Davies, n. 20, 143, in which he states: 'lower capital gains taxes seen in many countries since "supply side" reforms began in the Reagan/Thatcher years, have apparently made accumulation easier for the rich.' Martin J. McMahon, Jr confirms the role of the US tax system in the light of economic inequality; see Martin J. McMahon, Jr, 'The Matthew Effect and Federal Taxation', 45(5) *Boston College Law Review* (2004) 993–1128. Kaja Bonesmo Fredriksen also mentions the role of tax systems in enhancing inequality because of the preferential treatment of capital; see Kaja Bonesmo Fredriksen, n. 11, 16–18. Peter Hoeller et al. indicate the declining top income tax rates and the preferred treatment of capital gains as causes of inequality; see Peter Hoeller et al., 'Less Income Inequality and More Growth—Are they Compatible? Part 4, Top Incomes', *OECD Economics Department Working Papers* 927 (2012), http://dx.doi.org/10.1787/5k9h28wm6qmn-en, 9–11. For a technical critique on the current preferential tax treatment of capital gains, see Deborah Schenk, 'Saving the Income Tax with a Wealth Tax', 53(3) *Tax Law Review* (2000) 423–76.

II. Taxation of Capital and the Mark-to-Market Ideal in Income Tax Theory

Piketty thus triggered a debate on tax justice, causing politicians, organizations, and academics alike to examine measures to increase the fiscal burden on the wealthy. The debate has specifically revolved around examining various measures that could be upheld to increase fiscal contributions from capital owners. In order to conduct a specific analysis of tax justice, at least *three different types of taxation of capital* should be distinguished.

In order to overcome 'the indefinite increase of inequality of wealth', Piketty himself proposes the first type, the *wealth tax*: a levy on the value of one's holdings, irrespective of whether any revenue is being gained. In the absence of any transaction, a wealth tax is ideally levied on the market value of one's assets.[24]

Another possibility for targeting accumulative capital is to increase the taxation of revenue. Rather than taxing one's holdings, a capital gains tax is a form of income taxation, targeting only the gains that one's assets yield.[25] Capital gains taxation can take two forms depending on how income is assessed—and taxed.

One is the *market-to-market capitals gains tax*, which constitutes the second form of taxation of capital. This measure will tax capital as it accrues, and accordingly targets the annual increase in market value of one's holdings. The event that constitutes

[24] Limited forms of this wealth tax exist in many countries. For more information see Moris Lehner, 'The European Experience with a Wealth Tax: A Comparative Discussion', 53(615) *Tax Law Review* (1999–2000) 617–692. Piketty, however, endorses a global and universal wealth tax, which includes not only real estate but also all the components of capital, such as stocks, bonds, participations, shares pensions, annuities, intangible assets, and real estate; see Piketty, n. 15, 517. Such taxes exist in France and were, for example, proposed by the Belgian Francophone Socialist Party (PS), who brought a wealth tax bill into parliament to address the growing inequality; see Parti Socialiste, *Proposition de Loi Visant à introduire un impôt sur les grands patrimoines* (13 January 2015), www.dekamer.be/flwb/pdf/54/0770/54K0770001.pdf. For academic elaborations on wealth taxes in the light of inequality, see James Repetti, 'Democracy, Taxes, and Wealth', 76(3) *New York University Law Review* (2001) 825–73; Maureen Maloney, 'Distributive Justice: That is the Wealth Tax Issue', 20(3) *Ottawa Law Review* (1988) 601–35. An analysis of wealth taxation as an effective measure to tax capital gains is delivered in Schenk, n. 23, 423–76. From a different angle, see Stefan Bach et al., 'A Wealth Tax on the Rich to Bring Down Public Debt? Revenue and Distributional Effects of a Capital Levy in Germany', 35(1) *Fiscal Studies* (2014) 67–89.

[25] Several academics discuss the increased taxation of capital gains with reference to economic inequality. For instance, Piketty criticizes the decrease of capital gains' tax in many Western countries (see Piketty, n. 15, 495–6). Bankman and Shaviro also mention a surtax on capital income as the main candidate to mitigate wealth inequality; see Joseph Bankman and Daniel Shaviro, 'Piketty in America: A Tale of Two Literatures', 68(3) *Tax Law Review* (2015) 505. [Wijtvliet also champions the higher taxation of capital gains as an appropriate measure to mitigate wealth inequality; see Laurens Wijtvliet, 'Too Little, Too Late: The Uneasy Case for a Wealth Tax as a Means to Mitigate Inequality', 42(10) *Intertax* (2014) 642. Economists also propose that an increase in capital gains taxation—in the form of an equal taxation of income—is necessary in the light of equity and efficiency; see James Mirlees et al., 'The Mirrlees Review: Conclusions and Recommendations for Reform', 32(3) *Fiscal Studies* (2011) 331–59; Peter Diamond and Emmanuel Saez, 'The Case for a Progressive Tax: From Basic Research to Policy Recommendations', 25(4) *Journal of Economic Perspectives* (2011) 165–90. Such a tax shift was, for example, proposed by the OECD for Belgium; see *OECD*, Economic Survey of Belgium (February 2015), http://www.oecd.org/belgium/economic-survey-belgium.htm. President Obama also advanced an increase in capital gains taxation, up to 28 per cent; see Briefing Room, Press Release, The White House (17 January 2015), https://www.whitehouse.gov/the-press-office/2015/01/17/fact-sheet-simpler-fairer-tax-code-responsibly-invests-middle-class-fami.

taxation is thus the passing of a year and the increase in market value. This tax resembles the wealth tax in its assessment technique of focusing on the market value, but it remains an income tax nonetheless; a decrease in market value for a specific period will exclude taxation.

Finally, there is the *realization-based capital gains tax*, the third form of taxation of capital. Unlike the previous form of income taxation, which simply taxes value fluctuations, this measure presupposes the occurrence of a realization event, being the sale or exchange of an asset. The event that constitutes taxation is thus (agreement on) the receipt of a benefit (normally money) in exchange for the transfer of property. Both are income taxes and aim only to tax gains.

Within the theoretical distinction outlined above, this chapter deals primarily with the last two forms of taxation. The general increased interest in tax justice will thus be compressed to the issue of the taxation of capital income. To the extent that growing wealth inequality is caused by capital income and exacerbated by its preferential fiscal treatment, a primary solution appears to be increasing the use of the capital gains tax.[26]

Prior to any general increase in tax rates, one has to outline a particular conception of income. When do stocks, bonds, participations, shares, pensions, annuities, intangible assets, and real estate yield an income? Given the continued acceptance of—and renewed interest for—an income tax, one can detect a normative chasm in terms of which of the above-mentioned standards should apply in income taxation.

Most parts of current tax codes, and people's common intuitions alike, support the realization approach: income is the receipt—or at least a legal agreement over the receipt—of a tangible benefit.[27] Consequently, one should only be taxed when actually receiving contemporaneous benefits from a sale or exchange of property, or at least agreeing to such a receipt.

In contrast, taxation theory defines income as the sum of (1) the market value of rights exercised in consumption, and (2) the change in the value of the store of property rights between the beginning and end of the period in question.[28] This latter view on income includes the accretion of capital, and it consequently allows authorities to tax any increase in the market value of one's assets, irrespective of the occurrence of a sale or exchange.[29] Following this definition, scholars working in the field of income

[26] See Bankman and Shaviro, n. 25, 505; Wijtvliet, n. 25, 642.

[27] See, for example, Jeffrey L. Kwall, 'When Should Asset Appreciation Be Taxed? The Case for a Disposition Standard of Realization', 86(1) *Indiana Law Review* (2011) 79. People generally oppose a conception that follows the mark-to-market approach, since income is commonly conceived as an actual receipt, while an increase in value is regarded as a mere 'paper gain'; see Deborah Schenk, 'A Positive Account of the Realization Rule', 57(3) *Tax Law Review* (2004) 377.

[28] This highly influential definition is often called the 'Haig-Simons' concept of income, after Henry C. Simons and Robert Haig; see Henry Simons, *Personal Income Taxation: The Definition of Income as a Problem of Fiscal Policy* (Chicago: University of Chicago Press, 1938), 49–50; Robert Murray Haig, 'The Concept of Income—Economic and Legal Aspects', in Robert Murray Haig (ed.), *The Federal Income Tax* (New York: Columbia University Press, 1921), 27.

[29] The so-called Haig-Simmons concept of income logically justifies a mark-to-market tax; see, for example, John Robert H. Scarborough, 'Different Rules for Different Players and Products: The Patchwork Taxation of Derivatives', 72(12) *Taxes* (1994) 1031–49; Deborah H. Schenk, 'Taxation of Equity Derivatives: A Partial Integration Proposal', 50(4) *Tax Law Review* (1995) 571–642; John B. Shoven and Paul Taubman, 'Saving, Capital Income, and Taxation', in Henry J. Aaron and Michael J. Boskin

taxation embrace the mark-to-market approach as an ideal assessment method.[30] Whether or not one monetizes an increase of 10 per cent of one's fortune is of no importance to the ideal income tax. As income occurs with accretion, taxation merely demands an increase in market value.

Tax theory discerns the continued application of the realization principle in existing tax codes as 'the basic defect' of income taxation, and no serious scholar seems to ascribe it any normative foundation.[31] Vilified for reasons of both equity and efficiency, the 'Achilles' heel of the income tax' even led a group of tax scholars to support a shift in tax base.[32] In particular, an impressive amount of contributions have criticized the 'deferral' of the taxation of economic gains until realization, for creating substantial investment distortions and inefficiencies.[33] More specifically, the literature points at taxpayers' ability to manipulate their tax debt under the realization principle. In this sense the realization-based approach can be pinpointed as one of the elements causing inequality, as it enables capital owners to circumvent their tax duties. Imposing taxation only when investments generate gains leaves the possibility of debt-financed consumption, strategic trading, the strategic timing of asset dispositions, and portfolio adjustments for financial investments.[34]

Furthermore, the realization principle also conflicts with the traditional aims of equity, as it fails to treat different sources of income equally.[35] Once one adheres to the view that economic advantages for assets rise with the increase of their market value,

(eds), *The Economics of Taxation* (Washington, DC: Brookings Institute, 1980), 211–13; Reed Shuldiner, 'Consistency and the Taxation of Financial Products', 70(12) *Taxes* (1992) 781–93.

[30] Fred B. Brown, '"Complete" Accrual Taxation', 33(4) *San Diego Law Review* (1996) 1559–680; David J. Shakow, 'Taxation without Realization: A Proposal for Accrual Taxation', 134(5) *University of Pennsylvania Law Review* (1986) 1111–205.

[31] See, for example, William D. Andrews, 'The Achilles Heel of the Comprehensive Income Tax', in Charles E. Walker and Mark A. Bloomfield (eds), *New Directions in Federal Tax Policy for the 1980s* (Cambridge, MA: Ballinger, 1983), 278 (identifying the realization principle as one of the main culprits for the failure to adhere to a comprehensive income tax ideal); Gerard M. Brannon, 'Tax Loopholes as Original Sin: Lessons from Tax History', 31(6) *Villanova Law Review* (1986) 1763–85; and for a recent confirmation see Edward J. McCaffery, 'A New Understanding of Tax', 103(5) *Michigan Law Review* (2005) 889, in which he states: 'The realization requirement destroys the source of neutrality of an ideal income tax.'

[32] Most tax scholars see a possibility in obtaining a consumption tax; see Joseph Bankman and David Weisbach, 'Consumption Taxation Is Still Superior to Income Taxation', 60(3) *Stanford Law Review* (2007) 789–803; Daniel N. Shaviro, 'Replacing the Income Tax with a Progressive Consumption Tax', 103 *Tax Notes* (2004) 91–113.

[33] Brown, n. 30, 1559; Noel B. Cunningham and Deborah H. Schenk, 'Taxation without Realization: A "Revolutionary" Approach to Ownership', 47(4) *Tax Law Review* (1992) 725–814; Daniel Halperin, 'Saving the Income Tax: An Agenda for Research', 77 *Tax Notes* (1997): 967–77; Stephen B. Land, 'Defeating Deferral: A Proposal for Retrospective Taxation', 52(1) *Tax Law Review* (1996): 45–118; David M. Schizer, 'Realization as Subsidy', 73 *New York University Law Review* (1998) 1549–626; David A. Weisbach, 'A Partial Mark-to-Market Tax System', 53(1) *Tax Law Review* (1999), 95–136.

[34] On debt-financed consumption, see McCaffery, n. 31, 888. On strategic trading see David Elkins, 'The Myth of Realization: Mark-to-Market Taxation of Publicly-Traded Securities', 10(5) *Florida Tax Review* (2010) 375–407; Mark P. Gergen, 'The Effects of Price Volatility and Strategic Trading under Realization, Expected Return and Retrospective Taxation', 49(2) *Tax Law Review* (1994) 209–68. On timing see Myron Scholes et al., *Taxes and Business Strategy: A Planning Approach* (Upper Saddle River: Prentice Hall, 2009), 185–9. On portfolio adjustments see Bankman and Shaviro, n. 25, 477–85; Schenk, n. 27, 426–35.

[35] Ibid., 93; Kwall, n. 27, 93.

a realization-based tax can be seen as ignoring vital increases in one's well-being. The deferral of taxation until the moment of receipt is thus presented as a tax benefit in favour of capital.[36] Reluctance to tax capital as it fluctuates primarily benefits those whose assets contain capital, and this contributes to economic inequality.[37]

As hard as it will be to find a *principled* defence for the realization principle, many tax scholars do grant it some pragmatic support.[38] As expressed in the seminal work of Robert Haig, the realization principle is to be pictured as 'merely a concession made to the exigencies of a given situation'.[39] In particular, two reasons are acknowledged in support of this 'rule of convenience'.[40] First, the realization principle is deemed necessary because a tax on an increase in value without realization raises liquidity problems. Under a mark-to-market approach the event triggering the tax (the passage of a year and the increase in value) does not generate cash to pay the tax.[41] Consequently, taxes on accrued market values force taxpayers to sell their assets or to borrow money.[42] Second, a tax on accrued values requires an annual valuation of one's assets. In the absence of any actual receipt, tax administrators need to assess—and prove—the precise net value of one's gains. Moreover, many tax scholars recognize the difficulty and cost for tax authorities to monitor the market value of one's assets on a yearly basis.[43] Additionally, a market assessment might be difficult for some goods and might lead to much dispute with the tax authorities.[44] Hence the realization principle lingers on in most parts of our income tax systems.

Dominant income tax theory balances the ideals of a mark-to-market approach and the reality of the above-mentioned 'concession'. Researchers nonetheless plead for a prudent shift towards market assessment. In this regard, scholars are trying to convince policymakers that the taxation of value fluctuations would disturb taxpayers' affairs less than the liquidity argument assumes.[45] Concerning the valuation problem, proponents of the mark-to-market approach believe that for most assets a stable,

[36] This advantage is further discussed by Engler and Knoll; see Mitchell L. Engler and Michael S. Knoll, 'Simplifying the Transition to a (Progressive) Consumption Tax', 56(53) *Southern Methodist University Law Review* (2003) 53–81.

[37] Kwall, n. 27, 93.

[38] For confirmation of the non-normative nature of the realization principle, see Mitchell L. Engler, 'A Progressive Consumption Tax for Individuals: An Alternative Hybrid Approach', 54 *Alabama Law Review* (2003) 1210; Mary L. Heen, 'An Alternative Approach to the Taxation of Employment Discrimination Recoveries under Federal Civil Rights Statutes: Income from Human Capital, Realization, and Nonrecognition', 72 *North Carolina Law Review* (1994) 549–618; Stephen B. Land, 'Defeating Deferral: A Proposal for Retrospective Taxation', 52(1) *Tax Law Review* (1996) 45–118.

[39] Thomas Reed Powell, 'The Constitutional Aspects of Federal Income Taxation', in Haig (ed.), n. 28, 65.

[40] Schenk, n. 27, 358.

[41] Kwall, 27, 98.

[42] See, for example, Brown, n. 30, 1560, in which he states: 'Accrual taxation presents serious problems of its own—the difficulty of valuing assets and possible taxpayer illiquidity.'

[43] David M. Schizer, 'Realization as Subsidy', 73(5) *New York University Law Review* (1998) 1594; Schenk, n. 29, 630.

[44] See James Ripetti, 'Commentary: It's All About Valuation', 53(4) *Tax Law Review* (2000) 612.

[45] See Schenk, arguing that the liquidity problem is not considerable enough to justify realization: Schenk, n. 27, 360–436.

established market price can be detected, and the issue is less insurmountable than previously assumed.[46]

III. Towards a Deontological Defence of the Realization Principle

If the Piketty revolution results in concrete political eagerness to adopt a more ambitious tax on income from capital, the previous section has already outlined a theoretic consensus on the ideal assessment method. Although much of taxation theory grants no direct priority to mitigate inequality, it nonetheless alerts us to the fact that the realization principle is a benefit for capital owners.[47]

Any tax (or redistributive) system relies on two questions: what should be taxed and how should it be measured? Assuming the appropriateness of an income tax, this chapter will try to deliver a deontological defence of the realization principle. By explicating the moral problems of a mark-to-market approach I supplement the debate on tax justice. Moreover, I underwrite the moral impermissibility of a capital gains tax based on this assessment technique. To the extent that it relies on market values, the conclusions concerning the valuation standard for income also shed light on the permissibility of a wealth tax. Furthermore, by showing that the right to autonomy delivers a normative basis for the realization principle, I wish to challenge the consensus in taxation theory that the principle has no normative foundations.

The approach exemplified here will be different to the traditional normative framework governing taxation theory. Taxation will not be primarily presented as a means to optimize economic outcomes, but will also be seen as a matter of justice—here understood as legitimate (i.e. morally permissible) coercion. Rather than finding an *optimal* taxation, the aim here is to uncover a *just* taxation—a taxation policy that is consistent with people's fundamental rights and liberties. The latter are here accepted as 'prerequisites for the legitimate exercise of democratic authority' and create moral boundaries for governmental action.[48] Correspondingly, the sort of tax policies that are permissible depend on a prior analysis of people's rights over their holdings and their person. Importantly, as will be elaborated in Section III.F, the presented deontological framework does not disturb redistributive or efficiency-related reform, as it opens up strategies to revise the current interpretation of the realization principle.

This section will outline the constraints of the right to autonomy on the proper assessment standard of income. First, I will exemplify the common intuition of the

[46] Ibid., 365–70. See also Schmudde, mentioning the emergence of financial products that have a secure value: David Schmudde, 'Responding to the Subprime Mess: The New Regulatory Landscape for an Integrated Defense of Market Assessment', 14(4) *Fordham Journal of Corporate & Financial Law* (2009) 711. For an integrated defence of the mark-to-market approach, see Shakow and Shuldiner, who conclude that 7.5 per cent of all assets would be hard to value: David Shakow and Reed Shuldiner, 'A Comprehensive Wealth Tax', 53(4) *Tax Law Review* (2000) 529.

[47] The traditional prior aim of the dominant 'theory of optimal taxation' is to reduce inefficiencies and market distortions imposed by taxation. See, for example, Joel Slemrod, 'Optimal Taxation and Optimal Tax Systems', 4(1) *Journal of Economic Perspectives* (1990) 157–78. For an avowal on tax theories' disregard for relative inequality, see Bankman and Shaviro, n. 25, 455.

[48] John Tomasi, *Free Market Fairness* (Princeton: Princeton University Press, 2013), 76.

presumption of liberty (III.A), after which I will provide a general conceptualization of autonomy (III.B). Next, I will present valorizations as a function of autonomy (III.C). From this I will deduce the problematic nature of general market prices as a basis for interpersonal comparisons, and will articulate the normative basis for the realization principle (III.D). Finally, I will outline how the presented theory relates to some concurring work in taxation theory (III.E) and defend its unification with other aims in an integrated approach (III.F).

A. The Presumption of Liberty

Stanley Benn raises the example of a person named Alan sitting on a public beach. He has a pebble in each hand and is enjoying splitting them.[49] Benn asks us to envisage a second person, Betty, who prevents Alan from continuing his activity by handcuffing him or removing all the pebbles out of his reach. Benn notes that Alan would be within his rights to demand a justification from Betty, while Betty would not be within her rights to demand an explanation for Alan's pebble splitting. So while Alan might justifiably resent Betty's interference, Betty has no grounds for complaint against Alan. So if a third person were to observe this situation, she would not ask why Alan was splitting pebbles, but rather why Betty was preventing him from doing so.

Benn illuminates a basic *asymmetry* in our normative outlook: we seek justification not for why people act the way they do, but rather for why others would want to prevent them from doing so. The initial onus of justification lies not on the person acting but rather on the person interfering with those actions. Even if most people might find Alan engaging in a useless activity, they still think he is under no requirement to justify his actions. The onus lies on Betty, who will need to explain her justification for imposing restrictions on Alan's actions. This is exactly what Joel Feinberg calls presumption in favour of liberty: 'liberty should be the norm, [while] coercion always needs some special justification.'[50]

Interestingly, we have this attitudinal bias in favour of actions for *persons*. Imagine Betty interfering with some pebbles on a beach, preventing them from flowing back into the sea. An observer would not be inclined to ask her why she is intervening in the lives of the pebbles in the same way that would be asked if she were preventing other people from acting as they want. The principle of nonintervention that follows from the presumption of liberty is one we apply when we deal with adult persons. As long as there are no compelling reasons to intervene, all people have a moral claim to do as they wish until some justification is offered for limiting their liberty.[51] We do not ask why we can cross a border, why we can have consenting sexual contact, or why we can have the freedom to choose our occupation; rather, we would demand a justification if those liberties were curtailed.

[49] Stanley Benn, *A Theory of Freedom* (Cambridge: Cambridge University Press, 1988), 87.
[50] Joel Feinberg, *Harm to Others* (New York: Oxford University Press, 1984), 9.
[51] See Feinberg discussing some common justifications for intervention: Ibid., 10 ff.

B. The Right to Autonomy

But why is this the case? Why does the onus of justification lie on the interferer, rather than on the people who are acting the way they are? Why is freedom the norm, and why are we not allowed to act with people in the same way as we act with objects, plants, and animals?

The answer to these questions is tied to a fundamental quality of persons: *purposes*. We do not lie in a particular place in the same way that a pebble lies somewhere. We do not go and swim in the sea for the same reason that a crab does so. We consider humans to be 'persons' because their existence is not merely the outcome of external stimuli, but is embedded in 'purposes that [their] actions [are] designed to promote'.[52] We distinguish ourselves from objects and animals in this world because our actions are the outcome of intentions connected to personal goals. According to Benn this phenomenology of 'personal causation' delivers the moral underpinning of our conception of 'natural persons'.[53]

The axiom underlying the presumption of liberty is thus connected with an understanding that each person acts purposefully. The purpose underlying our actions is to attain our goals and the intention to do so is our motivation. However, this in itself does not entail a prescriptive attitude: one may, for example, hold the political view that every person's goals—and thus also their distinctive actions—should be matched to one common end. We can find the foundation of the presumption of liberty when we grant positive moral status to each person as a purposeful entity. Indeed, the right to autonomy arises from a normative appreciation of each person having an end of his or her own, which consequently acknowledges each person's *claim* to act in the light of this.

Hence, autonomy should be understood as the normative embodiment of purposeful behaviour. So, from an understanding that all people have their own purposes, we delineate the axiomatic right to act and live according to these. The reason that we do not demand justification for how Alan is acting, but rather for why Betty is intervening with his actions, is because each person has a separate end, and all people have the right to live and act accordingly.[54] In terms of autonomy, the focus lies not on the content of the act but on the fact that it counts as *one's own*.

The scope of one's rights is limited by the equal rights of one's fellow. Consequently, autonomy delineates a moral space around each person, which constructs the territory wherein interference is principally illegitimate.[55] Traditionally, the 'moral space' that demarcates people's sovereign domain is constructed by their body, their mind, and their property.[56] One's physical body parts, mental and physical capacities,

[52] Geoffrey Brennan and Loren Lomasky, *Democracy and Decision: The Pure Theory of Electoral Preference* (Cambridge, UK: Cambridge University Press, 1993), 9.

[53] Benn, n. 49, 91.

[54] See also Gaus, who connects the presumption of liberty with a Kantian conception of moral autonomy: Gerald Gaus, 'The Place of Autonomy within Liberalism', in Joel Anderson and John Christman (eds), *Autonomy and the Challenges to Liberalism: New Essays* (Cambridge, UK: Cambridge University Press, 2005), 272–306.

[55] See Feinberg using a 'territorial model' to conceptualize autonomy: Feinberg, n. 50, 53 ff.

[56] Ibid., 54.

knowledge, experience, and rightfully obtained external goods all form part of one's personal sphere, and can be used according to one's wishes in the pursuit of one's personal ends.[57]

The reason that we cannot forbid Alan to split pebbles or impose a religion on Betty, and that we oppose forced labour and prosecute rape, and even that we despise manipulation, is because we recognize each person as an embodied, a choosing being with the right to pursue his or her own distinctive purpose. This fundamental axiom discloses the underpinning of more specific principles, such as freedom of religion, freedom of speech, and the free movement of persons. But it is also the case that contract law (where people are only bound by consent) or the precepts of tort law (where people need to compensate for damage to another's sovereign domain) are an elaboration of the right of each person to live according his or her own ends.

C. Valorizations as a Function of Autonomy

The right to autonomy justifies the radical diversity in people's actions: people opt for different subjects of study, strive for different jobs, and develop different hobbies. People want different things because they have different goals and preferences, and the principle of autonomy defends this variety as a consequence of people's moral rights. This also entails consequences regarding goods. As stressed by one of the founding fathers of the theory of marginal utility, goods have no intrinsic value themselves—people attribute value to their own ends and consequently carry this over to economic goods as a means of satisfying these ends.[58] Given the fact that people have different goals and preferences, they will assign different values to the same goods. Because of people's divergent ends, they adopt distinctive standards of value (or 'utility'), which lead to different rankings. For someone who embraces rock and roll as the highest personal good, concerts might be the most important happening in a weekend, whereas another person might build his weekend around his football team. People's distinctive standards follow from their distinctive ends, which ultimately come down to their differing views on utility—and economically this leads to conflicting monetary valorizations. For the rock and roll fan, a £500 ticket to see the Rolling Stones might be a good buy, whereas a classical music adept might deride this price as a sign of the aesthetic decline of our times. Someone might consider the price of petrol to be absurd, given his preference for public transport, whereas a keen motorbiker might perceive it as a small price to pay for the feeling of liberty she gets from riding her motorbike. If everybody had the same goals and preferences then everybody would buy the same products, and goods sold to equally wealthy people would end up being the same

[57] The rights over one's body, mind, or external property do not necessarily involve the full right to income, so income taxation is not necessarily a violation of the sovereign domain. See, for example, Peter Vallentyne, 'Taxation, Redistribution and Property Rights', in Andrei Marmor (ed.), *The Routledge Companion to Philosophy of Law* (New York: Routledge, 2012), 291–301. For an elaboration of the difference between control and income ownership, see John Christman, *The Myth of Property: Toward an Egalitarian Theory of Ownership* (New York: Oxford University Press, 1994), 129–35.

[58] Carl Menger, *Principles of Economics*, James Dingwall and Bert F. Hoselitz (eds and trans) (Glencoe: The Free Press, 1950), 116.

price. Yet people assign different valorizations to goods and services, which reflect their different views on well-being flowing from their respective ends. For one person the £500,000 salary of a stockbroker would not compensate the missed opportunity to follow her natural calling to be an academic, whereas being a stockbroker might be another person's dream job, and he would gladly accept half that salary to be able to do it. We thus see that the valorizations we attach to goods are *a function of our autonomy.*

From the perspective outlined here, market prices have no 'objective' status. Although in our everyday lives we see fixed prices as secure features of goods and services, these should rather be seen as compressions of different valorizations that people give to goods. Moreover, the market price is the aggregate of the valorizations of all the consumers in a market.[59] As George Stigler makes clear, these can be conceived as an election result, whereby everybody has some minimal influence on the outcome, even though the result does not reflect anyone's valorizations.[60] The high wages of many football players and the low prices (compared to production costs) of academic books are signs of general consumer preferences in society, yet they do not reflect any individual valorizations. My personal ranking might put the purchase of an academic book much higher than obtaining a football ticket. Similarly, the low prices for real estate in the countryside express society's general preference to live in the city, but obviously individuals can have the opposite ranking of value.

General prices therefore do not tell us anything about the utility standards of potential suppliers. The high prices for corporate tax lawyers indicate the high value that many businesses attach to fiscal analyses. These do not spell out the value standard of a particular lawyer, who might prefer to deliver academic services for an average wage. And the high price of renting modern apartments in city centres merely informs us about the preferences of urban citizens and businesses to live or work in apartments—it does not give us any indication about the utility standards of the owners of these apartments, who might have completely different plans.

However, at the moment of effective *consent* over an amount of money in exchange for goods or services, prices transform into something that is more than sociological (the general market price) or psychological (a particular offer in an individual setting); they become information about people's utility standards. A consented price is a confirmation that a particular amount of money is seen as a valid valorization according to one's own utility standards. The fact that I effectively purchase an academic book confirms that I find this good valuable and I perceive the price as acceptable in view of my ends. And the fact that I accept a 'high' price for a house in the countryside counts as a confirmation of its value in the light of my somewhat deviant living preferences. So with regard to income, when the tenant of the city centre apartment effectively *accepts* the high rental price, she confirms this amount of money as a valid price according her own utility standards. If the well-established academic changes his profession because of a changed purpose (e.g. if he now has a family and wants to provide them

[59] See Hayek identifying a price as a result of how people valorize the same things differently: Friedrich Hayek, *The Mirage of Social Justice* (London: Routledge and Kegan Paul, 1976), 76.

[60] For prices as a result of individual consumer votes, see George Stigler, *The Theory of Price* (New York: Macmillan, 1987), 12.

with as high a standard of living as possible), he confirms the high price for corporate tax services as an appropriate benefit within his own standards of value.

To summarize, we can say that because people all have ends of their own, they will also have value standards of their own. Consequently, the right to autonomy recognizes that each person has personal valorizations as a function of his or her own subjective ends. From this perspective we have to downgrade market prices as an aggregate of other people's standards. At the occurrence of an exchange of property or services for money, people express their subjective standards in terms of a quantifiable homogeneous commodity: money.[61]

D. Autonomy and Taxation

Alan is not only a fan of pebble-splitting: he also works as an engineer for a medium-sized company. Considering his love for his family and his appetite for holidays and weekends, he did not opt for the highest-paying opportunity. Each year he earns £72,000 with his mathematical skills. Besides this he owns an apartment that he uses for artists' exhibitions, for which he paid £200,000. Additionally, he invested £20,000 to support his best friend's company.

During the hot summer months, however, a number of people discover Alan's capital (including his human capital), and express their value standards regarding some of his means. When he comes back he finds several offers in his mailbox. First, the raised general market value of his apartment translated into an offer: a local investor wishes to give him £400,000 to buy it and rent it to small businesses. Second, his friend's company managed to sign up a new big client, resulting in a doubling of the value of his shares. As if the summer has not already been profitable enough for Alan, an engineering company has tracked him down and given him an offer of working in a management position, earning three times his current wage. Finally, Alan has quite an unusual blood type, and an Indian businessman with an identical blood type offers him £1 million to buy his kidney via an intermediate company that commercializes human organs.

1. *The mark-to-market approach*

Most tax scholars will agree that Alan will come home a 'richer' man: income equals an increase in value of one's holdings for a period of time, and tax codes should not remain blind to Alan's very lucrative summer.[62] Concerning his external means, his shares undeniably went up £20,000 in value and the current market value of his

[61] As mentioned in Section III.F, the requirement of confirmation of a particular monetary benefit is not restricted to the sale or transfer of property.

[62] As mentioned above, for most tax scholars, a taxation of income merely demands an increase in market value. See, for example, Reed Shuldiner, 'Consistency and the Taxation of Financial Products', 70(12) *Taxes* (1992) 781, in which he states: 'The Haig-Simons definition of income, accretions to wealth plus the value of consumption, is generally accepted as an appropriate definition of income for purposes of a comprehensive income tax.' See also Schenk, where a global mark-to-market regime taxing accretions is presented as a normative ideal: Schenk, n. 30, 572–3.

apartment of approximately £400,000 means an increase in value of 100 per cent compared with last year. An ideal income tax, as supported in the cited literature, would include an end-of-year economic appreciation of these assets and would attribute Alan a capital income of £220,000. A tax targeting the value of his human capital, however, would not be advocated by most tax scholars due to the inevitable problems with conducting a proper valuation and to the possible lack of liquidity; a structural mark-to-market approach would seem insurmountable. It is indeed difficult to assess the market price of one's skills, and taxpayers who do not use their greatest earning potential would often not have the means to pay their tax debt. In our current example these 'administrative' concerns are not at stake, however: Alan has no liquidity problems (he inherited several million pounds) and we have a perfect example of the market price of his bio-capital (£1 million for his kidney and £216,000 for his mathematical skills).

Yet this analysis indicates that the absence of any valuation or liquidity problems does not overcome deeper normative objections concerning the *automatic* application of these market values in the assessment of income. From the perspective of autonomy, the challenge for the accretion-based tax is identical in all four of the above situations. As we saw, valorizations are a function of autonomy. The prices for Alan's kidney, apartment, and shares reflect the desires of others who want to acquire these means, and the price for his skills stems from people's wish to rely on his skills. All of these prices, however, conflict with Alan's own purposes: he does not perceive his kidney as a commodity and would not sell it at any price. He enjoys his current job and does not perceive three times his wage to be sufficient compensation for the loss of free time that the new job would entail. Likewise, he bought the apartment to cultivate his aesthetic passions and fund young artists, and the money the investor is willing to transfer does not fit into any of his plans. Finally, he sees his shares as a financial support for his friend, and so has no plans whatsoever to sell them; this rise in share value reflects the interest of other investors in the company rather than any of Alan's own interests.

The economist's view on taxation might stress the fact that Alan has come home to a new situation: given the valorizations for his apartment, shares, kidney, and skills his economic 'position' has changed. By contrast, the current subjectivist normative outlook would claim that *nothing* has changed for Alan; he has rejected all of these offers and has not altered any of his plans—these valorizations have no meaning from the perspective of his own utility standard.

Commencing from a viewpoint of people as active, choosing entities we can see that valorizations are embedded in a subjective life plan. Each price reflects particular decisions in the light of further ends, which are often unknown to others. Assigning valorizations that reflect decisions that one does not plan, and preferences that one does not hold, is incongruous to autonomy. Moreover, it defines one's tax liability according to a value standard that could be completely contradictory to one's own. In general, when we take market prices as the assessment basis for interpersonal comparisons, we ignore people's own vision of well-being and impose valorizations that are alien to their own. Under a mark-to-market approach, Alan's tax base is nothing more than a representation of what of others would like him to do; even if he had no liquidity problems, he would object to paying taxes on £1 million for his kidney, on £216,000 for his job offer, on £20,000 for his shares, and on £200,000 for his apartment. His objection would rely on the principle of autonomy, claiming that he was being assessed in terms of subjective utility calculations that were completely alien to the standards by which he governed his own life. The content of one's duties (the tax base) gets one-sidedly defined by prices reflecting other people's intentions over one's means. From the perspective outlined here, we can coin this practice as a *heteronomous tax base*: the taxpayer is being ordered to comply with fiscal duties on the basis of unconsented valorizations.

From this perspective, we can recast the commonly raised problems regarding a mark-to-market approach. The problem is not that one might not have the cash to pay one's tax debt, or that tax administrators might have a difficult time assessing a true market value. Rather, the fundamental problem is that there is no 'true value' in the sense that nothing has an intrinsic, objective value; consequently, mere market valorizations can conflict with one's own standards. When we grasp how this measurement technique attributes unconsented valorizations, the disturbing nature of the mark-to-market approach in the taxpayer's life, for example in terms of liquidity issues, is simply an unsurprising consequence.

In summary, our right to autonomy discloses our intuitive protest against a mark-to-market approach. Valorizations are a function of autonomy, and by calculating tax obligations on the basis of non-shared valorizations the market-to-market approach dictates the standard of the market and ignores people's own vision of well-being.

2. *The realization approach*

Imagine that Alan changes his life radically in a couple of years: he remarries and adopts an exuberant lifestyle after having lost half of his means due to the messy divorce with his ex-wife. His consumption now exceeds his income, but despite his hedonistic lifestyle he does not want to withdraw from his responsibility regarding his children, and so plans to finance their university studies. Given this situation, Alan decides to sacrifice his shares and apartment in order to be able to fund his two children's degrees. On top of this, he wants to maintain his high-flying lifestyle by acquiring an apartment in an upmarket neighbourhood.

Despite his need for money, he sells his shares back to his friend at 25 per cent below the market price for just £30,000. Since he is one of the few friends who supported Alan during the last two years, he perceives this as a nice way to thank him. Furthermore, he uses his excellent negotiating skills to sell his apartment at £450,000, exceeding its market value. Putting aside any maintenance costs that he may have incurred over the years, he realizes a profit of £260,000 following these transactions.

Contrary to the previous situation, this figure is not a general market price but a monetary benefit that Alan consented to by means of his own value standard. Each of the figures involved arises from particular intentions with respect to his purposes (paying for his children's studies, acquiring a new apartment, and thanking his friend). These figures do not reflect the estimations of what other people would want in order to acquire his means; rather, they resemble Alan's choices in the light of his subjective ends.

An appreciation of the right to live according to one's own purposes unravels the normative role of the realization principle. General prices reflect transactions and preferences that might or might not fit with one's ends. Real-life exchanges, on the other hand, consist of people's true actions whereby they exteriorize their own value standard. Consented prices are more than psychological information about other people's goals and preferences: they are confirmation of a particular valorization that is a function of autonomy. So the economic equilibrium reached when a person consents to a price reflects one's subjective preferences in terms of the most homogeneous and quantifiable commodity: money. The importance of the receipt of a benefit in exchange for the use or sale of property is that through this event people signal their utility standard in an observable way. The value of the realization principle is exactly that such a method does not invade one's tax liability on the basis of other people's valorizations; instead, it replicates a person's subjective valorizations as expressed in consented monetary benefits. By submitting one's own valorizations as administrative input for tax authorities, taxpayers are not forced to live—and pay taxes—according to market preferences. Instead, they are only required to pay a contribution according to their own value standard. The realization principle thus protects taxpayers' liability against external standards and guarantees that their obligations will be calculated in terms of their own utility calculations as expressed in market exchanges. Consequently, as the realization standard supervenes on their own consented valorizations, it will not impose any alien vision of well-being.

To summarize, we can state that the right to live according to one's own ends delivers normative justification for the generally reviled principle of taxation after realization. In particular, the right of each person to live according to one's own ends and preferences entails a duty for tax authorities not to impose any valorizations that one does not share. The moral status of the realization principle lies precisely in the fact that when people monetize certain assets and goods (such as via sales or transfers), they externalize their preferences in consented valorizations. So the realization event, meant as the contractual confirmation of a certain monetary benefit, is more than the point in time when one 'effectuates one's prior economic income' (i.e. when an asset merely increases in value);[63] it is the *morally decisive turning point* when one confirms a price or offer as being consistent with one's ends. In the absence of any general objective measure of utility, monetization yields a confirmation of valorization according to a person's own standard. Before such a moment, tax authorities fail to have any reliable information on a person's preferences and valorizations, and will fail to construe a tax base without violating the autonomy principle. As the realization principle supervenes on one's own consented valorizations, it consolidates the taxpayer's own view on well-being within the domain of income tax.

[63] For such an apprehension of income occurring irrespective of any realization, see for example, Kwall, n. 27, 80; Brown, n. 30, 1559–1680; Shakow, n. 30, 1111–205.

E. Personal and Market Goods

In an excellent article Ilan Benshalom and Kendra Stead make a distinction that might have come to the reader's mind by now. On the one hand, they picture 'investment goods' like portfolio holdings and company shares; for these 'emotionally non-fungible assets' they state that it is 'reasonable to assign tax liability for that asset's fluctuation in value according to a mark-to-market regime'.[64] Aiming at an equal taxation of increased well-being (as measured by welfare), the authors qualify the market price as a good proxy. On the other hand, they envisage personal goods like inherited jewellery, self-created artwork, residential homes, and family businesses; for these goods they dismiss the mark-to-market approach as a 'bad proxy for well-being'.[65] Moreover, the authors are convinced that for personal goods the taxpayer's 'subjective value is radically different (*that is, significantly higher*) than the assets' market value'.[66] Consequently, deferral until the time of monetization is required here, since the effective market return serves as a better standard for the extracted welfare. Benshalom and Stead acknowledge that this partial realization principle would be an exemption that would cause distortions and inequities.[67] Nevertheless, they note that personal assets represent a larger proportion of the wealth of low- and medium-income taxpayers than that of high-income taxpayers. Therefore, providing a tax benefit for personal assets would make the tax system as a whole more progressive.[68]

Benshalom and Stead's analysis is both illuminating and bold. In a clear fashion they identify both the aim of progressivity and the special character of personal goods as a normative bedrock for an exemption of these assets from the generally embraced mark-to-market approach. Nonetheless, for two reasons an overall defence of the realization principle can be found more convincing.

First, there is no general theory available that can provide policymakers with a comprehensive list that differentiates a small number of personal goods from the bulk of investment goods. As Benshalom and Stead acknowledge, the abstract distinction between personal and investment goods is in reality a continuum.[69] However, no ordinal continuum can be established: even goods that the authors confidently put at the extremes can be ordered alternatively by individual taxpayers.

For instance, many young urban professionals perceive their home (qualified under 'personal goods') as their only form of financial investment.[70] Consequently, their purchase will often reflect their anticipation of an increase in market value. Furthermore, families might perceive their family jewellery as a form of savings that could be sacrificed in the event of certain needs, such as university fees. Concerning the 'investment goods', generally, people might hold business shares and financial investments for financial reasons, yet it is not clear-cut that their market value will always coincide with people's personal value standards. Many shareholders who help to establish a company will have an emotional affiliation with its economic philosophy and produced goods that will transcend purely economic figures. Regarding investment

[64] Ilan Benshalom and Kendra Stead, 'Realization and Progressivity', 3(1) *Columbia Journal of Tax Law* (2011) 43–85, 68.
[65] Ibid., 66.
[66] Ibid., 64 (my emphasis).
[67] Ibid., 69.
[68] Ibid., 69.
[69] Ibid., 68.
[70] Ibid., 65.

portfolios, there are a rising number of people who combine the pursuit of profit with nonfinancial incentives, thereby obtaining portfolios that also reflect ethical, social, and ecological purposes. Such assets are not easily fungible with their more commercial counterparts, and the market value is not the sole standard by which people valorize these assets. Furthermore, Benshalom and Stead qualify family businesses as personal goods. Nonetheless, many of these tend to be sold to bigger entities, and many large companies arise from family businesses, so this does not seem to exclude the relevancy of market value as such. Conversely, many small businesses without any familial character—which the authors perceive as investment goods—do have personal value. Moreover, as the authors acknowledge, most goods fall between both extremes, and it will consequently be arbitrary to qualify them as one or the other.[71]

In other words, the reasons to reject a partial realization principle are similar to the reasons to reject the mark-to-market approach: the list of investments and personal goods upheld by policymakers and regulations will be incongruous to autonomy. The imposed distinction between market and personal goods will contain a standard of value that will often be inconsistent with the viewpoint of individual taxpayers and their ends. Many taxpayers will be taxed on the market value of goods that they hold for divergent reasons, and investors will obtain comparative benefits using the realization-based tax for so-called 'personal goods'.[72] The optimal decision from the viewpoint of autonomy is to put the authority over the distinction between both types of goods with the taxpayers themselves rather than with the legislator. When people agree on the receipt of a monetary benefit (via a market exchange), they signal that goods are fungible and so provide administrators with a valorization that adheres to their personal value standard (i.e. the agreed price). Additionally, given the fact that people's intentions are multidimensional (e.g. Alan selling his shares to his friend) and that most goods are partly personal and partly financial, the exact agreed price serves as the best reflection of people's ends and consequent value standards.

Second, the right to autonomy serves as a better explanation for our moral resistance to a mark-to-market approach than the reasons suggested by Benshalom and Stead. Envision once more Alan's apartment, which went up £200,000 in market value and became worth £400,000. His neighbour, who held a similar apartment, wished to rely on this price and sold it to a law firm. Alan, however, wanted to continue to use his apartment to accommodate young artists and their innovative exhibitions (prior to the break-up of his first marriage). He resented the reasons underlying the increased price (the corporate trend invading the neighbourhood) and perceived his decision as a way of rebelling against it. Our intuition tells us that it would have been very unjust to tax Alan on this increased market value. However, the real reason that we do not support Alan being taxed at a capital gain of £200,000 cannot lie in the fact that he attributed a 'higher value' to it than the current £400,000, as Benshalom and Stead endorse. This presumption would, for example, mean that he would be willing to pay a price for the apartment that exceeds this £400,000. But it could be perfectly possible that Alan would never consider buying his apartment at its current market price.

[71] Ibid., 68.

[72] The authors forecast these malpractices in Ibid., 82.

Furthermore, the assumption of a higher market value does not justify our intuitive position against taxing Alan. If anything, it provides a mandate for taxing him at this higher value rather than not at all.[73]

The proper theoretical explanation as to why we should refrain from taxing Alan on the increased market value is because a price supervenes on the taxpayer's intention to sell or rent an asset. The attribution of a certain amount of money presumes the relevancy of a specific market exchange within the subjective life plan of the person. However, in the absence of any real exchange we have no proof that this valorization will be consistent with any of the person's ends. The reason that we oppose Alan being taxed on the increase of £200,000 is because this price arises from plans that Alan did not intend to undertake, and consequently tied him to these external purposes. At the time, Alan held a deviant preference and the market value was inconsistent with his ends. So the reason that we oppose attributing income in the absence of real financial gains for these personal assets is not because the market value is a 'bad' proxy—it is because it is simply no proxy at all. Alan's preferences lay on a metric of value that was not expressible in any market price, since he did not engage in any market transactions. Any market valorization would have been incongruous to his autonomy, as it would have imposed a value standard that was contradictory to his own.

F. Autonomy-Friendly Optimization of Income Tax

I have tried to demonstrate that the realization principle is more than a pragmatic element: the logic that persons are taxed only when agreeing to the receipt of benefits can be seen as elucidating the right to autonomy. When tax scholars and egalitarian reformers aim at the optimal taxation of capital, such an endeavour ought to be implemented within the boundaries set by people's right to autonomy—that is, with respect for the realization principle.

As mentioned in Section II, the realization principle is nonetheless associated with practices such as the strategic trading and timing of asset dispositions, portfolio adjustments, and debt-financed consumption. These result in a decrease of the effective rate on capital-owners, causing inefficiencies and—among many other factors—adding to the accumulation of wealth, which egalitarian tax reformers wish to mitigate.

The theoretic framework elaborated here does not aspire to ignore these problems. Conversely, a renewed analysis can yield benefits in terms of how to deal with current defects. The realization principle protects taxpayers from liability for unconsented valorizations, not from taxation as such. Although the current contribution curtails authorities' taxing competences to some extent, it is not hostile to the promotion of efficiency or redistribution. Rather, an appraisal of the purpose of the realization principle can help to revise its current application in the light of these aims. Once we understand that confirmation of a certain monetary benefit is the prerequisite for an income tax, we can then begin to address its current problematic by-products.

[73] The granted exemption for personal goods is thus merely founded on the aim of progressivity, rather than on a higher attribution of value.

For instance, capital cannot only be sold or rented, but can also be applied to finance the acquisition of new goods by serving as security for a loan. One of the corollaries of the current income tax system is its disregard for the resulting debt-financed consumption or investment. Alan can put his apartment at risk and utilize its market value to borrow money to acquire a new apartment—without paying any income tax. If taxation is only triggered by a net cash flow, then taxpayers can utilize their assets to acquire loans, which allow them to consume or invest untaxed money. Most fiscal regimes thus permit taxpayers to enjoy the benefits of capital in the form of borrowed money used for consumption or investment, without being subject to income tax. Not only does this circumvention entail inefficiencies, but McCaffery also considers it to be a failure of the income tax 'to reach the propertied classes'.[74]

A renewed understanding of the realization principle provides insights to foreclose this inequitable tax advantage that is often enjoyed by more affluent taxpayers. In a secured debt agreement people can utilize their assets in a commercial exchange, whereby an asset is being collateralized in order to obtain a loan. Collateralization refers to an asset's market value, which serves as a security measure in case of default. Within such contracts a capital owner thus agrees to the market value of an asset. To the extent that this value exceeds the initial purchase price, this qualifies as the receipt of a particular monetary benefit. So, if Alan mortgages his apartment to acquire a loan from the bank, he forfeits his initial protection from non-shared valorizations—and the condition for permissible taxation of the occurred gain is therefore fulfilled.

In summary, tax scholars' righteous objectives of equity and efficiency could be unified in a research project on an autonomy-friendly income taxation of capital, which would demand confirmation of a particular monetary benefit as a moral condition for taxation. However, this condition is not restricted to current applications of the realization principle. For instance, the utilization of an increased market value of capital in the conclusion of a secured loan can be qualified as a realization event. Consequently, when one's assets are being used as security for a loan, this permits capital gains taxation in an autonomy-friendly fashion. Rather than being the unilateral attribution of a market value, such taxation merely replicates the market value appropriated by the parties in an agreement. Additionally, by broadening capital-owners' tax base, this measure would increase the progressive nature of our tax system, as demanded by Piketty and others.

IV. Conclusion

Thomas Piketty stated that taxation is 'not a technical matter, but preeminently a political and philosophical issue, perhaps the most important of all political issues'.[75] My analysis has advanced this insight and tried to implement a concept from moral and political philosophy to the domain of income tax. From the right of each person to live according to his or her own purposes I have codified a particular conceptualization of income. Moreover, I have shown that authorities cannot measure one's income with

[74] See McCaffery, n. 31, 888. [75] See Piketty, n. 15, 493.

alien utility standards, and should instead rely on shared valorizations. The fact that a mark-to-market approach leads to liquidity problems is merely the tip of the iceberg in this matter. I have demonstrated that a general market price often arises from exchanges that conflict with one's own purposes. Consequently, the attribution of this valorization ignores a person's own view on well-being, as it dictates the utility standard of the market. The value of the realization principle lies exactly in the fact that such a technique integrates with a person's autonomy, as it copies a person's consented monetary benefits within exchanges into the tax base.

By integrating normative insights from exterior domains, the current contribution has revealed a possible foundation for what is commonly described in taxation theory as a necessary evil. By clarifying acceptance over a monetary benefit as a moral prerequisite for income taxation, my deontological approach has tried to induce tax reformers to accomplish their aims *within* the boundaries of the realization principle, and to refute wealth and income taxation by means of a mark-to-market approach. Given this, I have presented the normative framework established here as not being hostile to egalitarian or efficiency-related perspectives. Rather, it is an appraisal of the right to autonomy as the proper foundation for the realization principle, which facilitates variations in its current interpretation in order to address the defects of the prevailing taxation of capital. An understanding of the normative bedrock of the realization principle, for example, underwrites the taxation of collateralized capital—a measure corresponding with the egalitarian aim of rendering our tax codes more progressive.

Index

Introductory Note

References such as '178–9' indicate (not necessarily continuous) discussion of a topic across a range of pages. Because the whole of this work is about 'taxation', use of this term (and certain others which occur throughout) as entry points has been restricted. Please look under the appropriate detailed entries. Wherever possible in the case of topics with many references, these have either been divided into sub-topics or only the most significant discussions of the topic are listed.